Ghost of a Pirate guarding his Treasure—Carol Rodriguez

SPOOKY TREASURE TROVES

UFOS, GHOSTS, CURSED PIECES OF EIGHT AND THE PARANORMAL

TIMOTHY GREEN BECKLEY and **SEAN CASTEEL**

With Paul Eno, Dr. Nandor Fodor, Scott Corrales,
Ted Owens and Paul Dale Roberts

Conspiracy Journal
PRODUCTIONS

SPOOKY TREASURE TROVES
UFOS, GHOSTS, CURSED PIECES OF EIGHT AND THE PARANORMAL

TIMOTHY GREEN BECKLEY and SEAN CASTEEL
With Paul Eno, Dr. Nandor Fodor, Scott Corrales,
Ted Owens and Paul Dale Roberts

This edition Copyright 2015 by Timothy Green Beckley
dba Global Communications/Conspiracy Journal

All rights reserved. No part of these manuscripts may be copied or reproduced by any mechanical or digital methods and no exerpts or quotes may be used in any other book or manuscript without permission in writing by the Publisher, Global Communications/Conspiracy Journal, except by a reviewer who may quote brief passages in a review.

Revised Edition

Published in the United States of America By
Global Communications/Conspiracy Journal
Box 753 · New Brunswick, NJ 08903

Staff Members
Timothy G. Beckley, Publisher
Carol Ann Rodriguez, Assistant to the Publisher
Sean Casteel, General Associate Editor
Tim R. Swartz, Graphics and Editorial Consultant
William Kern, Editorial and Art Consultant

Sign Up On The Web For Our Free Weekly Newsletter
and Mail Order Version of Conspiracy Journal
and Bizarre Bazaar
www.ConspiracyJournal.com

Order Hot Line: 1-732-602-3407
PayPal: MrUFO8@hotmail.com

Contents

HERE IS PROOF THE DECEASED CAN BE HELPFUL TO THE LIVING AND TURN AN INDIVIDUAL INTO AN INSTANT MILLIONAIRE! NEWS FLASH! DID SPIRITS LEAD TREASURE HUNTERS TO 4.5 MILLION IN SUNKEN TREASYRE FOUND OFF THE FLORIDA COAST? vii

BREAKING NEWS! FROM THE TOWN OF GAUNDIA KHERA IN THE UNNAO DISTRICT OF INDIA, A TEAM OF QUALIFIED ARCHAEOLOGISTS HUNT FOR BURIED TREASURE BASED ON THE VISION OF A 19TH CENTURY KING. ix

USING THE PARANORMAL TO FIND A TREASURE TROVE xi

THE UFO PROPHET "TALKS" TO A GHOST IN A HAUNTED ROOM 1

OREGON'S TREASURES GUARDED BY GHOSTS AND DEMONS 7

COWBOY GHOSTS AND SPECTRAL MINERS 15

COUNTING THE DEAD AT CAHUENGA PASS
    AND THE CURSES ON CHARLES ISLAND 21

RIDDLE OF THE TOMMYKNOCKERS 23

THAT WHICH GLISTENS: ACCURSED TREASURE 26

THE COMING OF THE GOLDEN GODS FROM OUTER SPACE 34

MAY THE FORCE—HOPEFULLY—BE WITH YOU:
TREASURES FOUND AND LOST THROUGH PSYCHIC MEANS 37

CURSE YOUR ANCESTORS TO THE EIGHTEENTH GENERATION 47

THE LOST DUSTCHMAN'S GOLD MINE—TALES OF MADNESS
            IN THE SUPERSTITION MOUNTAINS 49

UFOS, GHOSTS AND THE DREADED CURSE OF OAK ISLAND 54

THE CURSE OF COCOS ISLAND—
    COULD THIS BE THE LARGEST TREASURE TROVE IN THE WORLD? 61

TREASURE LADEN JEROME	71
GOLD MINING SLAVES OF THE ANCIENT ALIEN KIND	79
UFOS, CRYPTIDS AND GHOSTS: BRANCHES OF THE SAME TREE?	86
THE WORLD-WIDE HUNT FOR VANISHED RICHES	95
CAPTAIN KIDD IN FACT AND FICTION	110
CAPTAIN KIDD: HIS TREASURE	132
CAPTAIN KIDD: HIS TRIAL AND DEATH	157
THE WONDEROUS FORTUNE OF WILLIAM PHIPPS	179
THE BOLD SEA ROGUE, JOHN QUELCH	198
THE ARMADA GALLEON OF TOBERMORY BAY	214
THE LOST PLATE FLEET OF VIGO	239
THE PIRATE'S HOARD OF TRINIDAD	256
THE LURE OF COCOS ISLAND	271
THE MYSTERY OF THE LUTINE FRIGATE	282
THE TOILERS OF THE THETIS	294
THE QUEST OF EL DORADO	309
THE WIZARDRY OF THE DIVINING ROD	324
SUNDRY PIRATES AND THEIR BOOTY	338
PRACTICAL HINTS FOR TREASURE SEEKERS	359

HERE IS PROOF THE DECEASED CAN BE HELPFUL TO THE LIVING AND TURN AN INDIVIDUAL INTO AN INSTANT MILLIONAIRE

NEWS FLASH!
DID SPIRITS LEAD TREASURE HUNTERS TO 4.5 MILLION DOLLARS IN SUNKEN TREASURE FOUND OFF FLORIDA COAST?

The summer of 2015 brought a fascinating multimillion dollar treasure find that involved the spirits of the dead making themselves apparent on Florida's sunbaked Treasure Coast and had a salvage company's CEO talking about a case of what appeared to be "magical synchronicity."

Fee Fi Fo Fum - Brent Brisben (far right) and fellow treasure hunters from 1715 Fleet - Queens Jewels, LLC show off part of the sunken treasure trove that they recently found just off the shores of Vero Beach, Florida.

This astounding saga began when eleven Spanish galleons laden with treasure left Havana for Spain on July 30, 1715. Their mission was to deliver the "queen's jewels," at least $400 million worth of jewelry and gold, to King Philip V of Spain. They soon encountered a powerful hurricane and all the ships smashed against the reefs off Florida's east coast, sinking them in the early morning hours of the following day. As many as a thousand lives were lost in one of colonial Spain's biggest maritime disasters.

Among the lost coins were a special type called "Royals" that had been made specifically for King Philip in the early 1700s.

Fast forward 300 years to the day. Brent Brisben, the owner of a salvage company called 1715 Fleet – Queen's Jewels LLC, announced the discovery of $4.5 million worth of treasure that included nine "Royals" valued at $300,000 apiece. The treasure was found off the coast of Vero Beach in very shallow water.

"People love treasure stories," Brisben told reporters. "It resonates with everybody – every demographic, young and old, rich and poor. People freak out that we're literally ten to fifteen feet off the beach in two to three feet of water."

The timing of the treasure find has a significant meaning that will not be lost on the readers of this book, coming 300 years to the day after the ill-fated galleons went down.

Brisben said he believes some kind of magic played a role in his company's good fortune.

"Five years ago," he said, "before I got into this business, I would have told you that magic is in fairy tales."

Brisben cautioned that he did not want to put the find in "religious terms," but he acknowledged that, "I truly now believe that there is an energy that pervades these shipwrecks that I can't quantify. I truly believe that these shipwrecks wanted their story to continue, that this magically happened on this anniversary because this story still needs to be told and it's currently unfolding."

Did ghosts from among the 1,000 men lost in the 1715 hurricane purposely and consciously lead the treasure hunters to the buried wealth on the 300th anniversary of their demise? Is there some supernatural force reaching out that wanted the gold and jewelry to be found?

Brisben's company purchased the salvage rights to the shipwreck in 2010 from the family of treasure hunter Mel Fisher, who had won a lengthy court battle in the 1980s for the rights to the shipwrecks. During the litigation, the Spanish government did not assert an interest and thus has no claim to it now. The state of Florida did assert a claim and is entitled to 20 percent of the found artifacts for display in a museum in Tallahassee. The remaining 80 percent will be divided between Brisben and his diving crew.

"Things happen in strange occurrences," Brisben added. "It's been a magical anniversary year. But it's a tragedy that continues to tell its story every year."

Throughout this book the reader will learn that many treasures have a life of their own. Still, this news story out of Tallahassee, Florida, is about as impressive as one can get!

* * * * * *

BREAKING NEWS!
FROM THE TOWN OF DAUNDIA KHERA
IN THE UNNAO DISTRICT OF INDIA

A TEAM OF QUALIFIED ARCHAEOLOGISTS HUNT FOR BURIED TREASURE BASED ON THE VISION OF A 19TH CENTURY KING

Archaeologists in a small Indian village have been digging under a 19th-century palace hoping to find a massive treasure after a popular Hindu holy man told authorities that the ghost of King Ra Ram Baksh Singh appeared to him in a dream telling him about the exact location of a treasure worth over $50 billion in American currency!

Left: Gold Digging- Raja Ra Ram Baksh Singh

Below: The Indian palace beneath which the treasure is believed to be hidden

The digging began after Indian geological and archaeological officials found evidence of heavy metal about 66 feet underground.

Publicly, however, officials from the Archaeological Survey of India are strongly denying that they are digging based on a ghost's suggestion – but the dig continues nonetheless.

Virendra Verma, the aforementioned holy man, says that India is going through a "collapsing economy" and the village he came from is being particularly hard hit.

"In a dream," Virenda Verma said, "I spoke with my deceased gurus, the late Bhaskaranandi and the late Satsaganandji, and, shortly thereafter, wrote a letter to the Prime Minister about the treasure I know to be buried beneath the palace. I told him that the spirit of the king still roams around the palace and pleads to me to liberate it by digging out 1,000 tons of gold buried there."

He added that the discovery would by no means assist in his wellbeing but that a percentage should be given to the district.

But the influential body of archaeologists scoffed as they hedged their bets.

"Archaeology doesn't work according to the dreams of a holy man, or anybody else. Archaeology is a science. We are carrying out this excavation on the basis of our findings at the site," said Syed Jamal Hasan, an agency official.

Apparently, we are told, the timing was just a massive coincidence!

But the villagers are eager to see how this turns out as they reason that the holy man could be the "real thing!"

* * * * *

And so, dear seeker of fabulous fortunes, get ready to be continually astonished by the TRUE stories that will follow, for they are as awe-inspiring as the treasures with which they have come to be associated.

USING THE PARANORMAL TO FIND A TREASURE TROVE
By Timothy Green Beckley

Chris Bader, a Chapman University (Orange, CA) professor of sociology, is not what you would call a "true believer" by any stretch of the imagination. But he has made deep enough inroads into the paranormal community to realize that ghostly spirits do sometimes project a benevolent side in how they haunt.

"Ghosts go as far back as you can look for them; there are stories about ghosts from as far back as ancient Greece," said Bader. "The ghosts and their motives do change. It used to be, in some of the oldest reports, that the ghost would be hiding buried treasure. You would find it if you followed the ghost."

Apparently the agnostic-leaning author of Paranormal America failed to realize that such a "trend" amongst otherworldly apparitions has not changed all that much over the centuries and that some of the dearly departed still want to lead us to that pie in the sky or that sunken treasure trove, whichever is most relevant from where they now reside. We hope to show in the following pages that such is very much the case, though some spirits also seem – pardon the expression – hell bent on guarding their gold doubloons and there is always that cursed treasure or two up in the mountains or down around the cove to keep us on our toes and running fast if the opportunity presents itself.

* * * * * *

Wouldn't we all love to wake up one morning and be "as rich as Rockefeller?"

How might we go about accomplishing this major miracle?

We could win the lottery (except the person in line in front of us already won the "pick four" for the day).

Rob a bank (naughty, naughty – and you might get caught).

Invent something that everyone wants (I think there is already a patent on the ipod, so that's out of the question).

OK. I suppose as a last resort you could marry someone like Donald Trump, but could you wake up with a clear conscience the next day?

Oh, I forgot one way – find a long lost buried treasure!

I have long known that there are still places where you can go out and locate a "pot of gold" that will put you on top of life's mountain. Truth is, there are tens of BILLIONS of "dollars" in all sorts of swag just waiting to be recovered – maybe right in your own back yard, though most buried treasure admittedly will not be so easy to dig up. If it has been laying around for any prolonged period, chances are there could be a curse associated with the hoarded wealth and you had better watch your step.

In this book we will tell you where you can go to do your "digging," though you might have to bring in a bulldozer or two or a small submarine as well as get special permission from land owners or individual governments to go about your adventurous task. Even if you are a bit offshore, you could still be in territorial waters.

As far back as I can remember, I have been fascinated with the lore of pirates' booty and sunken vessels that rode the high seas, later being observed as ghost ships with their masts still hung high and proud, complete with phantom buccaneers on-deck and a blazing fire in the hull – no doubt from taking direct cannon fire.

OK, maybe I've seen too many horror movies, like the 1935 Bela Lugosi classic "Mystery of the Marie Celeste," but I guess I was also impressed by the works of Harold T. Wilkins when I was a kid (more later about Captain Kidd).

Wilkins was best known in later years for his books on flying saucers and lost worlds, but he was originally, in the 1940s, considered more than proficient when it came to penning tales of buried treasure, lost gold mines, hidden Inca jewels and pirate gold. He often wrote about vast underground treasure troves that were being guarded by a variety of denizens, from spear-chucking giants to super warriors from the lost continent of Atlantis

According to Wilkins, there exists a great tunnel system that stretches for thousands of miles less than half a mile beneath our feet. It is literally laden with all sorts of ancient artistic masterpieces, most of them of pure gold.

One elderly gentleman noted that his wife was once blindfolded and taken through many intricate passages cut in the rock, which led down into the subterranean gardens of the Inca. In due course, when the blindfold was removed, "The lady beheld, skillfully molded in the purest gold, trees laden with leaves and fruit, with birds perched on their branches. Among other things, she saw Atahualpa's gold sedan-chair (una de las undas) which had been so long searched for in vain and which is alleged to have sunk in the basin at the Baths of Pultamarca."

The husband commanded his wife not to touch any of these enchanted treasures, reminding her that the period fixed for the restoration of the Inca Empire had not yet arrived. No doubt she must have been tempted to try and retrace her steps at some later date to take back a "souvenir" from this fabulous underground treasure basin.

Are we all about ready to chime in with a hardy shiver me timbers?

I know I am!

THE GHOST AND FLYING SAUCER CONNECTION

Somewhere along the twisting path of the paranormal I discovered that UFOs and ghosts seemed to be attracted to buried treasure – either to guard it or lead to its discovery. Both phenomena have supposedly led prospectors directly to the proverbial "mother-load" or hovered so damn near it as to be beyond mere coincidence. I guess you could say they functioned as a sort of sign as to where to dig or dive – if the ultimate prize is underwater. Other times you better get your pistol or pick axe ready to protect yourself from the walking dead, though, come to think of it, neither instrument can wound or kill something that has already turned to dust. So it's better to hope you're light on your feet and can hightail it a safe distance away.

I have no statistics on any of these paranormal declamations, but I've heard an assortment of rumors. Now, in the case of UFOs, we're not talking about spaceships with humanoid pilots on board, but more likely ornery spook or ghost lights that seem to be under "intelligent control" but not piloted by "aliens" as we've come to imagine them – at least that is what I would assume.

With great difficulty, I "discovered" a saucer landing site on the Peruvian desert, 1954. (James W. Moseley)

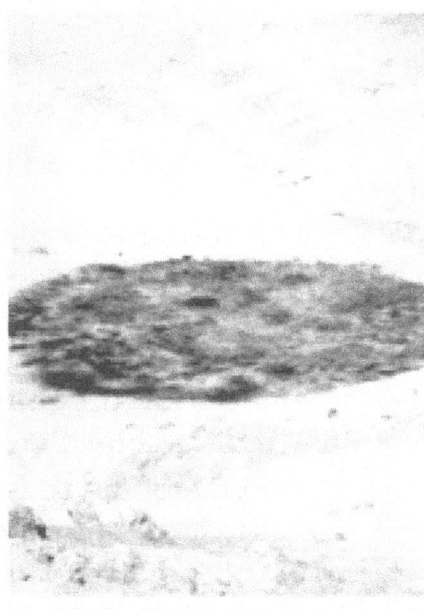

The mysterious Peruvian saucer-landing site seen from a nearby hill. This incident made the front page of Lima's most popular tabloid—twice. (James W. Moseley)

Though I must say that one scribe pointed out to me that if the ancient astronauts known as the Anunnaki were really coming here from Planet X thousands of years ago to take human slaves in order to mine for gold, perhaps they are still searching for this valuable substance – or perchance the slaves themselves are returning from the realm of spirits to haunt these particular locales as a form of retribution to their slave owners. It's all assuredly conjecture. Pure speculation. But something uncommonly bizarre does seem to be going on that connects some lost treasures with the eerie sector of the phantasmal.

In all honesty, I first started to put two and two together "treasure-wise" and to think about any possible connection with the supernatural (the supernatural would include UFOs, which I believe to be more psychic in natural than physical hardware from outer space) when I started working out of Jim W. Moseley's office in Manhattan. Jim was the editor/publisher of "Saucer News," a magazine devoted to the investigation of unidentified flying objects. Jim was a well-known media personality, pushing subscriptions on TV and radio shows like the popular Long John Nebel Party Line, a five-hour talk fest that was broadcast nightly over WOR, a station that pumped out wattage over thirty states, creating a huge audience in the tens of thousands.

Moseley had taken over my less-polished mimeographed zine – known as "The Interplanetary News Service Report" – and hired me as managing editor of his illustrious rag. JWM had garnered a somewhat "mysterious – lone wolf – reputation" among

certain incredulous types in the UFO field who accused him of being a government agent or a member of some global cabal they loosely referred to as the "International Bankers."

One of the reasons for this negative notoriety seems to have been Jim's ability to disappear for considerable periods of time, leaving behind his Fort Lee, New Jersey, digs (he actually resided in Guttenberg, the next town over, but picked up his mail from the same Post Office Box in Fort Lee for decades) and traveling overseas. Since his father had been in the military, this made him a prime contender for being a possible agent of darkness.

Truth is, Moseley and his father – U.S. Army

Major General George Van Horn Moseley – had not spoken in years because of their highly polarized political views. This included taking particular exception to his father's outspoken racist and anti-Semitic views, including his claims that America must "breed up" its own decaying population by copying Nazi eugenics practices and launching a program of "selective breeding, sterilization, the elimination of the unfit, and the elimination of those types which are inimical to the general welfare of the nation."

Some have accused Jimbo of being a "tomb raider" because some of the artifacts he dug up while on "saucer sabbatical" in Peru were indeed buried more or less "six feet under," which technically made him a grave robber. The treasures consisted of everything from pottery to beautiful gold burial masks that brought him a fabulous fortune once he bribed Peruvian authorities to smuggle the pieces out of their country and into the U.S. where such "foreign relics" were NOT considered to be contraband.

Flying saucer provocateur, and Moseley's friend, Curtis Collins, has summed up Jim's treasure hunting days thusly:

"For the next several years, Moseley divided his time between the U.S., 'Saucer News' and Peru treasure hunts. Jim's absences were a mystery to the flying saucer fans and 'Saucer News' readers and the subject of much speculation. This helped fuel fanciful rumors that he was a saucer spy! Also, while in Peru, Jim found time for both some real saucer work and also some mischief."

I knew Moseley very well on a personal basis from having worked with him daily out of his "Saucer News" office on Fifth Avenue. When he wasn't "out of town" on mysterious business dealings, I also partied until the wee hours with him and our sometimes wild gang of "saucer kooks" and had many discussions with Jim, both sober and inebriated.

At this stage, I don't profess to recall the intimate details, not having written them down, but Jim was certainly familiar with the lore and legends of Peru as far as ghost stories and flying saucers went. He said his frequent guide, a fellow by the name of Robert Kennedy, had told him that the spirits of the departed often guarded the places where they had been buried with valuables. I don't think they were intentionally hoarding these treasures from their position in the spirit world, but I am certain they had no intentions of having others dig them up centuries after they had been placed in the ground. That's sacrilegious in anyone's book.

Many a tomb, both in Peru and elsewhere, has a longstanding curse associated with it – especially ones that involve something valuable being buried underground. That's one of the reasons no one has ever located the Lost Dutchman Mine tucked away in the Superstition Mountain Range of Arizona outside of the heat-baked city of Phoenix. It's said that the spirits of the local native Indians, as appointed guardians, prevent anyone from getting anywhere near the cave where all the valuables are buried. Many have died and disappeared there, and some have even been abducted by UFOs, but that's another story for another time.

Regarding his treasure-hunting days in Peru, Jim had mentioned to me that mysterious flashing lights were being seen fairly frequently at high altitudes all over this South American country and there was some thought that flying saucers might be creating this unexplained phenomenon. Others have said that there is so much purportedly lost treasure in the mountainous regions around Machu Picchu that you can't possibly separate potential treasure from the UFOs hovering and streaking across the sky.

My friend and crystal skull explorer Joshua Shapiro said he became interested in the area near Lake Titicaca, Peru, after reading a book by Brother Philip (aka George Hunt Williamson) called "Secret of the Andes and the Golden Sun Disk of MU." In his book, Brother Philip describes a secret brotherhood in this area who administer a special school for those on the spiritual path.

"Lake Titicaca is even higher than Cusco. The Lake itself is very large and there are many islands within it. The large Peruvian city which is on the shore is called Puno, and this is where one stays. I know many of you have seen the derbies the women wear in Peru (which they got from the British, when they were there) and this is the case in Puno. Some of the local people have villages on the reed islands, and, in our last trip, we were able to go on one of their reed boats, which were very sturdy and comfortable. I asked our navigator if he ever saw UFOs in this area, and he said it is a common thing. Many people claim they have seen UFOs come in and go out of the water. Another friend told me that Jacques Cousteau once went in a submarine there to see what is under the water and was so shocked by what he saw that he has never spoken about this. My tour guide said the local people believe the Golden Sun Disk of the Inca is buried here. I think of all the places in Peru I visited, I saw more UFO-type 'clouds' here than everywhere else. Also, all the islands in the lake have stone terrace structures everywhere. The question I asked myself is, where did they get all these stones?"

Getting back to Moseley, as early as 1952 he was immersed in UFO research in Peru. The first incident that he became involved in actually involved a photograph of a UFO that trailed a column of smoke. This is the report he filed several years later with a noted UFO organization called NICAP, the National Investigations Committee on Aerial Phenomena.

In a letter dated August 10, 1957, Mr. Moseley gave NICAP the following account of the incident:

"In Lima, I met Señor Pedro Bardi, who is an agricultural engineer. On July 19, 1952, while on a farm in the Madre de Dios section of Peru, he and others saw a saucer. It was about 4:30 p.m. and they were talking to Lima by radio.

"Suddenly, according to Bardi, the radio went dead. They looked out the window and saw a round object going by at high speed. (The witnesses included Pedro Arellano, owner of the farm.) The object as such had passed; it was at an estimated 100 meters altitude and was a little smaller than a DC-3, according to Bardi. It made a buzzing sound as it went by."

The object's speed, Moseley explains, was determined by a report that it was seen four minutes later near Porto Maldonado, 120 kilometers distant. This speed was computed at 1117 miles per hour.

The photograph was secured from a customs administrator named Domingo Troncosco, who said he had taken it as the object flew near the port. Though the photo shows a cigar-shaped object instead of the round

Does a UFO over Machu Picchu indicate that so-called ancient astronauts are coming back to protect some golden artifacts said to be buried there?

shape Bardi described, this could possibly have been due to an elongated effect caused by speed.

"It seems obvious to me," Moseley told NICAP, "that the photo is genuine."

* * * * *

MORE UFO TREASURE TALES

Up around Mount Rainier, in Washington State, where Kenneth Arnold saw a string of nine crescent-shaped UFOs back in June of 1947, there is so much gold said to be buried in them there hills that you need a state guidebook to plot them all out on a map. From time to time some happy-go-lucky prospector – yes, there are still a few of the old breed around laying claim to some secluded grubstake – will come into town carrying a pouch of sparkling nuggets. But it doesn't seem like anything really to get excited about as the vast troves are still there for the taking if you happen to hit upon the right "ghost flame" to direct the way to the deep veins that exist below the earth, inside the mountain itself.

Actually, your best chance to come across a pocket of nuggets would be up around Yakima Indian Reservation, though the locals certainly would not think highly of you if you absconded with what rightfully might be theirs according to tradition. At one point in the 1970s there were so many UFO sightings in the area that the Parks Department built a viewing stand from which the phenomena was even photographed.

Paranormal investigator Ryan Dube gives these additional details: "The Yakima Indian Reservation is located in the southern part of Washington State and covers roughly 3,500 square miles of both forest and flat land. The first reports were made by forest rangers in 1960, and most impressively Chief Fire Control Officer Bill Vogel reported a ninety-minute sighting of a mysterious ghost light in the sky over Toppenish Ridge. The officer reported that the light had a teardrop appearance (like a flame). Air Force investigators also became involved and gathered information on the light, including photo and video footage. The lights attract both ghost enthusiasts and ghost hunters. Campers and rangers observed and reported the greatest level of activity throughout the 1970s, and a number of witnesses even reported receiving telepathic messages from the lights as well as electrical devices failing."

Maybe this "natural" or supernatural phenomenon persists because of the high concentration of certain minerals in the earth. I know from personal experience that a large crystal deposit can make any good spook light, as they are also called, jump to high heaven and attract a good deal of attention.

Fellow author and PSI proponent Preston Dennett says he has personally kept tabs on what has been called the Oriflamme Mountain Lights. "These lights," Dennett maintains, "have an ongoing reputation for hovering over areas where miners are known to have found gold and thus locally have become dubbed most appropriately 'Money Lights.'"

In his suspenseful book, "Supernatural California," Preston describes the Money Lights in rigorous detail.

"One famous location is the Oriflamme Mountain in the Southern California desert town of Anza-Borrego. Located on the western edge, the Oriflamme Mountain is composed of granite and schist bedrock. It has several streams which flow from it. Oriflamme Canyon is lined with oaks, sycamores, willow and cottonwoods. It is a popular site for hiking, camping and biking and remains a largely untouched wilderness area. The Oriflamme Mountain is also known for its mysterious ghost lights. The name 'Oriflamme' actually translates as 'Golden Flame.' Apparently, the accounts of these lights reach so far back in history that the mountain was actually named for them. The lights occur all over the mountain and range out over the adjacent Borrego Valley desert.

"While the oral traditions are well-established for centuries, the first recorded account came in 1858, when a stagecoach driver passing by the mountain observed "phantom lights" dancing on the mountain. From that point on, reports began to pour in from other witnesses, including settlers, prospectors and soldiers.

"At first, the lights were thought to be from the spirits of the Native Americans who once inhabited the area. Several ancient Indian burial grounds are located in Oriflamme Canyon and the surrounding areas. True to their profession, however, prospectors generally theorized that the money lights, as they called them, indicated the presence of treasure or gold, and in fact gold has been found in the area.

"One of the strangest and most famous of the sightings occurred in 1892 to a group of three prospectors camping near Grapevine Canyon. One of the men, Charles Knowles, described what happened. He and his companions suddenly observed three 'lights' which looked like 'fireworks' or balls of fire. The strange lights seemed to rise directly from the ground. They traveled in an arching pattern, reaching an elevation of about 100 feet. As they started to fall back down to the earth, the lights exploded. About thirty minutes later, the lights returned. On this occasion, the lights behaved very differently. They rose from the ground and arched up to 100 feet, but, instead of exploding, they returned to the ground where they stopped, reversed in direction, and traveled back to their starting location. Clearly these are not normal lights!

"The sightings continued. Miners periodically saw the lights over the adjacent Vallecito Mountains and across the Borrego desert. At times, the lights reportedly lit up the night sky like a fireworks show. During the Prohibition era, it was speculated that the lights were caused by bootleggers. And at one point, the Oriflamme lights again came under suspicion for indicating the presence of illegal immigration or smuggling activities.

"Still, the lights continued to appear. Reports have continued on and off reaching to the present day. In the 1930s, a sighting of one of the mysterious ghost lights bobbing up and down along San Felipe Creek was reported to the American Society for Psychical Research, which printed the account in their journal. More recently, in October 2002, the International Earthlight Alliance (IEA) conducted a field investigation into the lights. The IEA is composed of scientists with various disciplines devoted to studying the phenomenon of earth lights.

"On October 18, 2002, Marsha Adams of the IEA headed a team of researchers for an on-site investigation. While the team did not observe the lights, they were able to interview firsthand eyewitnesses from the nearby town of Butterfield who confirmed that the lights still appear. Still, no explanation to account for earth lights has ever been found. One recent scientific theory is as bizarre as any other theory.

It states that when strong winds blow sand up against large quartz outcroppings, they create a strong charge of static electricity. When the static-electric charge is strong enough, it discharges and causes the lights to flash.

"The area is now preserved as Anza-Borrego Desert State Park. To reach Oriflamme Canyon, take Highway S-2 one mile south of the Box Canyon Historical site. There is a small sign that reads 'Oriflamme Canyon.' It is a three-mile dirt road that may require four-wheel drive. Stay left as the road forks and it will lead you to the base of the canyon. Here you will find some of the ancient Indian 'morteros' or grave-sites. The canyon leads up to the southwest. The mountain itself can be observed from Highway S2, four miles west of Butterfield ranch. Two dirt roads lead up to the mountain. The Butterfield Ranch Resort is located at: 14925 Gt. S. Overland, Julian, CA, 92036. Phone: 760-765-2179."

I have been pleased to have Preston Dennett as a guest on Exploring The Bizarre, a weekly podcast I co-host with Emmy Award-winning producer Tim R. Swartz on the KCOR Digital Radio Network (all shows are archived at KCOR.com and can be found on my YouTube channel Mr. UFO's Secret Files – or simply under Tim Beckley. In the "golden days" of UFO newsstand publications, I relied on Preston to be a regular contributor to the now defunct UFO Universe and UFO Files magazines. I believe he told me last time we spoke that he had written seventeen books (don't hold me to that figure!) which included UFOs Over New Mexico, UFOs Over Arizona and the forthcoming UFOs Over Colorado. That's a hell of a lot of UFOs over somewhere.

Preston's conclusions: "UFOs definitely seem to be hovering over mines, and, in some instances, are actively digging there in gold mines, silver mines, copper mines, uranium mines, you name it."

Wild speculation? But certainly within the framework of this wondrous topic which hopefully will have you turning these pages till you have come to the end.

You're invited to step on over to Preston's website anytime – http://prestondennett.weebly.com/

A Wide And Perilous Sea—The Realm Of The Freebooters

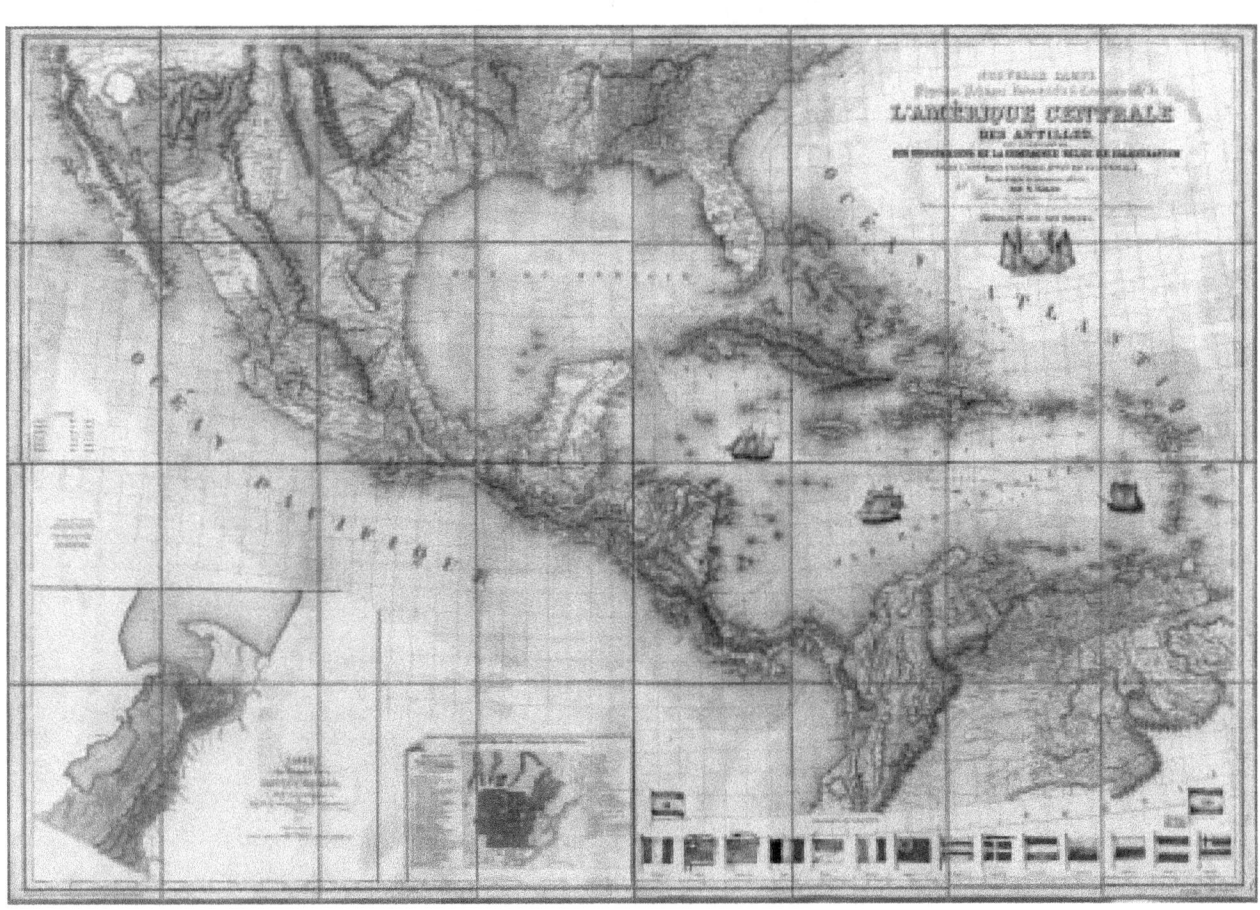

SPOOKY TREASURE TROVES

The late UFO Prophet Ted Owens was often in search of hidden treasure, seeking the guidance of his otherworldly friends for assistance in finding any hidden loot.

Ted Owens

THE UFO PROPHET "TALKS" TO A GHOST IN A HAUNTED ROOM
By Ted Owens

Note by coauthor Tim Beckley – There is no doubt that ghosts and treasure troves go together like salt and pepper. I remember the man they called the "UFO Prophet," Ted Owens, who would often talk about his exploits south of the border. One time he spilled the beans (bad pun) on how he had worked to hypnotize a woman who engaged a disembodied spirit that hopefully would lead all of them to a hidden treasure. I guess whatever they found was enough to enable Owens to drive onto the next town. Ted's story begins below here.

Some years ago I experienced several weird adventures in Mexico which I will never forget and never understand.

I had driven the long road across the Mexican desert from Texas down to Mexico City in an old Chevrolet. My purpose in going to Mexico City was to act as bodyguard for a lovely blonde girl trying to escape from a brutal man in Los Angeles. She paid me handsomely to deliver her to Mexico City, and I did. However, my real adventure began on the way back. I stopped over in Durango, Mexico, just at dusk, and asked a policeman on the street in my conversational Spanish where I could rent a room for the night in some place other than a tourist trap. He told me there was an old palace – which was not for touristas – but which he felt sure I would like. I thanked him, followed his directions, and entered the gate to the grounds of the palace. It wasn't really what I would call a palace but was indeed a huge mansion.

SPOOKY TREASURE TROVES

I was greeted by a gentleman in formal dress, with smooth, impeccable manners, who looked askance at my gringo attire – suede jacket, scuffed shoes, camera around my neck. But in a moment he smiled and told me to enter. He showed me to a suite of luxurious rooms with a high ceiling. And he told me to bathe and freshen up, that dinner would be served below in the dining room in an hour.

When I went down to the dining room, I was amazed to find that I was the only guest, seated myself at the end of a long, regal, glistening table. The meal was excellent – steak, salad, wine – and while I was dining this personable man stood nearby, ready to call the young waitress for anything I might want. And we chatted. He told me this mansion had been built up again from the ashes of a palace which had stood during the days of the Inquisition. The Spanish nobleman who owned the palace had to run for his life in the middle of the night, assembling his family and hiding his collection of fabulous jewels and his gold and silver at the bottom of an old well. Then, as the family fled, they put the torch to the palace, and it burned to the ground. Much later, the new mansion was constructed over the old site.

Many had tried to find the secret entrance to the old well and the treasure, but all had failed. But there was more. In one room of this mansion a ghost – a shimmery, moving, seemingly intelligent white cloud in a form somewhat like a human – had been seen to appear by maids, servants and various guests. The ghost always appeared in, or near, one certain room.

Well, as you might imagine, I was fascinated, intrigued. I had, some years before, attended Duke University and participated to some extent in the parapsychological experiments there. I had even tried my hand at being a spirit medium for the studies at Duke. So I suggested to my host that we assemble some persons in this haunted room later in the evening, at midnight, and see if we could attract the ghost. The gentleman stroked his chin, thought about it for a while, and then excused himself. He returned with his wife and told me that four others besides myself would volunteer to accompany me to the haunted room for the experiment. Well and good. I poured some more wine, lighted a good cigar, and patiently waited for the others to join us.

At midnight we were all seated in chairs inside the haunted room, which was an old storeroom high up in the top of the mansion. We locked the door on the inside. Our only light was a flickering candle on a table. Two of the group were an old crinkle-faced Spanish woman and her son, in his twenties, who spoke both English and Spanish and who attended a college in the United States.

At first, I asked them to be quiet, then called for any incorporeal spirits which might be there to signal us in some way. Perhaps by loud raps or knocks. Then the candle went out. We lighted it again and I had an inspiration. I asked my host if he

SPOOKY TREASURE TROVES

would like to try to find the hidden treasure on the grounds. He nodded. I explained that I would hypnotize the old Spanish woman and ask the spirit to guide her to the location of the treasure. It worked like a charm. She went into a somnambulistic state, rose, went to the door, unlocked it, and began descending the dark stairway, with us following. She led us down to an old, long-discarded fireplace, and stood there, pointing at the fireplace.

We thumped the walls and the floor trying to find a hollow space, but could find nothing. So I woke her, and we all went back up to the haunted room. I went through the same process, and the same thing happened. The old woman went back downstairs to the old fireplace and pointed. We gave up, and the séance ended. I went to my suite and had a wonderful sleep.

It was here that the marvelous thing happened. I packed my things, now ready to take them out to my car and resume my trip on the long, long road across the desert to San Antonio. But I recalled that up in the haunted room I had seen a very beautiful oil painting, full-size, of a nude reclining. So I took my camera and went up to the room. I took three shots of the nude painting, then, for some reason that didn't make sense, turned around and made pictures of the rest of the room and the balcony outside. Finally, feeling satisfied, I went down, assembled my belongings, got into my car and took off.

That night, at dark, a terrible storm came up, rain poured down and lightning crashed. I pulled into a lonely filling station where only a small boy, about 12, was on duty. He filled my gas tank, put in some oil, and then took me into the station to cash my bills and give me change. He had just handed me my change when a ghastly look came over his face. I turned and saw that a strange-looking, strangely-dressed man had entered the station. Another man stood just outside the door. The boy warned me, under his breath, that we were in great danger. I stuck my right hand down inside my coat, as if I had a pistol there.

The man spoke in rapid Spanish to the boy, who cringed. I figured that quick, bold action was needed on my part, so I talked loudly to the man, saying nothing that made sense, deliberately, hoping to confuse him. At the same time, I gestured with my left hand toward my coat pocket, stuck out my finger like I had a gun in the pocket, and edged around the man, who had taken out a knife and was eyeing me intently. I backed to the door, pushed aside the man who stood there,

SPOOKY TREASURE TROVES

Many a Western epic combined the lore of treasure, cowboys and outlaws and ghosts. The producers of "The Devil's Rain" took advantage of the macabre underground torture chambers and the lore of the unknown when they filmed around Durango in old Mexico.

and ran through the dark to my car. The men did not chase me and I drove off as fast as the old Chevy would go.

I drove all the next day and into the night. The next morning, I pulled out a blanket and decided to get some sleep. The last thing I remember is the hot sun beating down on me. When I awoke, I had no idea where I was. My hair stood straight up. If there is one thing I fear, it is spiders. And around me, forming an exact circle, was a ring of tarantulas. Huge, hairy things – each larger than my hand. They made no move toward me, nor to break the circle. I estimate there were about 20 of them.

Then I did another foolish thing. I leapt up, grabbed my blanket, and took a great jump over them. Later I discovered that any one of those tarantulas could have leapt clear over me. I jumped into car and took off, not even half-knowing what I was doing at the time.

Everything was in a haze. I had no notion what day it was, what time it was, or even what I was doing. Finally I came to a bridge. I looked into my rear view mirror. Nothing behind me and nothing ahead of me. So I slowed down and prepared to drive across the bridge. Again, that is all I know. When I came to I was lying beside my car with a hazy recollection of having been snapped backward and forward with a terrific force inside the car. I picked myself up and discovered a pickup truck behind my car. Two men were seated inside it. They didn't speak. They didn't even look at me. I figured they must have hit me from behind, but I had checked my mirror and no vehicle had been on the road. It was like being in a dream. I said nothing to the men, they said nothing to me. I got back into my car and drove ahead as if nothing had happened. In several hours, I reached San Antonio.

For some unknown reason, I drove to the Conrad Hilton and asked for a room, despite the fact that I didn't have more than $20 on me. The bellhop took

SPOOKY TREASURE TROVES

me to a floor high up in the hotel and threw open the door on a swank suite that couldn't have cost less than $100 a day. Before I could turn around and ask him why he had taken me to this room he had vanished.

It is not uncommon for skulls to be found buried in close proximity to a buried treasure, offering up evidence that perhaps spirits are close at hand, protecting what they had placed beneath the ground — or perhaps leading the way to its discovery.

Everything from that point on is a blur in my memory. I recall getting undressed and falling into bed. I recall somebody bringing me hot soup and something to eat. And I sent someone out with my pictures taken in Durango to have them developed. Days later, I awoke in a different room, a small room. My pictures were on the dresser. I picked them up. Good shots of Mexicans on their horses out in the desert . . . little children on the streets in Mexico City. Then I came to the Durango prints. Every photo I had taken in the haunted room had a black, shadowy figure, man-like, in it. It assumed different poses and shapes, but, no matter where I had pointed my camera in that room, that black figure was somewhere in the picture. Standing in the middle of that beautiful nude picture was the tall, shadowy shape!

Years have passed now. And as Ted Owens, "PK Man," I have become famous for my ability to communicate with UFO intelligence and PROVE it. Last summer at Brewer, Maine, I took some pictures in a mirror in an empty lodge beside a lake, and when the prints were developed, THERE WERE THE FACES OF CREATURES IN THE MIRROR WITH ME! Thus peculiar phenomena have happened to me twice in my life. These photos taken in Brewer are published in my book, "How to Communicate with Space People."

Looking back at the Mexico adventures, I now believe that during my long, lonely trip across the desert, I was captured and taken over by UFO creatures (for what purpose, I don't know), because my memory and mind up until I went to sleep in the desert that night were crystal clear. Who were the two men at the filling station? Who were the two men in the truck? What did the circle of spiders mean, and why didn't they attack me? How did I get that rich penthouse apartment in the Hilton Hotel? These are all questions I still can't answer. But, since

SPOOKY TREASURE TROVES

those days, my mind has miraculously gained astounding power. Until just recently I was accepted into Mensa, an international organization that will admit only those people into its group whose minds register in the top two percent of the general population.

Did the SIs do something to my mind, out there in the desert, to increase its power for their purposes? Yes, I am sure that they did. And only time will tell how this mental power increase on my part will be used to help bring about whatever it is the SIs want to bring about.

Note: Copies of *"How To Contact The Space People"* by Ted Owens can be obtained on Amazon. If you buy a copy and let us know, we will present you with a free SI disc which Ted claimed would assist in contacting his brand of ETs.

SPOOKY TREASURE TROVES

OREGON'S TREASURES GUARDED BY GHOSTS AND DEMONS
By Sean Casteel

Here is a buried treasure story with an abundance of macabre overtones and few equals in terms of overall treasure-related creepiness.

In an online posting on a site called "Pacific Northwest Photoblog," a contributor calling himself only "Rick" reports finding this story in the late 1980s to the early 1990s, but says he has no idea who wrote it originally.

The document Rick has unearthed is entitled *"A GHOST GUARDS THE TREASURE ON NEAHKAHNIE MOUNTAIN."*

"One summer afternoon," it begins, "many years ago, Indians near Neahkahnie Mountain were astonished to see two sailing ships approaching the coast. These were the first sailing ships ever seen along the Oregon Coast, and, to the Indians, they looked like 'great birds' as they raced in full sail toward the shore. Suddenly the ships drew close together, and, just beyond the breakers, they began to 'thunder' and puffs of smoke issued from their sides. After much noise and smoke, one of the ships began to list and was cast up on the beach near the foot of the mountain. The other sailed off over the horizon and was never seen again."

The one ship lurched onto the sand and men tumbled over its sides, staggering ashore through the surf. All of the men were white, except one, who was much larger than the others, a giant of sorts. He was black.

"To the Indians," the unknown author continues, "who assumed until then that there was only one race, these men of different colors were a frightening sight, and they regarded them much as we might regard visitors from another planet."

SPOOKY TREASURE TROVES

THE "BLACK DEMON" IS MURDERED

At low tide, the seafaring strangers straggled out to their ship and began to carry their belongings to the shore. Those items included a huge chest, so heavy and cumbersome that it took eight men to carry it. Struggling mightily, they carried the chest a short way up the mountain and dug a deep hole. Carefully, they lowered the chest into the hole. The black giant, whom the Indians believed was an evil demon, was told to step forward. When he did, he was killed and his body was thrown into the hole on top of the chest. The white men then filled the hole with sand and returned to the beach.

THE WHITE STRANGERS WEAR OUT THEIR WELCOME

"The Indians," the account says, "as usual in their initial dealings with white people, were friendly, generous and peaceful. They welcomed the strangers to their village, offered food and helped the men to obtain shelter for the coming winter. The white men, as usual in their dealings with people of another race, were quick to capitalize on the generosity of their hosts. They took food, land and other belongings from the Indians and offered venereal disease, measles and violence in return."

The sailors quarreled amongst themselves and with the Indians. Eventually an Indian was killed and the indigenous people retaliated by killing a white man. An uneasy balance was maintained by this method through two winters, but by

SPOOKY TREASURE TROVES

the third year the Indians could no longer tolerate their quick-tempered visitors, who had even begun to violate the native women at will.

A council among the local chiefs was held. One autumn morning, before dawn, 1500 warriors crept into the white men's camp and set fire to their dwellings. As the sailors ran from the blazing camp, the Indians killed them all. The white men were interred in a huge mound near the place where the chest and

the black man were buried. It is said that after this massacre the river ran red with blood for three days.

"The Indians, because of their reverence for the dead," the unknown writer explains, "never disturbed the burial place of the sailors, and, because of their fear of reprisal as the white presence grew in Oregon, refrained from talking about the massacre. Because of their fear of the 'black demon,' they never dug up the huge chest that the sailors buried near the beach. To this day, no one is sure what was in the chest, but many believed that the ship was a Spanish pirate ship and that the chest contained a fortune in gold."

HAS PROOF BEEN LEFT BEHIND?

The writer says there is considerable evidence supporting the belief in buried treasure near the Neahkahnie Mountain. Along with the Native-American

SPOOKY TREASURE TROVES

legends, there are records of Spanish ships, loaded with treasure gained in raids on South American cities, sailing northward from Peru, never to be heard from again.

Meanwhile, mysterious markings carved onto the rocks on the mountain could offer clues to the location of the treasure. At Three Rocks Beach, in North Lincoln County, skeletons and remnants of an old sailing vessel were discovered. Subsequent testing revealed that one of the skeletons belonged to a black man who was eight feet tall. Treasure hunters have also run across stone walls, masonry and giant mounds of rocks placed in the shape of an inverted "W" with a base nearly a mile long.

"If the treasure is there," the anonymous report concludes, "it has eluded an army of treasure hunters, most of whom came to Neahkahnie with a hunch, a shovel and a wheelbarrow. A few have come with bulldozers and backhoes. Many have come with metal detectors. Charles and Lynn Wood, a father and son, were killed when their 30-foot deep hole caved in on them in 1931. At least three others are known to have died in the attempt to find the treasure.

"Some say the treasure is there, but it will never be found. They believe that the ghosts of the black giant and his evil companions still guard the treasure of Neahkahnie and that they will keep the treasure hidden forever."

THE PIRATE MYSTERY ETCHED ON STONES

Another uncredited online article, called "Buried Treasure on Neahkahnie Mountain," begins by asking, "If you were a pirate stranded on the Oregon Coast, where would you hide your treasure chest? You'd have to have a landmark along

the coast that you could find again, keeping in mind it may be years – even decades – before you could recover your booty. What would you look for? A beach? A cave? A bay? How about the tallest formation on the coast – the 1,600-foot Neahkahnie Mountain? That might make a good landmark, even in the worst Oregon rain and fog."

The writer moves on to say that rumors that the lofty mountain concealed a pirate treasure date back well into the 19th century when the first European-American settlers came to the northern part of the west coast. The early pioneers were astounded to hear the story told to them by the local Clatsop and Tillamook Indians about a huge sailing vessel that had crashed onto Neahkahnie

SPOOKY TREASURE TROVES

Beach at least a century earlier, in the 1700s.

"The ship was ruined," the writer recounts, "but the men who sailed managed to salvage a large chest from the wreckage which they hauled up the forested slopes. Once they found a suitable spot, the men dug a deep hole and placed both the chest and a dead human body inside. The placement of a corpse along with a treasure chest was a well-known pirate custom. It was believed that the ghost of the dead man would guard the treasure until the pirates could return and collect it. With the gruesome task completed, the strangers left the area and were never seen again."

This is essentially the same story told at the beginning of this chapter, but in this version the pirates sail away and never return after burying the treasure with a corpse thrown in as a kind of ghostly burglar alarm. The part about the indigenous people being initially hospitable but later finding themselves driven to slaughter the evil pirates is not repeated here. Perhaps this is because of the tribes' reluctance to tell a story that might have invited vengeance from the white settlers who came later.

In any case, no one paid much attention to the old Indian tale until the early 1890s, when strange stones were found on the slopes of Neahkahnie Mountain. The stones were inscribed with odd images and symbols, like letters, arrows, numbers and crisscrossing lines. Some of the markings were carved in hard volcanic stone, others in softer sandstone.

"Treasure hunters immediately declared that the stones were left by the mysterious visitors, probably as markers to the buried pirate hoard," the article continues.

But Gary E. Allbright, a local historian, believes some of the pirate treasure legend was promoted by real estate developers eager to sell land to people from Portland and elsewhere. The developers would often advertise the legend, subtly suggesting that a lucky homeowner might actually find the treasure buried on their newly purchased property. Allbright also believes the inscribed stones are forgeries intended to keep the treasure rumors alive. He says this is especially true of the etched sandstone specimens that would have quickly disintegrated in the wet environment of the Oregon Coast.

If you want to make the trip to the Oregon beach and try your hand at finding the treasure yourself, the site provides the GPS coordinates to the Neahkahnie Mountain Overlook:

45.744600, -123.960851

A SPOOKY OREGON LAKE

In an article entitled *"Creepy Crater Lake, Oregon: Exploring the Legends, Lost Gold and a History of Mystery,"* writer Cody Meyocks opens with some humorous Oregonian self-deprecation.

"Oregon is famous for a few things," he begins. "Namely rain and being north of California."

But there is one wonder of the wild called Crater Lake, located in the Cascade Range of Southwest Oregon, that is worthy of our attention.

"It is a bright blue cistern of pure rainwater lying in the crater of a long-dormant volcano named Mount Mazama," Meyocks writes. "After violent eruptions exhausted the mountain's central spine of magma, Mazama's peak collapsed in on itself, leaving a giant bowl of ash and stone – known in geology as a 'caldera' – which now holds the majestic Crater Lake. In true Oregon fashion, it's more or less a famous puddle. But it's a beautiful puddle, attracting half a million visitors each year who come to admire its twelve square miles of heavenly blue. At one time, the lake was thought to be bottomless, but now it's measured at 1,943 feet, making it the deepest in the U.S."

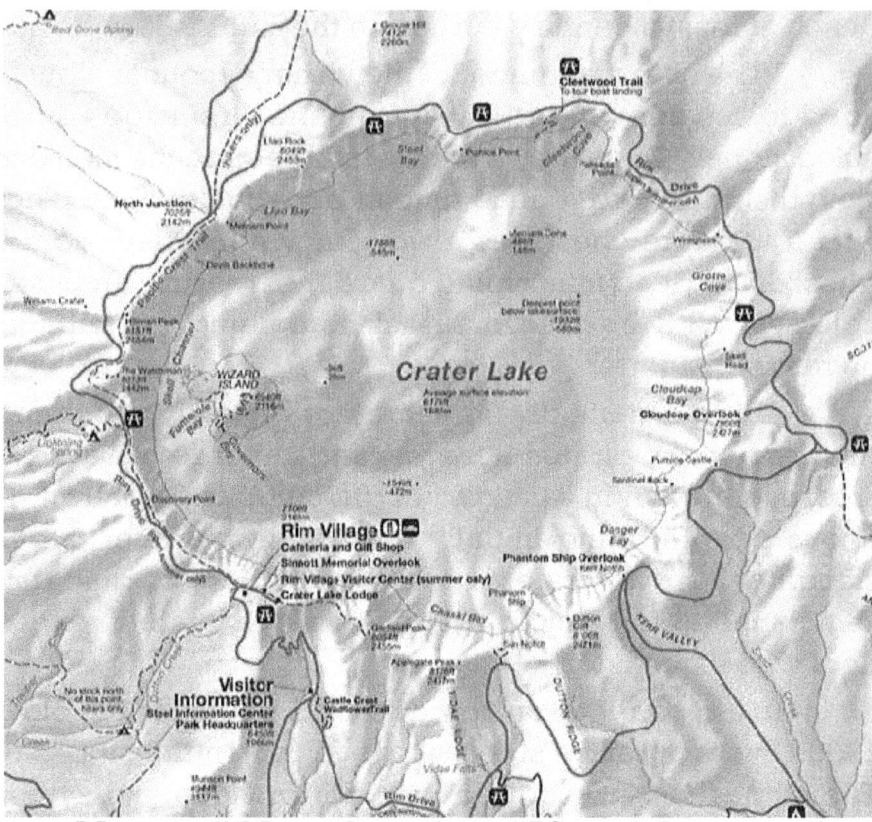

BIGFOOT, UFOs AND SPIRITS OF TERROR

According to Meyocks, Crater Lake is a hotbed for strange disappearances, ghostly encounters and legendary beasts.

"Bigfoot himself is known to show up here from time to time," Meyocks writes. "Rangers once reported following a large, dark, putrid-smelling creature through the woods until it started throwing pinecones at them. The area is also home to at least two claimed slayings of the Sasquatch. One was by car (the body was reportedly whisked away by the government), and one was by train. The train conductors didn't report slamming into something that looked like the legendary beast – for fear they'd be accused of drinking on the job.

"UFOs are no strangers to the area either," he goes on. "In February 1997 a jet pilot reported military aircraft pursuing UFOs above the lake. That night a loud sonic boom was heard all across Western Oregon. Strange lights make periodic appearances in the area."

There are also interesting Native-American legends about the area. The Klamath Indians say that to gaze upon the splendid blues of Crater Lake is to invite "Death and lasting sorrow." The Modoc tribe, who lived on the lake's borders for millennia, say it is an evil home of dark spirits and maintain a strict taboo against the place. It is essentially the home of the natives' version of the devil and it is said that people often disappear there.

Ghouls have been spotted in Crater Lake even in modern times. For instance, tourist Mattie Hatcher was rowing merrily along about the lake with her family when something "a block long" swam beneath their boat. "I have never been so scared in my life," she said. "What we saw that day was a monster. To me, it looked like a dragon. I know why the Indians call that place Lost Lake. They say monsters live in it. I believe them. I know, because I saw one there."

THE SEARCH FOR THE TREASURE OF "SET-'EM-UP"

"Whether the culprit is water monsters, Sasquatch, restless souls or something else, an abnormal amount of people have disappeared in and around Crater Lake," Meyocks writes. "The first settlers to find the lake were themselves investigating a mysterious disappearance – or, more likely, the treasure that went along with it."

The story revolves around a gold miner called "Set-'em-up," so named because he would come into the town of Yreka, California, with more than enough gold to buy the whole saloon a round. He would throw a little satchel of gold at the barkeep and holler, "Set-'em-up," which earned him his nickname. But his real name has been lost to history. His generosity also earned him a rabble of friends who were concerned about his safety when they hadn't heard from him for a couple of years.

Thinking that Set-'em-up was dead and having a rough idea of where his mine was located, they set out to find it. After stocking up on supplies in Jacksonville, Oregon, they headed off to the little-explored forests near Mount Mazama. While following the approximate directions they had to Set-'em-up's abode, they hit a fork in the trail. One party split to the left and one to the right, vowing to meet back at the spot before nightfall.

Isaac Skeeters, who had gone on the right fork, suddenly came to a spot where his horse refused to budge. Feeling curious, he dismounted to see what blocked their way.

"Much to his dread," Meyocks continues, "he found himself perched on the sheer rim of Crater Lake. Disappointed (he'd obviously chosen the wrong path), he took note of his grand discovery and hurried back to the rendezvous point to

SPOOKY TREASURE TROVES

see if anyone else had had better luck. When he reached the trail fork, a man named Hillman, who had taken the left path, rode up waving his arms. He'd spotted a small, decrepit cabin beside a stream coming from a shallow cavern."

Skeeters and Hillman were galloping back to the cabin to claim their fortune when Hillman's horse lost its footing on a rock and tumbled over the edge of a canyon, killing Hillman and the horse on impact. Despite their best efforts, Skeeters and the rest of the team never found a trace of the cabin by the creek. They soon ran low on provisions and were forced to return home, having found only an inconsequential lake. To this day the cabin has never been relocated, and old Set-'em-up became the first case among numerous others of mysterious disappearances in the Crater Lake region.

"What may have transpired (or expired) around the lake before the last hundred years of recorded history," Meyocks concludes, "brings us back to the stuff of legend, which, if those old tales had been heeded in the first place, might have avoided some of the misfortune surrounding this mountain today. Is Crater Lake cursed? Is Mount Mazama the abode of some ancient evil? You decide, but I won't be sightseeing at Crater Lake anytime soon."

SPOOKY TREASURE TROVES

COWBOY GHOSTS AND SPECTRAL MINERS:
Stories Collected By Paul Dale Roberts

Paul Dale Roberts is a longtime paranormal investigator who is sometimes called the world's foremost "Esoteric Detective" as he goes about seeking the truth behind mysteries that have as yet no final answers.

One of the stories he has collected involved his late half-brother Joseph "Joe" Anthony Soyo, a world traveler who at times worked alongside Greenpeace saving endangered species of animals on an international basis.

"My half-brother had a strong interest in the paranormal," Roberts writes, "and loved to dabble in magic. During his visit to Greenland he became fascinated with how the Vikings under Erik the Red created settlements in this cold, forbidding land."

Roberts points out that the Kingittorsuaq rune stone was discovered in Greenland, and there are numerous other artifacts and treasures believed to be buried there as well. Similar stories are told about the Isle of Man, located in the Irish Sea between the islands of Great Britain and Ireland. At the Isle of Man, a nice-sized gold ingot was found, along with a gold ring, a silver seal and other artifacts and treasures believed to have been left behind by seafaring Vikings.

But along with the tantalizing rumors of treasure comes a paranormal element. For example, a woman named Dana Goldberg claimed to have been abducted from her home in Portland, Maine, in 1972. Goldberg's abductors, the familiar gray aliens, took her to an underwater base in the ocean near Greenland. The alien leader told her that the base extended under Heart Mountain near Uummannaq in order for them to mine the basalt found in the volcanic rock.

"Greenland is known for its rich minerals," Roberts explains, "and would actually be a perfect place to harvest minerals if you were an extraterrestrial."

Reports of elves and fairies in Greenland are commonplace, and, according to Roberts' brother Joe, UFO sightings happen frequently in both Greenland

SPOOKY TREASURE TROVES

UFOs have become so engrained in the culture of Greenland that flying saucer-shaped structures have even been constructed in even the most remote, snow-laden, locales.

and the Isle of Man. One resident of Greenland told Joe that the UFO occupants are much interested in the buried treasures there because they contain some form of ancient, secret knowledge. Should mankind stumble on to this hidden wisdom, it would disturb the balance of power between humans and extraterrestrials, giving earthly people the upper hand.

"The extraterrestrials are very protective of these treasures," Roberts writes, "and if necessary will cause harm to treasure seekers. They do not want this hidden knowledge to be discovered. Some of these ancient treasures have been taken by the UFOs."

One Greenland witness has stated that he actually saw a UFO send down some kind of power beam with which it pulled up an object – which he believed to be some kind of hidden treasure – and then zipped away.

THE GHOST OF "RATTLESNAKE" DICK BARTER

That's a classic sounding Old West name, isn't it? "Rattlesnake" Dick Barter. But Barter was a genuine historical personage who operated as a highwayman – or roving thief – in the Gold Country that was California in the 1850s. Barter was also on friendly terms with Joaquin Murrieta Carrillo, who was often called the Mexican Robin Hood and is said to be the real life inspiration for Zorro, the hero of many a movie bearing his name. Barter was also a friend to Black Bart, aka Charles Earl Bowles, the Gentleman Bandit.

Black Bart and "Rattlesnake" Dick Barter allegedly robbed a stagecoach together in Placer County, which quickly drew the ire of Wells Fargo agents, who arrested Black Bart and left him doing time in the prison at San Quentin. But Barter was still a free man and continued to rob the gold being transported by stage coaches. He not only had Wells Fargo agents on his trail, but was also being sought by the Pinkerton Detective Agency.

Barter's adventures as a career criminal eventually brought him to Auburn, California, where the wife of Paul Dale Roberts was born. Her name is Deanna Jaxine Stinson, and she recalls to this day feeling a ghost in a peach orchard in Auburn.

"The sensation was strong," Roberts writes, "and it was like she'd stepped backward into time. It was known that 'Rattlesnake' Dick Barter buried a cache of gold in a peach orchard. Is it possible that Deanna, a sensitive, picked up on the spirit of 'Rattlesnake'?"

Plus there are other, more direct, witness reports. Misty Langford, of Placerville, says that one morning at 3 A.M. she saw a tall cowboy wearing a long coat.

Outlaw "Rattlesnake" Dick Barter's ghost is said to point in the direction of his stolen horde.

For the coat, the cowboy pulled out a bag that was tied and looked like it had coins inside. As Misty stared at the figure in shock, she realized she could see right through him. It was an ethereal apparition. The cowboy looked at her, then walked away, right through a wall of a building. Misty has no explanation for it, but firmly believes she saw "Rattlesnake." When she later described the figure she had seen to an Auburn historian, she was told she had described "Rattlesnake" to a tee.

The ghost of "Rattlesnake" has also been seen in numerous locations in Northern California. Ned Samuel of Yuba City claims to have seen the ghost at the Silver Dollar Saloon in Marysville. Ned is a psychic who has sighted many other ghostly figures from the Old West, like Virgil Earp's ghost and that of H.H. Holmes, the latter being famed for being America's first serial killer. When Ned Samuel saw the ghost of "Rattlesnake," the ethereal highwayman tried to whisper in Samuel's ear. Samuel said the voice was demonic and shook him to the core of his soul, but he has no idea what the "Rattlesnake" was hoping to communicate to him.

"Rattlesnake" tried for a time to live an honest life panning for gold, but he was continually blamed for every theft that took place along the river. He grew tired of being constantly under suspicion and decided to return to his life of crime,

SPOOKY TREASURE TROVES

earning the nickname of the "Pirate of Placer." It was part of his legend that no jail could hold him. Nevertheless, he died in a shootout with sheriff's deputies at 26 years of age. His lifeless body was displayed at the Masonic Hall's doorsteps for all the townsfolk to see, but the gold he took from the Wells Fargo stage coaches was never recovered.

Cynthia Tyler from Loomis says that she once saw the ghost of "Rattlesnake" Dick Barter pointing north. She still wonders if he was trying to point towards the buried gold. She tried to return to the location where she had seen the ghost but can't seem to remember it.

THE HAUNTED GRIFFITH QUARRY AT PENRYN, CALIFORNIA

Ghostly image photo taken at Griffith Quarry with possible spirit intervention or just ordinary double exposure?

Paul Dale Roberts begins his story on a haunted granite mine with a little historical background. The Penryn Granite Works office and quarry were established by Griffith Griffith, a native of Wales, in 1864. The park has three miles of trails, picnic sites and views of the old quarry pits. The quarry produced high-quality granite used to construct many of the buildings in San Francisco and Sacramento, including parts of the California State Capitol. The 23 acres that surround the two-story main building, made of granite blocks, are the remains of the quarry and its polishing mill. This was the first successful granite polishing mill in California.

In the years that quarry workers worked on the high quality granite, several accidents and deaths occurred. Which leads Roberts to speculate that a continually repeating residual energy would be left behind by the accidents, and the deaths would result in some kind of "intelligent energy" remaining on the scene as well. A Loomis resident named Leo Tanaka says that late at night you can hear banging on the rocks, a noise he calls the work of the Tommy Knockers, a supernatural phenomenon associated with mines that will be dealt with elsewhere in this book.

At the Griffith Quarry, one Gerald Reeves of Auburn says he witnessed two granite miners pounding on the rocks. Thinking they were actors, Gerald called out to them. The two "miners" looked up at him and then vanished into thin air.

Roberts and his "sensitive" wife, Deanna, made a visit to the quarry and stopped at several points to conduct EVP sessions, or to attempt to hear spirit voices by electronic means. At one point, a voice conjured in this way says, "Okay. Turn around. I'm here." Deanna began to use her crystal skulls to enhance her ability to detect whatever presence was there.

Roberts then instructed everyone in the party to take photos at every stop on the way in the hope they could capture various anomalies that would later be present when the photos were developed. A member of the party next begin to complain of nausea and dizziness and feeling as though she had been "blinded." Roberts commented that it might be a reaction to the heat that day, a blazing 104 degrees, or might have been brought on by the paranormal forces in the area. Since he is not a medical doctor, he could only offer his non-professional opinion.

The stricken woman would later write to Roberts, telling him that the various symptoms cleared up as soon as she left the area. "It was very weird," she says. "I wasn't tired or dizzy or anything like I was while we were walking the quarry. I know you said it could have been paranormal, but I brushed it off as just lack of food. But now that I look back, I feel like it might have been paranormal. I'm not sure."

Roberts speculates further that an entity or group of entities may have been draining the woman of her energy in order to communicate with the group through EVPs. Energy is a ghost or phantom's food, and the woman may have been used to provide enough "food" to allow the voices to speak. She may also have psychic abilities of which she is presently unaware which led the entities to focus on her like a moth to a flame.

In any case, Roberts makes a good case for the Griffith Quarry being a haunted mining location, rife with various otherworldly energies and residues. To

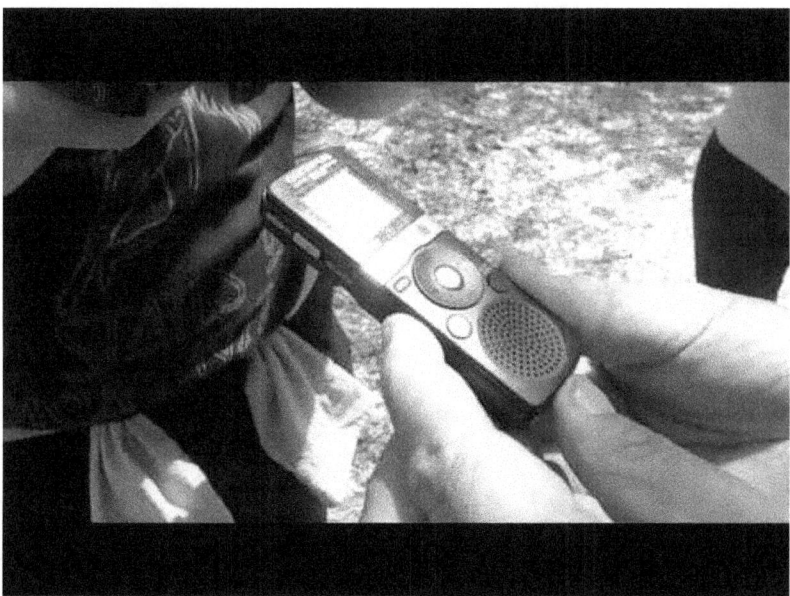

A member of Paul Dale Robert's investigative team tries to lock in on possible EVP transmission.

add a cherry to the cake, he passes along a UFO sighting that took place near the quarry on January 23, 1953.

"Linda Callahan and Mary Foxworth were near the granite quarry when they spotted three blue globes in the sky. The globes all rotated in the same direction. It was 3 P.M. As the two ladies stared at the globes, the globes went straight up in the air at an incredible speed and seemed to disappear.

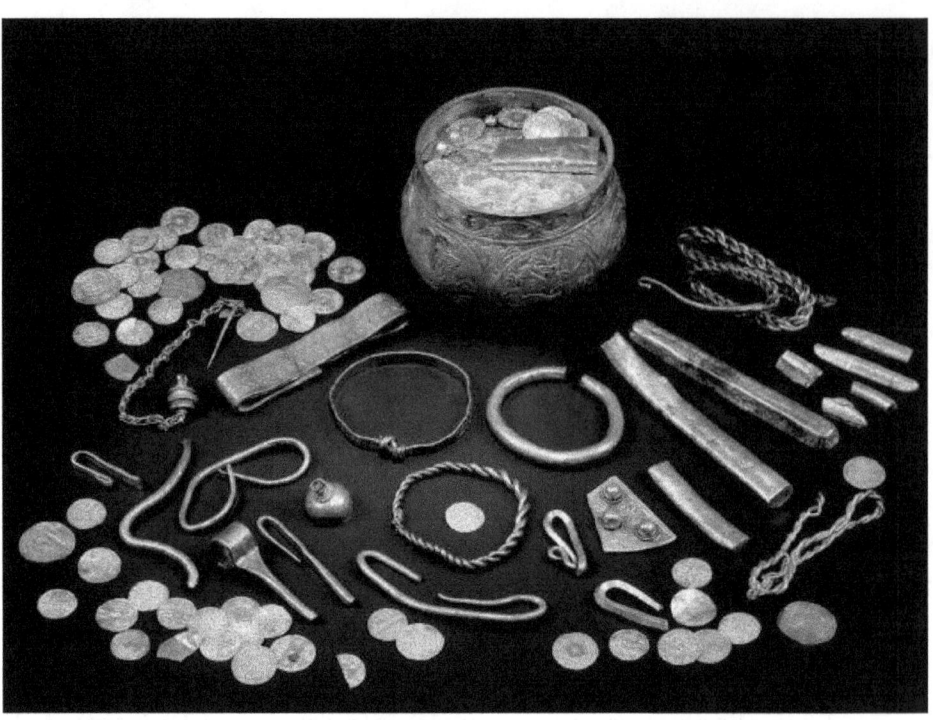

A few treasure "trinkets" left behind by the Vikings on U.K. soil which currently reside in the British Museum.

"Legend has it," the report goes on, "that extraterrestrials are interested in the following: 1. Gold. 2. Quartz – the quarry contains high quality granite that has quartz in it. 3. Human abduction that involves implanting alien implants, probing body parts, pregnancy, sexual/reproductive organs, the brain, etc. 4. Animal abductions and possible cattle mutilations. 5. Volcanoes, earthquake fault lines, ley lines – these could be refueling areas for their UFOs."

Do the aliens methodically and purposively seek out and protect minerals like gold and quartz? Are ghostly highwaymen part of the aliens' continuum of phenomena, which ranges freely between flying saucers and the world of the dead? Paul Dale Roberts doesn't offer definitive answers but he does offer tantalizing evidence in the affirmative to all of the above.

SPOOKY TREASURE TROVES

COUNTING THE DEAD IN CAHUENGA PASS AND THE CURSES ON CHARLES ISLAND

The treasure of Cahuenga Pass is a story of treasure lost and found. And, while the Pass goes on through the mountains for miles, there are some who say the treasure was buried near where the Hollywood sign is now located.

What constitutes a truly cursed treasure? One way to measure a treasure's "accursedness" is to examine the number of deaths related to its attempted recovery.

THE HOLLYWOOD BOWL DISAPPOINTMENT SUICIDE

In an online article written by Steve Moramarco about the Cahuenga Pass treasure and the large number of corpses that were laid on top of it, we see a particularly grisly example.

"With a story as winding as the Cahuenga mountains themselves," Moramarco writes, "it begins in 1864 when four soldiers sent by Benito Juarez went to San Francisco with a treasure trove of coins and jewels to purchase munitions for the Mexican War. Along the way, one of the men died and the other three buried the bounty for safekeeping. However, a wanderer named Diego Morena was watching, and he made off with the money soon afterward, traveling down south and stopping in Los Angeles in what was known as Cahuenga Pass."

SPOOKY TREASURE TROVES

That night, while staying in a local tavern, Morena dreamed that he would die if he took the loot with him to Los Angeles. In a state of panic, he buried the treasure but he died quickly afterward nonetheless. Before his passing, Morena told his friend Jesus Martinez where the treasure had been buried. Martinez set out to find the money with his stepson, but he had a heart attack and died when they began digging. Ten years later, the stepson was killed in a shootout in East Los Angeles.

A Basque shepherd found a small bit of the treasure in 1885, but he too perished when he fell overboard from a ship as he was trying to sail back to Spain. The gold in his pockets, ironically, only served to help sink him to the bottom of the ocean.

Oil expert Henry Jones attempted to dig for the treasure in an area that butted up against the Hollywood Bowl, which had been erected in the 1920s in the Cahuenga Pass region of Los Angeles. The year was 1939, and on November 27, a film crew was on-hand to record what turned out to be an excavation of mere dirt. Jones committed suicide because of the failure later that year, adding one more victim to the body count.

WHEN "THREE" IS NOT A CHARM BUT A CURSE

Moramarco also writes about the Charles Island Curse, explaining that in this instance the curse extended beyond just the area where the treasure was buried and included the entire island.

Found off the coast of Milford, Connecticut, Charles Island is also known as "Thrice Cursed Island."

"First, the chief of the Paugussett tribe considered the area sacred," Moramarco writes.

When Europeans tried to settle in the area, the chief warned that, "Any shelter will crumble to the Earth, and he shall be cursed."

The chief was apparently right. No buildings have ever stood there for any long period of time.

The pirate Captain Kidd was also said to have cursed the island in 1699 during his last voyage, and his treasure is said to be buried there. In 1721, a third hex was placed on the island, supposedly by Mexican Emperor Guatmozin, whose riches were stolen and allegedly hidden there by sailors.

Two treasure hunters managed to find a buried chest on Charles Island in 1850, but when they opened it they were greeted by a flaming skull. The two men were then either executed or spent the rest of their lives in an insane asylum, depending on which story you hear. In either case, no other treasure has been found, but people still report mysterious lights and sounds emanating from the island.

SPOOKY TREASURE TROVES

RIDDLE OF THE TOMMYKNOCKERS

Many readers will recognize the name "Tommyknockers" as being the title of Stephen King's 1987 book and a subsequent 1993 ABC miniseries. Actually, King's book did not involve Tommyknockers as mythical creatures but was instead more of an exercise in science fiction in which the residents of a Maine town gradually fall under the influence of a mysterious object buried in the woods. King himself thought his novel "The Tommyknockers" was "awful" and admitted he had written it while struggling with substance abuse.

In "real" life, Tommyknockers are described as impish, gnome-like men who guard over the precious metals of the Earth. They are said to be the equivalent of Irish leprechauns and English brownies. Germans called them Berggeister or Bergmannlein, meaning "mountains ghosts" or "little miners."

The Cornish miners of Southern England believed these wee little men were the souls of the Jews who crucified Christ and were sent by the Romans to work as slaves in the tin mines. This belief was so strong that the Tommyknockers were allegedly never heard on Saturdays or during Jewish holidays.

Tommyknockers are reported to be about two feet tall and greenish in color. They look like men and appear to wear a miniature traditional miner's outfit. They

23

SPOOKY TREASURE TROVES

live beneath the ground and have been credited with both good and evil deeds through the centuries. They play practical jokes and commit random acts of mischief, such as stealing unattended tools and food.

It was the Cornish miners who worked in the Pennsylvania coal mines in the 1820s who first brought the Tommyknockers myth to America. When the California gold rush began in the 1840s, these same Cornish miners were welcomed and even sought after by mine owners who valued the immigrants' many years of experience.

Mine owners would often approach the skilled Cornish workers and ask if they had relatives back in England who might also come to work the mines. The miners would reply something like this: "Well, me cousin Jack over in Cornwall wouldst come could ye pay 'is boat ride." Soon the miners took on the nickname "Cousin Jacks" and formed the core of America's early western mining force.

The Cousin Jacks, notorious for diving out of mine shafts just before they collapsed, attributed their luck to their diminutive friends, the Tommyknockers. The immigrant miners would refuse to enter a new mine until they were assured by the management that the Knockers were already on duty. Even non-Cornish miners – who also worked deep in the Earth where the noisy support timbers creaked and groaned – came to believe in the Tommyknockers, though the Americans put more of a ghostly spin on the phenomenon as opposed to the elvish creatures believed in by the Brits.

The knocking sounds said to come from the Tommyknockers were frequently interpreted as a warning that the mine was about to cave in. To some miners, the knockers were malevolent spirits hammering at walls and supports to actually CAUSE the cave-in, while others thought the knocking was a way to warn miners that a life-threatening collapse was imminent. To give thanks for the warnings, and to avoid future peril, the miners cast the last bite of their tasty pastries into the mines for the Tommyknockers.

When these grizzled little gnomes were good, they were thought to bring miners favors and wealth, even leading them to rich veins of gold and other metals. When they were bad, the Tommyknockers could bring misery, injury and death to those who doubted their powers or simply didn't believe in them. If a hammer was missing, it was the Tommyknockers who had taken it, but if a miner escaped collapse, the Tommyknockers were given credit.

In some mines, where the Tommyknockers' presence was known to be overwhelmingly evil, the mines were forced to close because of the miners' fear of the spirits. When a mine played out, the imps were said to find "work" in the homes surrounding the old mineshaft and would foretell a death in the family or local disaster with the same knocking method employed in the mines.

Luck has always been a factor in the dangerous life of the miner, and their collective mythology includes the idea that women seen in or near a mine were bad luck. Historically, women only came to the mines in times of tragedy, looking for lost loved ones. A red-haired woman was considered an omen of death. This belief may be a remnant of the aversion to the red-haired Danes who ravaged parts of Cornwall in 997 A.D.

With the coming of modern systems of education and scientific approaches to mining, belief in the Tommyknockers has faded away. Electric lights make the mines less gloomy and modern machinery drowns out the sounds of knocking against the wooden timbers and rock walls. The folklore of the underground has lost some of its meaning, but retains its ability to mystify and entertain.

SOURCES FOR THIS CHAPTER

Tommyknockers: The Spirits of the Underground, by Carl Barna, from the History Mystery Examiner on the website of the Bureau of Land Management.

Ghostly Legends and Mysteries: Tommyknockers of the Western Mines, by Kathy Weiser. http://www.legendsofamerica.com/gh-tommyknockers.html

Tommyknockers and Red-haired Women, by Daryl Burkhard http://www.darylburkhard.com/tommyknockers.html

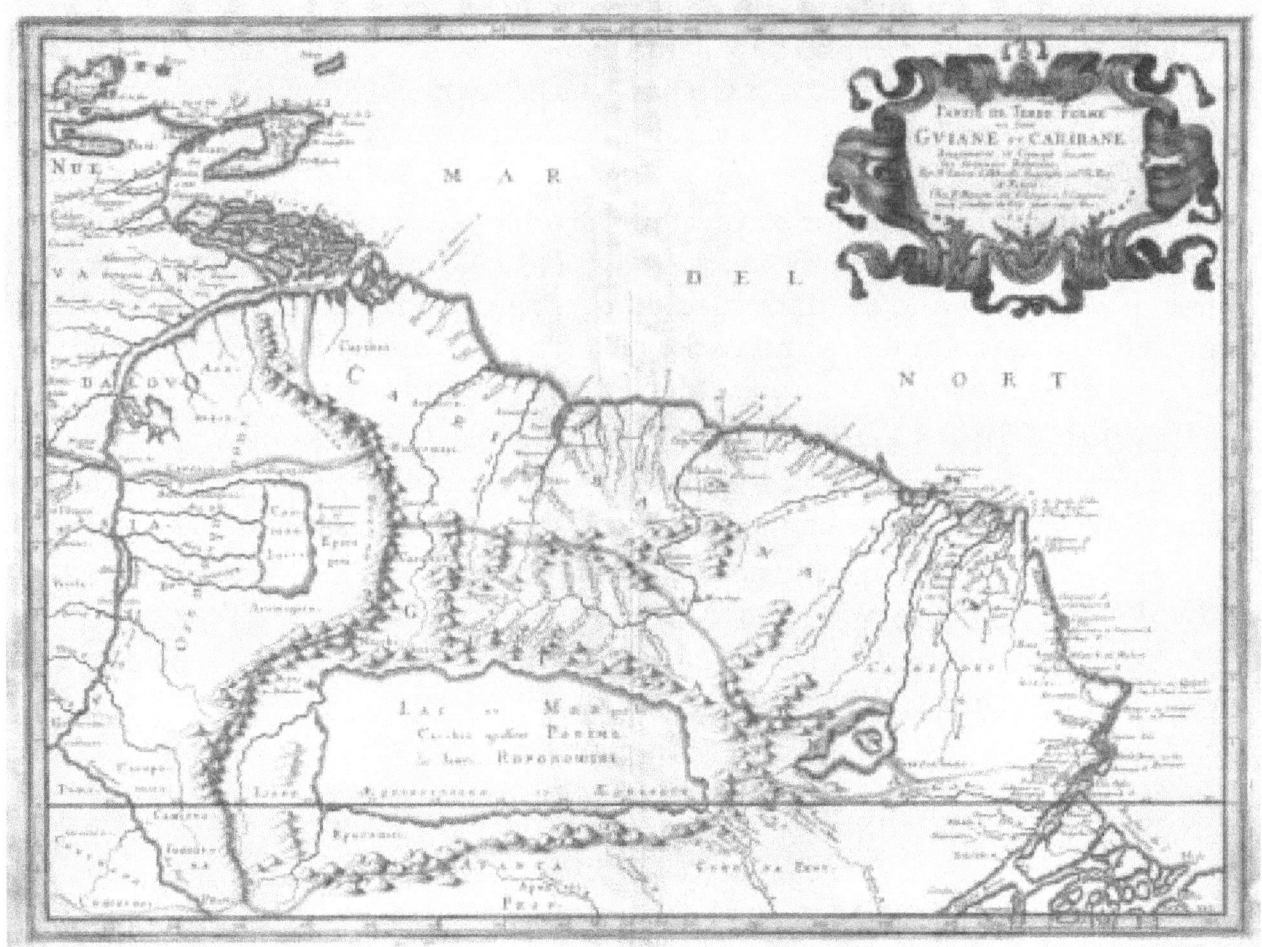

Unroll this 1630s map and you will certainly find El Dorado.

THAT WHICH GLISTENS: ACCURSED TREASURE
By Scott Corrales

Several legends have grown up about treasure chests covered in blood. There is, for example, a treasure in Argentina that is stained by the blood spilled in fighting over it and thus is cursed, inevitably bringing evil misfortune to the treasure hunter who finds it. It involves a nearly Shakespearean plot of a noble but childless marriage and a hurried flight with a caravan of forty mules burdened with the weight of untold wealth. Scott Corrales is the leading researcher in the US who devotes his time almost exclusively to gathering information on UFO incidents in Spanish-speaking nations. He has not for a moment missed the connection between a vast variety of paranormal manifestations and fascinating treasure lore.

Few things fire the human mind as much as the thought of treasure: hoards of gold and silver coins, precious jewels and adornments, exquisitely wrought decorations and other objects that bespeak the wealth of forgotten monarchs and

SPOOKY TREASURE TROVES

lost kingdoms. From a child's dream of peg-legged pirates burying oak chests filled with doubloons and pieces of eight on some lonely island to exhaustive searches by scholars and adventurers, the search for the concealed wealth of yore has been the source of poems, books and motion pictures.

The allure doubles, though, when the treasure is said to be cursed...

From the Lands of El Dorado

One of Latin America's fabled treasure hoards is the one belonging to the Marquis of Yaví y Tojo, which had to be hauled away by forty mules burdened with gold and silver.

In 1679, Juan José Campero de Herrera, a noble member of the knightly order of Calatrava (created from the remains of the Knights Templar), had the good fortune to marry well: his bride, Juana Bernardes de Obando, was the great-granddaughter of the famous General Zárate, who had been given enormous land-grants and money by the Spanish viceroy for having established a town in the Andean valley of Jujuy (modern Argentina). The Obando family's fiefdom extended from the vicinity of Humahuaca to the city of Tarija (modern Bolivia), giving the reader a fair idea of the extent of this land-grant. The knight of Calatrava therefore acquired, through marriage, a territory the size of Switzerland and Serbia combined, as well as the title of Marqués de Yaví y Tojo. After being pronounced man and wife, Campero de Herrera had acquired wealth, nobility and power in a single stroke.

Far from what one would expect after such unexpected bounty, Campero de Herrera did not sit back to enjoy his good fortune, but rather devoted himself to making improvements to his domain, building dams to control the flow of a nearby river, flour mills to feed the vast nations of natives under his sway, and installed facilities to retrieve abundant placer gold from the rivers. But even the best fairy tales have their downside: his wealthy bride proved barren, and hopes of perpetuating the family name were dashed. Ever pious, Campero de Herrera built two churches to seek divine intervention in the vicissitudes of biology.

Modern historians have found church documents attesting to the wealth of the childless marquis: a business contract makes mention of three hundred and thirty quintales of silver (an old unit of measure equivalent to 100 kilograms) being mined at Cochinoca – sixteen thousand kilograms of silver ore.

The marquis dug tunnels underneath his country house, Alicate, as a way to reach the mine workings and perhaps as exit routes in case of an attack by hostile natives. Perhaps Campero de Herrera could see the clouds gathering in the horizon; his excessive wealth and good fortune had led him to believe that it was possible to separate his fiefdom from the viceroyalty and run it as an independent domain. The plan failed, and Campero de Herrera was forced to set all of his business documents and books to the torch. But there would be no impoverished exile for the knight of Calatrava. Instead, he loaded his fortune onto the backs of forty mules and vanished, along with his wife and retainers, in 1696, never to be seen again.

After this lengthy prologue, it is here that the "legend of the lost treasure of the Marqués de Yaví y Tojo" begins. Tradition holds that the marquis, unable to cross the Andes with such a fabulous burden, decided to bury his kingly wealth in a place from which it could be recovered at a later date. In order to avoid any problems involving faulty recall or geographical changes, the marquis drew symbols marking the site. These can be seen in a canyon overlooking the Yaví River and resemble odd hieroglyphics showing what appears to be a sea anchor and a feline figure. The locals are adamant that the scrawls are not native petroglyphs but marks made by the marquis to show the location of the treasure.

Relieved of his burden, states the legend, the fugitive nobleman reached a wilderness known as Siete Corrales. There, it is said, Campero de Herrera and his wife were slain by natives who took the forty mules which still carried considerable quantities of food and valuables.

There are native structures in the La Mendieta mountain range which surrounds the area. Could these hold the marquis' lost silver treasure? Local ranchers believe that it would be possible to find the leather bags carried on muleback by dredging the Yuruma Creek, the body of water along which the ambush took place. This lost treasure awaits the brave souls willing to claim it.

An alien seems to be carefully watching children, but is he more concerned with protecting a lost treasure?

But the Marquis of Yaví y Tojo's lost treasure isn't Argentina's only lost treasure trove, according to retired school principal Christina Coccari, who cites the oral traditions of her country's Tuy region (a Guaraní word meaning "soft mud"), which includes the towns of Lavalle, Madariaga and Villa Gesell. In 1820, the fledgling Argentinean government built a series of forts to keep the nomadic tribes at bay. Wagons filled with bricks for this construction effort reached the area from Chascomús and three forts were erected: Juancho Viejo, Invernadas and La Porteña. The government then entrusted a military man, General Alzaga, with the task of colonizing the region and dispersing the Pampas tribesmen, who were known for their raids and for abducting the colonists' women and children. Ten years later, one such raid by the Pampean chieftain "Arbolito" (Little Tree) destroyed the forts and killed the settlers, except for one young woman who had survived along with a leather chest filled with silver and gold coins that was buried at the foot of a tree marked by a hanging Rosary.

The young survivor told the tragic story to a priest, Father Castañeda, who ordered that the treasure chest be located. Despite their best efforts, this was never accomplished, for a local child had found the Rosary dangling from the tree and taken it to her mother.

Contemporary belief holds that the treasure chest is located in the "El Rosario" lagoon, but that the hoard is "accursed" due to the blood that was spilled over it and will therefore represent a source of misfortune for anyone who comes across it.

Do UFOs guard solid gold figures like this one, thought to be worth millions upon million of dollars in today's pre-Colombian antiquities market?

Treasures of Old Mexico

Mexico reputedly holds a number of undiscovered treasures that are waiting to be claimed by an intrepid adventurer. One of them is the so-called "Tesoro del Fraile" (the Friar's Treasure) buried somewhere in the northern state of Coahuila. During the gold and silver boom times that pervaded throughout the Mexican vice-regal area, a number of treasure troves were stolen and concealed. This particular one, according to historian Rubén Dávila Farías, involves a series of letters written by Fray Pedro de Noyola, a priest who left Mexico during the country's War of Independence. In one missive, dated January 20, 1811, the priest asks Cipriano Lozoya, a resident of the port of Veracruz, to go north to Coahuila to find a buried treasure: "It will not be possible for me to return to that country in which I lived so joyfully...but perhaps chance may lead you, my friend, to a happy and wild region known as the Bolsón de Mapimí, where you shall find a hill known as La Bufa. On that hill, with its face toward the rising sun in the month of May, you can see a [mountain] range that dominates that height and two smaller hills not too far away. The point of reference I must give you is known as Antiguo Mineral de Mapimí..."

The priest goes on to explain that in a cave halfway up the small western hill, known as Guadalupe, there is a cave. The treasure hunter was to walk a distance of "twenty rods" from the cave entrance and dig "three rods down" to find four strongboxes containing gold and silvery jewelry belonging to the Church, plus an alleged 200 boxes of gold and silver coins "minted with the effigy" of King Charles V. A further, grislier find would also be the bones of the four mules used to haul this amazing wealth. Elena González, a resident of Torreón in the State of Coahuila, told television journalist Nino Canún in 1993 that she possessed the "gift of voices" and that one such voice had guided her and her friends to a series of caves where she found a "little bag of cloth containing sixteen silver pieces." Had Ms. González been given a foretaste of the greater wealth of the Friar's Treasure?

Nostradamus's "Accursed Hoard"

Michel de Nostradamus, born in 1503 in the village of Saint Remy, in Provence, has been considered by many as the most important post-Biblical prophet for the enigmatic verses known as the Centuries. Michel was the great-grandson of Pierre de Nostradamus, a court physician who attended the kings and dukes of France. Born into a family of mathematicians and philosophers, Nostradamus's work has been interpreted and re-interpreted to suit all manner of interests. Many have overlooked some of the lesser quatrains utterly unrelated to eschatology – and one of them has to do with lost treasure.

The 27th Quatrain (XXVII) reads thus:

Dessous de chaine Guien du Ciel frappé.
Non loing da lá est caché le tresor,
Qui par long siecles avoir esté grappé,
Trouver mourra, l'oeil crevé de ressor.

("Under the mountains of Guyana by heaven punished
Not far away there is treasure concealed,
Having for long ages being sealed
Death to he who finds it, eyes by springs pierced")

The 27th quatrain, a prophecy having nothing to do with the rise or fall of kings or great wars, has been ignored, as have been others, such as the 10th – interpreted by some as foretelling the rise of cinematography as an art ("serpents sealed in cages of iron"). The revelation of a hidden treasure trove in the Guyana Highlands is certainly fascinating, and no one has ever made an effort to find it. The treasure, says Nostradamus, will remain inviolate, and the curse upon the first one to lay eyes upon it shall remain in force. The "eyes by springs pierced" suggest some ingenious booby trap set by the filibuster or pirate who was forced to leave his wealth in this remote, inhospitable location. Such devices, reminiscent of the harrowing experiences of the fictional Indiana Jones in the opening

SPOOKY TREASURE TROVES

moments of Raiders of the Lost Ark, are known to have existed. It is believed that the tomb of Shi Huangdi, the legendary Yellow Emperor, is still defended by arrows set on hair-triggers.

A Succession of Spirit Guardians

It isn't enough for a hoard to be accursed by its previous owner or due to the violence that has characterized efforts at seeking its possession; sometimes supernatural guardians are appointed to guard the treasure and perform their task with chilling efficiency. Among the considerable holdings of the Cleveland Public Library, we come across two fascinating occult tomes, the Libellus Magicus and the Praxis Magica. These volumes apparently formed part of the collection of A. E. Waite, the renowned occultist. The Libellus, also known as "The True Magical Work of the Jesuits," contains a variety of conjurations and spells, among them "St. Cyprian's Invocation of Angels and his Conjuration of the Spirits Guarding Hidden Treasure" – a means by which a treasure hunter may adjure the paranormal forces to relinquish the treasures entrusted to their care.

Such supernatural aids would probably come in handy to the brave souls willing to dare some lost hoards, such as the one allegedly contained within the Khabriat Douma cave system in the mountains of Lebanon. Important due to its strategic value, the town of Douma attracted the attention of conquerors throughout the ages until it was finally burned down by the Ottoman Turks in the 17th century. According to local legends, a vast treasure of unknown origin can be found beneath the rocky outcropping known as Mar Nohra, and there are inscriptions and carvings nearby that are clues to its location. The intricate cave system, according to experts, was used in ancient times for military purposes and is linked to the fortress of Al-Hossein. Lebanese tradition holds that a princess hid her wealth in boxes inside this cave system, hence its name, "Cave of Boxes." It is further believed that the ancient hoard is protected by a type of local magic known as rasad, which punishes treasure hunters by ruining their businesses, possessions and families. Other Middle Eastern hoards are protected by more fearsome guardians, such as the efreeti.

Similar supernatural protectors are not unknown in the Americas, either. The cave known as La Malinche in the state of Veracruz is believed to contain a hidden treasure – whether Aztec or Spanish is unknown – that is protected by the ghost of La Malinche herself, the woman who aided the conquistador Hernán Cortes as a translator. Legend holds that the beautiful revenant offers the treasure to anyone unlucky enough to pass her way, warning them that if they are unable to extract the hoard, they will be trapped forever within the caves.

In Britain's Cornwall, tradition holds that the odd and still unexplained structures known as fogous play a role in supernatural treasure. These Celtic structures appear to have played a role in local folklore and were considered to contain evil spirits assigned to protecting a particular trove. Modern adventurers entering these structures have been treated to a host of paranormal events, ranging from hearing voices to encountering apparitions of what may be the reputed "guardians" of lost treasure.

American Spiritualist Emma Hardinge discussed the 19th century belief surrounding the discovery of gold or treasure: Spirits were able to lead mortals to uncover treasure troves or even lesser bounties like misplaced deeds or wills (Modern American Spiritualism, 439). If the treasure hunter placed his or her trust in spirit guides and treasure was indeed found, "it proved the belief in spirits by its fruits." Hardinge adds the interesting side note that American folklore had associated treasure with discarnate entities before the mid-19th century boom in such beliefs. It was believed that "Indian or pirate spirits" were protecting hidden wealth against unworthy seekers.

For hundreds of years, treasure hunters and historians alike have searched for El Dorado, the lost city of gold.

The Search for El Dorado

To the north of the Brazilian capital city of Brasilia lies the State of Tocantíns, which holds huge semi-desert regions crossed by the Balsas and Sono Rivers – not the image that comes to most people's minds when thinking about Brazil. This scarcely populated and seldom traversed region of the country is considered to be accursed: truck drivers on their way to make deliveries claim to have seen "beautiful women" emerge from nowhere, lights dancing among the sand dunes, and other lights that engage in vehicle chases. The region's reputation as an unholy location was only heightened in 1994 when, according to journalist Pablo Villarubia, a tractor-trailer suffered a mechanical breakdown in the middle of the desert. Twenty days later, the driver's corpse – half eaten by vultures – was found, clutching a stick with which he had tried to keep the carrion birds away. It is only fitting that an area such as this should have a "lost" source of wealth: the legendary Los Martirios gold mine.

In the 16th and 17th centuries, the bandeirantes, or expeditioners who cut their way into the forbidding Brazilian heartland, were looking for that country's version of El Dorado: a lagoon filled with gold, silver and emeralds, crowned by a city whose inhabitants lived like kings. The colonial explorers set out to find them and even established a number of towns to serve as bases for forays. While no city was found, the adventurers came across the Paraupava River and its gold deposits. A village named Araés was established and mineral wealth was exploited, but as it became increasingly harder to extract gold, the settlers became dispirited and the village was abandoned to the elements. In the mid-20th century, explorer and historian Manoel Rodrigues Ferreira was able to ascertain that the "lost" Los Martirios gold mine had been found. Over the centuries, the river had undergone a name change to Araguaia and the village of Araés had vanished from the maps.

Conclusion

Aside from the thrill of acquiring sudden wealth – a constant in almost every culture on earth – the notion of finding buried treasure, much like a child's fabled discovery of "pirate treasure" lying under a large black "X" on a tattered map, has led many adventurers to expend both capital and human lives on such endeavors.

From the dragon-hoards of Germanic myth to the treasures of Ali Baba and Aladdin, the belief that the gold of dead kings is tantalizingly within our reach will be with us forever, even if said riches are protected by forces beyond our imagination.

SPOOKY TREASURE TROVES

THE COMING OF THE GOLDEN GODS FROM OUTER SPACE
By Timothy Green Beckley and Sean Casteel

This story sounds almost like a remake of the 1964 classic James Bond film "Goldfinger" with its unforgettable image of the unfortunate beauty fatally painted gold by the titular villain. But here there is an alien twist. In researching this book, the authors came upon the following report, taken from the research of Albert Rosales as published in his online "Humanoid Catalogue." It recounts how a UFO witness saw a golden ship land and disgorge a golden humanoid.

Hey, this was in 1967, during the earliest beginnings of the glitter rock era,  so it could well have been my friend Arthur Kane, the bass player from the glam band the New York Dolls. When not performing around the world in his six-inch platform heels, Arthur would pop up at our various UFO conferences with his beautiful wife, Barbara, and their equally beauteous pure white pet wolf. But, all kidding aside, this certainly remains one of the most mysterious cases we've encountered, and it appears as if this particular humanoid brought some riches with him. Could it be that gold is abundant wherever he originated?

Looking like a space god in his gold lamé jump suit, New York Dolls bass player Arthur Kane in "real life" enjoyed attending the UFO conferences of his friend, publisher Tim Beckley.

SPOOKY TREASURE TROVES

Here then is the gist of Albert Rosales' report.

August 15, 1967

USA: Westport, Washington

Standing one hundred feet at just the other side of the top of the hill behind Kilahanna Campground, the witness saw a golden spacecraft land on the dunes about a third of a mile from the coastline. It was nearly completely silent when it landed 120 yards from his view.

He was looking down on a small grade at the landed craft. The ship was completely shiny, like 24-karat gold in color. It landed gracefully. The landing gear popped straight out like thin legs.

The witness just stared at it for about 30 seconds, wondering what to do. Just then a door opened and an alien dressed in a matching 24-karat gold spacesuit came out and walked down what looked like a ramp. The creature next flew straight through the air at about 20 miles-an-hour to a nearby fir tree branch. The witness could see the humanoid closely now and was shaking with fear.

The figure was standing a hundred feet from the witness while perched up in the tree about twenty feet above the ground. It looked like a human body in a gold space suit. It was 5 foot 8 inches tall, with a round helmet which did not permit the witness to see a face inside. It was holding what looked like a machine gun with a thick cable attached to it. Everything was, again, made completely of shiny gold.

The witness just stood motionless and very scared. He watched the figure stand there as if on guard duty; it was turning its head looking back down the hill to the south of the space craft. It was now a hundred feet northwest of the ship it had emerged from.

The frightened witness does not think the alien noticed him as it looked down the dunes. The witness then ran as fast as he could into the woods, down the hill and into the campground. He told a friend about what he had seen, and his friend went to the location a few minutes later but did not see anything.

Source:

Albert Rosales Humanoid Catalogue, 1967, entry #260; citing HBCC UFO Research – http://www.hbccufo.org

In attempting to understand this story, it would not be remiss of us to conjecture a little about possible alien motives for such a sighting. Perhaps they are attempting to symbolically show us that, whatever we may think of them, they are "made of gold," meaning they exist above our non-comprehending judgments about their nature and their purposes as they interact with humankind. Another possibility is that they, in their righteousness, are what we should be seeking – as opposed to the earthly riches we seem to waste our lives pursuing.

There is a passage in the Book of Matthew, chapter 6, beginning with verse 19, in which Jesus says, "Do not lay up for yourselves treasures on earth, where moth and rust consume and where thieves break in and steal, but lay up for yourselves treasures in heaven, where neither moth nor rust consumes and where thieves do not break in and steal. For where your treasure is, there will be your heart also."

Did the alien appear to the witness to warn us that they have the market cornered on this gold that is laid up in heaven?

A rather frightening apocalyptic verse is recorded in the Book of James, chapter 5, beginning with verse one.

"Come now, you rich, weep and howl for the miseries that are coming upon you. Your riches have rotted and your garments are moth-eaten. Your gold and silver have rusted, and their rust will be evidence against you and will eat your flesh like fire. You have laid up treasures for the last days. Behold, the wages of the laborers who mowed your fields, which you kept back by fraud, cry out; and the cries of the harvesters have reached the ears of the Lord of Hosts."

This almost sounds like the driving philosophy of the Occupy Wall Street Movement, who protested the disparity between the "one percent" who controlled so much of the country's wealth and the ninety-nine percent who suffered in relative poverty. Their memorable slogan, "We are the 99 percent," was first heard in 2011 when the movement began.

In any case, gold has formed the basis of many a simile and metaphor, and there are any number of meanings one can derive from the appearance of this golden humanoid in a golden ship. The witness who saw the events doesn't think the alien noticed him at all, but it is more likely that he was given to see a moment of what UFO abduction researcher Budd Hopkins once called "alien theater," or deliberate attempts by the aliens to communicate in symbolism that was obscure but most definitely intended to be seen.

SPOOKY TREASURE TROVES

MAY THE FORCE – HOPEFULLY – BE WITH YOU
TREASURES FOUND AND LOST THROUGH PSYCHIC MEANS
By Timothy Green Beckley

The exact details escape me with the fog of time. But I do know it was during the time that I was managing the New York School of Occult Arts and Sciences out of a 2200 square foot loft on 14th street on the outskirts of Greenwich Village. All manner of UFOlogist, psychic, palm reader, crystal ball gazer, seer and prophet passed through our second floor doorway in order to present their theories and concepts on the vast unexplained world of the paranormal. We're talking about the likes of Dr. Stanley Krippner, who did a pilot study in mental telepathy with the Grateful Dead; Clive Backster, an interrogation specialist for the Central Intelligence Agency, best known for his experiments with plants using a polygraph instrument in the 1960s; as well as the late Alan Vaughn, one of the best goddamn researchers and experiencers in parapsychology this side of the Brooklyn Bridge.

Shawn Robbins

SPOOKY TREASURE TROVES

But the one individual who stands out in my mind from those days is my longtime friend, Shawn Robbins, considered to be among the top ten psychics in America. Shawn and I worked together in the "glory days" of occultism in NYC. My metaphysical center was probably one of the first of its kind in the country (later on, such psychic "schools" could be found from coast to coast) and people were quite serious in their endeavors to make sense out of all the way-out, otherworldly phenomena that were taking place around them.

Shawn had quite a reputation as a both a psychic and a medium. When not teaching in our facility between Seventh and Eighth Avenues in Manhattan, she busied herself acting as a special consultant with the New York City Police Department and as one of the three original psychics in the CIA Stargate program, trained to spy on the Soviet Government. Her code name was Madame Zodiac.

Uri Geller outside his U.K. mansion showing off car with his private collection of bent utensils. UFOs could have led him to several treasures.

But, for most, Shawn was one of the original ghost hunters and mediums utilized by famed parapsychologist Hans Holzer in dozens of haunted houses across America. He would often hypnotize her and she would "remote-view" to one of the sites Hans indicated he was interested in obtaining some sort of validation on. During one of these hypnotic sessions, Shawn was asked about the possible location of a sunken treasure off the coast of Long Island. And even though she did get specific about its location, at the time no one bothered to check out the information that she had "tuned into."

When I heard about this supposed treasure trove that lay within fifty miles

SPOOKY TREASURE TROVES

of our door, I couldn't help but think that if we found the sunken loot we would be able to fund our fledgling metaphysical center. Perhaps convert some of our second-hand folding chairs to cushioned seats – which would make it far better to do out of the body travel and practice meditation techniques.

Using a divining rod and a map of Long Island, Shawn believed she had found the spot and we were both excited to go on our first treasure hunt. We "hijacked" a rowboat and started heading out to sea. We believed the treasure would be within easy reach. Well, we rowed and rowed and rowed and it was getting dark. We realized that, since we were not properly equipped for a nighttime vigil, we should head back. But the current was going in the wrong direction and we did not seem to be gaining any traction in our attempt to return to the dock. Our lack of experience on the open seas and our confusion in which way to paddle were taking their toll. Eventually we did make it back, totally exhausted and with the thrill of the hunt somewhat diminished – at least for that day.

For one reason or another we never went back to look for the sunken swag. But I did get my first taste of treasure hunting with a psychic and, to this day, when Shawn and I happen to chat we always look back upon this incident and have a good laugh. But I can't help but think that if we hadn't caught a good wave or two we would be out drifting in the Bermuda Triangle by now.

Uri Geller took this picture of three UFOs from his seat on a Lufthansa Jet.

URI GELLER BECOMES A TREASURE FINDING MILLIONAIRE

You have to hand it to Israeli born Uri Geller – luck just seems to come his way in utter abundance. And though he keeps it a closely guarded secret (except from someone like yours truly, your unrepentant seeker of fame and fortune), UFOs are at least partially responsible for uncovering a number of "treasures" in his career.

Hey, as everyone knows, Uri and I go way back to the time he first came to America under the guidance of the late Andrija Puharich, who had seen him performing catchpenny magic tricks in the basement of some Tel Aviv nightclub. Mixed in with these unremarkable feats of prestidigitation, however, there seemed

SPOOKY TREASURE TROVES

to be legitimate phenomena of the mind reading and metal bending type.

Now, I can attest to Uri's uncanny ability. I don't think he was faking it when he asked me to place one of my keys – not one of his! – on a desktop a good ten feet from where he was standing in the Manhattan apartment of health and fitness journalist Herbert Bailey. Herb, who was a rather well known science writer, had given Uri one of his spare keys, a fairly heavy one, and Geller proceeded to stroke it with his finger. The key began to slowly bend until it was bent over about maybe 30 degrees. When we checked later, my key on the faraway table also showed signs of bending, though its fold was a lot less critical than Herbert's, perhaps because of the distance between Geller and the key in question?

We even took Geller up to see boxing champion of the world, the great Muhammad Ali. The boxer had previously shared his immense interest in UFOs with us, telling our group about some of his 21 sightings, including a cigar-shaped vessel that passed directly in front of his limousine while driving toward his Cherry Hill, New Jersey, estate north along the New Jersey turnpike. While at Ali's training camp on another occasion, I observed Geller hold his hand over the ring finger of Ali's wife, Belinda, and make the stone inside of the ring she was wearing suddenly disappear and the setting it had been encased in to bend. He also put a deep indent into a heavy religious metal worn by Ali's sparring partner with only the push of his thumb. Of course, it could be trickery, like escape artist and illusionist the Amazing Randi claims. (Uri once shared a tiny office on Fifth Avenue back in the time when Randi was nowhere near as skeptical about such paranormal matters, and before Geller sued him and won in court!). But, hell, I am not so sure. It looked pretty legit to me, and I don't think I was under any hypnotic spell.

Frankly, Geller has never denied liking the good things in life. Perhaps "La Dolce Vita" should be his middle name. The charismatic mystic thinks of himself as a "psychic geologist," where we might playfully identify him as a fortune-telling fortune seeker. How did he get so wealthy? Well, apparently, by diving for oil and submerged wrecks, albeit with a little help from his extraterrestrial friends.

"I definitely believe UFOs – flying saucers – are responsible," Geller told me as we chatted away in his fashionably modern Manhattan apartment, where he lived before abandoning these digs for a plusher "palace" in England. "This is something I hesitate to talk about simply because of the sensational nature of what I am about to reveal. However, it is time, I believe, that the public should know what's going on."

Uri says that his first encounter with a "space ship" transpired in a quiet garden, right across the street from his parents' home in Tel Aviv. He was not even ten years old at the time. "One day, my ears perked up as I became conscious of a high-pitched, ringing noise in the air. Looking up, I saw a peculiar sight. There, overhead, was a silvery mass – a shiny object. It came down so low at one point

SPOOKY TREASURE TROVES

that I felt like I could almost reach up with my extended hand and touch it. Suddenly, I passed out. When I came to, I ran home and told my mother what I'd seen. She didn't believe me, but deep down I knew something of tremendous importance had just happened."

Shortly thereafter, Geller noticed strange things taking place around him. The minute and hour hands of his wristwatch would move forward or backward by themselves. Small household utensils would disappear and then show up elsewhere. He was even able to receive telepathic thoughts from complete strangers. Still later, Uri found he possessed the ability to make spoons, forks, keys and other metal bend – simply by thinking about what he wished to accomplish.

"I had ample reason to believe I was being prepared for some important mission, even as a young man." Uri says that on one occasion he was drawn to an open field just outside of Tel Aviv. "There was this sphere – a UFO – hanging as if from a string. I walked over to it and went inside. When I returned to my friends, they noticed that I was holding something in my tightly clenched fist. Opening my hand, we all saw that it was a cylindrical cartridge, the kind used in a certain brand of ballpoint pen. I gave it to one of those present. Later, in a tense voice, this individual announced that he believed the object belonged to a pen he had been writing with several days earlier. The cartridge had vanished as he sat writing a letter at his desk. 'Someone' had 'taken' it from him and returned it under very odd circumstances."

Another time, when Uri was riding in an airplane, he demanded proof. Lo and behold, a UFO pulled up outside his window and he managed to grab his camera and take a picture.

For a brief period Uri moved to the isolated skiing village of Ponte Di Legno and took up painting. "It was like something was guiding me. I did thirty canvases in twelve days, and they were huge paintings."

One evening, around dusk, a friend in another part of the building came and interrupted what Uri was doing and said that he should come immediately. "He had been standing outdoors, looking toward the nearby snow-covered mountains, when a large black disc-shaped object caught his attention. It was wobbling about over the nearby peaks. Following his gaze, I saw a brightly lit sphere headed toward us. We were not the only witnesses. There were twelve additional observers, all responsible people."

At this point, the most baffling event of Uri's paranormal career took place, the event that is the most germane to our writings. "A beam of light shot from out of the bottom section of the craft. It engulfed the entire house. Suddenly, we heard a clanging sound on the roof and on the pavement. There, falling from the sky, were 50 and 100 lira pieces. It was literally raining money!"

Uri says that altogether maybe 300 coins had fallen from the sky. The psychic and his companions gave chase and followed the UFO for miles out of town. The object seemed to come down in a clearing near where a decorated Christmas tree had been planted by someone or "something." It wasn't growing there. It was not planted in the soil. It had been stuck there and was over ten feet tall.

Over the years Geller has had numerous other UFO-related experiences. His first "big heist" was while seated in an airplane and peering out the window at the ground 15,000 feet below. He had been hired on a speculative basis to hunt for oil deep beneath the earth in South Africa. He would get paid nothing if he didn't come up with a site that could be drilled profitability. If he found oil, he would get a certain percentage. Apparently, Uri picked the exact spot where the crude black bubbly existed far below the earth and both he and his oil speculator associates hit it big. Uri became a millionaire and got himself a nice mansion in the U.K. where he married and has lived happily ever after.

And, while Geller is now in the process of selling his estate in England and taking a more reasonably-sized apartment in his homeland, he still dabbles in treasure hunting whenever the opportunity presents itself.

URI GELLER'S "TREASURE ISLAND"

A couple of years ago an article was posted on the website of "Scotland on Sunday," a Scottish newspaper, in which the reporter recounts a meeting with Uri. At the time, Geller said he prefers to call himself a "mystifier" – something more akin to an entertainer – as he obligingly bent spoons with only a gentle rubbing of the handle for the reporter and the staff of the restaurant where the interview was being conducted.

Geller was preparing to spend his first night on Scotland's Lamb Island, the tiny basalt outcrop he bought in 2009.

"There is a really powerful energy here," Geller told the reporter. "There is something about the ambiance, the atmosphere. It could be because of the geological forces. It could be because there is something mysterious here. I don't know. I just feel it."

Geller talked about climbing the hill that overlooks the town of North Berwick and the islands off its coast, including the Lamb. He joked with the reporter that he had not been winded by the effort involved in ascending the hill.

"I am in good shape," he said, aged 62 at the time. "That is what positive thinking does for you."

From the summit of the hill, he was rewarded by his first sight of the island, saying, "I was thrilled. It was quite amazing. I thought, 'What did I buy?' I can't believe the Scottish government let it go. But it's mine now!"

Lamb Island is considered a UFO hotspot, the flying saucer phenomena being one of Geller's great preoccupations over the course of his life, as we have observed

SPOOKY TREASURE TROVES

Then there is the legend of Scota. She was a sister of the Egyptian pharaoh, Tutankhamun, who fled her homeland and, the story goes, gave her name to a windswept land far to the northwest of Europe.

Geller has a theory that Scota moored her ships off Lamb Island and suspects she may have left some treasure behind her. The "mystifier" was set to camp on the tiny rock and to use the ancient art of dowsing to see if he could figure out where the hoard might be.

"I won't keep the treasure," Geller said. "And I won't go and start digging things up. I will see if I can feel where something might be. And, if I get a sense, I shall come back with the proper permission and dig. If I find anything, I'll give it to a Scottish museum."

Geller's buying Lamb Island with the intention of dowsing for treasure there is vaguely reminiscent of Jesus's words in Matthew 13, verse 44: "The kingdom of heaven is like treasure hidden in a field, which a man found and covered up; then in his joy he goes and sells all that he has and buys the field."

Has Geller purchased a UFO landing area that boasts the added bonus of potential buried Egyptian wealth? Knowing Uri as I do, I wouldn't be surprised. If the treasure is ever found, then assuredly it will add to Uri's wealth – before he gives it to some charity, of course!

BUT YOU CAN'T SPEND IT ON "MARS!" – DID THE VISITORS ABSCOND WITH WHITLEY STRIEBER'S BANK ACCOUNT?

I would have to say that Whitley Strieber is a decent enough person, someone you would like to trust. Certainly, his experiences belong in the "high strangeness" category, which might make them suspect to some people of a more skeptical frame of mind. But if Whitley's story about "missing money" is true, we'd better watch our P's and Q's.

Whitley Strieber first

Sean Casteel, on the right, hangs with Whitley Streiber at a book signing. Luckily, the Visitors had returned the bestselling author's vanished bank account.

wrote about his experiences of being abducted by aliens he called the "Visitors" in his 1987 bestseller "Communion." It was a wildly popular book that Strieber says brought him his "fifteen minutes of fame," along with tumultuous changes in his life and countless mysteries that remain largely unresolved even today. The first of the several sequels that followed was called "Transformation: The Breakthrough," published in 1988, in which he resumed the continuing saga of the changes being wrought in him by the Visitors.

"Transformation" includes a story about the aliens leading Strieber to confront his own arrogance and hubris, an experience that began with a visit from Strieber's brother, Richard.

Strieber had recently sent Richard the book "Communion" in manuscript form. The book caused Richard some degree of discomfort, though he did not doubt that his brother Whitley had experienced something quite real. Richard decided to visit Whitley, his wife, Anne, and their son, Andrew, at the Strieber's upstate New York cabin where many of the events recorded in "Communion" had taken place.

"At about eight in the evening," Strieber writes, "we all went for a walk to the meadow that lies beyond our woods. As we moved through the woods, I was feeling quite proud of my place and of the bestsellers like 'Warday' that had enabled me to buy it. Perhaps I was doing a little too much prideful explaining to my younger brother. Suddenly I heard a loud, very old and low voice say, 'Arrogance! I can do what I wish to you.' I practically jumped out of my skin. The others had gotten ahead of me on the path. Their total lack of reaction told me they hadn't heard a thing."

After reaching the meadow, the moon began to rise, with a beautiful star shining near it that Strieber assumed was Jupiter. Then Richard noticed the "star" was moving and told the others, who began to pay closer attention. The object moved toward the moon, disappeared as it crossed the face, and then reappeared on the other side. At one point it seemed to increase in size and move toward the group before finally disappearing for good.

"The next moment," Strieber writes, "it seemed to me that there was a light fog around us in the meadow. I had the impression that three people were coming out of the woods toward us. I called to my son, momentarily confused as to his whereabouts even though he was standing right beside me."

Richard would later tell Strieber that he had had that same impression about there being three people standing where Strieber had been looking. The group returned to the cabin and the rest of the night passed uneventfully.

Strieber's thoughts returned to the voice he had heard just before they all saw the traveling "star."

"The voice had been so loud and so real – and so incredibly stern," he mar-

SPOOKY TREASURE TROVES

veled. "WAS I getting too arrogant? I didn't feel particularly prideful. One doesn't, I suppose, when one is."

The previous Friday Strieber had made a large transfer of funds from one bank to another. This represented all the cash he had. Without the money, he would have been unable to meet his obligations and would have been forced into bankruptcy.

"Late Monday afternoon," he continued, "my accountant called to tell me that the money had disappeared. My agent told me it was a computer error of some kind. Nobody could understand what had happened. I was frantic. Beside myself. But before I could get a fuller explanation the banks all closed for the day."

Strieber sweated through Monday night in a state of terrible agitation. He possessed only what was in his wallet and he saw visions of he and his family being tossed out into the streets. On Tuesday morning he was told that an "inexplicable computer error" had caused the money literally "to evaporate into electronic oblivion." However, sufficient paper records were eventually found and the money was recovered.

"Nobody at the banks had ever seen anything like it," Strieber writes. "As I put down the phone after being told this good news, Anne came into my office. She'd just seen another disk, going in the same direction as the first, at just the moment that the call had come through. It was like the period at the end of a sentence.

"My frame of mind was such that I became convinced that the Visitors had just made a show of strength. It was like a lesson in humility, expertly designed and managed, and incredibly effective. After seeing all that money evaporate before my eyes, I was a chastened man. I might well have had a taste of what they could do to me unless I admitted my arrogance and made an effort to change."

WHERE DID THE DIAMONDS GO?

One last account to keep you on the edge of your seat.

Back in the late 1960s and early 70s I shared an office on Fifth Avenue with Jim Moseley (it was actually HIS office) and the Amazing Randi. We were listed in the phone book under "Saucer News," so people could find us and did pop in from time to time unannounced.

Sometime during the middle of the week I think it was the front door to the office creaked open (there was no back or side door as this was a one room affair) and a gentlemen sporting a long black coat and hat walked into our space. He had a long gray beard, and I knew right away he was a Hasidic Jew from the way he dressed. He wanted to know if he could tell me something. I knew that Jews don't try to convert gentiles so I was curious as to what he wanted. He began to tell me a story about how he was in Israel driving alone along a darkened stretch of road

45

SPOOKY TREASURE TROVES

at night. He was carrying with him a pouch full of rather valuable diamonds that had been given to him by a jewelry wholesaler on approval with the understanding that if he sold them he would get a nice commission. This is a normal transaction in the diamond business, especially if you have known someone for a while and trust them.

Anyway, the gentleman came upon a fog bank as he was driving; he slowed down but did not stop. He said that while in the fog bank he could see a brilliant white light in front of him. The next day he discovered that the pouch with the diamonds had gone missing. He looked all over the car and went through his many pockets, but they did not turn up. He was afraid that the individuals would think he had stolen their valuables and would harm him if he did not return the valuable sparklers post haste – something which he could not possibly do since he did not possess them any longer.

The gentleman was quite anxious and wanted to know how he might go about finding them. Could the spirit world perhaps be approached? Were UFOs behind all of this? What should he do?

I told him point blank that I wasn't sure, but in other cases of "mysterious disappearances" similar to this one, the objects usually turned up sometime later in a roundabout way. My sister once had a ring disappear after a UFO hovered near her apartment and it showed up inside a breadbox.

He stopped in the next time he was in New York City and thanked me for taking away at least part of his anxiety. The diamonds did eventually show up, though I can't remember where they eventually transported themselves to.

So here are your treasure-hunting stories involving UFOs, both positive and negative. Hopefully, you will have a positive story to relate to us next time around. Drop us at line at mrufo8@hotmail.com and we will tell the world but keep your identity confidential if you so desire.

SPOOKY TREASURE TROVES

CURSE YOUR ANCESTORS TO THE EIGHTEENTH GENERATION

Our chapter title (with the replacement of the first word with a popular expletive) is a favorite ancient curse among the Chinese which has been adapted by just about every nationality, give or take a word here or there.

And curses seem to work pretty damn well in a lot of instances. In fact, the para-creature known as Mothman may have risen from the dead after the Native American Chief Cornstalk placed a curse on the area around Point Pleasant, West Virginia. History tells us that Cornstalk opposed European expansionism west of the Ohio River, but he later became an advocate for peace after the Battle of Point Pleasant. For his role in the peace movement, he was murdered by American militiamen at Fort Randolph during a diplomatic visit in November 1777, which outraged both American Indians and the colonial Virginians. Before his death, he placed a shamanistic curse that seems to have worked its negative magic, thank you very much. It is believed the curse was finally fulfilled with the collapse of the Silver Bridge across the Ohio River, best portrayed in the 2002 film "The Mothman Prophecies," starring Richard Gere.

So, after all this time, we finally have gotten around to the subject of dreaded curses – a topic long associated with buried treasure, be it on land or sea. Of

SPOOKY TREASURE TROVES

The Hope Diamond (45.52 carat)

Despite its being cursed, this treasure is one that every wealthy socialite would like to wear – regardless of the possible deadly consequences.

all the various paranormal aspects of treasure hunting, curses seem to go hand-in-hand – or skeleton to skeleton – with what lies buried beneath the ground or at the bottom of the ocean. Seems you can't have a good treasure without some raging spirit trying to make your life as miserable as possible in an attempt to keep your mitts off what they assume is their rightful property, though they may have been dead for centuries and even though their ownership might be in question anyway.

There have always been plenty of curses to go around, especially as related to anything valuable or "worth a king's ransom," as they might say.

Take everyone's favorite diamond – the Hope Diamond. Dozens are believed to have been killed outright because they dared to wear this sparkling gem that is said to have been stolen from the statue of a Hindi god. Maria Antoinette and King Louis XVI went running around without their heads because they dared to wear this priceless "trinket," while the likes of Princess de Lambelle was beaten to death, so she wasn't going to look so hot no matter what she wore to the ball.

The Hope Diamond has passed through numerous and various hands and I don't believe there has ever been a positive outcome. Today it lays locked up in a vault somewhere where it can harm no one.

But all of this is mere prologue to the next few chapters, all of which deal with curses made terrifying by the simple fact that no one seems to be able to ignore them without suffering the exact consequences to which they so arrogantly thought they would be immune.

Somewhere within the vast expanse of the Superstition Mountains rests the Lost Dutchman Mine with a vast treasure trove worth millions and millions of dollars.

THE LOST DUTCHMAN'S GOLD MINE – TALES OF MADNESS IN THE SUPERSTITION MOUNTAINS
By Timothy Green Beckley and Sean Casteel

According to legend, the Lost Dutchman's Gold Mine contains a vast amount of gold hidden somewhere in the Southwestern United States. Its location is popularly believed to be in the Superstition Mountains, near Apache Junction and east of Phoenix, Arizona. There have been numerous stories and theories about how to locate the mine, and people still make the trek to the mountains seeking the mine to harvest its fabled, bounteous gold. It goes without saying that some people have died in that frustrated effort.

The mine gets its name from a German immigrant named Jacob Waltz (1810-1891), who is alleged to have discovered it in the 1800s and kept its location a

secret. Waltz was not, in fact, Dutch, but "Dutchman" was a common American term for "German," derived from the German word "Deutsch." There are a great many variations among the legends told of the gold mine. Some say it belonged originally to the Apaches who lived in the area and that their spirits are still the force guarding it to this day.

In "Subterranean Worlds Inside Earth," Timothy Green Beckley's paranormal classic, there are stories that are both fascinating and frightening regarding the strange twists of fate and sudden bouts of madness that have befallen would-be gold prospectors in the area.

"Those who have braved the shadows of the Superstition Mountains," Beckley writes, "say that there is something there that puts evil in the minds of people who go into the mountains to search for the Lost Dutchman Mine! Probably the richest treasure yet to be found by man is located somewhere within the bowels of the Earth in these mysterious mountains. In the search for this treasure many people have been killed; many others have died from mysterious causes, while still others have met death at the hands of fellow prospectors who crave – GOLD!"

Just what is it, Beckley asks, that causes men to go stark raving mad upon the mountains that make up the Superstition Range? Is it simple greed or lust for gold, or is it something far more sinister and perhaps supernatural?

In 1959, a prospector named Benjamin M. Ferrira, of Honolulu, Hawaii, was serving a jail sentence for the murder of his gold-seeking partner when he told

SPOOKY TREASURE TROVES

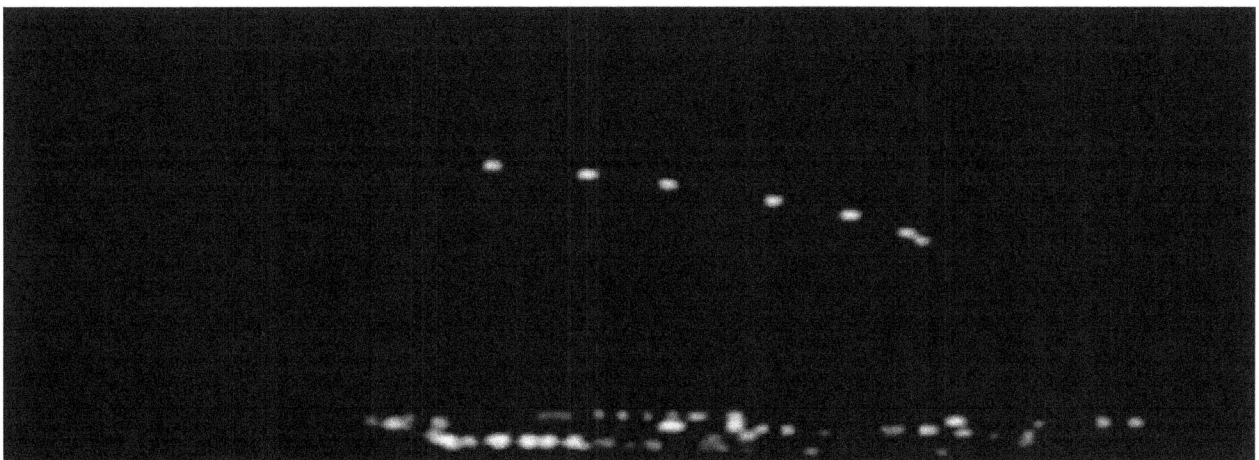

There have been many major UFO sightings as well as abductions by aliens inside the Superstition Mountains Range. The Phoenix Lights no doubt passed within miles —perhaps coming back to make sure their gold was still safe?

staff reporter Jack Karie of the Arizona Republic that, "There is something that happens to the minds of people going into that mountain to look for gold. People just get started hating each other, and first thing you know they're at each other's throats. It doesn't make sense! There's something on that mountain that makes men foolish. I know from experience – from a very sad experience – that mountain does things to the minds of men. At least I think I went completely nuts. One time I thought those canyon walls were moving in on me."

Grab a map and join the search for the treasure yourself — but play it safe and don't go out in the noonday sun!

Later in 1959, Laven Rowlee of Phoenix was shot to death by Ralph Thomas after a life-and-death struggle that took place just southeast of the famous Weaver's Needle, named for its discoverer Pauline Weaver. Mrs. Thomas, Ralph's wife, according to a report in the Arizona Republic, said that Rowlee first approached the couple "jabbering something about us trying to kill him. He said my husband was

Various gold artifacts have been discovered buried near where the Lost Dutchman Mine is said to be located.

an FBI agent. I really didn't understand what he was talking about. It sounded like a lot of gibberish."

After Rowlee attacked the couple, they somehow managed to grab his gun and overpower him. As the two proceeded to march Rowlee to a nearby prospectors' camp, he screamed, "I've got another one." Thinking Rowlee meant a gun, Thomas fired and knocked Rowlee down with a shot from his own gun. Rowlee died a few hours later.

Meanwhile, there have been numerous sightings of childlike creatures in the area. Was it a matter of overworked imaginations succumbing to the hot sun and cruel winds?

"In May of 1959," Beckley writes, "two dingy, dirty, sweaty prospectors told a strange story while visiting with an old-time resident of the Phoenix area. They claimed that for several days they noticed what they at first thought to be several small children playing near and in a small creek which had water in it only during the early spring season. To find children so far from any desert dwelling or residential area puzzled the two. They were quite familiar with the many 'strange' deaths that had occurred in this area and wisely felt that children had no business there.

"These small 'children,'" Beckley continues, "appeared to be about five or six years old and would be seen in the same dry creek bed day after day as the prospectors went about their digging. One day they decided to investigate and see what children could possibly be doing in such an area."

When they reached the creek bed, the "children" had completely disappeared but had left behind, fresh in the sand, footprints that indicated they had been wearing miniature duplicates of engineer boots. The two miners visited the spot the next day but never saw the diminutive creatures again.

Other witnesses say they've seen the "children" at closer range and that the creatures look more like men than children. Ranchers in the region say they could clearly see "little men" on the tops of ridges and mountains of the Superstition Range looking down and watching them.

Sometime in the 1970s, a teenage boy working with a large ranch concern on roundup was lost from the rest of the crew and wandered without food or water, which could quite easily have been fatal. As he wandered the barren wastes, the youth passed into a semi-conscious twilight between sleep and wakefulness.

While lying there in that near-comatose state, he was aware of several little men around him giving help and directions. They were finally able to lead him out of the mountains to the town of Globe, Arizona, about 50 miles from where he had been lost. The strange helpers did not give him food or water but somehow he had the strength to travel to safety. He could not see the little men clearly and thus he was not sure whether they were "ghosts" or real creatures, but he did manage to exchange a few words with his rescuers.

The foregoing stories clearly reinforce the connection between hidden treasure and the supernatural or alien creatures who take an interest of some kind in that treasure, most often appearing to guard the concealed wealth quite jealously. But for whom? And to what purpose? What manner of creatures are they that they should value Earth's precious metals at all?

If we could answer those questions, there would be no need for this book. We can only present the various mysteries, not their solutions.

Rick and Marty make up part of the History Channel's "Curse of Oak Island" dig team.

UFOS, GHOSTS AND THE DREADED CURSE OF OAK ISLAND

Did the lights of low-hanging flying saucers lead a teenage boy to the possible location of one of the world's richest buried treasure troves over two hundreds ago? And are apparitions of one type or another "camping out" to make sure no one is successful in finding whatever is buried on this isolated, windswept locale? And, furthermore, did this same supernatural force at play here put a curse on that treasure that has doomed so many seekers after its hidden hoard?

Oak Island is a 140-acre tree-covered spit of an island on the south shore of Nova Scotia, Canada, one of over 350 islands in Mahone Bay. Rising to a height of only 36 feet above sea level, it is situated 660 feet from shore and connected to the mainland by a modern causeway. It is currently privately owned, though several teams of treasure hunters make their home there, trying to figure out ingenious ways to get to the source of all this drama, which has become known as North America's most infamous treasure trove.

None of the above geographical statistics are particularly impressive, but

SPOOKY TREASURE TROVES

nevertheless Oak Island has been the source of much interest for over 200 years, beginning with the aforementioned inquisitive adolescent. And the interest does more than just merely linger to this very day; a whole new generation of the curious have found out what all the excitement is about as they tune into a TV series on the History Channel.

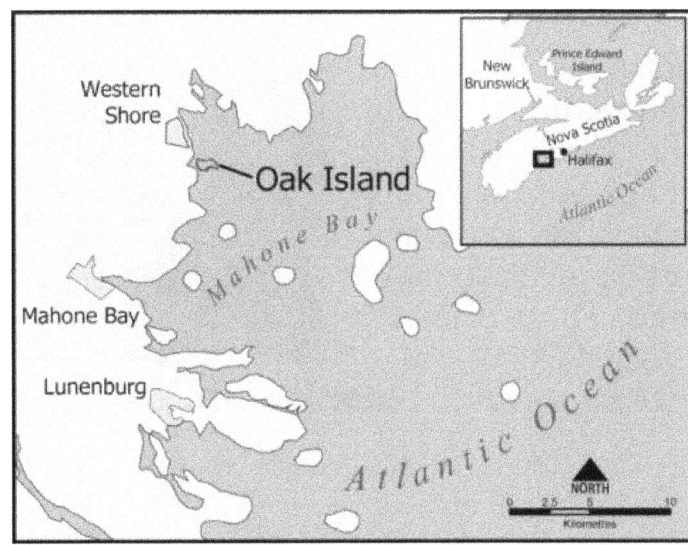

"The Curse of Oak Island" is as riveting a reality melodrama as you are likely to find anywhere. Now in its third season, every week the excitement continues to mount. In particular, 2015 holds several extraordinary milestones for the Oak Island team. It's been 50 years since an article about the Money Pit appeared in Reader's Digest, which not only sparked the imaginations of the lead players in the series, brothers Rick and Marty Lagina, but also compelled "old timer" Dan Blankenship — now joined by his son on the island — to devote his life to solving this great mystery.

It is also the 50th anniversary of the Restall tragedy, which claimed four of the six lives lost in search of the Oak Island treasure. It's easy to get hooked on the series and it's doubly easy to see why so many have gone to such lengths to find out not only where the treasure might be buried, but what it actually consists of.

An aerial view of Oak Island.

Some say it's a conventional swashbuckler's horde. Others insist the Knights Templar sailed the mighty seas to bury the likes of gold crosses, bespectacled jewels, and perhaps even the Holy Grail and/or the mighty Ark of the Covenant. And if that isn't enough to blow your ever-loving treasure-hunting mind, some proclaim that Shakespeare's "lost sonnets" could be sealed in a vault deep underground. Of course, in this account, Shakespeare isn't really Shakespeare but the likes of Francis Bacon, First Viscount of Saint Alban, who was an English philosopher, statesman, scientist, jurist, orator, essayist and author. He served both as Attorney General and Lord Chancellor of England. And since the Bard was really illiterate and could only just

SPOOKY TREASURE TROVES

about sign his name, someone else had to be responsible for his penmanship. But that's another story which we have covered previously in our published tract by Sean Casteel, called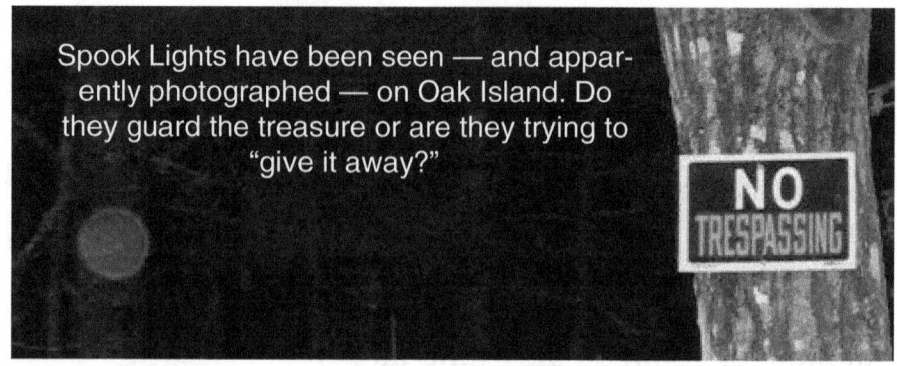

Spook Lights have been seen — and apparently photographed — on Oak Island. Do they guard the treasure or are they trying to "give it away?"

"Shakespeare's Confidential Dossier: To Be Or Not To Be?"

Who inscribed an unknown message on large boulders found throughout the island off the coast of Nova Scotia?

Regardless of what is buried on Oak Island, it has to be more valuable than the Queen's Jewels as no one in their bloody mind would go to the extreme efforts that were made to render the treasure inaccessible by an elaborate series of booby traps that have kept the treasure out of the hands of dozens and dozens of treasure seekers and killed a half dozen individuals in the process.

But what exactly is the story behind the curse of Oak Island?

"It all started one dark night way back in 1795 when a teenage boy named Daniel McGinnis witnessed ethereal nocturnal lights winding their way amongst the trees on a little island across the water from his family's home in Nova Scotia. His interest aroused, he rowed out to the island the next day to try to figure out the source of the lights," says a posting on "The Witching Hour" website.

McGinnis most likely never found out the mystery of what we might today identify as "spook lights" or "ghost lights," but he did find a circular impression in the ground about a dozen feet across. One's first thought is that the circular impression might have been the familiar landing traces sometimes left behind by a UFO, but the mystery is a little different here.

"Daniel was excited about his find for good reason," the story continues. "A hundred years earlier, in that very location, it was well known that pirates had used the scantily populated shores of eastern Canada to hide their illicit treasures.

SPOOKY TREASURE TROVES

It was then, in 1795, that Oak Island seduced its first innocent."

To continue we look to the website "The Museum of Unnatural History," which tells the next part of the story.

McGinnis recruited two of his friends and they began digging into the depression. After digging just two feet, they hit a floor of carefully laid flagstones made from a slate not found on the island. They concluded the flagstones must have been brought from a location at least two miles north. Below the stones, they discovered that they were digging down a shaft that had been refilled. The walls of the shaft were scored with the marks of pick axes, which further proved that the shaft was manmade and not some natural sinkhole.

At the ten foot level they hit wood, which they thought at first was some sort of buried treasure chest, but they soon realized it was only a platform of oaken logs sunk into the sides of the shaft. After pulling up the logs, they discovered a two-foot depression and more of the shaft. At 25 feet, they decided they could not continue without more help and better planning. After covering the pit over, they departed, but they remained convinced that something must be at the bottom of the pit since no one would dig such a shaft unless he had something very valuable to hide.

Nothing much happened with the pit until 1802, when Simeon Lynds visited the area and was impressed with the story. He formed a company to support the excavation, and work started in the summer of 1803. Having dug down nearly a hundred feet, the Lynds dig team discovered a flat stone, three feet long and a foot wide. The stone had strange letters and figures cut into it.

After removing the inscribed stone, they probed the bottom of the shaft with a crowbar and hit a barrier as wide and long as the shaft. The group believed they'd finally reached the treasure vault and left the site, expecting that the next day the treasure would be theirs for the taking. When they returned, the crew was shocked to find that overnight the pit had filled with 60 feet of water. Bailing was useless. As soon as water was removed from the pit, more flowed in to take its place. They tried digging another shaft nearby to get at the treasure by running a tunnel underneath the pit, but the new shaft flooded as soon as the tunnel got close to its goal.

It was theorized that the flooding was a kind of booby-trap intentionally left by whoever designed the shaft. There appeared to be intricate workings laid out in advance that seemed to anticipate the thoughts and actions of those who would follow. Such an elaborate system would seem similar to the builders of Egypt's great pyramids and most certainly not some rum-swigging pirates who had never heard of Johnny Depp and with breath so bad that if you got close enough it would send you reeling back to the Rock of Gibraltar.

Later attempts to get around the flooding problem by various mechanical means did not succeed any better. In 1861, searchers tried to pump out the pit using a steam-engine device, a high-tech piece of equipment back in those days. A boiler on the engine burst, and one worker was scalded to death. And so the curse of Oak Island seemed to continue!

In a subsequent attempt by another group, just before the turn of the century, a worker was returning to the surface after descending into one of the many holes that pocked the land around what had come to be called "The Money Pit." As they brought him to the surface, the rope unraveled from the pulley they were using and he plummeted to his death.

The 18 stories deep, 10-X shaft was bored down near the original "Money Pit" when the pit itself continued to flood with sea water.

In 1965, former daredevil motorcyclist Robert Restall and his 18-year-old son were killed by the carbon monoxide fumes of a gasoline pump being used in another futile attempt to rid the shaft of the water. Restall's business partner and a worker they had hired also died attempting to rescue Restall and his son. The pit had taken four lives in a single day, and the total number of fatalities had come to six. There is a legendary curse that declares that seven must die before the treasure is recovered, and, as of this writing, there is one left to go.

After the first death in 1861, there were whispers that ghosts were protecting their treasure and would claim more souls if the digging continued. One little girl, Peggy, who had come to the island with her parents, saw something that greatly frightened her. It was winter and there was snow on the ground. Peggy was playing by a little storage cabin near the Money Pit. One morning she came running into the house where she resided with her parents, her father being the foremen of the then-contemporary dig. Very excitedly she said, "Mommy, there's a crowd of men coming up from the shore (toward the cove). What pretty clothing one of them has got on! There's big stripes down his pants." She was too young, we are told, to know that these were the type of pants that one of the men who had died on the island in a tragic accident was usually seen wearing. Peggy once said she saw a man sitting on the wharf with a patch over his eyes. She would have still been too young to have heard about the exploits of Long John Silver and "Treasure Island."

But the digging has continued despite the ghost stories and the inability to unravel the secrets of the island and its supposed massive treasure, and there is never a shortage of people willing to invest their money and years of their lives to keep digging deeper and deeper for the answer.

But what exactly are they digging for?

The stone with the strange markings found in 1803 has been translated to read, "Forty feet below two million pounds is buried," but that translation is still disputed, and there are some that think that the slab was a hoax and that the lettering had been carved into it in recent times. There are also those who said the strange markings on the rock were really a secret cipher that concealed the truth about the treasure.

Some believe the pit holds a pirate treasure hoard buried by Captain Kidd or possibly Edward Teach, known more familiarly as "Blackbeard." Teach boasted he had buried his treasure "where none but Satan and myself can find it." Another possibility is that the pit was dug not by pirates but by Spanish sailors from a wrecked galleon or British troops during the American Revolution.

The priceless jewels of Marie Antoinette, historically said to be missing still, may have made their way to the Nova Scotia region via a maid whom the queen instructed to gather the royal jewels and flee just before the Palace of Versailles was stormed by revolutionaries in 1789. Supposedly the maid fled to London and from there escaped to Nova Scotia. Using her contacts formed during her service to the Queen, she was able to persuade the French navy deployed to northern America to construct the famed "pit" on the island and conceal the jewelry.

As previously stated, one of the wilder theories comes from writer Penn Leary, who contends that the pit is being used to hide manuscripts that prove Francis Bacon to be the true author of Shakespeare's works.

And, as stated, perhaps the exiled Knights Templar dug the pit and made it the last resting place of the Holy Grail or even the Holy Ark of the Covenant. There may be a Templar tomb on the island as well. Others argue that the shaft and its mysterious contents seem to echo aspects of a Masonic initiation rite involving a hidden vault containing a sacred treasure. Many of the prominent excavators were Freemasons and a number of stories told about the pit explicitly include Masonic imagery.

Several individuals have the rights to dig and drill on the island, though the History Channel treasure hunting team are the currently the main players in this exploration. And, while they have not found the apparently accursed loot, they have the financial backing to bring in the most modern of sonar and metal detecting equipment, tools that the average "prospector" could not even get near enough

SPOOKY TREASURE TROVES

to touch. A few miscellaneous coins have been found in the swamp, and a drill bit in the 10-X chamber has bought up coconut fibers. And, of course, coconuts are not native to the area and must have been bought up all the way from the Caribbean back whenever. One can only hope that the Rick and Marty and their team will finally unravel the mystery that has intrigued so many, especially the authors, for a damn long period of time.

And so we ask, is the treasure on Oak Island guarded by the restless spirits of whomever left it behind? Or do the aliens who first led young Daniel McGinnis to the location with their ethereal lights still jealously guard the wealth there, as they apparently do at other alleged treasure sites around the world? We are perhaps dealing here with a complex of unknowable extraterrestrial motivations intermingled with the mysteries of ghosts and the terrifyingly "real" curses that so often bedevil the greedy seekers of treasure that was never intended to be theirs.

As for Oak Island, will a seventh victim of the curse be the key that unlocks the pit's mysterious gates? We can only hope that there is a happier ending to this story and that the treasure will finally be located. And that no one else will have to die!

SPOOKY TREASURE TROVES

THE CURSE OF COCOS ISLAND
Could This Be The Largest Treasure Trove In The World?
By Dr. Nandor Fodor

Dr. Nandor Fodor, born in 1895, was a British and American parapsychologist, psychoanalyst, author and journalist of Hungarian origin. After receiving a doctorate in law from the Royal Hungarian University of Science in Budapest, he moved to New York to work as a journalist and to Britain in 1929, where he worked for a newspaper company.

Fodor became one of the leading authorities on poltergeists, hauntings and paranormal phenomena. He was also an associate of Dr. Sigmund Freud. The field of psychoanalysis, as pioneered by Freud, was, on the surface, disdainful of the occult, but it is said that even Freud secretly believed that there could be paranormal aspects to some cases of mental illness and neuroses.

Fodor began to embrace paranormal phenomena in the 1930s and by the next decade was advocating a psychoanalytic approach to psychic phenomena, which quickly drew the ire of the spiritualist community. So virulent were the attacks that Fodor eventually filed a lawsuit for libel against a spiritualist newspaper called "The Psychic News."

He is best known for his magnum opus, "Encyclopedia of Psychic Science," first published in 1934. His other titles include "The Haunted Mind: A Psychoanalyst Looks at the Supernatural" and "Haunted People: The Story of the Poltergeist Down the Centuries," the latter being coauthored with Hereward Carrington. Fodor died in 1964 shortly after his 69th birthday.

There is a tremendous fortune buried on the Island of Cocos; the spirit of "John King" will guide the brave explorer to it...

SPOOKY TREASURE TROVES

THE MYSTERY OF COCOS ISLAND

A RECENT OUTBREAK of interest in treasure-hunting on Cocos Island sent me searching through papers I had preserved from my old days of psychical research in England. I read the book, "The Lost Treasure of Cocos Island," by Ralph Hancock and Julian A. Weston, which had renewed interest in the perennial mystery of what has happened to the immense treasures hidden on a scrap of land about 550 miles due west from Panama City, and I compared its latest findings with my unpublished writing on the quest for treasure there which Sir Malcolm Campbell (then Captain Campbell) had undertaken in 1926.

My writing also told about two mediums through whose help I had tried to find the location of the treasure on Cocos Island, which Sir Malcolm Campbell so conspicuously failed to find. Yes, it would be worthwhile at last to publish the contents of my old paper, for as Hancock and Weston conclusively show, somewhere in the steaming jungle of Cocos Island lies the greatest treasure hoard on earth, yet in 140 years expedition after expedition has failed to find a trace of it.

Under the circumstances, any possible clue should be given. The consensus is that there are three treasure troves on Cocos Island, and this is what Sir Malcolm Campbell believed when I happened to travel with him in 1933 from London to Budapest on the Orient Express. We were bound for an international newspaper congress where the great speed king – Sir Malcolm was the first man to travel over 300 miles per hour in an automobile – was to represent Lord Rotherrnere and the Daily Mail. He gave me his book, "My Greatest Adventure" (1931), to read, and talked freely as the Orient Express sped along about the mystery of Cocos Island.

"The first [treasure trove]," said Sir Malcolm, "is that of Captain Edward Davis, a partner with Damphier in his privateering adventures, when he blockaded the Bay of Panama and sacked the City of Leon in Nicaragua in 1685."

Hancock and Weston add to the Davis story. "Captain Davis and his men made Cocos Island their headquarters and raided the coast from Baja California to Guayaquil. From time to time the Bachelor's Delight was joined by the ships of other freebooters. All these made stops at Cocos Island to bury the plunder of their raids. And when one considers the tons of silver ingots, the chests stuffed with jewels and pieces-of-eight, and the leathern bags filled with gold that must have been buried all over the island, the marvel is that so little of it has ever been found."

Captain Davis "surrendered to his Majesty's mercy," accepted the amnesty offered to all pirates by King James II, and retired to Virginia to await a chance to return to Cocos Island and recover his treasure. He finally started back in a small ship, took to piracy along the way, and mysteriously disappeared.

The second treasure trove was deposited on Cocos Island by Captain Benito Benito, the notorious "Benito of the Bloody Sword." He operated in the waters off Central America in the years 1818-1820 and is thought to have buried several large fortunes on Cocos. In 1819 his cutthroat crew came ashore and hijacked a rich cargo of gold that was being taken from Mexico City to Acapulco. This netted treasure estimated to be worth eleven million dollars—all of which Captain Bonito buried on Cocos Island. In 1821 "Bonito of the Bloody Sword" died in a mutiny of his men in the West Indies.

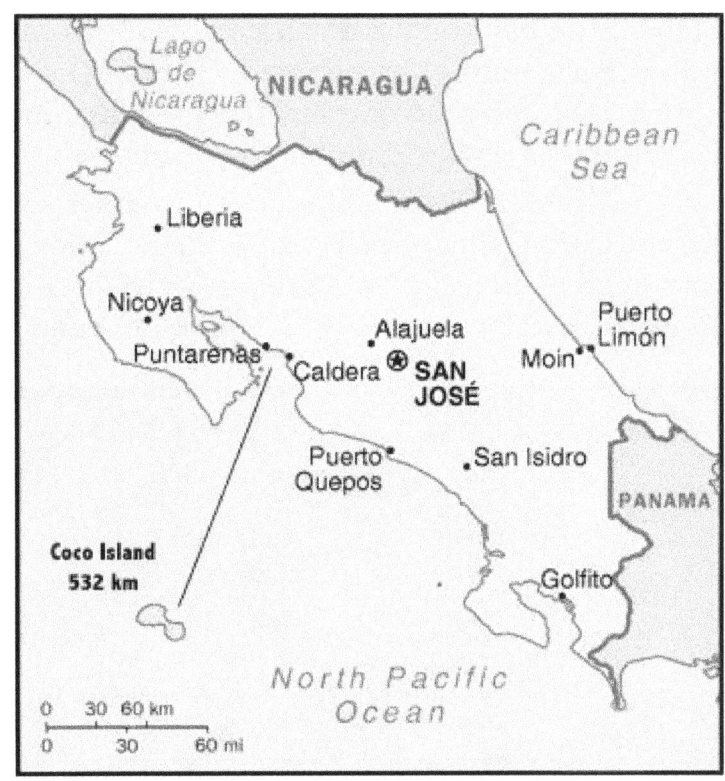

BUT THE GREATEST treasure trove on this small tropical island – it's only four miles long by three wide – is the "Lima" treasure which is estimated to be worth one hundred million dollars! In 1820 the Spanish Viceroy of Peru became alarmed when a rebel army under José de San Martin invaded his province. He hastily emptied the mint and its storehouse of gold and silver and stripped the churches of their solid gold and silver accoutrements, and transported all this treasure to Lima's seaport, Callao. Here it was put on board the British merchantman, Mary Dear, which was commanded by a Scot, Captain Thompson.

It was arranged that Captain Thompson should put to sea and cruise about for a couple of months. Then, if the Spanish regime at Lima were still secure, he should return to Callao and restore the treasure; otherwise he should deliver the treasure to the Spanish authorities in Panama. A half dozen men, including two priests, came on board to guard the fabulously rich cargo.

Out to sea went the Mary Dear and the next morning the gold-crazed crew murdered the guards and the priests. Captain Thompson headed for Cocos Island in lat. 5° 32" 57" North, long. 87° 2' 10" West in the Pacific Ocean. He thought that the treasure could be buried without interference in this uninhabited place and that after a year or two, he could reassemble his men and they could go back to Cocos, recover the treasure and take it home to England.

Only the first part of this plan was effected. The Mary Dean anchored in one

SPOOKY TREASURE TROVES

of the three bays on the north side of Cocos Island and her longboat, loaded to the gunwales, made eleven trips to shore. The immense treasure was hidden in a spot selected by the captain and the mate, and only a small amount of coins was kept back and shared among the crew.

The Mary Dear sailed away to disaster. A Spanish man-of-war picked her up and made acutely embarrassing inquiries about the missing treasure. Captain Thompson and his crew were put on trial for murder and piracy on the high seas. Everyone was sentenced to be hanged and the sentence was carried out until

Future President Franklin D. Roosevelt (aged 27) and friends on Cocos Island searching for the treasure in 1910. Image courtesy of the National Archives and Records Administration

only the captain and the mate remained. They then made a deal. If their lives were spared, they would lead the Spaniards to the spot where they had buried the "Lima" treasure. Which in due course they did.

And here begins the thick mystery of Cocos Island. For when the "expedicionarios" landed on Cocos, the captain and the mate promptly disappeared into the thick jungle that comes right down to the water's edge. For days the expedicionarios hunted for them but finally had to sail back, disappointed in their treasure-lust.

The self-marooned men lived on coconuts, birds' eggs, fish and small game for several months and were rescued sometime in 1822 by a British Whaler which stopped at the island for fresh water.

SPOOKY TREASURE TROVES

The captain and the mate said simply that they had been shipwrecked on the island, and to avoid raising any suspicion, they refrained from taking with them even an ounce of gold. The next item in this fascinating story is the death of the mate in Costa Rica, and then a sequence of stories about the treasure coming from 'Captain Thompson. But did the mate die at Puntarenas, as generally accepted until Hancock and Weston came along with their new book? Is there also a chain of evidence coming from him as a source? The Cocos Island story from 1822 to the present is a tangle of legends, fancies, facts and fictions, and scores of unsuccessful treasure hunts, some extremely well-organized and some one-man, completely amateur affairs.

THIS IS A BUSINESS of ancient descent. From time immemorial man has searched for buried treasure. From time immemorial spirits have been alleged to hover over hidden hoards. The air of the supernatural circulates over treasure troves, and uncanny happenings have chilled the blood of many brave adventurers, as happened with Sir Malcolm Campbell in 1926. He discussed with me the Unknown into which he felt he had strayed on that little tropical island.

According to him, he had gone there for romantic reasons. As he put it, "what able-bodied man is there with time, money, and imagination, who would not trim his sails and set his course for salty horizons tomorrow, if he had a clue in

Has part of the treasure been found? Fabulous $200 million dollar treasure hoard unearthed recently in Cocos Island. Some have reported that the find is a hoax and that there is still a curse on the loot.

his pocket, a treasure to find?" He camped on the island with two fellow-adventurers and a mongrel dog. One night, aching in every limb from the day's exertions, he was trying to sleep in the terrible heat. He writes in "My Greatest Adventure": "Suddenly the dog, who had been sleeping beside me, twitching occasionally in his sleep as dogs sometimes do, but otherwise normal, leapt to his feet with a terrifying howl and dashed to the open flap of the tent door, barking and chattering with rage and fear. He was almost beside himself. I have never seen a dog in such a paroxysm of terror. It was as though he had seen a ghost. He stood there barking and yapping into the blackness of the night, every hair on end, his voice vibrant with fear and defiance.

"Both men awoke and sat up. I took my revolver from the holster and crawled to the tent door, expecting to meet anything from a ghost to a wild pig or an Indian on his belly. There was nothing. The great wood fire, built to keep off the insects, leapt and flickered redly against the velvet background of the tropic dark. Overhead a million stars shone and twinkled like points of fire. The trees, like a tapestry of black velvet, stood brooding and motionless around the tiny camp. A million insects filled the night with a throbbing hum. The sea broke with the swish of silk gently on the beach. There were no other sounds.

"I stepped quietly outside the radius of the firelight and sneaked among the trees, expecting at any moment to surprise some lurking enemy. It may seem a little melodramatic to recount it now, but I can only say that Cocos possesses such an indefinable influence of evil that when once you are on it, your nerves are on the edge for anything. It is a haunted island. I could find nothing, although I scouted cautiously round all the camp, slipping and sliding among the trees, finger on trigger ready to shoot. All the time the dog was standing in the tent door, whining and shivering, I had the feeling that somewhere in the blackness someone was watching me, following my every movement. I returned to the tent with a prickly feeling down my spine.

"When I got inside the dog quieted down after a time, and presently went to sleep. I lay awake for an hour or so with my revolver handy, waiting for something to happen. Nothing did. Finally I fell off to sleep.

"The next night the same thing happened again. Round about midnight the dog sprang suddenly to the tent door, yapping, barking, and shivering with fear. He stood there, frothing at the mouth, half-paralyzed with fright. Again I reconnoitered, revolver in hand. Again I had the feeling that something was crouching in the bush watching me. But I could find nothing and nothing happened.

"Twice after this the same thing happened in the middle of the night. We could not account for it then, and I cannot explain it now. There are no animals on the island, so far as I know, except

wild pig, and they are not stealthy beasts. There is no subtlety about them. When they move it is for all the world to hear. They plunge and crash and do not care who listens to them. I saw no rats, no snakes, in fact, no reptiles or mammals

SPOOKY TREASURE TROVES

of any sort apart from pig. What then, or who, can have been our mysterious midnight visitor?"

In our conversation on the Orient Express, Sir Malcolm would subtract nothing from this account of an extraordinary experience. He knew that psychical research was my preoccupation, and he assured me that his account was a faithful and unembellished rendering of what had occurred. He was not a spiritualist, nor did he believe in ghosts or evil spirits; but he frankly confessed that hewould not like to spend many nights alone on Cocos Island. He also noted that almost every one of the major expeditions that in the last century had landed on Cocos Island and searched for the treasure had met with disaster, and not one had succeeded in finding anything. Even his own party had suffered in a small way from misfortune: one of his companions hurt his leg, and another was badly lamed for a fortnight.

OF WHAT was the dog afraid? Sir Malcolm could advance only one explanation. It is romantic, and it stirs one's imagination. (Incidentally, it is not included in the lore that Hancock and Weston put in "The Lost Treasure of Cocos Island.") There is a legend in the South Seas that at the time of the Spanish Conquistadors some of the Incas of the Peruvian mainland fled from the appalling cruelty of the invader, and found refuge on Cocos. When the pirates came on their irregular visits, these Incas retreated to the top of the highest mountain on the island, nearly 2800 feet high, where, according to one of the pirate chroniclers, there is a crater lake, teeming with fish. Here, the legend says, the descendants of the mighty Inca race still dwell. They are in deadly fear of the white man and the moment their sentries descry a ship upon the horizon, they damp their fires, and every member of the group takes to the high hills.

I frankly told Sir Malcolm that I did not believe a lurking Inca spy could send his dog into a paroxysm of terror. To me the signs pointed to a "supernatural" visitation. We talked long into the night. I told him that, as an experiment, it would be well worthwhile to attempt an inquiry through psychic channels into the treasure's location. Of course, he was rather skeptical, but agreed to lend me the Admiralty map he had used in his treasure hunt.

The map showed a mountainous island of less than 20 square miles in area. It rises almost vertically out of the sea and has only two adequate landing places, Chatham Bay and Wafer Bay, on its north side. It is said that there are only two seasons – the rainy season and the wet season – and the island is obscured much of the time by heavy rainfall or by fog. I covered a top corner of this map, to hide the name of the island, and took it to the British College of Psychic Science, where I had a sitting with Miss Jacqueline. I took shorthand notes. The map was still unrolled when Miss Jacqueline said: "Is that concerning a place? Is it an initial H or K?"

SPOOKY TREASURE TROVES

I said that K, according to the sound, was correct.

She then took the map, which could have conveyed little more to her than that it represented an island, and continued: "I don't know whether it is connected with something hidden. I see three or four people trying to discover something, to look for something. I see very great possibilities. It is almost as if I were going up to hidden treasure."

After I had partly unrolled the map, she pointed at various spots on it and, asked: "Has there been any writing on this place? Nothing to do with Glastonbury Abbey? No name of any person like that?"

This was an error, but nevertheless a good proof that the idea of hidden treasure was not conveyed from my mind to hers. The spots she pointed out were different from those Sir Malcolm had picked as likely. I told Miss Jacqueline nothing whatsoever. Two days later I visited her again. She then said that at almost the instant I had left her, she had heard her "guide" say, "Coco... Coco Island."

This time she tried her divining rod over the map. It went into oscillation over certain spots, indicating, as she believed, the presence of gold. She pointed to the highest peak, Mount Iglesias, and said that some people were there. This was in curious agreement with the legend that descendants of the Incas may still be surviving on this mountain top. I found this interview encouraging.

With the map rolled up, I next called on Mrs. Eileen Garrett. When she passed into trance and "Uvani," one of her spirit controls, introduced himself, I asked him if he could put me in touch with "John King," a picturesque old-timer in spirit "controls," who is said to have been in the flesh Sir Henry Morgan, the pirate. "Uvani" said that he would try, and after a little while, said that he had found him. He announced that he would speak in his behalf.

"This contact gives him the impression of a great deal of adventure. This is a map. The map of an island. Off Penzance. I feel an island to which this map takes me. There is some idea of exploration here. He is glad to see that adventure is still left in the hearts of some people. There is treasure. He has the feeling of buried treasure. This was the haunt of pirates in the old days. There have been many shipwrecks here, and nobles fleeing from the court with their jewelry and documents give him the impression that this island has a great history. Legends are current, it even being suspected that many of the royal fugitives had taken up residence here until they were taken off from this hotbed of treasure. I do not know if any treasure has been found, but he is definite that much had been put there, especially under the little church to which there was a path from the waterfront."

I said that there must be some mistake: the island is nowhere near England and is uninhabited.

"Uvani" was puzzled. Was I sure that there was no channel at all? Then to

SPOOKY TREASURE TROVES

my surprise:

"Is it anything like C . . . O . . . C?"

Then slowly: "Cocos. He speaks of Cocos Island as connected with the peninsula by an ancient civilization. Peruvian. The habitation of the ancient In _ _ [struggling] _ _ Inc _ . . . A religious sect like the Aztecs which he calls White Indians. At one time it was the headquarters of the occult tribe of the Aztecs . . . it was only approachable from two sides. There is an extinct volcano and the remains of a church. For a long time it was thought that there were inhabitants on that island, on the other side of the volcano, on the west where there is no landing-place. The western side is sheer cliff. In the old days there was a port on the other side for traders between South America and the Southern Archipelago. The treasure was taken to the western side of the island. It meant days of dwelling there and carrying provisions. There was a time when it was a place of refuge. Many Inca pilgrims went there. No treasure has been taken off. He could help to find it. It would give him great joy, like old days. But one would have to make a safari and take it very seriously."

THERE ARE SOME remarkable points in this statement. Remember that the map was rolled up. Nothing indicated the nature of the roll. If Mrs. Garrett or "Uvani" was reading my mind, how did the confusion at the beginning of the description come about? Moreover, in my romantic imagination, I would have preferred that the ancient Incas were still living on the island to their being wiped out by a volcanic eruption. There are two high peaks on the island, Mount Iglesias, 2,788 feet, and another, unnamed, rising 1,574 feet. Whether they are volcanic, I cannot tell, nor do Hancock and Weston tell us. It is plain from the map that the west side of the island is unapproachable. It is curious, too, that another clairvoyant, a Mrs. Pollock, of whom Sir Malcolm Campbell writes in his book, should have said that "the treasure lies high up, perhaps a thousand feet above sea-level."

I was given no precise indication of where the treasure is to be found. But "John King" had said that he could lead to it. He asked for a meeting with the owner of the map. Had I known the topography of the island, had I possessed myself of all the available information about the pirates and their evil deeds on this island, I believe I should have obtained more help. Why I would have, I cannot tell. All I know is that in mediumistic communications the sitter's imagination, if deeply exercised, appears to act as a relay, and is able to glean more definite indications than does a barren mind. Mrs. Pollock, for instance, gave Sir Malcolm fairly precise indications of the whereabouts of the treasure, indications that were almost as important as the pirate clue which he possessed. Though, owing to shortness of time, Sir Malcolm returned from Cocos with empty hands, he was sufficiently impressed by Mrs. Pollock to write in his book: "Mrs. Pollock's indication will very likely either lead to the subsequent discovery of the treasure or will be amply justified, should it be found without their help."

I wanted to arrange a meeting between "John King" and Sir Malcolm. He had written: "One of these days I shall return to Cocos, and when I do I shall not give up the search until I have either found the treasure or convinced myself that it is humanly impossible to discover it." But now in the nineteen-thirties he was afraid to expose himself to a fresh treasure-hunting temptation. He never again outfitted an expedition to Cocos Island, and the prize piece of the "Lima" treasure – a solid gold, gem-encrusted, life-sized image of the Virgin Mary – still lies unfound on that secretive speck of land midway between San Francisco and Valparaiso.

A Wide And Perilous Sea: The Realm Of The Freebooters

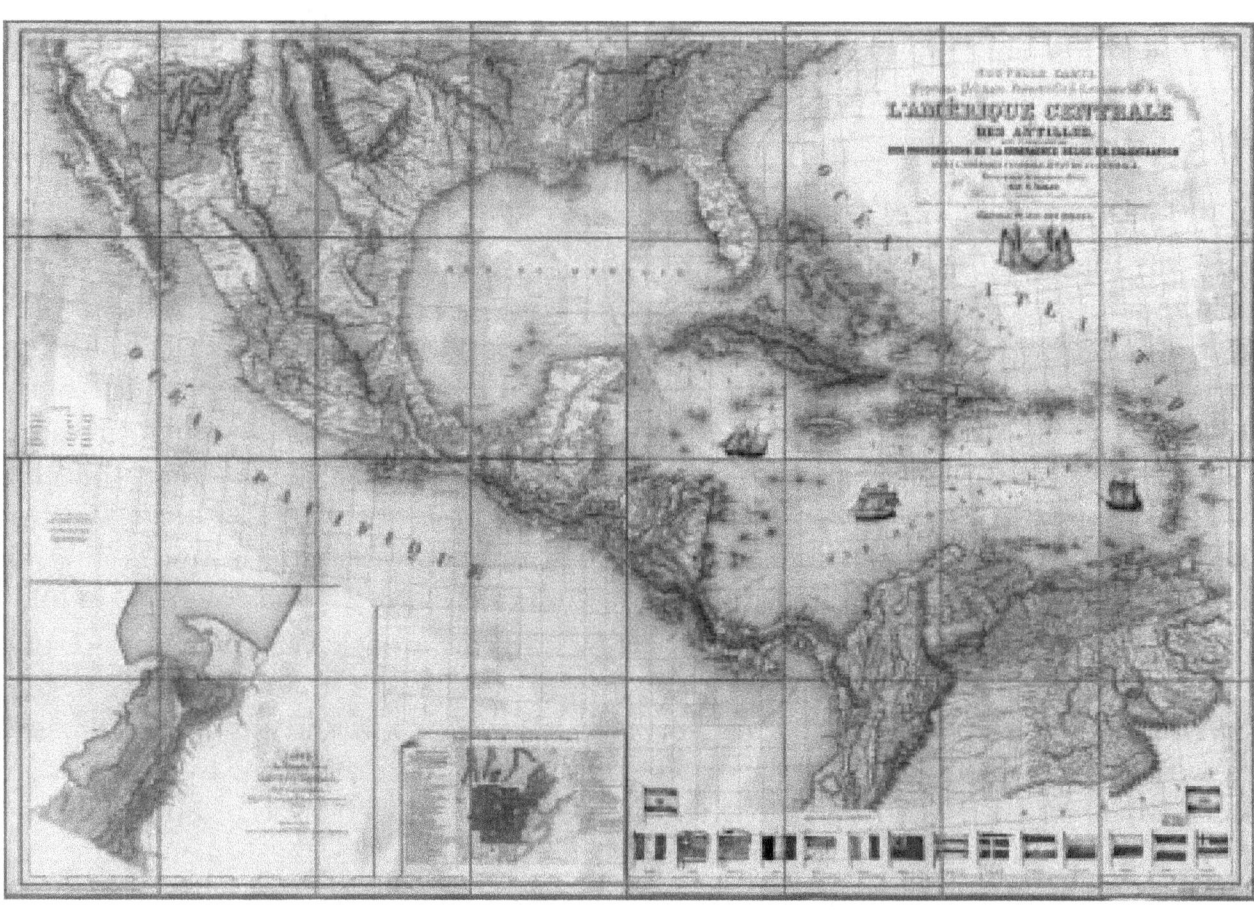

SPOOKY TREASURE TROVES

Shutterbug and fellow investigator Charla Gene snapped the photo of author Tim Beckley on the main street of Jerome at a time when it certainly appears to be a "ghost" town.

TREASURE-LADEN JEROME
By Timothy Green Beckley

Some call it the wickedest city in the old West. The town, during its heyday, was full of drunks, prostitutes and murderers. In fact, because of its outrageous bawdiness, Jerome burned, or nearly burned, to the ground eight times.

And, as far as treasure goes – and the ghosts that guard it – there are said to be more spirits in the town than members of the living who, at last tally, totaled 444, which is a rather mystical number in itself.

There is all sorts of treasure buried around here – gold, silver and copper – and many have laid down their lives digging up the troves or prospecting for them.

Jerome winds along one of Arizona's scorching and dusty trails. As Charla Gene and I drove the length of Highway 89A that stretches between Sedona and Phoenix, I couldn't help but feel compassion for the Spanish Conquistadors led by Antonio de Espejo, who passed through the Verde Valley in the mid-16th Century dressed to honor the King in heavy metal helmets and confining, polished armament. If it was anything like what today's modern traveler experiences, it had to have been like trekking through the embers of hell. It's the land where the temperature rises to 102 degrees by the time you awake, and the air becomes so

SPOOKY TREASURE TROVES

hot by midday that you want to crawl under a rock – if you could find one!

Historians tell us things were a bit more temperate back in the days of the Conquistadors, so we don't think Espejo and his men were hallucinating or had heat stroke when they told the local Yavapai Indians that they had come to lay claim to the vast fortune that was theirs through God's grace. They had heard as far away as Spain about the existence of El Cibola, better known as the Seven Cities of Gold. Some conjecture that El Cibola was the stronghold of a band of the Knights Templar, who had fled from Europe with a vast treasure of religious artifacts and set up shop in the territory around 1150. It is said that seven Bishops assigned to Cibola (thus the distinction of seven cities) amassed a bloody fortune which they buried in the earth for safekeeping. Though worthy of only minor consideration, this tale of vast wealth buried in the ground does add a mystique to our sojourn and makes us wonder if Espejo didn't know a little something more than academia might credit to him.

Spanish conquistadors trudged across the hot land only to bury a vast fortune somewhere around Jerome. No doubt their spirits could be guarding this vast fortune, but you might still stumble upon a gold relic or two.

Over a period of the next couple of hundred years various artifacts of considerable value were found and polished. There was enough copper and gold

SPOOKY TREASURE TROVES

lying about to make even the biggest fool's heart flutter. And, in addition, those traversing the region had conferred with the local Indians, who showed them an opening in the mountain that was filled with treasures. This landmark became known as Cleopatra Hill, and eventually word spread far and wide of a possible huge mother-load. By 1876, the town had been established and multitudes were coming to stake their claims. In 1889 the United Verde Copper Company opened up several mines around Jerome, and those not wishing to prospect for prosperity on their own had as much work as they wanted – though toiling under the prevailing conditions at the mines could easily be dangerous to life and limb. An estimated ONE BILLION DOLLARS worth of valuable minerals – gold, copper and silver – were extracted from the earth over the decades, but many a determined young man died in the process of making a few elite individuals exceedingly wealthy.

A fellow ghost hunter, paranormal enthusiast, shutterbug and insatiable Arizona explorer, Charla Gene was the perfect travel companion to hit the ghostly byways with. Inquisitive and adventuresome, she was primed to see if the stories of spirits rumored to abound in Jerome were overly exaggerated or on the level.

As we put our gas guzzling Ford Explorer into second gear to climb the rather steep scenic back mountain roads that lead into Jerome, we did not have to remind ourselves why we were heading to a place where time ostensibly has elapsed. We thought of ourselves as tried and true "ghost hunters" on a mission to reveal to the world the plight of those residing directly across from us on the opposite side of the veil. You might wonder what might make it easier to establish contact with spirits in Jerome than most other places – and our answer would be that it must have something to do with what many say is an indefinable energy in the earth in these parts.

In a sense, we were representing the downtrodden: prostitutes, underpaid miners working under hazardous conditions, Mexican immigrants, gunslingers, out-of-luck gamblers and hopeless alcoholics who could not afford a decent legal defense. In short, any and all troubled spirits, many of whom sacrificed their lives to settle what became an essential part of America's Wild West.

We had made special arrangements with the hosts of Higher Vibrations to stream a live ghost hunt from Jerome's Ghost City Inn, which was to serve as base camp while staying in town. Previously a creaky boarding house and illegal distillery, the multiple-story landmark has a history of legitimate haunts that we were anxious, if possible, to verify firsthand. The program's offbeat hosts, Alex "Friend of Putin" Scully and King Ron, have been broadcasting locally in Las Vegas, Nevada, on KLAV-AM, 1230, every Tuesday at 9 PM. This was to be their first Saturday night broadcast, which they had heavily promoted for weeks, hoping to have a larger than normal audience. Streaming worldwide over the Internet, their show

SPOOKY TREASURE TROVES

is dedicated to educating people on the subjects of UFOs and other paranormal activity. Thus, as it turned out, we were – as Jake Blues proclaims in the "Blues Brothers" musical comedy – "On a mission from God," to be the "messengers of choice" on the evening of June 18, 2011.

Built on a hillside, several times parts of the town have slid further and further down into the valley below. Many miners, prospectors and even a few prostitutes have met their untimely death in Jerome — though they might come back to haunt!

THE MANY GHOSTS OF JEROME

The structure that is now the Ghost City Inn was initially established in 1885 as a place for the mine's middle management to reside. The town was expanding to and fro with construction going on day after day, and the Inn was an attempt to provide adequate space for everyone to live, even if it was under strained and crowded conditions.

After numerous devastating fires, a landslide and various other upheavals in Jerome, the entire structure of the city and the land it stood on shifted significantly, as did the town's population, which expanded and shrunk like an accordion at various intervals in its history. In fact, a number of the town's structures actually slid down the mountainside to a lower altitude, including the town's jail, which ended up down the ridge 225 feet below its original position.

Outside in the still-balmy evening air, Shotgun Sadie was conversing with a group of tourists who had gathered for the Haunted Tours of Jerome, for which Sadie is a knowledgeable tour guide. They were in the process of walking around town taking in the chilling sites when we came across them congregating on the corner of Main and First Streets. Each of the tour's guests had been given a rather impressive ghost detector that theoretically flashes rapidly when a spirit is present. The detectors were going crazy!

Shotgun Sadie explained that we were standing in a particularly active "hot

SPOOKY TREASURE TROVES

spot," thus the noticeable disturbance.

"A hotspot?"

"Oh yes!" she replied. "You see, when the town was booming, its residents were out on the streets drinking at all hours of the day and night. There were maybe three or four shifts at the mines which let out at various hours. Midnight might have been as busy as noon in the alleyways around town where people went to sleep it off. The bars and gambling halls never closed. Fights were pretty common, as were knifings and shootouts. People were dying pretty appalling deaths."

Shotgun says she has stood on this spot on Main and First and actually heard disembodied voices. "A number of times I have heard someone say very loud, 'Liar! Liar!'" The voice gives her chills.

A bit of investigation provoked another possibility.

A check of the town's records tells a horrific tale of fires that almost destroyed this wild and wooly town on more than more than just a few occasions. The Jerome Volunteer Fire Department list these as major historical blazes:

In the late 1890's the town was devastated by one conflagration after another:

April 24, 1894 - Two blocks in the commercial district burned down.

December 24, 1897 - Christmas fire destroyed the business district and many homes.

September 17, 1898 - Once again the business district and many homes went up in flames.

I mentioned to Sadie that I was getting a rather strong psychic impression that the voice she heard might actually have been shouting "Fire! Fire!" instead of "Liar!" She concurred that this was indeed a good possibility and a matter of what could be a misinterpretation. Were the spirits speaking forthrightly, trying to get a message across to us that they did not want to be incinerated in one of the infernos that swept over Jerome?

THE MYSTERIOUS LEDGER

During our stay in Jerome, having set up shop in the immensely popular bed and breakfast, The Ghost City Inn, we were still attempting to lock horns with an unadulterated spirit. Was there a phantom of any sort in the Miners Suite that would like to communicate with either Charla or myself?

We had been told that every room in the Inn had its own presence that was – pardon the expression – dying to get through to the living. Could ours be any different? During the broadcast, the hosts of Higher Frequency wanted to know if I could feel the presence of anything unusual in the Miners Suite where we had hunkered down. I was seated in an antique chair, telephone in hand, answering

SPOOKY TREASURE TROVES

Ghosts are quite frequently seen — and apparently photographed — like this one in the hallway of the Hotel Jerome. Don't think the owners would like you digging there for buried treasure, even if there could be something valuable several feet beneath the structure's foundation.

any and all questions that King Ron and his paranormal partner Alex Scully tossed my way.

And while I have to confess I wasn't getting the vibe – perhaps it was too early in the evening – across the room from me Charla was holding a ghost detector supplied to us by paranormal investigator and "Speaking of Strange" talk show host Joshua P. Warren – and it was flashing on and off as she held it in the doorway. Later, we learned from the manager on duty that this is the exact spot where an apparition has been seen or felt from time to time in the Miners Suite.

So were we alone or not? I am no expert on the sensitivity of ghost detectors and prefer my own psychic intuition. Apparently, others who had stayed in the Miners Suite had been determined to do precisely the same thing.

A ledger near the bed seemed to flip open, though it was probably a gust from the air-conditioning unit that was operating on a thermostat system that made the AC go on and off. Nonetheless, I figured that a closer look at the journal's pages might be in order.

As it turns out, there were numerous references to phenomena reportedly seen, felt, sensed and smelled in our cozy quarters. The following are random postings made by previous guests over a period of about five or six years. These are just a few examples:

MICHELLE AND SCOTT
PEORIA, AZ

Two years ago we came to Jerome for my birthday with my two sisters. We stayed in Room 33 at the Grand (the former hospital where 9000 came to expire). My sister was awakened by moans and sounds of carts.

SPOOKY TREASURE TROVES

LINDA M.

Something pulled the covers off on the left side of the bed. I saw a dark shadow and I began to scream.

MARRY ANN
BURBANK, CA

We had a ghost with us last night. As I sat quietly in bed, I noticed the bathroom door move and it scared me to death.

RANDY AND KATHY
SURPRIZE, AZ

My wife was tired and went to bed before I did. I went to bed at 11 PM. About a half hour later, I was awakened by noises in the ceiling and in the wall near our headboard. It sounded like a large party and people talking. I could hear someone running across the floor. I saw a figure standing in our bedroom at the foot of the bed. I quickly got up out of bed and turned on the light and the figure just vanished. I checked the bathroom, ground floor and even the front door to make certain it was locked. Later, I felt a hand on my chest. It wasn't my wife's hand as she was turned away from me on the bed.

The Inn's proprietor, Jackie, says that she once had a run-in with a vanishing cowboy. She was cleaning in one of the vacant rooms when she observed a man standing in the doorway. He was wearing a heavy canvas or leather coat, which reminded her of a trench coat and was visibly dusty. He had long gray hair that hung to his shoulders, unkempt and naturally curly. The cowboy vanished as quickly as he had appeared. Other times, the radio went on by itself even when the electric cord was pulled out of the wall.

Others have also seen this dusty trail blazer, who some think is the spirit of a prospector who is protecting a satchel of his valuable treasure.

There are many other tales to tell about our trip to Jerome. The full story is in our book ***"The Bell Witch Project"*** which you can easily obtain on Amazon.

Eventually, Charla and I fell asleep, exhausted from the evening's ghostly activities. However, the next morning, as we dragged our equipment down the stairs, we were overcome by a feeling of "resilience," as if the spirits at the Ghost City Inn and in the entire city of Jerome were not harmful as much as they were anxious to get their tragic tales across to the world . . . to allow the living to know that the departed do not forget what has occurred to them in life after shuffling off this mortal coil. Despite their former standing in life, they deserve the same treatment and respect as anyone else, regardless of that individual's fancier clothes or his inherent wealth.

The "old" mining town of Jerome came to a kind of halt in 1951, when the mines dried up and almost everyone began drifting away. But Jerome and its residents – the living and the dead – are not about to give up as they venture into a new era of cooperation between spirits and those still residing in the physical realm. And, besides, who would guard all that treasure buried around town? Maybe if you stay at the Ghost City Inn, you can find a cooperative spirit who will not harass you but share his treasure with you. The possibility is surely worth the price of an overnight stay!

Gaining speed as we wound our way back down to the highway, we couldn't help but feel as if we had left another world – a world where the living and the dead share many of the same concerns. The spirits had entrusted us with a story to tell, and, although there is much more that could be said, we are more than happy to present this important part of their legacy to you until another opportunity to relate more of the spirits' stories comes along!

REFERENCES

www.ToursOfJerome.com

www.Sawaufo.com/higher-vibrations-special-ghost-hunt-with-tim-beckley-live-from-the-ghost-city-inn/

www.GhostCityInn.Com

www.Jeromefd.org/

www.JeromeHistoricalSociety.com

SPOOKY TREASURE TROVES

GOLD MINING SLAVES OF THE ANCIENT ALIEN KIND

After all of our research and our storytelling, the question remains, what exactly is the substance known as gold and why is it so valuable to our way of thinking? One "expert" gave this explanation:

"Pure gold – like, for example, pure mercury, lead, silver, copper, iron or aluminum – is classified as a metallic element. (By definition, an element comprises only a single type of atom.) For comparable volumes, gold weighs some 19.3 times more than water, 1.4 times more than mercury, 1.7 times more than lead, 1.8 times more than silver, 2.2 times more than copper, 2.4 times more than iron and 7.1 times more than aluminum.

"If comparatively rare, gold nevertheless occurs on every continent on earth and in the waters of the sea. It is, according to the Prospectors Paradise Internet site, 'mined in deserts, high mountain ranges, in the deeply weathered soil of the tropics and in the permanently frozen ground of the Arctic.'

"In America, nature was extremely generous. Thirty-two states have recorded significant commercial gold production. The highest yield areas are located within the western states. The recreational gold prospector can find gold in practically every state of the union.

"Treasured by the craftsman, gold, more than any of the other pure metals, can be hammered, bent, drawn and carved into shapes as massive as the dome of an Islamic mosque and as delicate as the web of a spider. 'A solitary ounce of gold,' says Prospectors Paradise, 'can be drawn and stretched into an ultrafine wire of 50 miles in length, without breaking or hammering, to the amazing thinness of one hundred thousandth of an inch without disintegrating.' Further, gold resists corrosion and rust even when exposed for thousands of years to seawater, soil, air, heat or cold.

"Also treasured by scientists and technologists, gold has been used to treat some forms of arthritis and related conditions. It has been used to tag proteins in studies of human disease. It has been used to tint the visors of astronauts' helmets, coat the impellers in the space shuttles' liquid hydrogen pumps, and to coat the mirror of the Mars Global Surveyor telescope."

Reference: http://www.antelopevalleyhaunts.com/

Now that we have clarified that matter, another question presents itself – why is there so much UFO and ghostly activity around treasure troves? Certainly, the Ultra-Terrestrials are not about to walk into a 7-11 and buy a slice of cold pizza. There must be some other attraction. Furthermore, why would ghosts and UFOs form a union of sorts to work in tandem either to guide us to a treasure or to keep us as far away as "humanly" possible?

Zecharia Sitchin professes that the Anunnaki came in ancient times to rape and plunder our planet.

For those who haven't studied these mysteries extensively – nor devoted their entire lives to such phenomena – there wouldn't seem to be an obvious connection between "spook lights," as UFOs are sometimes referred to, and just ordinary spooks of the life after death variety. But someone such as the present authors who are steeped in such spiritual vagaries might say otherwise.

The fact of the matter is that what takes place in a haunted house is also likely to take place in a field where a UFO has landed. For example, objects float around freely, including humans, who have been known to ascend on a beam of

SPOOKY TREASURE TROVES

light to a hovering UFO, as well as possibly passing through solid objects such as a wall or a door – just like a ghost would. In the case of one of the authors, Tim Beckley, members of his own family were sucked into a whirlwind of poltergeist-like activity following the appearance of a UFO that hovered across the street from their residence. There were voices in the basement, specters in the woods behind their residence, and objects were vanishing and reappearing days later in the strangest of places. As reported by the prestigious British UFO Research Organization (BUFORA), a UK family was besieged by the sounds of moaning in their bedroom and the appearance of small humanoid creatures in various rooms of their house. They thought the dwelling to be haunted until they put two and two together and realized their world was turned upside down only after several family members had encountered a UFO out on the road after dark. It's as if the "visitor" followed them back to their lair.

While there was no treasure involved in either of these instances, mainly what we are trying to do is make a meager comparison between UFOs and other weird phenomena that go bump in the night (well some of them create a bit more noise, clamoring and clanging their way through a darkened household). The veil is thin between the scary duo of UFO and poltergeist and it would appear that such interrelated occurrences are increasing in number in the last few years. Those readers seeking further verification and validation are pointed in the direction of several of our books available on Amazon, including "Evil Empire of The ETs and the Ultra-Terrestrials," which is the focal point of our "Dark Side Of UFOlogy Series."

Knowing that readers would be interested in exploring this fascinating connection along with us, we have asked paranormal talk show host and author Paul Eno, whose show "Behind the Paranormal" has become a fixture on station WOON out of Woonsocket, Rhode Island (where it can be heard every Monday evening at 6 PM before being archived at www.BehindTheParanormal.com) to add his understanding and knowledge of this budding relationship between supposed phantoms of the deceased and some very strange cosmic journeymen who might be a little bit "stranger" than we have even begun to suspect. The concluding chapter, "UFOs, Cryptids & Ghosts: Branches of the Same Tree?" by our buddy Paul is certainly in a league all its own.

And while we claim to have no simple answer to this rather perplexing question as to why a legion of phantoms of one variety or another would be so closely aligned with treasure hunting, one individual might provide us with a few compelling clues to this quandary.

The late Zecharia Sitchin is still considered to be among the preeminent scholars of the ancient astronauts theory of the creation of mankind. His books have sold millions of copies worldwide and been translated into more than 25

SPOOKY TREASURE TROVES

languages, beginning with "The 12th Planet" in 1976.

Sitchin attributes the creation of the ancient Sumerian culture to the Anunnaki, which he states was a race of extraterrestrials from a planet beyond Neptune called Nibiru. He believed this hypothetical planet of Nibiru to be in an elongated elliptical orbit in the Earth's own solar system, which he said is clearly stated in Sumerian mythology.

In an online article by Neil Freer entitled "Sumerian Culture and the Anunnaki," Freer gives some more essential historical background.

"Working from the same archeological discoveries, artifacts and recovered records as archeologists and linguists have for two hundred years," Freer writes, "Sitchin propounds that the Anunnaki (a name translated from the ancient Sumerian as "those who came down from the heavens," with equivalents in Old Testament Hebrew and Egyptian), an advanced civilization from the tenth planet in our solar system splashed down in the Persian Gulf area around 432,000 years ago and colonized the planet with the purpose of obtaining large quantities of gold.

The Anunnaki came in antiquity to mine gold using human slaves. They could return soon.

"Some 250,000 years ago," Freer continues, "the recovered documents tell us that their lower echelon miners rebelled against conditions in the mines, and the Anunnaki directorate decided to create a creature to take their place."

So began a period of experimentation. Enki, the chief scientist of the alien race, and Ninhursdag, their chief medical officer, first tried splicing animal genes with that of the extremely primitive precursor of man, Homo Erectus. But the results failed to achieve their goals. It was then decided to merge their Anunnaki genes with Homo Erectus, which produced mankind as we know him today, the species Homo Sapiens. Because we were a hybrid, we could not procreate.

When the demand for people as workers increased, we were genetically manipulated to allow us to reproduce.

"For thousands of years," Freer writes, "we were their slaves, their workers, their servants and their soldiers in their political battles among themselves.

SPOOKY TREASURE TROVES

The Anunnaki used us in the construction of their palaces (we retro-project the religious notion of temple on these now), their cities, their mining and refining complexes and their astronomical installations on all the continents. They expanded from Mesopotamia to Egypt to South and Central America, and the stamp of their presence can be found in the farthest reaches of the planet."

Another writer, Andy Lloyd, also takes up the subject of Sitchin's race of gold-hungry aliens.

"One of the most curious things about Zecharia Sitchin's theories is his description of the Anunnaki's search for gold," Lloyd writes. "Their descent to Earth was triggered by a worsening environmental disaster on their own world, Nibiru. They came here with the explicit need to collect one thing: Gold. Why? Not for jewelry, certainly. Their plundering of the Earth's gold supplies was necessary in order to achieve just one end. They needed to pump the stuff into the atmosphere of Nibiru. This is one of the strangest aspects of a very strange story."

Lloyd wrote his article around the same time that the U.S. was pressuring scientists to recommend high-tech solutions to the threat of global warming. The ideas included space "mirrors" to reflect some small percentage of the light of the sun away from the Earth. It was felt this could compensate for the greenhouse gas effects we are suffering from the industrial and domestic output of carbon gases.

"One of the ways to reflect light into space," Lloyd continues, "would be to introduce reflective material into the highest part of Earth's atmosphere. Such a solution is being considered seriously. This all suddenly sounds rather familiar. This is pure Sitchin! It's what the Anunnaki did with our gold. They spent hundreds of thousands of years purportedly mining the stuff and shipping it back to Nibiru when that planet's elongated orbit brought it round to the planetary zone of our star every 3,600 years. Once they had enough of the stuff, the Anunnaki left. It now seems that the purpose for the gold was not to keep the home world's planetary heat in, but to keep the light out!"

As Freer explains, around 6,000 years ago, the Anunnaki chose to phase out their presence on Earth and began to gradually help mankind develop a functioning independence. Sumer, a human civilization, amazing in its "sudden" appearance, was set up under the extraterrestrials' guidance in Mesopotamia. Human kings were inaugurated as go-betweens, foremen of the human populations that answered to the Anunnaki. Designated humans were taught technology, mathematics, astronomy, advanced crafts and the ways of advanced civilized society.

This is all, admittedly, a more "unsentimental" view of mankind's creation than is usually taught to us by our various religions. But it may go a long way to explain the interest of UFOs and their alien occupants in our present day gold mines and why they are seen so often in areas where vast stores of gold and other precious metals are alleged to have been buried. Even the ghosts, demons and various spirits reputed to guard certain buried treasures could be an expression of the aliens' paranormal abilities, phantasms projected from some other dimension where aliens can move freely among the living and the dead.

On the History Channel's program "Ancient Aliens," season 6, episode 7, this theory is discussed in further detail.

"Many ancient cultures were in the pursuit of precious gold, silver and jewels," the program explains. "They always did this under the premise that they were gathering it for their gods. Zecharia Sitchin speculates that gold is absolutely necessary for the people of the tenth planet. Gold has proven to be a valuable element for space travel. Gold is highly conductive, and you would probably have a lot of electrical-based equipment on your ship. Gold has great thermal properties, and it's incredibly easy to work with. You can make it very thin."

Might our ancestors have secreted away vast caches of gold on the orders of extraterrestrial gods?

The same episode of "Ancient Aliens" also takes up the subject of the Copper Scroll, part of an extraordinary cache of first century documents first discovered in caves at Qumran and popularly known as the Dead Sea Scrolls.

According to writer April Holloway, "The Copper Scroll, however, is very different from the other documents in the Qumran library. In fact, it is so anomalous among the Dead Sea Scrolls – its author, script, style, language, genre, content and medium all differ to the other scrolls – that scholars believe it must have been placed in the cave at a different time than the rest of the ancient documents. While the other scrolls were written on parchment or papyrus, this scroll was written on metal: copper mixed with about one percent tin."

The Copper Scroll was also not a literary work, as the other scrolls were, but was instead a list of 64 locations where staggering quantities of treasure could be found. Over 4,600 talents of precious metal are listed on the scroll, making the total haul in excess of a billion dollars. It is assumed that the treasure is from the Jewish Temple, though there is disagreement as to whether that would be Solomon's Temple, destroyed by Babylon in 586 B.C., or the Second Temple, lost to the Romans around the time of Christ.

"There are many, though, who are not so concerned about where it came from," Holloway writes, "but much more interested in where it is now. The Copper Scroll has led to one of the biggest treasure hunts in history, with numerous expeditions setting out to find the valuable hoard."

However, the locations are written as if the reader would have an intimate knowledge of what are now obscure references nearly impossible to decipher in our time. But this hasn't stopped the enthusiasts. An extensive treasure hunt was conducted in 1962, led by one John Allegro, whose team excavated many poten-

SPOOKY TREASURE TROVES

tial burial places for the treasure but returned empty handed. Despite being available for several decades, the Copper Scroll has not yielded a single material find.

Holloway concludes by saying, "Nevertheless, to anyone who has a little bit of the Indiana Jones spirit inside them, it remains a fascinating and tantalizing artifact, and will no doubt continue to tempt the imaginations of scholars and the public alike for centuries to come."

But we must get to the main purpose at hand – finding some buried or sunken treasure of our very own. The following pages are filled with rich prizes to be sought after. And there remains many an undiscovered hoard to be packed up and displayed in a museum. There are vast treasures all around us. Though some of the hidden stores of fabulous riches described in the following pages may have already been taken, most still await the time when they will again be touched by human hands. And, perhaps, with a bit of luck, we will have some hands from the other side of reality to help in our search for wealth as well as a deeper understanding of the unexplained.

Not one to travel much lately, co-author Tim Beckley didn't have to uncover the rare Ark of the Covenant at the bottom of Oak Island's "Money Pit," where it is said to be waiting for a fortune seeker to unseal its fate. Instead, he found one on display at a Bible study program show in Fort Lauderdale.

SPOOKY TREASURE TROVES

UFOS, CRYPTIDS AND GHOSTS: BRANCHES OF THE SAME TREE?
By Paul Eno

Our intrepid investigator gives the smack down on the close connection between all the vexing inhabitants of what appears to be a "goblin universe."

Budd Hopkins was there to talk about aliens and I was there to talk about ghosts. It was the 2003 West Virginia Paranormal Conference in Parkersburg, and we were so intrigued by what the other had to say that we found a quiet corner to talk. The prominent alien-abduction researcher brought an album full of photos illustrating bruises, scoop marks and other physical traces on the bodies of what he believed were abductees.

"Budd, these marks are exactly what I've seen in many poltergeist* cases!" I stated. We talked about doing some collaborative research, but Hopkins was overtaken by his tragic illness before we could begin.

The questions, however, remain. Are there connections between seemingly unrelated phenomena within the broader paranormal realm? Do the labels we place on paranormal experiences and entities depend on the context in which we experience them? Is there a single "tree" of which all paranormal phenomena are "branches"?

More specifically, why do so many ghost and poltergeist cases – once one thinks to look beyond a single home or family – sometimes involve large areas, many homes and many people? Why do so many – again, if one thinks to look – turn into UFO cases that often enough involve "grays" and cryptids? Perhaps most importantly: Why does the military seem to take an interest in such areas?

Or is it all just coincidence?

To even ask these questions, never mind answer them, one must somehow get past the mob of assumptions that derive from the modern epistemological paradigm, and which I feel stand squarely in the way of progress in paranormal understanding. Among these virtually unquestioned assumptions:

UFOs are nuts-and-bolts craft from other planets.

SPOOKY TREASURE TROVES

Being "advanced" means having more and better technology, as opposed to being advanced morally or spiritually.

There's a material world and a spirit world.

Ghosts are spirits of the dead. But they can walk, talk, dress up, think, remember and drive cars even though they don't have bodies or brains anymore.

Nasty spirits are demons and very good theologians because they know all about God and are afraid of holy water.

Cryptids like Nessie and Yeti are just really good at playing hide-and-seek.

Paranormal entities, including aliens, have the same motivations we do and can be understood from our own anthropocentric framework of knowledge.

UFOs, cryptids and ghosts are entirely separate phenomena.

Additional assumptions include:

Eyewitnesses have bad eyesight.

The paranormal can be made acceptable to mainstream science.

Our science and the materialism on which it's based can fully define reality. Anything "supernatural" must therefore be undiscovered materialistic science.

And the most fundamental assumption of all:

The Island Theory. Within our bodies and brains, we are totally self-contained life-forms. Few of the assumptions above can be embraced unless we first accept the Island Theory.

I'm not saying that "none of the above" are true. I'm suggesting that some may be untrue (or at least misinterpreted), others might be partially true, and none are complete explanations for anything.

I first began researching ghosts in 1970 while, believe it or not, studying for the priesthood. As early as my very first case in the field, involving ultra-bizarre doings at an abandoned and overgrown village in northeast Connecticut, it became disconcertingly obvious, at least to me, that the classical explanations for paranormal events just didn't do it. Somehow, the theology, the spiritualism, the fumbling attempts at science, the superstition, and cer-

New England talk show host and paranormal author Paul Eno stands proudly in his private library.

tainly the assumptions, simply weren't good enough.

Even the "experts" at the time seemed mired in the assumptions. I was working with Fr. John Nicola, a Jesuit priest who was the technical advisor for the film The Exorcist, and one of the Roman Catholic Church's leading experts on the subject. He couldn't get beyond the theology. It was all about the devil and demons, with some psychology thrown in beforehand to make sure the victim wasn't bonkers instead of possessed.

Then there was Dr. Louisa Rhine, the renowned and pioneering parapsychologist at Duke University, with whom I corresponded. She and her colleagues were straining and sweating to make paranormal phenomena fit the materialist scientific paradigm, the "square peg in the round hole" if ever there was one.

Among my other mentors were the grandparents of modern "ghost hunting," Ed & Lorraine Warren, now household names because of the 2013 film The Conjuring. They couldn't get beyond pop-theology mixed with spiritualism.

Other than some nods toward transpersonal psychology and theoretical physics, most of today's experts are still married to the same assumptions in their respective fields, and from what I can see they're still getting nowhere.

By the beginning of the 1980s, I'd run into poltergeists, ghosts of people both living and dead, phantom buildings and vehicles, possession and exorcism, appearing and disappearing animals and people, space/time displacements and, of course, UFOs. I had worked in psychiatric hospitals as a seminarian and a student in abnormal psychology, and I'd seen what appeared to be psychoses and paranormal phenomena intertwined. Out went the assumptions and in came the only possible solution I could discern: quantum mechanics.

I emphasize that I'm not a scientist, let alone a theoretical physicist. My degree is in philosophy, with additional postgraduate work in theology, psychology, history and law. Nevertheless, philosophy is supposed to teach one to think, and to bring together diverse facts and ideas to discover new facts and ideas, all in the midst of a society whose supposedly great thinkers are wildly overspecialized. And besides, I wasn't born yesterday. I was seeing what I was seeing.

For me, quantum mechanics all pointed to a single explanation: multiple parallel worlds, an open system with relatively free exchanges of energy and, at times, inhabitants. Couple this with the contention of some physicists, including Hugh Everett and Bryce DeWitt, that this "multiverse" contains all possible possibilities, and the broader idea that all things, past and future included, exist simultaneously, and we have the beginning of a more complete and less naive explanation for the paranormal.

This suggested to me that "ghosts" weren't dead people but actual people living in parallel worlds that happened to intersect ours at certain times, places and states. This explained why many ghosts seem afraid of us, thinking we are

SPOOKY TREASURE TROVES

ghosts haunting them, and why many have such physical characteristics. "Spirits of the dead," however, is the only way our two-dimensional modern paradigm can deal with them.

It suggested that "demons," whose action I'd seen with my own eyes many times over, aren't servants of Satan but multiversal life forms, "parasites" feeding on the energy of other life forms.

Photo by Allen Greenfield of spector outside parish of Christ Church, Georgia, rectory.

This explains why I have occasional physical encounters with them, why they don't all respond to exorcisms, and why they leave their victims drained, often with chronic fatigue. Our folklore explains them as evil spirits, ghouls or even vampires because that's the best we can do.

Additionally, it suggested that UFOs and aliens might be far more than beings in nuts-and-bolts craft from other planets. We often scratch our heads about how they can travel such enormous distances. If they have the ability, technologically or otherwise, to traverse world boundaries to wherever or whenever they want to be, distance doesn't matter.

As for cryptids coming and going...there we have it – maybe.

It should be made clear that, while most physicists today acknowledge the multiverse idea in some form, not all interpret it the way I do. But seeing, as they say, is believing, and I don't know a single theoretical physicist who works in the paranormal "trenches" as I have for nearly 45 years.

So if there are entire regions where world intersects are common or even semi- permanent, it might explain paranormal "flaps" – multiple, seemingly unrelated paranormal events taking place in profusion in the same area. Several of these areas are legendary.

The "Mothman" affair in the Ohio Valley of the US in the 1960s is associated with the appearance of one or more huge, moth-like or bird-like creatures that terrified local residents. But as journalist and author John Keel pointed out, there were a great many additional and concurrent phenomena. These included nightly UFOs seen by hundreds of people, "men in black" and other strange visitors such as the self-styled alien known as Indrid Cold, ghosts, poltergeists, and clairvoyance and heightened psychic abilities among some residents.

SPOOKY TREASURE TROVES

Local witnesses I interviewed in the early 2000s, children at the time of the Mothman events, reported the above, along with things like red eyes looking in their windows and something walking heavily on their roofs at night.

More recently, Utah's "Skinwalker Ranch" situation has come to light, with teams of scientists supposedly witnessing nightly UFOs, things coming through holes in the sky and air, apportations of objects and animals, ultra-bizarre cryptids, alien encounters, poltergeist activity, time slips, ghostly encounters and more.

Since 2005, my son and partner, Ben, and I have been studying other areas where we believe this sort of flap might be taking place. These include a large section of Litchfield County, Connecticut; Freetown State Forest and the Hockomock Swamp Wildlife Management Area in Massachusetts (the so-called Bridgewater Triangle), and Rendlesham Forest in the UK.

Especially in the minds of UFO researchers, Rendlesham Forest is associated primarily with the reported December 1980 sightings and landings at the twin NATO air bases straddling the forest, RAF Bentwaters and RAF Woodbridge. Looking deeper, however, one finds bizarre events in the area going back to Saxon times. These include strange lights in the sky and on the ground, cryptids and, yes, downloads of binary codes reported by local witnesses.

While researching the area after dark in September 2012, accompanied by 1980 UFO witness Larry Warren and several local listeners to our radio show, Ben and I had a sort of "alien encounter" before even leaving the parking lot to head toward the famous "East Gate" of the erstwhile Woodbridge air base. Photos from that night revealed odd lights among the trees.

Our most active investigation, now approaching 10 years in process, is the Litchfield County, Connecticut, flap. This began in 2005 when rural homeowners contacted us after reading my 2002 book Footsteps in the Attic, saying that the multiverse approach was the only thing they felt could explain the outlandish and seemingly unrelated phenomena taking place in their 1793 farmhouse.

By 2009, we found that the entire area was affected. Other families were reporting ghost and poltergeist activity. UFOs were being seen by hundreds of witnesses, to the point where the local media got involved. "Grays" were seen in people's homes and there were at least two Yeti sightings.

Mass changes in public behavior were reported as well, such as people driving on the wrong side of the road to a degree way beyond the statistical probability. When this was noticed in local media, the behavior changed, and people reportedly began driving off the road and hitting trees.

As in every other case mentioned here, there seems to be a military component. In 2009 and 2010, there was substantial military activity in the flap area. People reported taking walks and being turned back at certain points by armed troops. Unusual aircraft seemed to join the UFO sightings and continue to do so, including black helicopters. It all seems to center on an "abandoned" farm along a rural road a few miles from the farmhouse where our involvement began.

In November 2010, Ben and I joined a New York producer and camera crew in the area to make a pilot for a possible television show. We found no activity at the farm at that point, but the entire property was well kept, and the fields mown. Since then, there has been substantial vehicular activity, the central farm buildings have been torn down and replaced with a huge, flat metal sheet of several thousand square feet, visible only from the air. For some reason, the two silos have been left standing and repainted.

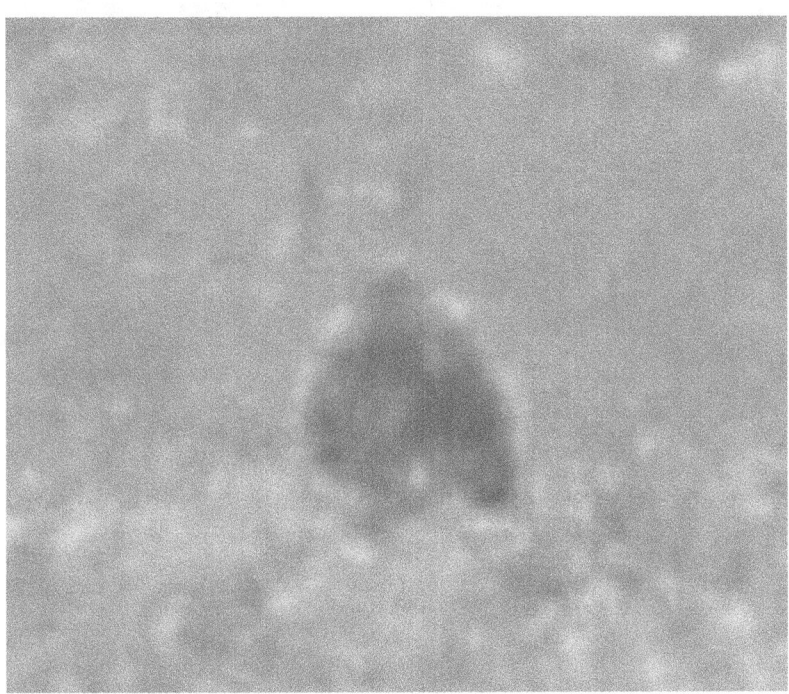

Could Bigfoot be called upon to assist in guarding a treasure buried in some wood hollow?
(Photo by Bruce Cornet in El Paso).

The dirt road leading to the farm is sometimes closed, and the unexplained aerial activity continues and includes large, black, double-rotor freight aircraft. We have been unable to obtain any official confirmation that actual military activity was or is taking place, either by regular, National Guard or Reserve forces. And we have never been allowed to see the footage from the pilot, which produced no subsequent television show.

The question of the multiversal nature of paranormal phenomena aside, why the military activity in flap areas? We suspect a simple answer: Wouldn't we just love to weaponize the paranormal? That's nothing new. It's been going on since at least the Stargate Project in the 1970s, and probably before. Why would the research be centered in relatively populous areas such as the Ohio Valley; Suffolk, England, or central Connecticut? Perhaps because the researchers must go where the world intersects are.

So why the manic secrecy and the military muscle in guarding such areas? Aside from keeping people guessing, throwing them off the scent and simply keeping them out, there might be a more visceral reason.

We live in a world where people long ago came to grips with the Klingons, ET and the Planet of the Apes. Rather than creating global panic and social collapse, the announcement of alien life, even alien visitors, might very well be greeted with enthusiasm. But only if that great assumption were confirmed: They come from some far-off planet.

What if they don't? Suppose these multiverse ideas are true and the government, or some other powerful entity, knows that our aliens – in every possible form and attitude – come from parallel worlds that are right next to us all the time, that all the demons and monsters of our darkest folklore are real in some form after all. That would surely be cause for panic and ample cause for secrecy, in my opinion.

The Sedona/Jerome, Arizona, area is overrun with mysterious phenomena and is the site of various groups of buried minerals from gold to silver to cooper (Courtesy Tom Dongo Collection).

Perhaps Ben and I are wrong. Perhaps everything we've described above is as coincidental as it is circumstantial. Maybe other, far more competent, UFO researchers than ourselves, such as Richard Dolan, Marc D'Antonio and Robert Schroeder, who have approached the multiverse idea in some of their own work, will shed further light on it.

In the meantime, Ben and I, and people like us, will continue to watch from the trenches.

*In parapsychology, a poltergeist (German: "a spirit that rants or thrashes about") is believed to be produced by the energy from a frustrated human "agent." The authors believe they are parasitic, ultraterrestrial life-forms.

SPOOKY TREASURE TROVES

AN AFTERTHOUGHT ON THE TREASURE HUNTING ASPECTS OF THE PARANORMAL

What are the possible reasons for interest in treasure by members of the "goblin universe?"

1) Extra-planetary mining. There is some opinion among what might be called paleo-ufologists that certain alien races have come here in the past to obtain gold. I suppose that's possible.

2) More likely to me is the parasite connection as evidenced in folklore. What we might interpret as anything from aliens to ghosts to leprechauns, but which actually might be energy-eating parasites, might lead us to sites where "X" might or might not "mark the spot," then literally feed on any resulting frustration. In the Bell Witch case (1817-1821) in Tennessee, for example, there are stories of the "witch," which I believe was in fact four parasites, leading treasure hunters on wild-good chases, then laughing at the results. So the real goal of whatever might be leading people to buried treasure might be helping themselves to us rather than helping us to the loot.

3) As to "spirits" or whatever guarding treasure, wealth of any kind often brings out the worst in people. Horrific events such as murder and mayhem tend to echo across the various parallel worlds of the multiverse (which I think is a far better explanation for the paranormal than any veil or spirit world). People who are attuned to that will tend to pick up the actual event as it takes place in a close parallel world where dear old Blackbeard is still running through the poor drudges who buried the booty, and there can even be rudimentary contact.

Copyright 2014 by Paul F. Eno. All rights reserved.

But we must get to the main purpose at hand – finding some buried or sunken treasure of our very own. The following pages are filled with rich prizes to be sought after. And there remains many an undiscovered hoard to be packed up and displayed in a museum. There are vast treasures all around us. Though some of the hidden stores of fabulous riches described in the following pages may have already been taken, most still await the time when they will again be touched by human hands. And, perhaps, with a bit of luck, we will have some hands from the other side of reality to help in our search for wealth as well as a deeper understanding of the unexplained.

SPOOKY TREASURE TROVES

NOTES

SPOOKY TREASURE TROVES

H.M.S. *Lutine* leaving Yarmouth Roads, Oct. 9, 1799, on her last voyage. (*From the painting by Frank Mason, R.A., in the Committee Room of Lloyd's, London.*) See Chapter XI.

THE BOOK OF BURIED TREASURE

CHAPTER I
THE WORLD-WIDE HUNT FOR VANISHED RICHES

The language has no more boldly romantic words than *pirate* and *galleon* and the dullest imagination is apt to be kindled by any plausible dream of finding their lost treasures hidden on lonely beach or tropic key, or sunk fathoms deep in salt water. In the preface of that rare and exceedingly diverting volume, "The Pirates' Own Book," the unnamed author sums up the matter with so much gusto and with so gorgeously appetizing a flavor that he is worth quoting to this extent:

"With the name of pirate is also associated ideas of rich plunder, caskets of buried jewels, chests of gold ingots, bags of outlandish coins, secreted in lonely,

SPOOKY TREASURE TROVES

out of the way places, or buried about the wild shores of rivers and unexplored sea coasts, near rocks and trees bearing mysterious marks indicating where the treasure was hid. And as it is his invariable practice to secrete and bury his booty, and from the perilous life he leads, being often killed or captured, he can never revisit the spot again, therefore immense sums remain buried in those places and are irrevocably lost. Search is often made by persons who labor in anticipation of throwing up with their spade and pickaxe, gold bars, diamond crosses sparkling amongst the dirt, bags of golden doubloons and chests wedged close with moidores, ducats and pearls; but although great treasures lie hid in this way, it seldom happens that any is recovered."[1]

In this tamed, prosaic age of ours, treasure-seeking might seem to be the peculiar province of fiction, but the fact is that expeditions are fitting out every little while, and mysterious schooners flitting from many ports, lured by grimy, tattered charts presumed to show where the hoards were hidden, or steering their courses by nothing more tangible than legend and surmise. As the Kidd tradition survives along the Atlantic coast, so on divers shores of other seas persist the same kind of wild tales, the more convincing of which are strikingly alike in that the lone survivor of the red-handed crew, having somehow escaped the hanging, shooting, or drowning that he handsomely merited, preserved a chart showing where the treasure had been hid. Unable to return to the place, he gave the parchment to some friend or shipmate, this dramatic transfer usually happening as a death-bed ceremony. The recipient, after digging in vain and heartily damning the departed pirate for his misleading landmarks and bearings, handed the chart down to the next generation.

It will be readily perceived that this is the stock motive of almost all buried treasure fiction, the trademark of a certain brand of adventure story, but it is really more entertaining to know that such charts and records exist and are made use of by the expeditions of the present day. Opportunity knocks at the door. He who would gamble in shares of such a speculation may find sun-burned, tarry gentlemen, from Seattle to Singapore, and from Capetown to New Zealand, eager to whisper curious information of charts and sailing directions, and to make sail and away.

Some of them are still seeking booty lost on Cocos Island off the coast of Costa Rica where a dozen expeditions have futilely sweated and dug; others have cast anchor in harbors of Guam and the Carolines; while as you run from Aden to Vladivostock, sailormen are never done with spinning yarns of treasure buried by the pirates of the Indian Ocean and the China Sea. Out from Callao the treasure hunters fare to Clipperton Island, or the Gallapagos group where the buccaneers with Dampier and Davis used to careen their ships, and from Valparaiso many an expedition has found its way to Juan Fernandez and Magellan Straits. The topsails of these salty argonauts have been sighted in recent years off the Salvages to the southward of Madeira where two millions of Spanish gold were buried in chests, and pick and shovel have been busy on rocky Trinidad in the South Atlantic which conceals vast stores of plate and jewels left there by pirates who looted the galleons of Lima.

Near Cape Vidal, on the coast of Zululand, lies the wreck of the notorious sailing vessel *Dorothea*, in whose hold is treasure to the amount of two million dollars in gold bars concealed beneath a flooring of cement. It was believed for some time that the ill-fated *Dorothea* was fleeing with the fortune of Oom Paul Kruger on board when she was cast ashore. The evidence goes to show, however, that certain officials of the Transvaal Government, before the Boer War, issued permits to several lawless adventurers, allowing them to engage in buying stolen gold from the mines. This illicit traffic flourished largely, and so successful was this particular combination that a ship was bought, the *Ernestine*, and after being overhauled and renamed the *Dorothea*, she secretly shipped the treasure on board in Delagoa Bay.

It was only the other day that a party of restless young Americans sailed in the old racing yacht *Mayflower* bound out to seek the wreck of a treasure galleon on the coast of Jamaica. Their vessel was dismasted and abandoned at sea, and they had all the adventure they yearned for. One of them, Roger Derby of Boston, of a family famed for its deep-water mariners in the olden times, ingenuously confessed some time later, and here you have the spirit of the true treasure-seeker:

"I am afraid that there is no information accessible in documentary or printed form of the wreck that we investigated a year ago. Most of it is hearsay, and when we went down there on a second trip after losing the *Mayflower*, we found little to prove that a galleon had been lost, barring some old cannon, flint rock ballast, and square iron bolts. We found absolutely no gold."

The coast of Madagascar, once haunted by free-booters who plundered the rich East Indiamen, is still ransacked by treasure seekers, and American soldiers in the Philippines indefatigably excavate the landscape of Luzon in the hope of finding the hoard of Spanish gold buried by the Chinese mandarin Chan Lu Suey in the eighteenth century. Every island of the West Indies and port of the Spanish Main abounds in legends of the mighty sea rogues whose hard fate it was to be laid by the heels before they could squander the gold that had been won with cutlass, boarding pike and carronade.

The spirit of true adventure lives in the soul of the treasure hunter. The odds may be a thousand to one that he will unearth a solitary doubloon, yet he is lured to undertake the most prodigious exertions by the keen zest of the game itself. The English novelist, George R. Sims, once expressed this state of mind very exactly. "Respectable citizens, tired of the melancholy sameness of a drab existence, cannot take to crape masks, dark lanterns, silent matches, and rope lad-

Treasure-seekers' Camp at Cape Vidal on African coast.

Divers searching wreck of Treasure ship *Dorothea*, Cape Vidal, Africa.

ders, but they can all be off to a pirate island and search for treasure and return laden or empty without a stain upon their characters. I know a fine old pirate who sings a good song and has treasure islands at his fingers' ends. I think I can get together a band of adventurers, middle-aged men of established reputation in whom the public would have confidence, who would be only too glad to enjoy a year's romance."

Robert Louis Stevenson who dearly loved a pirate and wrote the finest treasure story of them all around a proper chart of his own devising, took Henry James to task for confessing that although he had been a child he had never been on a quest for buried treasure. "Here is indeed a willful paradox," exclaimed the author of "Treasure Island," "for if he has never been on a quest for buried treasure, it can be demonstrated that he has never been a child. There never was a child (unless Master James), but has hunted gold, and been a pirate, and a military commander, and a bandit of the mountains; but has fought, and suffered shipwreck and prison, and imbrued its little hands in gore, and gallantly retrieved the lost battle, and triumphantly protected innocence and beauty."

Mark Twain also indicated the singular isolation of Henry James by expressing precisely the same opinion in his immortal chronicle of the adventures of Tom Sawyer. "There comes a time in every rightly constructed boy's life when he has a raging desire to go somewhere and dig for buried treasure." And what an entrancing career Tom had planned for himself in an earlier chapter! "At the zenith of his fame, how he would suddenly appear at the old village and stalk into church, brown and weather-beaten, in his black velvet doublet and trunks, his great jackboots, his crimson sash, his belt bristling with horse-pistols, his crime-rusted cutlass at his side, his slouch hat with waving plumes, his black flag unfurled, with the skull and cross-bones on it, and hear with swelling ecstasy the whisperings, 'It's Tom Sawyer the Pirate!—The Black Avenger of the Spanish Main.'"

When Tom and Huck Finn went treasure seeking they observed the time-honored rules of the game, as the following dialogue will recall to mind:

"Where'll we dig?" said Huck.

"Oh, most anywhere."

"Why, is it hid all around?"

"No, indeed it ain't. It's hid in mighty particular places, Huck, sometimes on islands, sometimes in rotten chests under the limb of an old dead tree, just where the shadow falls at midnight; but mostly under the floor in ha'nted houses."

"Who hides it?"

"Why, robbers, of course. Who'd you reckon, Sunday-school superintendents?"

"I don't know. If 'twas mine I wouldn't hide it; I'd spend it and have a good time."

SPOOKY TREASURE TROVES

"So would I. But robbers don't do that way. They always hide it and leave it there."

"Don't they come after it any more!"

"No, they think they will, but they generally forget the marks or else they die. Anyway, it lays there a long time and gets rusty; and by and by somebody finds an old yellow paper that tells how to find the marks,—a paper that's got to be ciphered over about a week because it's mostly signs and hy'roglyphics."

Hunting lost treasure is not work but a fascinating kind of play that belongs to the world of make believe. It appeals to that strain of boyishness which survives in the average man even though his pow be frosted, his reputation starched and conservative. It is, after all, an inherited taste handed down from the golden age of fairies. The folk-lore of almost every race is rich in buried treasure stories. The pirate with his stout sea chest hidden above high-water mark is lineally descended from the enchanting characters who lived in the shadow land of myth and fable. The hoard of Captain Kidd, although he was turned off at Execution Dock only two hundred years ago, has become as legendary as the dream of the pot of gold at the end of the rainbow.

Many a hard-headed farmer and fisherman of the New England coast believes that it is rash business to go digging for Kidd's treasure unless one carefully performs certain incantations designed to placate the ghostly guardian who aforetime sailed with Kidd and was slain by him after the hole was dug lest the secret might thus be revealed. And it is of course well known that if a word is spoken after the pick has clinked against the iron-bound chest or metal pot, the devil flies away with the treasure, leaving behind him only panic and a strong smell of brimstone.

Such curious superstitions as these, strongly surviving wherever pirate gold is sought, have been the common property of buried-treasure stories in all ages. The country-folk of Japan will tell you that if a pot of money is found a rice cake must be left in place of every coin taken away, and imitation money burned as an offering to any spirit that may be offended by the removal of the hoard. The negroes of the West Indies explain that the buried wealth of the buccaneers is seldom found because the spirits that watch over it have a habit of whisking the treasure away to parts unknown as soon as ever the hiding-place is disturbed. Among the Bedouins is current the legend that immense treasures were concealed by Solomon beneath the foundations of Palmyra and that sapient monarch took the precaution of enlisting an army of jinns to guard the gold forever more.

In parts of Bohemia the peasants are convinced that a blue light hovers above the location of buried treasure, invisible to all mortal eyes save those of the person destined to find it. In many corners of the world there has long existed the belief in the occult efficacy of a black cock or a black cat in the equipment of a

SPOOKY TREASURE TROVES

treasure quest which is also influenced by the particular phases of the moon. A letter written from Bombay as long ago as 1707, contained a quaint account of an incident inspired by this particular superstition.

"Upon a dream of a Negro girl of Mahim that there was a Mine of Treasure, who being overheard relating it, Domo, Alvares, and some others went to the place and sacrificed a Cock and dugg the ground but found nothing. They go to Bundarra at Salsett, where disagreeing, the Government there takes notice of the same, and one of them, an inhabitant of Bombay, is sent to the Inquisition at Goa, which proceedings will discourage the Inhabitants. Wherefore the General is desired to issue a proclamation to release him, and if not restored in twenty days, no Roman Catholick Worship to be allowed on the Island."

A more recent chronicler, writing in *The Ceylon Times*, had this to say:

"It is the belief of all Orientals that hidden treasures are under the guardianship of supernatural beings. The Cingalese divide the charge between the demons and the cobra da capello (guardian of the king's ankus in Kipling's story). Various charms are resorted to by those who wish to gain the treasure because the demons require a sacrifice. The blood of a human being is the most important, but so far as is known, the Cappowas have hitherto confined themselves to the sacrifice of a white cock, combining its blood with their own drawn from the hand or foot."

No more fantastic than this are the legends of which the British Isles yield a plentiful harvest. Thomas of Walsingham tells the tale of a Saracen physician who betook himself to Earl Warren of the fourteenth century to ask courteous permission that he might slay a dragon, or "loathly worm" which had its den at Bromfield near Ludlow and had wrought sad ravages on the Earl's lands. The Saracen overcame the monster, whether by means of his medicine chest or his trusty steel the narrator sayeth not, and then it was learned that a great hoard of gold was hidden in its foul den. Some men of Herefordshire sallied forth by night to search for the treasure, and were about to lay hands on it when retainers of the Earl of Warwick captured them and took the booty to their lord.

Blenkinsopp Castle is haunted by a very sorrowful White Lady. Her husband, Bryan de Blenkinsopp, was uncommonly greedy of gold, which he loved better than his wife, and she, being very jealous and angry, was mad enough to hide from him a chest of treasure so heavy that twelve strong men were needed to lift it. Later she was overtaken by remorse because of this undutiful behavior and to this day her uneasy ghost flits about the castle, supposedly seeking the spirit of Bryan de Blenkinsopp in order that she may tell him what she did with his pelf.

When Corfe Castle in Dorsetshire was besieged by Cromwell's troops, Lady Bankes conducted a heroic defense. Betrayed by one of her own garrison, and despairing of holding out longer, she threw all the plate and jewels into a very

SPOOKY TREASURE TROVES

deep well in the castle yard, and pronounced a curse against anyone who should try to find it ere she returned. She then ordered the traitor to be hanged, and surrendered the place. The treasure was never found, and perhaps later owners have been afraid of the militant ghost of Lady Bankes.

From time immemorial, tradition had it that a great treasure was buried near the Kibble in Lancashire. A saying had been handed down that anyone standing on the hill at Walton-le-Dale and looking up the valley toward the site of ancient Richester would gaze over the greatest treasure that England had ever known. Digging was undertaken at intervals during several centuries, until in 1841 laborers accidentally excavated a mass of silver ornaments, armlets, neck-chains, amulets and rings, weighing together about a thousand ounces, and more than seven thousand silver coins, mostly of King Alfred's time, all enclosed in a leaden case only three feet beneath the surface of the ground. Many of these ornaments and coins are to be seen at the British Museum.

On a farm in the Scotch parish of Lesmahagow is a boulder beneath which is what local tradition calls "a kettle full, a boat full, and a bull's hide full of gold that is Katie Nevin's hoord." And for ages past 'tis well known that a pot of gold has lain at the bottom of a pool at the tail of a water-fall under Crawfurdland Bridge, three miles from Kilmarnock. The last attempt to fish it up was made by one of the lairds of the place who diverted the stream and emptied the pool, and the implements of the workmen actually rang against the precious kettle when a mysterious voice was heard to cry:

"Paw! Paw! Crawfurdland's tower's in a law."

The laird and his servants scampered home to find out whether the tower had been "laid law," but the alarm was only a stratagem of the spirit that did sentry duty over the treasure. When the party returned to the pool, it was filled to the brim and the water was "running o'er the linn," which was an uncanny thing to see, and the laird would have nothing more to do with treasure seeking.

The people of Glenary in the Highlands long swore by the legend that golden treasure was hidden in their valley and that it would not be found until sought for by the son of a stranger. At length, while a newly drained field was being plowed, a large rock was shattered by blasting, and under it were found many solid gold bracelets of antique pattern and cunningly ornamented. The old people knew that the prophecy had come true, for the youth who held the plow was the son of an Englishman, a rare being in those parts a few generations ago.

Everyone knows that Ireland is fairly peppered with "crocks o' goold" which the peasantry would have dug up long before this, but the treasure is invariably in the keeping of "the little black men" and they raise the divil and all with the bold intruder, and lucky he is if he is not snatched away, body, soul, and breeches. Many a fine lad has left home just before midnight with a mattock under his arm, and maybe there was a terrible clap of thunder and that was the last of him except the empty hole and the mattock beside it which his friends found next morning.

In France treasure seeking has been at times a popular madness. The traditions of the country are singularly alluring, and perhaps the most romantic of them is that of the "Great Treasure of Gourdon" which is said to have existed since the reign of Clovis in the sixth century. The chronicle of all the wealth buried in the cemetery of this convent at Gourdon in the Department of the Lot has been preserved, including detailed lists of gold and silver, rubies, emeralds and pearls. The convent was sacked and plundered by the Normans, and the treasurer, or custodian, who had buried all the valuables of the religious houses under the sway of the same abbot, was murdered while trying to escape to the feudal seignor of Gourdon with the crosier of the lord abbott. "The head of the crosier was of solid gold," says an ancient manuscript, "and the rubies with which it was studded of such wondrous size that at one single blow the soldier who tore it from the monk's grasp and used it as a weapon against him, beat in his brains as with a sledgehammer."

Not only through the Middle Ages was the search resumed from time to time, but from the latter days of the reign of Louis XIV until the Revolution, tradition relates that the cemetery of the convent was ransacked at frequent intervals. At length, in 1842, the quest was abandoned after antiquarians, geologists, and engineers had gravely agreed that further excavation would be futile. The French treasure seekers went elsewhere and then a peasant girl confused the savants by discovering what was undeniably a part of the lost riches of Gourdon. She was driving home the cows from a pasture of the abbey lands when a shower caused her to take shelter in a hollow scooped out of a sand-bank by laborers mending the road. Some of the earth caved in upon her and while she was freeing herself, down rolled a salver, a paten, and a flagon, all of pure gold, richly chased and studded with emeralds and rubies. These articles were taken to Paris and advertised for sale by auction, the Government bidding them in and placing them in the museum of the Bibliotheque.

During the reign of Napoleon III there died a very famous treasure seeker, one Ducasse, who believed that he was about to discover "the master treasure" (*le maitre tresor*) said to be among the ruins of the ancient Belgian Abbey of Orval. Ducasse was a builder by trade and had gained a large fortune in government contracts every sou of which he wasted in exploring at Orval. It was alleged that the treasure had been buried by the monks and that the word NEMO carved on the tomb of the last abbott held the key to the location of the hiding-place.

In Mexico one hears similar tales of vast riches buried by religious orders when menaced by war or expulsion. One of these is to be found in the southwestern part of the state of Chihuahua where a great gorge is cut by the Rio Verde.

SPOOKY TREASURE TROVES

In this remote valley are the ruins of a church built by the Jesuits, and when they were about to be driven from their settlement they sealed up and destroyed all traces of a fabulously rich mine in which was buried millions of bullion. Instead of the more or less stereotyped ghosts familiar as sentinels over buried treasure, these lost hoards of Mexico are haunted by a specter even more disquieting than phantom pirates or "little black men." It is "The Weeping Woman" who makes strong men cross themselves and shiver in their serapes, and many have heard or seen her. A member of a party seeking buried treasure in the heart of the Sierra Madre mountains solemnly affirmed as follows:

"We were to measure, at night, a certain distance from a cliff which was to be found by the relative positions of three tall trees. It was on a bleak tableland nine thousand feet above the sea. The wind chilled us to the marrow, although we were only a little to the north of the Tropic of Cancer. We rode all night and waited for the dawn in the darkest and coldest hours of those altitudes. By the light of pitch pine torches we consulted a map and decided that we had found the right place. We rode forward a little and brushed against three soft warm things. Turning in our saddles, by the flare of our torches held high above our heads we beheld three corpses swaying in the wind. A wailing cry of a woman's voice came from close at hand, and we fled as if pursued by a thousand demons. My comrades assured me that the Weeping Woman had brushed past us in her eternal flight."

This is a singular narrative but it would not be playing fair to doubt it. To be over-critical of buried treasure stories is to clip the wings of romance and to condemn the spirit of adventure to a pedestrian gait. All these tales are true, or men of sane and sober repute would not go a-treasure hunting by land and sea, and so long as they have a high-hearted, boyish faith in their mysterious charts and hazy information, doubters make a poor show of themselves and stand confessed as thin-blooded dullards who never were young. Scattered legends of many climes have been mentioned at random to show that treasure is everywhere enveloped in a glamour peculiarly its own. The base iconoclast may perhaps demolish Santa Claus (which God forbid), but industrious dreamers will be digging for the gold of Captain Kidd, long after the last Christmas stocking shall have been pinned above the fireplace.

There are no conscious liars among the tellers of treasure tales. The spell is upon them. They believe their own yarns, and they prove their faith by their back-breaking works with pick and shovel. Here, for example, is a specimen, chosen at hazard, one from a thousand cut from the same cloth. This is no modern Ananias speaking but a gray-bearded, God-fearing clam-digger of Jewell's Island in Casco Bay on the coast of Maine.

"I can't remember when the treasure hunters first began coming to this island, but as long ago as my father's earliest memories they used to dig for gold up and down the shore. That was in the days when they were superstitious enough to spill lamb's blood along the ground where they dug in order to keep away the devil and his imps. I can remember fifty years ago when they brought a girl down here and mesmerized her to see if she could not lead them to the hidden wealth.

"The biggest mystery, though, of all the queer things that have happened here in the last hundred years was the arrival of the man from St. John's when I was a youngster. He claimed to have the very chart showing the exact spot where Kidd's gold was buried. He said he had got it from an old negro in St. John's who was with Captain Kidd when he was coasting the islands in this bay. He showed up here when old Captain Chase that lived here then was off to sea in his vessel. So he waited around a few days till the captain returned, for he wanted to use a mariner's compass to locate the spot according to the directions on the chart.

"When Captain Chase came ashore the two went off up the beach together, and the man from St. John's was never seen again, neither hide nor hair of him, and it is plumb certain that he wasn't set off in a boat from Jewell's.

"The folks here found a great hole dug on the southeast shore which looked as if a large chest had been lifted out of it. Of course conclusions were drawn, but nobody got at the truth. Four years ago someone found a skeleton in the woods, unburied, simply dropped into a crevice in the rocks with a few stones thrown over it. No one knows whose body it was, although some say,—but never mind about that. This old Captain Jonathan Chase was said to have been a pirate, and his house was full of underground passages and sliding panels and queer contraptions, such as no honest, law-abiding man could have any use for."

The worthy Benjamin Franklin was an admirable guide for young men, a sound philosopher, and a sagacious statesman, but he cannot be credited with romantic imagination. He would have been the last person in the world to lead a buried treasure expedition or to find pleasure in the company of the most eminent and secretive pirate that ever scuttled a ship or made mysterious marks upon a well-thumbed chart plentifully spattered with candle-grease and rum. He even took pains to discourage the diverting industry of treasure seeking as it flourished among his Quaker neighbors and discharged this formidable broadside in the course of a series of essays known as "The Busy-Body Series":

"... There are among us great numbers of honest artificers and laboring people, who, fed with a vain hope of suddenly growing rich, neglect their business, almost to the ruining of themselves and families, and voluntarily endure abundance of fatigue in a fruitless search after imaginary hidden treasure. They wander through the woods and bushes by day to discover the marks and signs; at midnight they repair to the hopeful spots with spades and pickaxes; full of expectation, they labor violently, trembling at the same time in every joint through fear of certain malicious demons, who are said to haunt and guard such places.

"At length a mighty hole is dug, and perhaps several cart-loads of earth thrown out; but, alas, no keg or iron pot is found. No seaman's chest crammed with Spanish pistoles, or weighty pieces of eight! They conclude that, through some mistake in the procedure, some rash word spoken, or some rule of art neglected, the guardian spirit had power to sink it deeper into the earth, and convey it out of their reach. Yet, when a man is once infatuated, he is so far from being discouraged by ill success that he is rather animated to double his industry, and will try again and again in a hundred different places in hopes of meeting at last with some lucky hit, that shall at once sufficiently reward him for all his expenses of time and labor.

"This odd humor of digging for money, through a belief that much has been hidden by pirates formerly frequenting the (Schuylkill) river, has for several years been mighty prevalent among us; insomuch that you can hardly walk half a mile out of the town on any side without observing several pits dug with that design, and perhaps some lately opened. Men otherwise of very good sense have been drawn into this practice through an overweening desire of sudden wealth, and an easy credulity of what they so earnestly wished might be true. There seems to be some peculiar charm in the conceit of finding money and if the sands of Schuylkill were so much mixed with small grains of gold that a man might in a day's time with care and application get together to the value of half a crown, I make no question but we should find several people employed there that can with ease earn five shillings a day at their proper trade.

"Many are the idle stories told of the private success of some people, by which others are encouraged to proceed; and the astrologers, with whom the country swarms at this time, are either in the belief of these things themselves, or find their advantage in persuading others to believe them; for they are often consulted about the critical times for digging, the methods of laying the spirit, and the like whimseys, which renders them very necessary to, and very much caressed by these poor, deluded money hunters.

"There is certainly something very bewitching in the pursuit after mines of gold and silver and other valuable metals, and many have been ruined by it....

"Let honest Peter Buckram, who has long without success been a searcher after hidden money, reflect on this, and be reclaimed from that unaccountable folly. Let him consider that every stitch he takes when he is on his shopboard, is picking up part of a grain of gold that will in a few days' time amount to a pistole; and let Faber think the same of every nail he drives, or every stroke with his plane. Such thoughts may make them industrious, and, in consequence, in time they may be wealthy.

"But how absurd it is to neglect a certain profit for such a ridiculous whimsey; to spend whole days at the 'George' in company with an idle pretender to astrology, contriving schemes to discover what was never hidden, and forgetful how carelessly business is managed at home in their absence; to leave their wives and a warm bed at midnight (no matter if it rain, hail, snow, or blow a hurricane, provided that be the critical hour), and fatigue themselves with the violent digging for what they shall never find, and perhaps getting a cold that may cost their lives, or at least disordering themselves so as to be fit for no business beside for some days after. Surely this is nothing less than the most egregious folly and madness.

"I shall conclude with the words of the discreet friend Agricola of Chester County when he gave his son a good plantation. 'My son,' said he, 'I give thee now a valuable parcel of land; I assure thee I have found a considerable quantity of gold by digging there; thee mayest do the same; but thee must carefully observe this, *Never to dig more than plough-deep.*"

For once the illustrious Franklin shot wide of the mark. These treasure hunters of Philadelphia, who had seen with their own eyes more than one notorious pirate, even Blackbeard himself, swagger along Front Street or come roaring out of the Blue Anchor Tavern by Dock Creek, were finding their reward in the coin of romance. Digging mighty holes for a taskmaster would have been irksome, stupid business indeed, even for five shillings a day. They got a fearsome kind of enjoyment in "trembling violently through fear of certain malicious demons." And honest Peter Buckram no doubt discovered that life was more zestful when he was plying shovel and pickaxe, or whispering with an astrologer in a corner of the "George" than during the flat hours of toil with shears and goose. If the world had charted its course by Poor Richard's Almanac, there would be a vast deal more thrift and sober industry than exists, but no room for the spirit of adventure which reckons not its returns in dollars and cents.

There are many kinds of lost treasure, by sea and by land. Some of them, however, lacking the color of romance and the proper backgrounds of motive and incident, have no stories worth telling. For instance, there were almost five thousand wrecks on the Great Lakes during a period of twenty years, and these lost vessels carried down millions of treasure or property worth trying to recover. One steamer had five hundred thousand dollars' worth of copper in her hold. Divers and submarine craft and wrecking companies have made many attempts to recover these vanished riches, and with considerable success, now and then fishing up large amounts of gold coin and bullion. It goes without saying that the average sixteen-year-old boy could extract not one solitary thrill from a tale of lost treasure in the Great Lakes, even though the value might be fairly fabulous. But let him hear that a number of Spanish coins have been washed up by the waves on a beach of Yucatan and the discovery has set the natives to searching for the buried treasure of Jean Lafitte, the "Pirate of the Gulf," and our youngster pricks up

SPOOKY TREASURE TROVES

his ears.

Many noble merchantmen in modern times have foundered or crashed ashore in various seas with large fortunes in their treasure rooms, and these are sought by expeditions, but because these ships were not galleons nor carried a freightage of doubloons and pieces of eight, most of them must be listed in the catalogue of undistinguished sea tragedies. The distinction is really obvious. The treasure story must have the picaresque flavor or at least concern itself with bold deeds done by strong men in days gone by. Like wine its bouquet is improved by age.

It is the fashion to consider lost treasure as the peculiar property of pirates and galleons, and yet what has become of the incredibly vast riches of all the vanished kings, despots, and soldiers who plundered the races of men from the beginnings of history? Where is the loot of ancient Home that was buried with Alaric! Where is the dazzling treasure of Samarcand? Where is the wealth of Antioch, and where the jewels which Solomon gave the Queen of Sheba? During thousands of years of warfare the treasures of the Old World could be saved from the conqueror only by hiding them underground, and in countless instances the sword must have slain those who knew the secret. When Genghis Khan swept across Russia with his hordes of savage Mongols towns and cities were blotted out as by fire, and doubtless those of the slaughtered population who had gold and precious stones buried them and there they still await the treasure seeker. What was happening everywhere during the ruthless ages of conquest and spoliation[2] is indicated by this bit of narrative told by a native banker of India to W. Forbes Mitchell, author of "Reminiscences of the Great Mutiny":

"You know how anxious the late Maharajah Scindia was to get back the fortress of Gwalior, but very few knew the real cause prompting him. That was a concealed horde of sixty *crores* (sixty millions sterling) of rupees in certain vaults within the fortress, over which British sentinels had been walking for thirty years, never suspecting the wealth hidden under their feet. Long before the British Government restored the fortress to the Maharajah everyone who knew the entrance to the vaults was dead except one man and he was extremely old. Although he was in good health he might have died any day. If this had happened, the treasure might have been lost to the owner forever and to the world for ages, because there was only one method of entrance and it was most cunningly concealed. On all sides, except for this series of blind passages, the vaults were surrounded by solid rock.

"The Maharajah was in such a situation that he must either get back his fortress or divulge the secret of the existence of the treasure to the British Government, and risk losing it by confiscation. As soon as possession of the fortress was restored to him, and even before the British troops had left Gwalior territory, masons were brought from Benares, after being sworn to secrecy in the Temple of the Holy Cow. They were blindfolded and driven to the place where they were to labor. There they were kept as prisoners until the hidden treasure had been examined and verified when the hole was again sealed up and the workmen were once more blindfolded and taken back to Benares in the custody of an armed escort."

[1] "The Pirates' Own Book" was published at Portland, Maine, 1837, and largely reprinted from Captain Charles Johnson's "General History of the Pyrates of the New Providence," etc., first edition, London, 1724. His second edition of two volumes, published in 1727, contained the lives of Kidd and Blackbeard. "The Pirates' Own Book," while largely indebted to Captain Johnson's work, contains a great deal of material concerning other noted sea rogues who flourished later than 1727.

[2] "As to Clive, there was no limit to his acquisitions but his own moderation. The treasury of Bengal was thrown open to him. There were piled up, after the usage of Indian princes, immense masses of coin, among which might not seldom be detected the florins and byzants with which, before any European ship had turned the Cape of Good Hope, the Venetians purchased the stuffs and spices of the East. Clive walked between heaps of gold and silver, crowned with rubies and diamonds, and was at liberty to help himself."—Macauley.

SPOOKY TREASURE TROVES

CHAPTER II
CAPTAIN KIDD IN FACT AND FICTION

Doomed to an infamy undeserved, his name reddened with crimes he never committed, and made wildly romantic by tales of treasure which he did not bury, Captain William Kidd is fairly entitled to the sympathy of posterity and the apologies of all the ballad-makers and alleged historians who have obscured the facts in a cloud of fable. For two centuries his grisly phantom has stalked through the legends and literature of the black flag as the king of pirates and the most industrious depositor of ill-gotten gold and jewels that ever wielded pick and shovel. His reputation is simply prodigious, his name has frightened children wherever English is spoken, and the Kidd tradition, or myth, is still potent to send treasure-seekers exploring and excavating almost every beach, cove, and headland between Nova Scotia and the Gulf of Mexico.

Fate has played the strangest tricks imaginable with the memory of this seventeenth century seafarer who never cut a throat or made a victim walk the plank, who was no more than a third or fourth rate pirate in an era when this interesting profession was in its heyday, and who was hanged at Execution Dock for the excessively unromantic crime of cracking the skull of his gunner with a wooden bucket.

As for the riches of Captain Kidd, the original documents in his case, preserved among the state papers of the Public Record Office in London, relate with much detail what booty he had and what he did with it. Alas, they reveal the futility of the searches after the stout sea-chest buried above high water mark. The only authentic Kidd treasure was dug up and inventoried more than two hundred years ago, nor has the slightest clue to any other been found since then.

These curious documents, faded and sometimes tattered, invite the reader to thresh out his own conclusions as to how great a scoundrel Kidd really was, and how far he was a scapegoat who had to be hanged to clear the fair names of those noble lords in high places who were partners and promoters of that most unlucky sea venture in which Kidd, sent out to catch pirates, was said to have turned amateur pirate himself rather than sail home empty-handed. Certain it is that these words of the immortal ballad are cruelly, grotesquely unjust:

I made a solemn vow, when I sail'd, when I sail'd, I made a solemn vow when I sail'd. I made a solemn vow, to God I would not bow, Nor myself a prayer allow, as I sail'd.

I'd a Bible in my hand, when I sail'd, when I sail'd, I'd a Bible in my hand when I sail'd. I'd a Bible in my hand, by my father's great command, And I sunk it in the sand when I sail'd.

In English fiction there are three treasure stories of surpassing merit for ingenious contrivance and convincing illusion. These are Stevenson's "Treasure Island"; Poe's "Gold Bug"; and Washington Irving's "Wolfert Webber." Differing widely in plot and literary treatment, each peculiar to the genius of its author, they are blood kin, sprung from a common ancestor, namely, the Kidd legend. Why this half-hearted pirate who was neither red-handed nor of heroic dimensions even in his badness, should have inspired more romantic fiction than any other character in American history is past all explaining.

Strangely enough, no more than a generation or two after Kidd's sorry remnants were swinging in chains for the birds to pick at, there began to cluster around his memory the folklore and superstitions col-

Captain Kidd burying his Bible.

Carousing at Old Calabar River.
(From The Pirates' Own Book.)

ored by the supernatural which had been long current in many lands in respect of buried treasure. It was a kind of diabolism which still survives in many a corner of the Atlantic coast where tales of Kidd are told. Irving took these legends as he heard them from the long-winded ancients of his own acquaintance and wove them into delightfully entertaining fiction with a proper seasoning of the ghostly and the uncanny. His formidable hero is an old pirate with a sea chest, aforetime one of Kidd's rogues, who appears at the Dutch tavern near Corlear's Hook, and there awaits tidings of his shipmates and the hidden treasure. It is well known that Stevenson employed a strikingly similar character and setting to get "Treasure Island" under way in the opening chapter. As a literary coincidence, a comparison of these pieces of fiction is of curious interest. The similarity is to be explained on the ground that both authors made use of the same material whose groundwork was the Kidd legend in its various forms as it has been commonly circulated.

Stevenson confessed in his preface:

"It is my debt to Washington Irving that exercises my conscience, and justly so, for I believe plagiarism was rarely carried farther. I chanced to pick up the 'Tales of a Traveler' some years ago, with a view to an anthology of prose narrative, and the book flew up and struck me: Billy Bones, his chest, the company in the parlor, the whole inner spirit and a good deal of the material detail of my first chapters—all were there, all were the property of Washington Irving. But I had no guess of it then as I sat writing by the fireside, in what seemed the springtides of a somewhat pedestrian fancy; nor yet day by day, after lunch, as I read aloud my morning's work to the family. It seemed to me original as sin; it seemed to belong to me like my right eye."

After the opening scenes the two stories veer off on diverging tacks, the plot of Stevenson moving briskly along to the treasure voyage with no inclusion of the supernatural features of the Kidd tradition. Irving, however, narrates at a leisurely pace all the gossip and legend that were rife concerning Kidd in the Manhattan of the worthy Knickerbockers. And he could stock a treasure chest as cleverly as Stevenson, for when Wolfert Webber dreamed that he had discovered an immense treasure in the center of his garden, "at every stroke of the spade he laid bare a golden ingot; diamond crosses sparkled out of the dust; bags of money turned up their bellies, corpulent with pieces of eight, or venerable doubloons; and chests, wedged close with moidores, ducats, and pistareens, yawned before his ravished eyes and vomited forth their glittering contents."

The warp and woof of "Wolfert Webber" is the still persistent legend that Kidd buried treasure near the Highlands of the lower Hudson, or that his ship, the *Quedah Merchant*, was fetched from San Domingo by his men after he left her and they sailed her into the Hudson and there scuttled the vessel, scattering ashore and dividing a vast amount of plunder, some of which was hidden nearby. Many years ago a pamphlet was published, purporting to be true, which was entitled, "An Account of Some of the Traditions and Experiments Respecting Captain Kidd's Piratical Vessel." In this it was soberly asserted that Kidd in the *Quedah Merchant* was chased into the North River by an English man-of-war, and finding himself cornered he and his crew took to the boats with what treasure they could carry, after setting fire to the ship, and fled up the Hudson, thence footing it through the wilderness to Boston.

The sunken ship was searched for from time to time, and the explorers were no doubt assisted by another pamphlet published early in the nineteenth century which proclaimed itself as:

"A Wonderful Mesmeric Revelation, giving an Account of the Discovery and Description of a Sunken Vessel, near Caldwell's Landing, supposed to be that of the Pirate Kidd; including an Account of his Character and Death, at a distance of nearly three hundred miles from the place."

This psychic information came from a woman by the name of Chester living in Lynn, Mass., who swore she had never heard of the sunken treasure ship until while in a trance she beheld its shattered timbers covered with sand, and "bars of massive gold, heaps of silver coin, and precious jewels including many large and brilliant diamonds. The jewels had been enclosed in shot bags of stout canvas. There were also gold watches, like duck's eggs in a pond of water, and the wonderfully preserved remains of a very beautiful woman, with a necklace of diamonds around her neck."

As Irving takes pains to indicate, the basis of the legend of the sunken pirate ship came not from Kidd but from another freebooter who flourished at the same time. Says Peechy Prauw, daring to hold converse with the old buccaneer in the tavern, "Kidd never did bury money up the Hudson, nor indeed in any of those parts, though many affirmed such to be the fact. It was Bradish and others of the buccaneers who had buried money; some said in Turtle Bay, others on Long Island, others in the neighborhood of Hell-gate."

This Bradish was caught by Governor Bellomont and sent to England where he was hanged at Execution Dock. He had begun his career of crime afloat as boatswain of a ship called the *Adventure* (not Kidd's vessel). While on a voyage from London to Borneo he helped other mutineers to take the vessel from her skipper and go a-cruising as gentlemen of fortune. They split up forty thousand dollars of specie found on board, snapped up a few merchantmen to fatten their dividends, and at length came to the American coast and touched at Long Island.

The *Adventure* ship was abandoned, and there is reason to think that she was taken possession of by the crew of the purchased sloop, who worked her around to New York and beached and sunk her after stripping her of fittings and gear. Bradish and his crew also cruised along the Sound for some time in their

SPOOKY TREASURE TROVES

small craft, landing and buying supplies at several places, until nineteen of them were caught and taken to Boston. That there should have been some confusion of facts relating to Kidd and Bradish is not at all improbable.

Among the Dutch of New Amsterdam was to be found that world-wide superstition of the ghostly guardians of buried treasure, and Irving interpolates the distressful experience of Cobus Quackenbos "who dug for a whole night and met with incredible difficulty, for as fast as he threw one shovelful of earth out of the hole, two were thrown in by invisible hands. He succeeded so far, however, as to uncover an iron chest, when there was a terrible roaring, ramping, and raging of uncouth figures about the hole, and at length a shower of blows, dealt by invisible cudgels, fairly belabored him off of the forbidden ground. This Cobus Quackenbos had declared on his death bed, so that there could not be any doubt of it. He was a man that had devoted many years of his life to money-digging, and it was thought would have ultimately succeeded, had he not died recently of a brain fever in the almshouse."

A story built around the Kidd tradition but of a wholly different kind is that masterpiece of curious deductive analysis, "The Gold Bug," with its cryptogram and elaborate mystification. In making use of an historical character to serve the ends of fiction it is customary to make him move among the episodes of the story with some regard for the probabilities. For example, it would hardly do to have Napoleon win the Battle of Waterloo as the hero of a novel. What really happened and what the author imagines might have happened must be dovetailed with an eye to avoid contradicting the known facts. Like almost everyone else, however, Poe took the most reckless liberties with the career of poor Captain Kidd and his buried treasure and cared not a rap for historical evidence to the contrary. Although Stevenson is ready to admit that his "skeleton is conveyed from Poe," the author of "Treasure Island" is not wholly fair to himself. The tradition that secretive pirates were wont to knock a shipmate or two on the head as a feature of the program of burying treasure is as old as the hills. The purpose was either to get rid of the witnesses who had helped dig the hole, or to cause the spot to be properly haunted by ghosts as an additional precaution against the discovery of the hoard.

What Stevenson "conveyed" from Poe was the employment of a skeleton to indicate the bearings and location of the treasure, although, to be accurate, it was a skull that figured in "The Gold Bug." Otherwise, in the discovery of the remains of slain pirates, both were using a stock incident of buried treasure lore most generally fastened upon the unfortunate Captain Kidd.

Most of the treasure legends of the Atlantic coast are fable and moonshine, with no more foundation than what somebody heard from his grandfather who may have dreamed that Captain Kidd or Blackbeard once landed in a nearby cove.

SPOOKY TREASURE TROVES

The treasure seeker needs no evidence, however, and with him "faith is the substance of things hoped for." There is a marsh of the Penobscot river, a few miles inland from the bay of that name, which has been indefatigably explored for more than a century. A native of a statistical turn of mind not long ago expressed himself in this common-sense manner:

"Thousands of tons of soil have been shovelled over time and again. I figure that these treasure hunters have handled enough earth in turning up Codlead Marsh to build embankments and fill cuts for a railroad grade twenty miles long. In other words, if these lunatics that have tried to find Kidd's money had hired out with railroad contractors, they could have earned thirty thousand dollars at regular day wages instead of the few battered old coins discovered in 1798 which started all this terrible waste of energy."

The most convincing evidence of the existence of a pirates' rendezvous and hoard has been found on Oak Island, Nova Scotia. In fact, this is the true treasure story, *par excellence*, of the whole Atlantic coast, with sufficient mystery to give it precisely the proper flavor. Local tradition has long credited Captain Kidd with having been responsible for the indubitable remains of piratical activity, but it has been proved that Kidd went nowhere near Nova Scotia after he came sailing home from the East Indies, and the industrious visitors to Oak Island are therefore unknown to history.

The island has a sheltered haven called Mahone Bay, snugly secluded from the Atlantic, with deep water, and a century ago the region was wild and unsettled. Near the head of the bay is a small cove which was visited in the year of 1795 by three young men named Smith, MacGinnis, and Vaughan who drew their canoes ashore and explored at random the noble groves of oaks. Soon they came to a spot whose peculiar appearance aroused their curiosity. The ground had been cleared many years before; this was indicated by the second growth of trees and the kind of vegetation which is foreign to the primeval condition of the soil. In the center of the little clearing was a huge oak whose bark was gashed with markings made by an axe. One of the stout lower branches had been sawn off at some distance from the trunk and to this natural derrick-arm had been attached a heavy block and tackle as shown by the furrowed scar in the bark. Directly beneath this was a perceptible circular depression of the turf, perhaps a dozen feet in diameter.

The three young men were curious, and made further investigation. The tide chanced to be uncommonly low, and while ranging along the beach of the cove they discovered a huge iron ring-bolt fastened to a rock which was invisible at ordinary low water. They reasonably surmised that this had been a mooring place in days gone by. Not far distant a boatswain's whistle of an ancient pattern and a copper coin bearing the date of 1713 were picked up.

SPOOKY TREASURE TROVES

The trio scented pirates' treasure and shortly returned to the cove to dig in the clearing hard by the great oak. It was soon found that they were excavating in a clearly defined shaft, the walls of which were of the solid, undisturbed earth in which the cleavage of other picks and shovels could be distinguished. The soil within the shaft was much looser and easily removed. Ten feet below the surface they came to a covering of heavy oak plank which was ripped out with much difficulty.

At a depth of twenty feet another layer of planking was uncovered, and digging ten feet deeper, a third horizontal bulkhead of timber was laid bare. The excavation was now thirty feet down, and the three men had done all they could without a larger force, hoisting machinery, and other equipment. The natives of Mahone Bay, however, were singularly reluctant to aid the enterprise. Hair-raising stories were afloat of ghostly guardians, of strange cries, of unearthly fires that flickered along the cove, and all that sort of thing. Superstition effectually fortified the place, and those bold spirits, Smith, MacGinnis, and Vaughan were forced to abandon their task for lack of reinforcements.

Half a dozen years later a young physician of Truro, Dr. Lynds, visited Oak Island, having got wind of the treasure story, and talked with the three men aforesaid. He took their report seriously, made an investigation of his own, and straightway organized a company backed by considerable capital. Prominent persons of Truro and the neighborhood were among the investors, including Colonel Robert Archibald, Captain David Archibald, and Sheriff Harris. A gang of laborers was mustered at the cove, and the dirt began to fly. The shaft was opened to a depth of ninety-five feet, and, as before, some kind of covering, or significant traces thereof, was disclosed every ten feet or so. One layer was of charcoal spread over a matting of a substance resembling cocoa fibre, while another was of putty, some of which was used in glazing the windows of a house then building on the nearby coast.

Ninety feet below the surface, the laborers found a large flat stone or quarried slab, three feet long and sixteen inches wide, upon which was chiselled the traces of an inscription. This stone was used in the jamb of a fireplace of a new house belonging to Smith, and was later taken to Halifax in the hope of having the mysterious inscription deciphered. One wise man declared that the letters read, "Ten feet below two million pounds lie buried," but this verdict was mostly guesswork. The stone is still in Halifax, where it was used for beating leather in a bookbinder's shop until the inscription had been worn away.

When the workmen were down ninety-five feet, they came to a wooden platform covering the shaft. Until then the hole had been clear of water, but overnight it filled within twenty-five feet of the top. Persistent efforts were made to bail out the flood but with such poor success that the shaft was abandoned and another sunk nearby, the plan being to tunnel into the first pit and thereby drain it and get at the treasure. The second shaft was driven to a depth of a hundred and ten feet, but while the tunnel was in progress the water broke through and made the laborers flee for their lives. The company had spent all its money, and the results were so discouraging that the work was abandoned.

It was not until 1849 that another attempt was made to fathom the meaning of the extraordinary mystery of Oak Island. Dr. Lynds and Vaughan were still alive and their narratives inspired the organization of another treasure-seeking company. Vaughan easily found the old "Money Pit" as it was called, and the original shaft was opened and cleared to a depth of eighty-six feet when an inrush of water stopped the undertaking. Again the work ceased for lack of adequate pumping machinery, and it was decided to use a boring apparatus such as was employed in prospecting for coal. A platform was rigged in the old shaft, and the large auger bit its way in a manner described by the manager of the enterprise as follows:

"The platform was struck at ninety-eight feet, just as the old diggers found it. After going through this platform, which was five inches thick and proved to be of spruce, the auger dropped twelve inches and then went through four inches of oak; then it went through twenty-two inches of metal in pieces, but the auger failed to take any of it except three links resembling an ancient watch-chain. It then went through eight inches of oak, which was thought to be the bottom of the first box and the top of the next; then through twenty-two inches of metal the same as before; then four inches of oak and six inches of spruce, then into clay seven feet without striking anything. In the next boring, the platform was struck as before at ninety-eight feet; passing through this, the auger fell about eighteen inches, and came in contact with, as supposed, the side of a cask. The flat chisel revolving close to the side of the cask gave it a jerk and irregular motion. On withdrawing the auger several splinters of oak, such as might come from the side of an oak stave, and a small quantity of a brown fibrous substance resembling the husk of a cocoa-nut, were brought up. The distance between the upper and lower platforms was found to be six feet."

In the summer of 1850 a third shaft was sunk just to the west of the Money Pit, but this also filled with water which was discovered to be salt and effected by the rise and fall of the tide in the cove. It was reasoned that if a natural inlet existed, those who had buried the treasure must have encountered the inflow which would have made their undertaking impossible. Therefore the pirates must have driven some kind of a tunnel or passage from the cove with the object of flooding out any subsequent intruders. Search was made along the beach, and near where the ring-bolt was fastened in the rock a bed of the brown, fibrous material was uncovered and beneath it a mass of small rock unlike the surrounding sand and gravel.

SPOOKY TREASURE TROVES

It was decided to build a coffer-dam around this place which appeared to be a concealed entrance to a tunnel connecting the cove with the Money Pit. In removing the rock, a series of well-constructed drains was found, extending from a common center, and fashioned of carefully laid stone. Before the coffer-dam was finished, it was overflowed by a very high tide and collapsed under pressure. The explorers did not rebuild it but set to work sinking a shaft which was intended to cut into this tunnel and dam the inlet from the cove. One failure, however, followed on the heels of another, and shaft after shaft was dug only to be caved in or filled by salt water. In one of these was found an oak plank, several pieces of timber bearing the marks of tools, and many hewn chips. A powerful pumping engine was installed, timber cribbing put into the bottom of the shafts, and a vast amount of clay dumped on the beach in an effort to block up the inlet of the sea-water tunnel. Baffled in spite of all this exertion, the treasure-seekers spent their money and had to quit empty-handed.

Forty years passed, and the crumbling earth almost filled the numerous and costly excavations and the grass grew green under the sentinel oaks. Then, in 1896, the cove was once more astir with boats and the shore populous with toilers. The old records had been overhauled and their evidence was so alluring that fresh capital was subscribed and many shares eagerly snapped up in Truro, Halifax and elsewhere. The promoters became convinced that former attempts had failed because of crude appliances and insufficient engineering skill, and this time the treasure was sought in up-to-date fashion.

Almost twenty deep shafts were dug, one after the other, in a ring about the Money Pit, and tunnels driven in a net-work. It was the purpose of the engineers to intercept the underground channel and also to drain the pirates' excavation. Hundreds of pounds of dynamite were used and thousands of feet of heavy timber. Further traces of the work of the ancient contrivers of this elaborate hiding-place were discovered, but the funds of the company were exhausted before the secret of the Money Pit could be revealed.

Considerable boring was done under the direction of the manager, Captain Welling. The results confirmed the previous disclosures achieved by the auger. At a depth of one hundred and twenty-six feet, Captain Welling's crew drilled through oak wood, and struck a piece of iron past which they could not drive the encasing pipe. A smaller auger was then used and at one hundred and fifty-three feet cement was found of a thickness of seven inches, covering another layer of oak. Beyond was some soft metal, and the drill brought to the surface a small fragment of sheepskin parchment upon which was written in ink the syllable, "vi" or "wi." Other curious samples, wood and iron, were fished up, but the "soft metal," presumed to be gold or silver, refused to cling to the auger. It was of course taken for granted that the various layers of oak planking and spruce were chests containing the treasure.

SPOOKY TREASURE TROVES

During the various borings, seven different chests or casks, or whatever they may be, have been encountered. It seems incredible that any pirates or buccaneers known to the American coast should have been at such prodigious pains to conceal their plunder as to dig a hole a good deal more than a hundred feet deep, connect it with the sea by an underground passage, and safeguard it by many layers of timber, cement, and other material. Possibly some of the famous freebooters of the Spanish Main in Henry Morgan's time might have achieved such a task, but Nova Scotia was a coast unknown to them and thousands of miles from their track. Poor Kidd had neither the men, the treasure, nor the opportunity to make such a memorial of his career as this.

Quite recently a new company was formed to grapple with the secret of Oak Island which has already swallowed at least a hundred thousand dollars in labor and machinery. For more than a century, sane, hard-headed Nova Scotians have tried to reach the bottom of the "Money Pit," and as an attractive speculation it has no rival in the field of treasure-seeking. There may be documents somewhere in existence, a chart or memorandum mouldering in a sea chest in some attic or cellar of France, England, or Spain, that will furnish the key to this rarely picturesque and tantalizing puzzle. The unbeliever has only to go to Nova Scotia in the summer time and seek out Oak Island, which is reached by way of the town of Chester, to find the deeply pitted area of the treasure hunt, and very probably engines and workmen busy at the fine old game of digging for pirates' gold.

Let us now give the real Captain Kidd his due, painting him no blacker than the facts warrant, and at the same time uncover the true story of his treasure, which is the plum in the pudding. He had been a merchant shipmaster of brave and honorable repute in an age when every deep-water voyage was a hazard of privateers and freebooters of all flags, or none at all. In one stout square-rigger after another, well armed and heavily manned, he had sailed out of the port of New York, in which he dwelt as early as 1689. He had a comfortable, even prosperous home in Liberty Street, was married to a widow of good family, and was highly thought of by the Dutch and English merchants of the town. A shrewd trader who made money for his owners, he was also a fighting seaman of such proven mettle that he was given command of privateers which cruised along the coasts of the Colonies and harried the French in the West Indies. His excellent reputation and character are attested by official documents. In the records of the Proceedings of the Provincial Assembly of New York is the following entry under date of April 18, 1691:

"Gabriel Monville, Esq. and Thomas Willet, Esq. are appointed to attend the House of Representatives and acquaint them of the many good services done to this Province by Captain William Kidd in his attending here with his Vessels before His Excellency's[1] arrival, and that it would be acceptable to His Excellency and this Board that they consider of some suitable reward to him for his good services."

This indicates that Captain Kidd had been in command of a small squadron engaged in protecting the commerce of the colony. On May 14, the following was adopted by the House of Representatives:

"Ordered, that His Excellency be addressed unto, to order the Receiver General to pay to Captain William Kidd, One Hundred and Fifty Pounds current money of this Province, as a suitable reward for the many good services done to this Province."

In June, only a month after this, Captain Kidd was asked by the Colony of Massachusetts to punish the pirates who were pestering the shipping of Boston and Salem. The negotiations were conducted in this wise:

By the Governor and Council.

Proposals offered to Captain Kidd and Captain Walkington to encourage their going forth in their Majesties' Service to suppress an Enemy Privateer now upon this Coast.

That they have liberty to beat up drums for forty men apiece to go forth on this present Expedition, not taking any Children or Servants without their Parents' or Masters' Consent. A list of the names of such as go in the said Vessels to be presented to the Governor before their departure.

That they cruise upon the Coast for the space of ten or fifteen days in search of the said Privateer, and then come in again and land the men supplied them from hence.

That what Provisions shall be expended within the said time, for so many men as are in both the said Vessels, be made good to them on their return, in case they take no purchase;[2] but if they shall take the Privateer, or any other Vessels, then only a proportion of Provisions for so many men as they take in here.

If any of our men happen to be wounded in the engagement with the Privateer, that they be cured at the public charge.

That the men supplied from hence be proportionable sharers with the other men belonging to said Vessels, of all purchase that shall be taken.

Besides the promise of a Gratuity to the Captains, Twenty Pounds apiece in money.

Boston, June 8th, 1691.

To this thrifty set of terms, Captain Kidd made reply:

"*Imprimis*, To have forty men, with their arms, provisions, and ammunition.

"*2dly*. All the men that shall be wounded, which have been put in by the Country, shall be put on shore, and the Country to take care of them. And if so

SPOOKY TREASURE TROVES

fortunate as to take the Pirate and her prizes, then to bring them to Boston.

"*3rdly*. For myself, to have One Hundred Pounds in money; Thirty Pounds thereof to be paid down, the rest upon my return to Boston; and if we bring in said Ship and her Prizes, then the same to be divided amongst our men.

"*4thly*. The Provisions put on board must be ten barrels Pork and Beef, ten barrels of Flour, two hogsheads of Peas, and one barrel of Gunpowder for the great guns.

"*5thly*. That I will cruise on the coast for ten days' time; and if so that he is gone off the coast, that I cannot hear of him, I will then, at my return, take care and set what men on shore that I have had, and are willing to leave me or the Ship."

These records serve to show in what esteem Captain Kidd was held by the highest officials of the Colonies. Such men as he were sailing out of Boston, New York, and Salem to trade in uncharted seas on remote coasts and fight their way home again with rich cargoes. They hammered out the beginnings of a mighty commerce for the New World and created, by the stern stress of circumstances, as fine a race of seamen as ever filled cabin and forecastle.

The Idle Apprentice goes to sea. (From Hogarth's series, "Industry and Idleness.") On the shore of this reach of the Thames, at Tilbury, is shown a gibbeted pirate hanging in chains, just as it befell Captain William Kidd.

SPOOKY TREASURE TROVES

In the year 1695, Captain Kidd chanced to be anchored in London port in his brigantine *Antigoa*, busy with loading merchandise and shipping a crew for the return voyage across the Atlantic. Now, Richard Coote, Earl of Bellomont, an ambitious and energetic Irishman, had just then been appointed royal governor of the Colonies of New York and Massachusetts, and he was particularly bent on suppressing the swarm of pirates who infested the American coast and waxed rich on the English commerce of the Indian Ocean. Their booty was carried to Rhode Island, New York, and Boston, even from far-away Madagascar, and many a colonial merchant, outwardly the pattern of respectability, was secretly trafficking in this plunder.

"I send you, my Lord, to New York," said King William III to Bellomont, "because an honest and intrepid man is wanted to put these abuses down, and because I believe you to be such a man."

Thereupon Bellomont asked for a frigate to send in chase of the bold sea rogues, but the king referred him to the Lords of the Admiralty who discovered sundry obstacles bound in red tape, the fact being that official England was at all times singularly indifferent, or covertly hostile, toward the maritime commerce of her American colonies. Being denied a man-of-war, Bellomont conceived the plan of privately equipping an armed ship as a syndicate enterprise without cost to the government. The promoters were to divide the swag captured from pirates as dividends on their investment.

The enterprise was an alluring one, and six thousand pounds sterling were subscribed by Bellomont and his friends, including such illustrious personages as Somers, the Lord Chancellor and leader of the Whig party; the Earl of Shrewsbury, the Earl of Orford, First Lord of the Admiralty; the Earl of Romney, and Sir Richard Harrison, a wealthy merchant. According to Bishop Burnet, it was the king who "proposed managing it by a private enterprise, and said he would lay down three thousand pounds himself, and recommended it to his Ministers to find out the refit. In compliance with this, the Lord Somers, the Earl of Orford, Romney, Bellomont and others, contributed the whole expense, for the King excused himself by reason of other accidents, and did not advance the sum he had promised."

Macauley, discussing in his "History of England" the famous scandal which later involved these partners of Kidd, defends them in this spirited fashion:

"The worst that could be imputed even to Bellomont, who had drawn in all the rest, was that he had been led into a fault by his ardent zeal for the public service, and by the generosity of a nature as little prone to suspect as to devise villainies. His friends in England might surely be pardoned for giving credit to his recommendations. It is highly probable that the motive which induced some of them to aid his designs was a genuine public spirit. But if we suppose them to have had a view to gain, it would be legitimate gain. Their conduct was the very opposite of corrupt. Not only had they taken no money. They had disbursed money largely, and had disbursed it with the certainty that they should never be reimbursed unless the outlay proved beneficial to the public."

It would be easy to pick flaws in this argument. Bellomont's partners, no matter how public spirited, hoped to reimburse themselves, and something over, as receivers of stolen goods. It was a dashing speculation, characteristic of its century, and neither better nor worse than the privateering of that time. What raised the subsequent row in Parliament and made of Kidd a political issue and a party scapegoat, was the fact that his commission was given under the Great Seal of England, thus stamping a private business with the public sanction of His Majesty's Government. For this Somers, as Lord Chancellor, was responsible, and it later became a difficult transaction for his partisans to defend.

There was in London, at that time, one Robert Livingston, founder of a family long notable in the Colony and State of New York, a man of large property and solid station. He was asked to recommend a shipmaster fitted for the task in hand and named Captain Kidd, who was reluctant to accept. His circumstances were prosperous, he had a home and family in New York, and he was by no means anxious to go roving after pirates who were pretty certain to fight for their necks. His consent was won by the promise of a share of the profits (Kidd was a canny Scot by birth) and by the offer of Livingston to be his security and his partner in the venture.

An elaborate contract was drawn up with the title of "Articles of Agreement made this Tenth day of October in the year of Our Lord, 1695, between the Right Honorable Richard, Earl of Bellomont, of the one part, and Robert Livingston Esq., and Captain William Kidd of the other part."

In the first article, "the said Earl of Bellomont doth covenant and agree at his proper charge to procure from the King's Majesty or from the Lords Commissioners of the Admiralty, as the case may require, one or more Commissions impowering him, the said Captain Kidd, to act against the King's enemies, and to take prizes from them as a private man-of-war, in the usual manner, and also to fight with, conquer and subdue pyrates, and to take them and their goods, *with such large and beneficial powers and clauses in such commissions as may be most proper and effectual in such cases.*"

Bellomont agreed to pay four-fifths of the cost of the ship, with its furnishings and provisions, Kidd and Livingston to contribute the remainder, "in pursuance of which Bellomont was to pay down 1600 pounds on or before the 6th of November, in order to the speedy buying of said ship." The Earl agreed to pay such further sums as should "complete and make up the said four parts of five of the charge of the said ship's apparel, furniture, and victualling, within seven weeks after date of the agreement," and Kidd and Livingston bound themselves to do likewise in respect of their fifth part of the expense. Other articles of the agreement read:

"7. The said Captain Kidd doth covenant and agree to procure and take with him on board of the said ship, one hundred mariners, or seamen, or thereabout, and to make what reasonable and convenient speed he can to set out to sea with the said ship, and to sail to such parts and places where he may meet with the said Pyrates, and to use his utmost endeavor to meet with, subdue, and conquer the said Pyrates, and to take from them their goods, merchandise, and treasures; also to take what prizes he can from the King's enemies, and forthwith to make the best of his way to Boston in New England, and that without touching at any other port or harbor whatsoever, or without breaking bulk, or diminishing any part of what he shall so take or obtain; (of which he shall make oath in case the same is desired by the said Earl of Bellomont), and there to deliver the same into the hands or possession of the said Earl.

"8. The said Captain Kidd doth agree that the contract and bargain which he will make with the said ship's crew shall be no purchase,[3] no pay, and not otherwise; and that the share and proportion which his said crew shall, by such contract, have of such prizes, goods, merchandise and treasure, as he shall take as prize, or from any Pyrates, shall not at the most exceed a fourth part of the same, and shall be less than a fourth part, in case the same may reasonably and conveniently be agreed upon.

"9. Robert Livingston Esq. and Captain William Kidd agree that if they catch no Pyrates, they will refund to the said Earl of Bellomont all the money advanced by him on or before March 25th, 1697, and they will keep the said ship."

Article 10 allotted the captured goods and treasures, after deducting no more than one-fourth for the crew. The remainder was to be divided into five equal parts, of which Bellomont was to receive four parts, leaving a fifth to be shared between Kidd and Livingston. The stake of Captain Kidd was therefore to be three one-fortieths of the whole, or seven and one-half per cent. of the booty.

It is apparent from these singular articles of agreement that Robert Livingston, in the role of Kidd's financial backer, was willing to run boldly speculative chances of success, and was also confident that a rich crop of "pyrates" could be caught for the seeking. If Kidd should sail home empty-handed, then these two partners stood to lose a large amount, by virtue of the contract which provided that Bellomont and his partners must be reimbursed for their outlay, less the value of the ship itself. Livingston also gave bonds in the sum of ten thousand pounds that Kidd would be faithful to his trust and obedient to his orders, which in itself is sufficient to show that this shipmaster was a man of the best intentions, and of thoroughly proven worth.

SPOOKY TREASURE TROVES

Captain Kidd's privateering commission was issued by the High Court of Admiralty on December 11, 1695, and licensed and authorized him to "set forth in war-like manner in the said ship called the *Adventure Galley*, under his own command, and therewith, by force of arms, to apprehend, seize, and take the ships, vessels, and goods belonging to the French King and his subjects, or inhabitants within the dominion of the said French King, and such other ships, vessels, and goods as are or shall be liable to confiscation," etc.

This document was of the usual tenor, but in addition, Captain Kidd was granted a special royal commission, under the Great Seal, which is given herewith because it so intimately concerned the later fortunes of his noble partners:

WILLIAM REX.

WILLIAM THE THIRD, by the Grace of God, King of England, Scotland, France, and Ireland, Defender of the Faith, etc. To our trusty and well beloved Captain William Kidd, Commander of the ship *Adventure Galley*, or to any other, the commander of the same for the time being, GREETING:

Whereas, we are informed that Captain Thomas Tew, John Ireland, Capt. Thomas Wake, and Capt. William Maze, and other subjects, natives, or inhabitants of New York and elsewhere, in our plantations in America, have associated themselves with divers other wicked and ill-disposed persons, and do, against the law of nations, commit many and great piracies, robberies, and depredations on the seas upon the parts of America and in other parts, to the great hindrance and discouragement of trade and navigation, and to the great danger and hurt of our loving subjects, our allies, and of all others navigating the seas upon their lawful occasions,

NOW, KNOW YE, that we being desirous to prevent the aforesaid mischief, and as much as in us lies, to bring the said pirates, freebooters, and sea rovers to justice, have thought fit, and do hereby give and grant to the said Robert Kidd (to whom our Commissioners for exercising the office of Lord High Admiral of England have granted a commission as a private man-of-war, bearing date of the 11th day of December, 1695), and unto the Commander of the said ship for the time being, and unto the Officers, Mariners, and others which shall be under your command, full power and authority to apprehend, seize, and take into your custody, as well the said Captain Tew, John Ireland, Capt. Thomas Wake, and Capt. William Maze, or Mace, and all such pirates, freebooters, and sea rovers, being either our subjects or of other nations associated with them, which you shall meet with upon the seas or coasts of America, or upon any other seas or coasts, with all their ships and vessels, and all such merchandizes, money, goods, and wares as shall be found on board, or with them, in case they shall willingly yield themselves up, but if they will not yield without fighting, then you are by force to compel to yield.

And we also require you to bring, or cause to be brought, such pirates, freebooters, or sea rovers as you shall seize, to a legal trial to the end that they may be proceeded against according to the law in such cases. And we do hereby command all our Officers, Ministers, and others our loving subjects whatsoever to be aiding and assisting you in the premises, and we do hereby enjoin you to keep an exact journal of your proceedings in execution of the premises, and set down the names of such pirates and of their officers and company, and the names of such ships and vessels as you shall by virtue of these presents take and seize, and the quantity of arms, ammunition, provisions, and lading of such ships, and the true value of the same, as near as you judge.

And we do hereby strictly charge and command, and you will answer the contrary to your peril, that you do not, in any manner, offend or molest our friends and allies, their ships or subjects, by colour or pretense of these presents, or the authority thereof granted. *In witness* whereof, we have caused our Great Seal of England to be affixed to these presents. Given at our Court in Kensington, the 26th day of January, 1696, in the seventh Year of our Reign.

It was privately understood that the King was to receive one-tenth of the proceeds of the voyage, although this stipulation does not appear in the articles of agreement. By a subsequent grant from the Crown, this understanding was publicly ratified and all money and property taken from pirates, except the King's tenth, was to be made over to the owners of the *Adventure Galley*, to wit, Bellomont and his partners, and Kidd and Livingston, as they had agreed among themselves.

The *Adventure Galley*, the ship selected for the cruise, was of 287 tons and thirty-four guns, a powerful privateer for her day, which Kidd fitted out at Plymouth, England. Finding difficulty in recruiting a full crew of mettlesome lads, he sailed from that port for New York in April of 1696, with only seventy hands. While anchored in the Hudson, he increased his company to 155 men, many of them the riff-raff of the water-front, deserters, wastrels, brawlers, and broken seamen who may have sailed under the black flag aforetime. It was a desperate venture, the pay was to be in shares of the booty taken, "no prizes, no money," and sober, respectable sailors looked askance at it. Kidd was impatient to make an offing. Livingston and Bellomont were chafing at the delay, and he had to ship what men he could find at short notice.

The *Adventure Galley* cruised first among the West Indies, honestly in quest of "pirates, freebooters and sea rovers," and not falling in with any of these gentry, Kidd took his departure for the Cape of Good Hope and the Indian Ocean. This was in accordance with his instructions, for in the preamble of the articles of agreement it was stated that "certain persons did some time since depart from

SPOOKY TREASURE TROVES

New England, Rhode Island, New York, and other parts in America and elsewhere with an intention to pyrate and to commit spoyles and depredations in the Red Sea and elsewhere, and to return with such riches and goods as they should get to certain places by them agreed upon, of which said persons and places the said Captain Kidd hath notice."

This long voyage was soundly planned. Madagascar was the most notorious haunt of pirates in the world. Their palm-thatched villages fringed its beaches and the blue harbors sheltered many sail which sallied forth to play havoc with the precious argosies of the English, French, and Dutch East India Companies. Kidd hoped to win both favor and fortune by ridding these populous trade routes of the perils that menaced every honest skipper.

When, at length, Madagascar was sighted, the *Adventure Galley* was nine months from home, and not a prize had been taken. Kidd was short of provisions and of money with which to purchase supplies. His crew was in a grumbling, mutinous temper, as they rammed their tarry fists into their empty pockets and stared into the empty hold. The captain quieted them with promises of dazzling spoil, and the *Adventure Galley* vainly skirted the coast, only to find that some of the pirates had got wind of her coming while others were gone a-cruising. From the crew of a wrecked French ship, Kidd took enough gold to buy provisions in a Malabar port. This deed was hardly generous, but by virtue of his letters of marque Kidd was authorized to despoil a Frenchman wherever he caught him.

After more futile cruising to and fro, Kidd fell from grace and crossed the very tenuous line that divided privateering from piracy in his century. His first unlawful capture was a small native vessel owned by Aden merchants and commanded by one Parker, an Englishman, the mate being a Portuguese. The plunder was no more than a bale or two of pepper and coffee, and a few gold pieces. It was petty larceny committed to quiet a turbulent crew and to pay operating expenses. Parker made loud outcry ashore and a little later Kidd was overtaken by a vengeful Portuguese man-of-war off the port of Carawar. The two ships hammered each other with broad-sides and bow-chasers six hours on end, when Kidd went his way with several men wounded.

Sundry other small craft were made to stand and deliver after this without harm to their crews, but no treasure was lifted until Kidd ventured to molest the shipping of the Great Mogul. That fabled potentate of Asia whose empire had been found by Genghis Khan and extended by Tamerlane, and whose gorgeous palaces were at Samarcand, had a mighty commerce between the Red Sea and China, and his rich freights also swelled the business of the English East India Company. His ships were often convoyed by the English and the Dutch. It was from two of these vessels that Kidd took his treasure and thus achieved the brief career which rove the halter around his neck.

SPOOKY TREASURE TROVES

The first of these ships of the Great Mogul he looted and burned, and to the second, the *Quedah Merchant*, he transferred his flag after forsaking the leaky, unseaworthy *Adventure Galley* on the Madagascar coast. Out of this capture he took almost a half million dollars' worth of gold, jewels, plate, silks, and other precious merchandise of which his crew ran away with by far the greater share, leaving Kidd with about one hundred thousand dollars in booty.

It was charged that while on this coast Kidd amicably consorted with a very notorious pirate named Culliford, instead of blowing him out of the water as he properly deserved. This was the most damning feature of his indictment, and there is no doubt that he sold Culliford cannon and munitions and received him in his cabin. On the other hand, Kidd declared that he would have attacked the pirate but he was overpowered by his mutinous crew who caroused with Culliford's rogues and were wholly out of hand. And Kidd's story is lent the color of truth by the fact that ninety-five of his men deserted to join the *Mocha Frigate* of Culliford and sail with him under the Jolly Roger. It is fair to assume that if William Kidd had been the successful pirate he is portrayed, his own rascals would have stayed with him in the *Quedah Merchant* which was a large and splendidly armed and equipped ship of between four and five hundred tons.

Abandoned by two-thirds of his crew, and unable to find trustworthy men to fill their places, Kidd was in sore straits and decided to sail for home and square accounts with Bellomont, trusting to his powerful friends to keep him out of trouble. In the meantime, the Great Mogul and the English East India Company had made vigorous complaint and Kidd was proclaimed a pirate. The royal pardon was offered all pirates that should repent of their sins, barring Kidd who was particularly excepted by name. Many a villain whose hands were red with the slaughter of ships' crews was thus officially forgiven, while Kidd who had killed no man barring that mutineer, the gunner, William Moore, was hunted in every sea, with a price on his head.

On April 1, 1699, after an absence of almost two years, Kidd arrived at Anguilla,[4] his first port of call in the West Indies, and went ashore to buy provisions. There he learned, to his consternation, that he had been officially declared a pirate and stood in peril of his life. The people refused to have any dealings with him, and he sailed to St. Thomas, and thence to Curacoa where he was able to get supplies through the friendship of an English merchant of Antigua, Henry Bolton by name, who was not hampered by scruples or fear of the authorities. Under date of February 3, the Governor of Barbadoes had written to Mr. Vernon, Secretary of the Lords of the Council of Trade and Plantations in London:

"I received Yours of the 23rd. of November in relation to the apprehending your notorious Pyrat Kidd. He has not been heard of in these Seas of late, nor do I believe he will think it safe to venture himself here, where his Villainies are so

SPOOKY TREASURE TROVES

well known; but if he does, all the dilligence and application to find him out and seize him shall be used on my part that can be, with the assistance of a heavy, crazy Vessell, miscalled a Cruizer, that is ordered to attend upon me."

The first news of Kidd was received from the officials of the island of Nevis who wrote Secretary Vernon on May 18, 1699, as follows:

Your letter of 23rd, November last in relation to that notorious Pirate Capt. Kidd came safe to our hands ... have sent copies thereof to the Lieut, or Deputy Governor of each respective island under this Government: since which we have had this following acct. of the said Kidd:

That he lately came from Mallagascoe,[5] in a large Gennowese vessel of about foure hundred Tons; Thirty Guns mounted and eighty men. And in his way from those partes his men mutiny 'd and thirty of them lost their lives: That his Vessell is very leaky; and that several of his men have deserted him soe that he has not above five and twenty or thirty hands on board. About twenty days since he landed at Anguilla ... where he tarry'd about foure hours; but being refused Succour sailed thence for the Island of St. Thomas ... and anchored off that harbour three dayes, in which time he treated with them alsoe for relief; but the Governor absolutely Denying him, he bore away further to Leeward (as tis believ'd) for Porto Rico or Crabb Island. Upon which advice We forthwith ordered his Majestie's Ship *Queensborough*, now attending this Government, Capt. Rupert Billingsly, Commander, to make the best of his way after him. And in case he met with his men, vessell and effects, to bring them upp hither.

That no Imbezzlem't may be made, but that they may be secured until we have given you advice thereof, and his Majestie's pleasure relating thereto can be knowne, we shall by the first conveyance transmitt ye like account of him to the Governor of Jamaica. So that if he goes farther to Leeward due care may be taken to secure him there. As for those men who have deserted him, we have taken all possible care to apprehend them, especially if they come within the districts of this Government, and hope on return of his Majestie's frigate we shall be able to give you a more ample acct. hereof.

We are with all due Respect:

Rt. Hon'ble,   YOUR MOST OBEDT. HUMBLE SERVANTS.

Kidd dodged all this hue and cry and was mightily anxious to get in touch with Bellomont without loss of time. He bought at Curacoa, through the accommodating Henry Bolton, a Yankee sloop called the *San Antonio* and transferred his treasure and part of his crew to her. The *Quedah Merchant* he convoyed as far as Hispaniola, now San Domingo, and hid her in a small harbor with considerable cargo, in charge of a handful of his men under direction of Bolton.

SPOOKY TREASURE TROVES

Then warily and of an uneasy mind, Captain Kidd steered his sloop for the American coast and first touched at the fishing hamlet of Lewes at the mouth of Delaware Bay. All legend to the contrary, he made no calls along the Carolinas and Virginia to bury treasure. The testimony of Kidd's crew and passengers cannot be demolished on this score, besides which he expected to come to terms with Bellomont and adjust his affairs within the law, so there was no sane reason for his stopping to hide his valuables.

The first episode that smacks in the least of buried treasure occurred while the sloop was anchored off Lewes. There had come from the East Indies as a passenger one James Gillam, pirate by profession, and he wished no dealings with the authorities. He therefore sent ashore in Delaware Bay his sea chest which we may presume contained his private store of stolen gold. Gillam and his chest bob up in the letters of Bellomont, but for the present let this reference suffice, as covered by the statement of Edward Davis of London, mariner, made during the proceedings against Kidd in Boston:

That in or about the month of November, 1697, the Examinant came Boatswain of the ship *Fidelia*, Tempest Rogers, Commander, bound on a trading voyage for India, and in the month of July following arrived at the Island of Madagascar and after having been there about five weeks the Ship sailed thence and left this Examinant in the Island, and being desirous to get off, enter'd himself on board the Ship whereof Capt. Kidd was Commander to worke for his passage, and accordingly came with him in the sd. Ship to Hispaniola, and from thence in the Sloop *Antonio* to this place.

And that upon their arrival at the Hoor Kills, in Delaware Bay, there was a chest belonging to one James Gillam put ashore there and at Gard'ner's Island, there was several chests and packages put out of Capt. Kidd's Sloop into a Sloop belonging to New Yorke. He knows not the quantity, nor anything sent on Shore at the sd. Island nor doth he know that anything was put on Shore at any Island or place in this Country, only two Guns of ... weight apeace or thereabout at Block Island.

Signed, (his mark)   EDWARD (E* D.) DAVIS.

In Delaware Bay Kidd bought stores, and five of the people of Lewes were thrown into jail by the Pennsylvania authorities for having traded with him. Thence he sailed for Long Island Sound, entered it from the eastward end, and made for New York, cautiously anchoring in Oyster Bay, nowadays sedulously avoided by malefactors of great wealth. It was his purpose to open negotiations with Bellomont at long range, holding his treasure as an inducement for a pardon. From Oyster Bay he sent a letter to a lawyer in New York, James Emmot who had before then

SPOOKY TREASURE TROVES

defended pirates, and also a message to his wife. Emmot was asked to serve as a go-between, and he hastened to join Kidd on the sloop, explaining that Bellomont was in Boston. Thereupon the *Antonio* weighed anchor and sailed westward as far as Narragansett Bay where Emmot landed and went overland to find Bellomont.

[1] Governor Henry Sloughter.

[2] Prizes.

[3] Prizes.

[4] Anguilla, or Snake Island, is a small island of the Leeward Group of the West Indies, considerably east of Porto Rico, and near St. Martin. It belongs to England.

[5] Madagascar.

SPOOKY TREASURE TROVES

CHAPTER III
CAPTAIN KIDD, HIS TREASURE[1]

"You captains brave and bold, hear our cries, hear our cries,You captains brave and bold, hear our cries.You captains brave and bold, though you seem uncontrolled,Don't for the sake of gold lose your souls, lose your souls,Don't for the sake of gold lose your souls."(*From the old Kidd ballad.*)

The negotiations between Kidd and the Earl of Bellomont were no more creditable to the royal governor than to the alleged pirate. Already the noble partners in England were bombarded with awkward questions concerning the luckless enterprise, and Bellomont, anxious to clear himself and his friends, was for getting hold of Kidd and putting him in Boston jail at the earliest possible moment. He dared not reveal the true status of affairs to Kidd by means of correspondence lest that wary bird escape him, and he therefore tried to coax him nearer in a letter sent back in care of Emmot, that experienced legal adviser of pirates in distress. This letter of Bellomont was dated June 19, 1699, and had this to say:

Captain Kidd:

Mr. Emmot came to me last Tuesday night late, telling me he came from you, but was shy of telling me where he parted with you, nor did I press him to it. He told me you came to Oyster Bay in Nassau Island and sent for him to New York. He proposed to me from you that I would grant you a pardon. I answered that I had never granted one yet, and that I had set myself a safe rule not to grant a pardon to anybody whatsoever without the King's express leave or command. He told me you declared and protested your innocence, and that if your men could be persuaded to follow your example, you would make no manner of scruple of coming to this port or any other within her Majestie's Dominions; that you owned there were two ships taken but that your men did it violently against your will and had us'd you barbarously in imprisoning you and treating you ill most part of the Voyage, and often attempting to murder you.

SPOOKY TREASURE TROVES

Mr. Emmot delivered me two French passes taken on board the two ships which your men rifled, which passes I have in my custody and I am apt to believe they will be a good Article to justifie you if the peace were not, by the Treaty between England and France, to operate in that part of the world at the time the hostility was committed, as I almost confident it was not to do! Mr. Emmot also told me that you had to about the value of 10,000 pounds in the Sloop with you, and that you had left a Ship somewhere off the coast of Hispaniola in which there was to the Value of 30,000 pounds more which you had left in safe hands and had promised to go to your people in that Ship within three months to fetch them with you to a safe harbour.

These are all the material particulars I can recollect that passed between Mr. Emmot and me, only this, that you showed a great sense of Honour and Justice in professing with many asseverations your settled and serious design all along to do honor to your Commission and never to do the least thing contrary to your duty and allegiance to the King. And this I have to say in your defense that several persons at New York who I can bring to evidence it, if there be occasion, did tell me that by several advices from Madagascar and that part of the world, they were informed of your men revolting from you in one place, which I am pretty sure they said was at Madagascar; and that others of them compelled you much against your will to take and rifle two Ships.

I have advised with his Majesty's Council and showed them this letter this afternoon, and they are of opinion that if your case be so clear as you (or Mr. Emmot for you) have said, that you may safely come hither, and be equipped and fitted out to go and fetch the other Ship, and I make no manner of doubt but to obtain the King's pardon for you and those few men you have left, who I understand have been faithful to you and refused as well as you to dishonor the Commission you had from England.

I assure you on my word and on my honor I will performe nicely what I have now promised, tho' this I declare before hand that whatever treasure of goods you bring hither, I will not meddle with the least bit of them, but they shall be left with such trusty persons as the Council will advise until I receive orders from England how they shall be disposed of. Mr. Campbell will satisfie you that this that I have now written is the Sense of the Council and of

YOUR HUMBLE SERVANT.(Not signed but endorsed, "A true copy, Bellomont.")

These were fair words but not as sincere as might have been. Governor Bellomont was anxious to lay hands on Kidd by fair means or foul, and in the light of subsequent events this letter appears as a disingenuous decoy. It was carried back to Narragansett Bay by Emmot, and with him Bellomont sent one Duncan Campbell, postmaster of Boston, as an authorized agent to advance the negotiations. Campbell was a Scotchman who had been a friend of Kidd. He is mentioned in John Dunton's "Letter Written from New England, A. D. 1686."

"I rambled to the Scotch book-seller, one Campbell. He is a brisk young fellow that dresses All-a-mode, and sets himself off to the best Advantage, and yet thrives apace. I am told (and for his sake I wish it may be true) that a Young Lady of Great Fortune has married him."

In reply to Bellomont's letter, thus delivered, Captain Kidd replied as follows:

FROM BLOCK ISLAND ROAD, ON BOARD THE SLOOP ST. ANTONIO,
June 24th, 1699.

May It please your Excellencie:

I am hon'rd with your Lordship's kind letter of ye 19th., Current by Mr. Campbell which came to my hands this day, for which I return my most hearty thanks. I cannot but blame myself for not writing to your Lordship before this time, knowing it was my duty, but the clamorous and false stories that has been reported of me made me fearful of writing or coming into any harbor till I could hear from your Lordship. I note the contents of your Lordship's letter as to what Mr. Emmot and Mr. Campbell Informed your Lordship of my proceedings. I do affirm it to be true, and a great deal more may be said of the abuses of my men and the hardships I have undergone to preserve the Ship and what goods my men had left. Ninety-five men went away from me in one day and went on board the *Moca Frigott*, Captain Robert Cullifer, Commander, who went away to the Red Seas and committed several acts of pyracy as I am informed, and am afraid that because of the men formerly belonging to my Galley, the report is gone home against me to the East India Companee.

A Sheet of paper will not contain what may be said of the care I took to preserve the Owners' interest and to come home to clear up my own Innocency. I do further declare and protest that I never did in the least act Contrary to the King's Commission, nor to the Reputation of my honorable Owners, and doubt not but I shall be able to make my Innocency appear, or else I had no need to come to these parts of the world, if it were not for that, and my owners' Interest.

There is five or six passengers that came from Madagascar to assist me in bringing the Ship home, and about ten of my own men that came with me would not venture to go into Boston till Mr. Campbell had Ingaged body for body for them that they should not be molested while I staid at Boston, or till I returned with the ship. I doubt not but your Lordship will write to England in my favor and for these few men that are left. I wish your Lordship would persuade Mr. Campbell to go home to England with your Lordship's letters, who will be able to give account of our affairs and diligently forward the same that there may be speedy answer from England.

I desired Mr. Campbell to buy a thousand weight of rigging for the fitting of the Ship, to bring her to Boston, that I may not be delay'd when I come there. Upon receiving your Lordship's letter I am making the best of my way for Boston. This with my humble duty to your Lordship and the Countess is what offers from,

My Lord, Your Excellency'sMost humble and dutyfull Servant,WM. KIDD.

Notwithstanding these expressions of confidence, Kidd suspected Bellomont's intentions and decided to leave his treasure in safe hands instead of carrying it to Boston with him. Now follows the documentary narrative of the only authenticated buried treasure of Captain Kidd and the proofs that he had no other booty of any account. At the eastern end of Long Island Sound is a beautiful wooded island of three thousand acres which has been owned by the Gardiner family as a manor since the first of them, Lionel Gardiner, obtained a royal grant almost three centuries ago. In June of 1699, John Gardiner, third of the line of proprietors, sighted a strange sloop anchored in his island harbor, and rowed out to make the acquaintance of Captain William Kidd who had crossed from Narragansett Bay in the San Antonio. What happened between them and how the treasure was buried and dug up is told in the official testimony of John Gardiner, dated July 17th, 1699.

"THE NARRATIVE OF JOHN GARD(I)NER OF GARD(I)NER ISLAND, ALIAS ISLE OF WIGHT, RELATING TO CAPTAIN WILLIAM KIDD.

That about twenty days ago Mr. Emmot of New York came to the Narrator's house and desired a boat to go to New York, telling the Narrator he came from my Lord at Boston, whereupon the Narrator furnished Mr. Emmot with a boat and he went for New York. And that evening the Narrator saw a Sloop with six guns riding an Anchor off Gardiner's Island and two days afterwards in the evening the Narrator went on board said Sloop to enquire what she was.

And so soon as he came on board, Capt. Kidd (then unknown to the Narrator) asked him how himself and family did, telling him that he, the said Kidd, was going to my Lord at Boston, and desired the Narrator to carry three Negroes, two boys and a girl ashore to keep till he, the said Kidd, or his order should call for them, which the Narrator accordingly did.

That about two hours after the Narrator had got the said Negroes ashore, Capt. Kidd sent his boat ashore with two bales of goods and a Negro boy; and the morning after, the said Kidd desired the Narrator to come immediately on board and bring six Sheep with him for his voyage for Boston, which the Narrator did. Kidd asked him to spare a barrel of Cyder, which the Narrator with great importunity consented to, and sent two of his men for it, who brought the Cyder on board said Sloop. Whilst the men were gone for the Cyder, Capt. Kidd offered the Narrator several pieces of damnified[2] Muslin and Bengali as a present to his Wife, which the said Kidd put in a bagg and gave the Narrator. And about a quarter of an hour afterwards the said Kidd took up two or three (more) pieces of damnified Muslin and gave the Narrator for his proper use.

And the Narrator's men then coming on board with the said barrel of Cyder as aforesaid, Kidd gave them a piece of Arabian gold for their trouble and also for bringing him word. Then the said Kidd, ready to sail, told this Narrator he would pay him for the Cyder, to which the Narrator answered that he was already satisfied for it by the Present made to his wife. And it was observed that some of Kidd's men gave to the Narrator's men some inconsiderable things of small value which were Muslins for neck-cloths.

And then the Narrator tooke leave of the said Kidd and went ashore and at parting the said Kidd fired four guns and stood for Block Island. About three days afterwards, said Kidd sent the Master of the Sloop and one Clark in his boat for the Narrator who went on board with them, and the said Kidd desired him to take ashore with him and keep for him a Chest and a box of Gold and a bundle of Quilts and four bales of Goods, which box of Gold the said Kidd told the Narrator was intended for my Lord. And the Narrator complied with the request and took on Shore the said Chest, box of Gold, quilts and bales goods.

And the Narrator further saith that two of Kidd's crew who went by the names of Cooke and Parrat delivered to him, the Narrator, two baggs of Silver which they said weighed thirty pound weight, for which he gave receipt. And that another of Kidd's men delivered to the Narrator a small bundle of gold and gold dust of about a pound weight to keep for him, and did present the Narrator with a sash and a pair of wortsed stockins. And just before the Sloop sailed, Capt. Kidd presented the Narrator with a bagg of Sugar, and then took leave and sailed for Boston.

And the Narrator further saith he knew nothing of Kidd's being proclaimed a Pyrate, and if he had, he durst not have acted otherwise than he had done, having no force to oppose them and for that he hath formerly been threatened to be killed by Privateers if he should carry unkindly to them.

The within named Narrator further saith that while Capt. Kidd lay with his Sloop at Gardner's Island, there was a New York Sloop whereof one Coster is master, and his mate was a little black man, unknown by name, who as it is was said, had been formerly Capt. Kidd's quartermaster, and another Sloop belonging to New Yorke, Jacob Fenick, Master, both which lay near to Kidd's Sloop three days together. And whilst the Narrator was on board with Capt. Kidd, there was several bales of Goods put on board the other two Sloops aforesaid, and the said two Sloops sailed up the Sound. After which Kidd sailed with his sloop for Block Island; and being absent by the space of three days, returned to Gardner's Island again in Company of another Sloop belonging to New York, Cornelius Quick,

SPOOKY TREASURE TROVES

Master, on board of which were one Thomas Clarke of Setauket, commonly called Whisking Clarke, and one Harrison of Jamaica, father to a boy that was with Capt. Kidd, and Capt. Kidd's Wife was then on board his own Sloop.

And Quick remained with his Sloop there from noon to the evening of the same day, and took on board two Chests that came out of Kidd's Sloop, under the observance of this Narrator, and he believes several Goods more and then Sailed up the Sound. Kidd remained there with his Sloop until next morning, and then set sail intending, as he said, for Boston. Further the Narrator saith that the next day after Quick sailed with his Sloop from Gardner's Island he saw him turning out of a Bay called Oyster Pan Bay, altho' the wind was all the time fair to carry him up the Sound. The Narrator supposes he went in thither to land some Goods.

JOHN GARDINER.

Boston, July 17th, 1699.

The Narrator, John Gardiner, under Oath before his Excellency and Council unto the truth of his Narrative in this sheet of paper.

ADDINGTON, Sec'ry."

This artless recital has every earmark of truth, and it was confirmed in detail by other witnesses and later events. Before we fall to digging up the treasure of Gardiner's Island, carried ashore in the "Chest and box of Gold," it is well to follow those other goods which were carried away in the sloops about which so much has been said by John Gardiner. No more is heard of that alluring figure, "the little black man, unknown by name, who as it was said had been formerly Capt. Kidd's Quarter-Master," but "Whisking" Clarke was duly overhauled. All of the plunder transferred from Kidd's sloop to those other craft was consigned to him, and some of it was put ashore at Stamford, Conn., in charge of a Major Sellick who had a warehouse hard by the Sound. Clarke was arrested by order of Bellomont and gave a bond of £12,000 that he would deliver up all to the government. This he did, without doubt, but legend has been busy with this enterprising "Whisking" Clarke.

In the Connecticut River off the "upper end of Pine Meadow," near Northfield, Mass., is Clarke's Island which was granted by the town to William Clarke in 1686, and confirmed to his heirs in 1723, It then contained ten and three-fourth acres, and was a secluded spot, well covered with trees. Later, what with cutting off the woods and the work of the freshets, a large part of the island was washed away. It was here, tradition has it, that some of Kidd's treasure was hidden by "Whisking" Clarke.

The local story is that Kidd and his men ascended the river, though how they got over the series of falls is not explained, and made a landing at Clarke's Island. Here, having placed the chest in a hole, they sacrificed by lot one of their number and laid his body on top of the treasure in order that his ghost might forever defend it from fortune-seekers. One Abner Field, after consulting a conjurer who showed him precisely where the chest was buried resolved to risk a tussle with the pirate's ghost, and with two friends waited in fear and trembling for the auspicious time when the moon should be directly overhead at midnight.

They were to work in silence, and to pray that no cock should crow within earshot and break the spell. At length, one of them raised his crowbar for a mighty stroke, down it went, and clinked against metal. "You've hit it," cried another, and alas, instantly the chest sank out of reach, and the ghost appeared, and very angry it was. A moment later, the devil himself popped from under the bank, ripped across the island like a tornado and plunged into the river with a

John Gardiner's sworn statement of the goods and treasure left with him by Kidd.

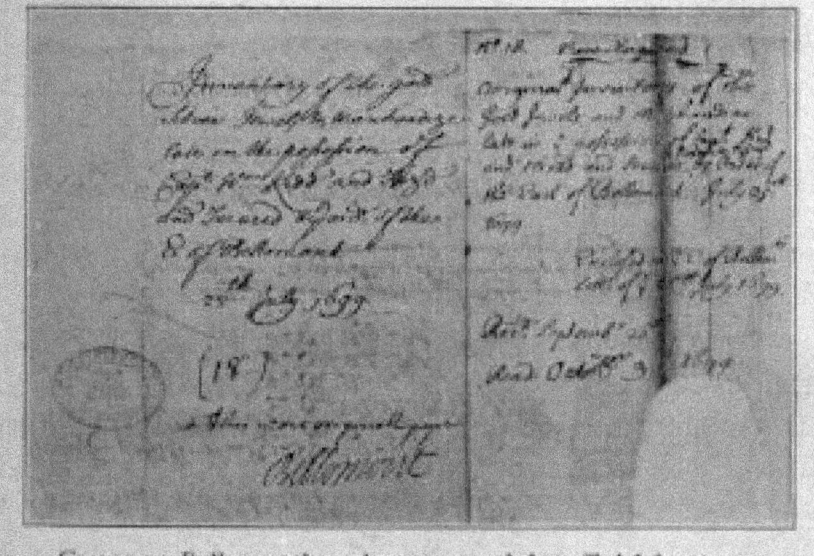

Governor Bellomont's endorsement of the official inventory of Kidd's treasure found on Gardiner's Island.

prodigious, hissing splash. The treasure hunters flew for home, and told their tale, but village rumor whispered it about that one Oliver Smith and a confederate had impersonated the ghost and the energetic Evil One.

On October 20, 1699, Bellomont wrote in a letter to England:

SPOOKY TREASURE TROVES

"I have prevailed with Governor Winthrop of Connecticut to seize and send Thomas Clarke of N. York prisoner hither. He has been on board Kidd's sloop at the east end of Long Island and carried off to the value of about 5000 pounds in goods and treasure (that we know of and perhaps a great deal more) into Connecticut Colony; and thinking himself safe from under our power, writ my Lt. Governor of New York a very saucy letter and bade us defiance. I have ordered him to be safely kept prisoner in the fort, because the gaol of New York is weak and insufficient. And when orders come to me to send Kidd and his men to England (which I long for impatiently), I will also send Clarke[3] as an associate of Kidd."

Three days later, the Lieutenant Governor of New York wrote Bellomont as follows:

"Clarke proffers 12,000 pounds good Security and will on oath deliver up all the goods he hath been entrusted with from Kidd, provided he may go and fetch them himself, but says he will rather die or be undone than to bring his friends into a Predicament. I told him if he would let me know where I might secure these goods or Bullion, I would recommend his case to your Lordship's favour. He answered 'twas impossible to recover anything until he went himself."

After leaving the bulk of his treasure on Gardiner's Island, Kidd received another friendly message from Lord Bellomont, and was by now persuaded that he could go to Boston without danger. With his wife on board his sloop, and she stood by him staunchly, he laid a course around Cape Cod and made port on the first day of July. Captain and Mrs. William Kidd found lodgings in the house of their friend, Duncan Campbell, and he walked unmolested for a week, passing some of the time in the Blue Anchor tavern. "Being a very resolute fellow," wrote Hutchinson, "when the officer arrested him in his lodgings, he attempted to draw his sword, but a young gentleman who accompanied the officer, laying hold of his arm, prevented him and he submitted."

In the letters of Lord Bellomont to the Lords of Plantations and Colonies are fully related the particulars of Kidd's downfall and of the finding of his treasure. On July 26th, he stated:

"*My Lords:*

"I gave your Lordships a short account of my taking Capt. Kidd in my letter of the 8th. Inst. I shall in this letter confine myself wholly to an account of my proceedings with him. On the 13th, of last month Mr. Emmot, a lawyer of N. York came to me late at night and told me he came from Capt. Kidd who was on the Coast with a Sloop, but would not tell me where; that Kidd had brought 60 pounds weight of gold, about 100 weight of silver, and 17 bales of East India goods (which was less by 24 bales than we have since got out of the sloop). That Kidd had left behind him a great Ship near the coast of Hispaniola that nobody but himself could find out, on board whereof there were in bale goods, saltpetre, and other things to the value of at least 30,000 pounds. That if I would give him a pardon, he would bring in the sloop and goods hither and fetch his great ship and goods afterwards.

"Mr. Emmot delivered me that night two French passes which Kidd took on board the two Moors' ships which were taken by him in the seas of India (or as he alleged by his men against his will). One of the passes wants a date in the original as in the copy I sent your Lordships, and they go (No. 1) and (No. 2). On the said 19th. of June as I sat in Council I wrote a letter to Capt. Kidd and showed it to the Council, and they approving of it I despatched Mr. Campbell again to Kidd with my said letter, a copy whereof goes (No. 4). Your Lordships may observe that the promise I made Capt. Kidd in my said letter of a kind reception and procuring the King's pardon for him, is conditional, that is, provided he were as Innocent as he pretended to be. But I quickly found sufficient cause to suspect him very guilty, by the many lies and contradictions he told me.

"I was so much upon my guard with Kidd that he arriving here on Saturday of this month, I would not see him but before witnesses; nor have I ever seen him but in Council twice or thrice that we examined him, and the day he was taken up by the Constable. It happened to be by the door of my Lodging, and he rush'd in and came rushing to me, the Constable after him. I had him not seiz'd till Thursday, the 6th Inst. for I had a mind to discover where he had left the great Ship, and I thought myself secure enough from his running away because I took care not to give him the least umbrage or design of seizing him. Nor had I till that day (that I produced my orders from Court for apprehending) communicated them to anybody and I found it necessary to show my order to the Council to animate them to join heartily with me in securing Kidd and examining his affairs nicely,[4] ... discover what we could of his behaviour in his whole voyage. Another reason why I took him up no sooner was that he had brought his wife and children hither in his Sloop with him who I believ'd he would not easily forsake.

"He being examined twice or thrice by me and the Council, and also some of his men, I observed he seemed much disturbed, and the last time we examined him I fancied he looked as if he were upon the wing and resolved to run away. And the Gentlemen of the Council had some of them the same thought with mine, so that I took their consent in seizing and committing him. But the officers appointed to seize his men were so careless as to let three or four of his men escape which troubled me the more because they were old N. York Pyrates. The next thing the Council and I did was to appoint a Committee of trusty persons to search for the goods and treasure brought by Kidd and to secure what they should find till the King's pleasure should be known as to the disposition thereof, as my orders from Mr. Secretary Vernon import. The said Committee were made up of two Gentlemen of the Council, two merchants, and the Deputy Collector, whose names are to the enclosed Inventory of the goods and treasure.

SPOOKY TREASURE TROVES

"They searched Kidd's lodgings and found hid and made up in two sea beds a bag of gold dust and Ingots of the value of about 1000 pounds and a bag of silver, part money and part pieces and piggs of silver, value as set down in the said Inventory. In the above bag of gold were several little bags of gold; all particulars are very justly and exactly set down in the Inventory. For my part I have meddled with no matter of thing under the management of the Council, and into the Custody of the aforementioned Committee, that I might be free from the suspicion and censure of the world.

"The enamel'd box mentioned in the beginning of the Inventory is that which Kidd made a present of to my wife by Mr. Campbell, which I delivered in Council to the said Committee to keep with the rest of the treasure. There was in it a stone ring which we take to be a Bristol stone. If it was true[5] it would be worth about 40 pounds, and there was a small stone unset which we believe is also counterfeit, and a sort of a Locket with four sparks which seem to be right diamonds: for there's nobody that understands Jewels[6] ... box and all that's in it were right, they cannot be worth above 60 pounds.

"Your Lordships will see in the middle of the Inventory a parcel of treasure and Jewels delivered up by Mr. Gardiner of Gardiner's Island in the province of New York and at the East end of Nassau Island, the recovery and saving of which treasure is owing to my own care and quickness. I heard by the greatest accident in the world the day Capt. Kidd was committed, that a man... offered 30 pounds for a sloop to carry him to Gardiner's Island, and Kidd having owned to burying some gold on that Island (though he never mentioned to us any jewels nor do I believe he would have own'd to the gold there but that he thought he should himself be sent for it), I privately posted away a messenger to Mr. Gardiner in the King's name to come forthwith and deliver up such treasure as Kidd or any of his crew had lodg'd with him, acquainting him that I had committed Kidd to Gaol as I was ordered to do by the King.

"My messenger made great haste and was with Gardiner before anybody, and Gardiner, who is a very substantial man, brought away the treasure without delay; and by my direction delivered it into the hands of the Committee. If the Jewels be right, as 'tis suppos'd they are, but I never saw them nor the gold and silver brought by Gardiner, then we guess that the parcel brought by him may be worth (gold, silver, and Jewels) 4500 pounds. And besides Kidd had left six bales of goods with him, one of which was twice as big as any of the rest, and Kidd gave him a particular charge of that bale and told him 'twas worth 2000 pounds. The six bales Gardiner could not bring, but I have ordered him to send 'em by a Sloop that is since gone from hence to N. York, and which is to return speedily.

"We are not able to set an exact value on the goods and treasure we have got because we have not open'd the bales we took on board the (Kidd's) sloop, but we hope when the six bales are sent in by Gardiner, what will be in the hands of the Gentlemen appointed to that trust will amount to about 14,000 pounds.

"I have sent strict orders to my Lt. Governor at N. York to make diligent search for the goods and treasure sent by Kidd to N. York in three Sloops mentioned in Gardiner's affidavit.[7] ... I have directed him where to find a purchase[8] in a house in N. York which I am apt to believe will be found in that house. I have sent to search elsewhere a certain place strongly suspected to have received another deposition of gold from Kidd.

"I am also upon the hunt after two or three Arch-Pyrates which I hope to give your Lordships a good account of by the next conveyance. If I could have but a good able Judge and Attorney General at N. York, a man-of-war there and another here, and the companies recruited and well paid, I will rout Pyrates and pyracy entirely out of this North part of America, but as I have too often told your Lordships 'tis impossible for me to do all this alone in my single person.

"I wrote your Lordships in my last letter of the 8th. Inst. that Bradish, the Pyrate, and one of his crew were escap'd out of the gaol in this town. We have since found that the Gaoler was Bradish's kinsman, and the Gaoler confessed they went out at the prison door and that he found it wide open. We had all the reason in the world to believe the Gaoler was consenting to the escape. By much ado I could get the Council to resent the Gaoler's behavior, and by my Importunity I had the fellow before us. We examin'd him, and by his own story and account given us of his suffering other prisoners formerly to escape, I prevailed to have him turn'd out and a prosecution order'd against him to the Attorney Gen'l. I have also with some difficulty this last session of Assembly here, got a bill to pass that the Gaol be committed to the care of the High Sheriff of the County, as in England with a salary of 30 pounds paid to the said Sheriff.

"I am forced to allow the Sheriff 40 Shillings per week for keeping Kidd safe. Otherwise I should be in some doubt about him. He has without doubt a great deal of gold, which is apt to corrupt men that have not principles of honour. I have therefore, to try the power of Iron against Gold, put him into irons that weigh 16 pounds. I thought it moderate enough, for I remember poor Dr. Gates[9] had a 100 weight of Iron on him while he was a prisoner in the late reign.

"There never was a greater liar or thief in the world than this Kidd; notwithstanding he assured the Council and me every time we examined him that the great Ship and her cargo awaited his return to bring her hither, and now your Lordships will see by the several informations of Masters of Ships from Curacoa that the cargo has been sold there, and in one of them 'tis said they have burnt that noble ship. And without doubt, it was by Kidd's order, that the ship might not be an evidence against him, for he would not own to us that her name was the *Quedah Merchant*, tho' his men did.

SPOOKY TREASURE TROVES

"Andres ...[10] eyne and two more brought the first news to New York of the sale of that cargo at Curacoa, nor was ever such pennyworths heard for cheapness. Captain Evertz is he who has brought the news of the ship's being burnt. She was about 500 tons, and Kidd told us at Council that never was there a stronger or stauncher ship seen. His lying had like to have involved me in a contract that would have been very chargeable and to no manner of purpose. I was advised by the Council to dispatch a Ship of good condition to go and fetch away that ship and cargo. I had agreed for a ship of 300 tons, 22 guns, and I was to man her with 60 men to force (if there had been need of it) the men to yield who were left with the ship.

"I was just going to seal the writing, when I bethought myself 'twere best to press Kidd once more to tell me the truth. I therefore sent to him two gentlemen of the Council to the gaol, and he at last own'd that he had left a power (of attorney) with one Henry Bolton, a Merchant of Antigua, to whom he had committed the care of the ship, to sell and dispose of all the cargo. Upon which confession of Kidd's I held my hand from hiring that great ship which would have cost 1700 pounds by computation, and now to-morrow I send the sloop Kidd came in with letters to the Lieut. Govn'r of Antigua, Col. Yoemans, and to the Governors of St. Thomas Island and Curacoa to seize and secure what effects they can that were late in the possession of Kidd and on board the *Quedah Merchant*.

"There is one Burt, an Englishman, that lives at St. Thomas, who has got a great store of the goods and money for Kidd's account. St. Thomas belongs to the Danes, but I hope to retrieve what Burt has in his hands. The sending this Sloop will cost but about 300 pounds, if she be out three months. I hope your Lordships will take care that immediate orders will be sent to Antigua to secure Bolton who must have played the Knave egregiously, for he could not but know that Kidd came knavishly by the ship and goods.

"'Tis reported that the Dutch at Curacoa have loaded three sloops with goods and sent them to Holland. Perhaps 'twere not amiss to send and watch their arrival in Holland, if it be practicable to lay claim to 'em there.

"Since my commitment of Kidd, I heard that upon his approach to this port, his heart misgave him and he proposed to his men putting out to sea again, and going to Caledonia, the new Scotch settlement near Darien, but they refused. I desire I may have orders what to do with Kidd and all his and Bradish's crew, for as the Law stands in this Country, if a Pyrate were convicted, yet he cannot suffer death; and the Council here refused the bill to punish Privateers and Pyrates, which your Lordships sent with me from England with a direction to recommend it at N. York and here, to be passed into a Law....

"You will observe by some of the information I now send that Kidd did not only rob the two Moors' ships, but also a Portuguese ship, which he denied absolutely to the Council and me. I send your Lordships 24 several papers and evidences relating to Capt. Kidd. 'Tis impossible for me to animadvert and make remarks on the several matters contain'd in the said papers in the weak condition I am at present...."

My Lord Bellomont was in the grip of the gout at this time, which misfortune perhaps increased his irritation toward his partner, Captain William Kidd. In a previous letter to the authorities in London, this royal governor had explained quite frankly that he was trying to lure the troublesome pirate into his clutches, and called Emmot, the lawyer, "a cunning Jacobite, a fast friend of Fletcher's[11] and my avowed enemie." He also made this interesting statement:

"I must not forget to tell your Lordships that Campbell brought three or four small Jewels to my Wife which I was to know nothing of, but she came quickly and discover'd them to me and asked me whether she would keep them, which I advised her to do for the present, for I reflected that my showing an over nicety might do hurt before I had made a full discovery what goods and treasure were in the Sloop....

"Mr. Livingston also came to me in a peremptory manner and demanded up his Bond and the articles which he seal'd to me upon Kidd's Expedition, and told me that Kidd swore all the Oaths in the world that unless I did immediately indemnify Mr. Livingston by giving up his Securities, he would never bring in that great ship and cargo. I thought this was such an Impertinence in both Kidd and Livingston that it was time for me to look about me, and to secure Kidd. I had noticed that he designed my wife a thousand pounds in gold dust and Ingotts last Thursday, but I spoil'd his compliment by ordering him to be arrested and committed that day, showing the Council's orders from Court for that purpose....

"If I had kept Mr. Secretary Vernon's orders for seizing and securing Kidd and his associates with all their effects with less secrecy, I had never got him to come in, for his countrymen, Mr. Graham and Livingston, would have been sure to caution him to shift for himself and would have been well paid for their pains."

One by one, Kidd's plans for clearing himself were knocked into a cocked hat. His lawyer did him no good, his hope of bribing the Countess of Bellomont with jewels, "gold dust and Ingotts" went wrong, and his buried treasure of Gardiner's Island was dug up and confiscated by officers of the Crown. It is regrettable that history, by one of its curious omissions, tells us no more about this titled lady. Did Kidd have reason to suppose that she would take his gifts and try to befriend him? When he was in high favor she may, perchance, have admired this dashing shipmaster and privateer as he spun his adventurous yarns in the Governor's mansion. He may have jestingly promised to fetch her home jewels and rich silk stuffs of the Indies filched from pirates. At any rate, she was not to be bought over, and Kidd sat in jail anchored by those sixteen-pound irons, and bit-

SPOOKY TREASURE TROVES

ing his nails in sullen wrath and disappointment, while a messenger was posting to Gardiner's Island with this order from Bellomont to the proprietor:

BOSTON IN NEW ENGLAND, 8th July, 1699...

Mr. Gardiner:

Having received the King's express Orders for Seizing and Securing the body of Capt. Kidd and all his associates together with all their effects till I should receive his Majesty's Royal pleasure how to dispose of the same, I have accordingly secured Capt. Kidd in the Gaol of this Town and some of his men. He has been examined by myself and the Council and has confessed among other things that he left with you a parcel of gold made up in a box and some other parcels besides, all of which I require you in his Majesty's name immediately to fetch hither to me, that I may secure them for his Majesty's use, and I shall recompense your pains in coming hither.

I am,

Your friend and servant, BELLOMONT.

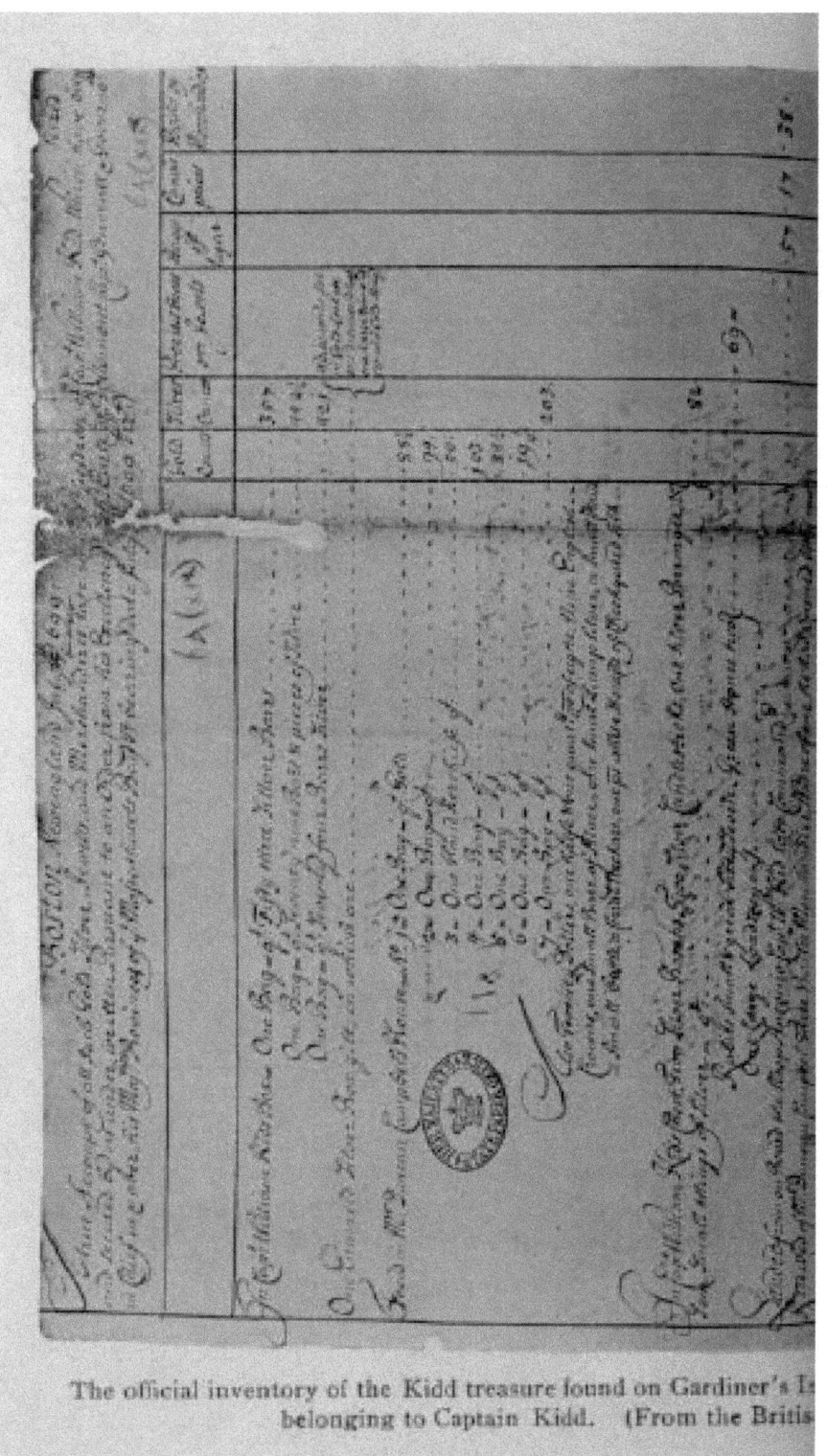

The official inventory of the Kidd treasure found on Gardiner's Island belonging to Captain Kidd. (From the British...)

SPOOKY TREASURE TROVES

The official inventory of the Kidd treasure found on Gardiner's Island. This is the only original and authenticated record of any treasure belonging to Captain Kidd. (From the British State Papers in the Public Record Office, London.)

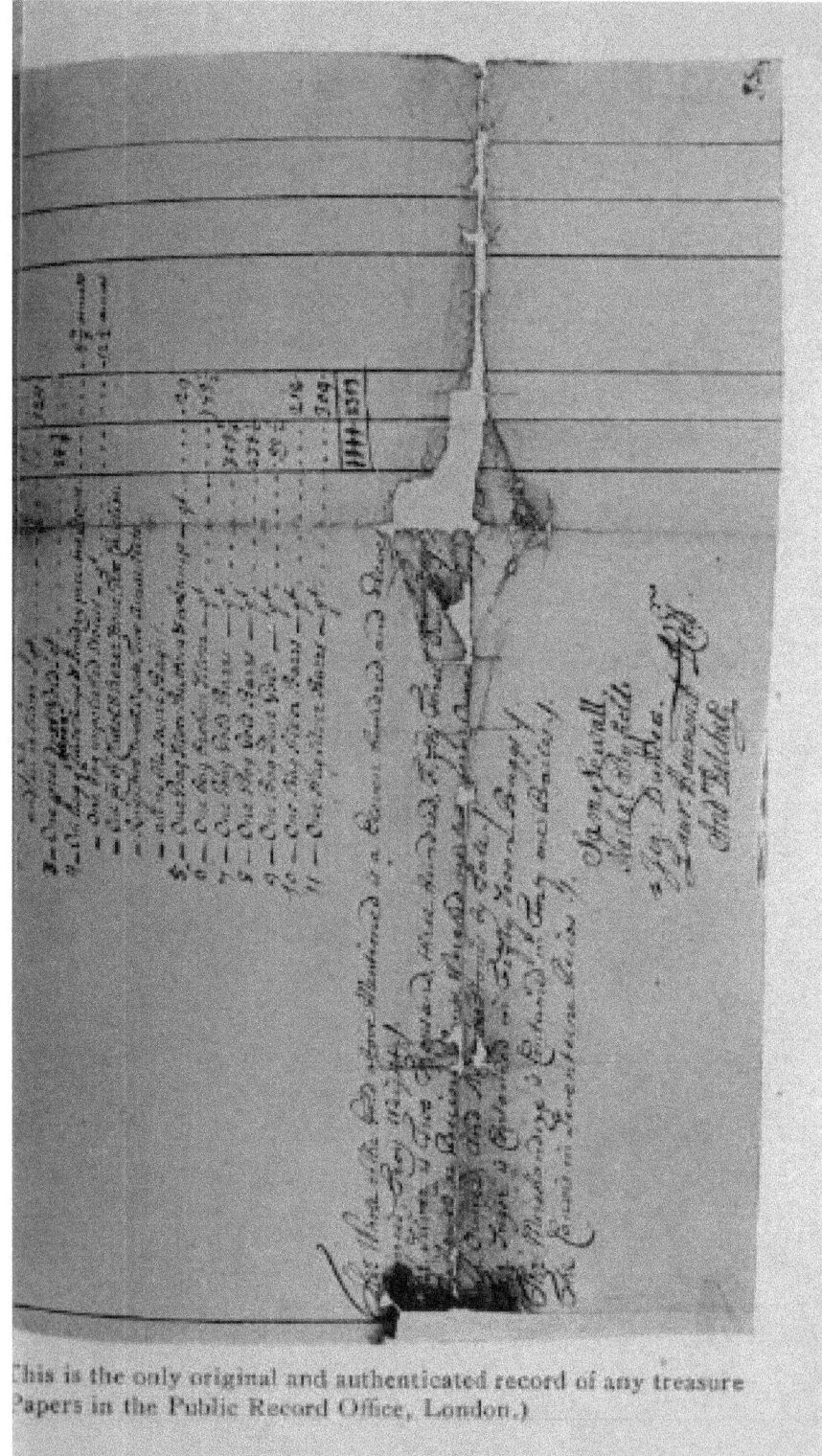

This is the only original and authenticated record of any treasure Papers in the Public Record Office, London.)

The box and the chest were promptly delivered by honest John Gardiner, who had no mind to be mixed in the affairs of the now notorious Kidd, together with the bales of goods left in his care. This booty was inventoried by order of Bellomont and the Governor's Council and the original document is photographed herewith, as found in the Public Record Office, London. It possessed a singular interest because it records and vouches for the only Kidd treasure ever discovered. Nor are its detailed items a mere dusty catalogue of figures and merchandise. This is a document to gloat over. If one has a spark of imagination, he smacks his lips. Instead of legend and myth, here is a veritable pirate's hoard, exactly as it should be, with its bags of gold, bars of silver, "Rubies great and

SPOOKY TREASURE TROVES

small," candlesticks and porringers, diamonds and so on. The inventory contains also other booty found in the course of the treasure hunt, and lest the document itself may prove too hard reading, its contents are transcribed as follows to convince the most skeptical mind that there was a real Kidd treasure and that it was found in the Year of our Lord, 1699.

BOSTON, NEW ENGLAND, July 25th, 1699.

A true Accompt. of all such Gold, Silver, Jewels, and Merchandises in the Possession of Capt. William Kidd, Which have been seized and secured by us under-writing Pursuant to an Order from his Excellency, Richard, Earle of Bellomont, Capt. Generall and Governor-in-Chief in and over his Majestie's Province of ye Massachusetts Bay, etc., bearing date[12] ... 1699, Vizt.

In Capt. William Kid's Box—

One Bag Fifty-three Silver Barrs.One Bag Seventy-nine Barrs and pieces of silver....One Bag Seventy-four Bars Silver.

One Enamel'd Silver Box in which are 4 diamondsset in gold Lockets, one diamond loose,one large diamond set in a gold ring.

Found in Mr. Duncan Campbell's House,

No. 1. One Bag Gold.2. One Bag Gold.3. One Handkerchief Gold.4. One Bag Gold.5. One Bag Gold.6. One Bag Gold.7. One Bag Gold.

Also Twenty Dollars, one halfe and one quart. pcs. of eight, Nine English Crowns, one small Barr of Silver, one small Lump Silver, a small Chaine, a small bottle, a Corral Necklace, one pc. white and one pc. of Checkquer'd Silk....

In Capt. William Kidd's Chests—Two Silver Boxons, Two Silver Candlesticks, one Silver Porringer, and some small things of Silver—Rubies small and great Sixty-seven, Green Stones two. One large Load Stone....

Landed from on board the Sloop *Antonio* Capt. Wm. Kidd late Command.... 57 Baggs of Sugar, 17 pieces canvis, 38 Bales of Merchandize.

Received from Mr. Duncan Campbell Three Bailes Merchandise, Whereof one he had opened being much damnified by water.... Eighty-five ps. Silk Rumals and Bengalis, Sixty ps. Callicoes and Muslins.

Received the 17th. instant of Mr. John Gardiner.

No. 1. One Bag dust Gold.2. One Bag Coyned Gold and in it silver.3. One p'cl dust Gold.4. One Bag three Silver Rings and Sundry preciousstones. One bag of unpolished Stones. Oneps. of Cristol and Bazer Stone, Two CornelionRings, two small Agats. Two Amathests all inthe same Bag.5. One Bag Silver Buttons and a Lamp.6. One Bag broken Silver.7. One Bag Gold Bars.8. One Bag Gold Barrs.9. One Bag Dust Gold.10. One Bag of Silver Bars.11. One Bag Silver Bars.

SPOOKY TREASURE TROVES

The whole of the Gold above mentioned is Eleven hundred, and Eleven ounces, Troy Weight.

The silver is Two Thousand, three Hundred, Fifty-three ounces.

The Jewels or Precious Stones Weight are seventeen Ounces ... an Ounce, and Six[13] ... Stone by Tale.

The Sugar is Contained in Fifty-Seven Baggs.

The Merchandize is Contained in Forty-one Bailes.

The Canvis is Seventeen pieces.

SAM. SEWALL.NATH'L BYFIELD.JER. DUMMER.LAUR. HAMMOND, Lt. Coll.ANDR. BELCHER.

Endorsed:

Inventory of the Gold, Silver, Jewels and Merchandize late in the possession of Capt. Wm. Kidd and Seiz'd and secured by ordr. of the E. of Bellomont, 28th of July 1699. This is an original paper.

BELLOMONT."

A memorandum of Captain Kidd's treasure left on Gardiner's Island. This is his own declaration, signed and sworn.

SPOOKY TREASURE TROVES

That famous sloop, the *San Antonio*, was also carefully inventoried but her contents were for the most part sea gear and rough furnishings, barring a picturesque entry of "ye boy Barleycorn," an apprentice seaman who had sailed with Kidd. Robert Livingston has something to say about Kidd's property in his statement under examination, which has been preserved as follows:

"Robert Livingston, Esq. being notified to appear before his Excellency and Council this day and sworn to give a true Narrative and Relation of his knowledge or information of any Goods, Gold, Silver, Bullion, or other Treasure lately imported by Capt. William Kidd, his Company and Accomplices, or any of them, into this Province, or any other of his Majesty's Provinces, Colonies, or Territories in America, and by them or any of them imbezelled, concealed, conveyed away, or any ways disposed of, saith:

"That hearing Capt. Kidd was come into these parts to apply himself unto his Excellency the Earl of Bellomont, the said Narrator came directly from Albany ye nearest way through the woods to meet the said Kidd here and to wait upon his Lordship. And at his arrival at Boston Capt. Kidd informed him there was on board his Sloop then in Port forty bales of Goods, and some Sugar, and also said he had about eighty pound weight in Plate. The Narrator does not remember whether he said this was on board the Sloop or not. And further the sd. Kidd said he had Forty pound weight in Gold which he hid and secured in some place in the Sound betwixt this and New York, not naming any particular place, which nobody could find but himself. And that all the said Goods, Gold, Plate and Sloop was for accompt. of the Owners of the *Adventure Galley*, whereof this Narrator was one.

"And upon further discourse, Kidd acknowledged that several Chests and bundles of Goods belonging to the men were taken out of his Sloop betwixt this place and New York, and put into other sloops, saying he was forced thereto, that his men would otherwise have run the Sloop on shore. And he likewise acknowledged that he had given Mr. Duncan Campbell one hundred pieces of eight when he was on board his Sloop at Rhode Island. And he knows no further of any concealment, imbezelment, or disposal made by said Kidd, his Company, or accomplices of any Goods, Gold, money, or Treasure whatsoever, saving that Kidd did yesterday acknowledge to this Narrator that ye Gold aforementioned was hid upon Gardiner's Island. He believed there was about fifty pound weight of it and that in the same box with it there was about three or four hundred pieces of eight and some pieces of Plate belonging to his boy Barleycorn and his Negro man which he had gotten by[14] ... for the men. Also the said Kidd gave this Narrator a negro boy and another to Mr. Duncan Campbell."

There is reproduced herewith the original statement of Kidd touching this Gardiner Island treasure. The document is badly torn and disfigured, but the gaps can be supplied from a copy made at that time, and here is what he had to say under oath:

BOSTON, Sept. 4th. 1699.

Captain William Kidd declareth and Saith that in his Chest which he left at Gardiner's Island there were three small baggs or more of Jasper Antonio, or Stone of Goa, several pieces of silk stript with Silver and gold Cloth of Silver, about a Bushell of Cloves and Nutmegs mixed together, and strawed up and down, several books of fine white Callicoa, several pieces of fine Muzlins, several pieces more of flowered silk. He does not well remember what further was in it. He had an invoice thereof in his other chest. All that was contained in ye said Chest was bought by him and some given him at Madagascar. Nothing thereof was taken in ye ship Quidah Merchant. He esteemed it to be of greater value than all else that he left at Gardiner's Island except ye Gold and Silver. There was neither Gold nor Silver in ye Chest. It was fastened with a Padlock and nailed and corded about.

Further saith that he left at said Gardiner's Island a bundle of nine or ten fine Indian quilts, some of ye silk with fringes and Tassels.

WM. KIDD.

The Earl of Bellomont was as keen as a bloodhound on the scent of treasure and it is improbable that any of the Kidd plunder escaped his search. He lost no time in the quest of that James Gillam whose chest had been landed in Delaware Bay, and a singularly diverting episode is related by Bellomont in one of his written reports to the Council of Trade and Plantations:

"I gave you an account, Oct. 24th, of my taking Joseph Bradish and Wetherly, and writ that I hoped in a little time to be able to send News of my taking James Gillam, the Pyrate that killed Capt. Edgecomb, commander of the *Mocha Frigate* for the East India Co., and that with his own hand, while the captain was asleep. Gillam is supposed to be the man that encouraged the Ship's Company to turn pyrates, and the ship has ever since been robbing in the Red Sea and Seas of India. If I may believe the report of men lately come from Madagascar, she has taken above 2,000,000 pounds sterling.

"I have been so lucky as to take James Gillam, and he is now in irons in the gaol of this town. And at the same time we seized on Francis Dole, in whose house he was harboured, who proved to be one of Hore's crew. My taking of Gillam was so very accidental one would believe there was a strange fatality in the man's stars. On Saturday, 11th inst., late in the evening, I had a letter from Col. Sanford, Judge of the Admiralty Court in Rhode Island, giving me an account that Gillam had been there, but was come towards Boston a fortnight before, in order to ship himself for some of the Islands, Jamaica or Barbadoes.

SPOOKY TREASURE TROVES

"I was in despair of finding the man. However, I sent for an honest Constable I had made use of in apprehending Kidd and his men, and sent him with Col. Sanford's messenger to search all the Inns in town and at the first Inn they found the mare on which Gillam had rode into town, tied up in the yard. The people of the Inn reported that the man who brought her hither had alighted off her about a quarter of an hour before, and went away without saying anything.

"I gave orders to the master of the Inn that if anybody came to look after the mare, he should be sure to seize him, but nobody came for her. Next morning I summoned a Council, and we published a Proclamation, wherein I promised a reward of 200 Pieces of Eight for the seizing and securing of Gillam, whereupon there was the strictest search made all that day and the next that was ever made in this part of the world. But we would have missed had I not been informed of one Capt. Knott as an old Pyrate and therefore likely to know where Gillam was conceal'd. I sent for Knott and examined him, promising if he would make an ingenious Confession I would not molest him.

"He seemed much disturbed but would not confess anything to purpose. I then sent for his wife and examined her on oath apart from her husband, and she confessed that one who went by the name of James Kelly had lodged several nights in her house, but for some nights past he lodged, as she believed, in Charlestown, cross the River. I knew that he (Gillam) went by the name of Kelly. Then I examined Captain Knott again, telling him his wife had been more free and ingenious than him, which made him believe she had told all. And then he told me of Francis Dole in Charlestown, and that he believed that Gillam would be found there.

"I sent half a dozen men immediately, and Knott with 'em. They beset the House and searched it, but found not the man. Two of the men went through a field behind Dole's house and ... met a man in the dark whom they seized at all adventure, and it happened as oddly as luckily to be Gillam. He had been treating two young women some few miles off in the Country, and was returning at night to his landlord Dole's house.

"I examined him but he denied everything, even that he came with Kidd from Madagascar, or even saw him in his life; but Capt. Davis who came thence with Kidd's men is positive he is the man and that he went by his true name Gillam all the while he was on the voyage with 'em. And Mr. Campbell, Postmaster of this town, whom I sent to treat with Kidd, offers to swear this is the man he saw on board Kidd's sloop under the name of Gillam. He is the most impudent, hardened Villain I ever saw....

"In searching Captain Knott's house a small trunk was found with some remnants of East India Goods and a letter from Kidd's Wife to Capt. Thomas Paine, an old pyrate living on Canonicut Island in Rhode Island Government. He made an affidavit to me when I was in Rhode Island that he had received nothing from Kidd's sloop, when she lay at anchor there, yet by Knott's deposition, he was sent with Mrs. Kidd's letter to Paine for 24 ounces of Gold, which Kidd accordingly brought, and Mrs. Kidd's injunction to Paine to keep all the rest that was left with him till further notice was a plain indication that there was a good deal of treasure still left behind in Paine's Custody.

"Therefore I posted away a messenger to Gov. Cranston and Col. Sanford to make a strict search of Paine's house before he could have notice. It seems nothing was then found, but Paine has since produced 18 ounces and odd weight of Gold, as appears by Gov. Cranston's letter, Nov. 25, and pretends 'twas bestowed on him by Kidd, hoping that may pass as a salve for the oath he has made. I think it is plain he foreswore himself. I am of opinion he has a great deal more of Kidd's goods still in his hands, but he is out of my Power and being in that Government I cannot compel him to deliver up the rest...."

That "Edward Davis, Mariner," who came home with Kidd and who made the statement already quoted concerning Gillam's chest, found himself in trouble with the others of that crew, and the tireless Bellomont refers to him in this fashion:

"When Capt Kidd was committed to Gaol, there was also a Pyrate committed who goes by the name of Captain Davis, that came passenger with Kidd from Madagascar. I suppose him to be that Captain Davis that Dampier and Wafer speak of, in their printed relations of Voyages, for an extraordinary stout man; but let him be as stout as he will, here he is a prisoner, and shall be forthcoming upon the order I receive from England concerning Kidd and his men.

"When I was at Rhode Island there was one Palmer, a Pyrate, that was out upon Bail, for they cannot be persuaded there to keep a Pyrate in Gaol, they love 'em too well. He went out with Kidd from London and forsook him at Madagascar to go on board the *Mocha Frigate*, where he was a considerable time, committing several Robberies with the rest of the Pyrates in that Ship, and was brought home by Shelly of New York.

"I asked Gov. Cranston how he could answer taking bail for him, when he had received so strict Orders from Mr. Secretary Vernon to seize and secure Kidd and his associates with their effects. I desired Col. Sanford to examine Palmer on oath. I enclose his Examination where your Lordships may please to observe that he accuses Kidd of murdering his Gunner, which I never heard before."

SPOOKY TREASURE TROVES

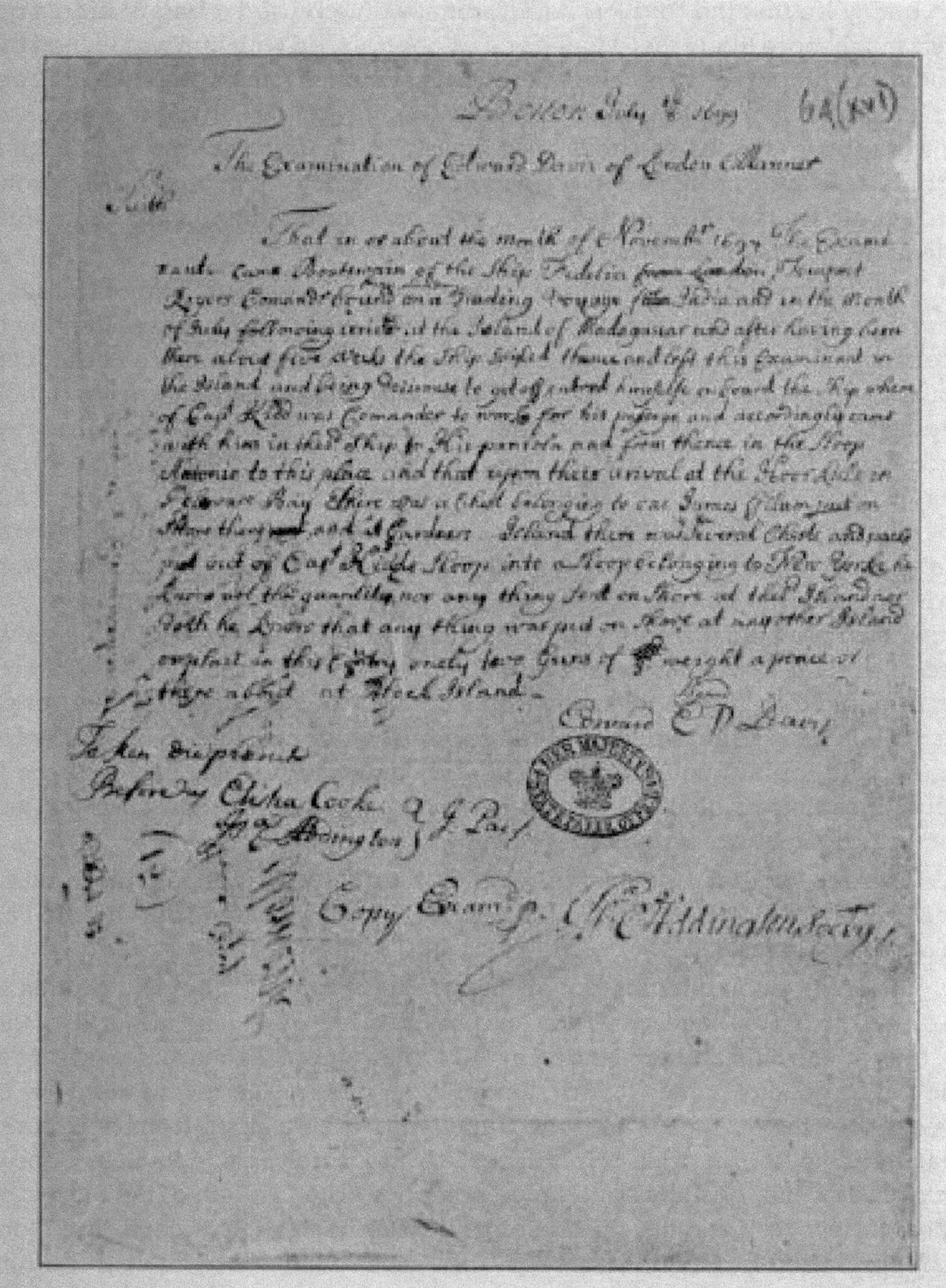

Statement of Edward Davis, who sailed home with Kidd, concerning the landing of the treasure and goods.

SPOOKY TREASURE TROVES

It may be that the "old Pyrate," Thomas Paine buried a bag of Kidd's gold but it is much more likely that whatever had been stored with him was turned over to that astute helpmeet, Mrs. William Kidd, for whom it has been left in his keeping. As for that "most impudent, hardened Villain," James Gillam, it is unreasonable to suppose that his sea chest was buried by the friends who took it off his hands in Delaware Bay. Indeed, there was no motive for putting booty underground when it could be readily disposed of in the open market. Bellomont complained in one of his letters of this same eventful summer:

"There are about thirty Pyrates come lately into the East end of Nassau Island and have a great deal of Money with them, but so cherished are they by the Inhabitants that not a man among them is taken up. Several of them I hear, came with Shelly from Madagascar. Mr. Hackshaw, one of the Merchants in London that plotted against me, is one of the owners of Shelley's Sloop, and Mr. De Lancey, a Frenchman at New York is another. I hear that Capt. Kidd dropped some Pyrates in that Island (Madagascar). Till there be a good Judge or two, and an honest, active Attorney General to prosecute for the King, all my Labour to suppress Pyracy will signify even just nothing. When Fred Phillip's ship and the other two come from Madagascar, which are expected every day, New York will abound with Gold. 'Tis the most beneficial Trade, that to Madagascar with the Pyrates, that ever was heard of, and I believe there's more got that way than by turning Pirates and robbing. I am told this Shelley sold rum, which cost but 2 s. per Gallon in New York for 50 s. at Madagascar, and a pipe of Madeira wine, which cost him 19 pounds at New York, he sold for 300 pounds. Strong liquors and gun powder and ball are the commodities that go off there to best Advantage, and those four ships last summer carried thither great quantities of things."

There is another authentic glimpse of Kidd and his men and his spoils, as viewed by Colonel Robert Quarry,[15] Judge of the Admiralty Court for the Province of Pennsylvania.

"There is arrived in this Government," he reported, "about 60 pirates in a ship directly from Madagascar. They are part of Kidd's gang, and about 20 of them have quitted the Ship and are landed in this Government. About sixteen more are landed at Cape May in the Government of West Jersey. The rest of them are still on board the ship at Anchor near the Cape waiting for a sloop from New York to unload her. She is a very rich Ship. All her loading is rich East India Bale Goods to a very great value, besides abundance of money. The Captain of the Ship is one Shelley of New York and the ship belongs to Merchants of that place. The Goods are all purchased from the Pirates at Madagascar which pernicious trade gives encouragement to the Pirates to continue in those parts, having a Market for all the Goods they plunder and rob in the Red Sea and several other parts of East India."

SPOOKY TREASURE TROVES

Colonel Quarry caught two of these pirates and lodged them in jail at Burlington, New Jersey, and later tucked away two others in Philadelphia jail. From the former two thousand pieces of eight were taken, a neat little fortune to show that piracy was a paying business. A few days later Colonel Quarry got wind of no other than Kidd himself and would have caught him ahead of Bellomont had he been properly supported. He protested indignantly:

"Since my writing the enclosed I have by the assistance of Col. Bass, Governor of the Jerseys, apprehended four more of the Pirates at Cape May and might have with ease secured all the rest of them and the Ship too, had this Government (Pennsylvania) given me the least aid or assistance. But they would not so much as issue a Proclamation, but on the contrary the people have entertained the Pirates, convey'd them from place to place, furnished them with provisions and liquors, and given them intelligence, and sheltered them from justice. And now the greater part of them are conveyed away in boats to Rhode Island. All the persons I have employed in searching for and apprehending these Pirates are abused and affronted and called Enemies of the Country for disturbing and hindering honest men (as they are pleased to call the Pirates) from bringing their money and settling amongst them....

"Since my writing this, Capt. Kidd is come in this (Delaware) Bay. He hath been here about ten days. He sends his boat ashore to the Hore Kills where he is supplied with what he wants and the people frequently go on board him. He is in a Sloop with about forty men with a Vast Treasure, I hope the express which I sent to his Excellency Governor Nicholson will be in time enough to send the man-of-war to come up with Kidd....

"The Pirates that I brought to this Government have the liberty to confine themselves to a tavern, which is what I expected. The six other Pirates that are in Burlington are at liberty, for the Quakers there will not suffer the Government to send them to Gaol. Thus his Majesty may expect to be obeyed in all places where the Government is in Quakers' hands...."

[1] Mr. F. L. Gay of Boston very kindly gave the author the use of his valuable collection of documentary material concerning Captain Kidd, some of which is contained in this chapter. In addition, the author consulted many of the original documents among the state papers in the Public Record Office, London.

[2] Damaged.

[3] Clarke managed to clear himself and this threat was not carried out.

[4] Ms. torn.

[5] Genuine.

[6] Ms. torn.

[7] Ms. torn.

[8] Prize, or plunder.

SPOOKY TREASURE TROVES

[9] Titus Gates, the notorious informer, who revealed an alleged "Papist plot" to massacre the English Protestants in the reign of Charles II. He was later denounced, pilloried, and publicly flogged within an inch of his life.

[10] Ms. torn.

[11] Lieutenant-governor at New York.

[12] Ms. torn.

[13] Ms. torn.

[14] Ms. torn.

[15] Colonel Robert Quarry cut a rather odd figure as a prosecutor of pirates in New Jersey and Pennsylvania. He had been secretary to the Governor of Carolina and assumed that office without authority from the proprietors, at the death of Sir Richard Kyle who was appointed in 1684.

"A few months before it had been recommended that 'as the Governor will not in all probability always reside in Charles Town, which is so near the sea as to be in danger from a sudden invasion of Pirates,' Governor Kyle should commissionate a particular Governor for Charles Town who may act in his absence." (South Carolina Historical Society Collections.)

Governor Kyle suggested as a suitable person for this office his secretary, Robert Quarry, and "probably this recommendation made Quarry feel justified in assuming control when Kyle died. So flagrant was Quarry's encouragement of pirates, and his cupidity so notorious that he was removed from office after two months. Later "he went north and was appointed Admiralty Judge for New York and Pennsylvania." ("The Carolina Pirates," by S. C. Hughson, Johns Hopkins University Studies.)

SPOOKY TREASURE TROVES

CHAPTER IV
CAPTAIN KIDD, HIS TRIAL, AND DEATH

As the under dog in a situation where the most powerful influences of England conspired to blacken his name and take his life, Captain William Kidd, even at this late day, deserves to be heard in his own defense. That he was unfairly tried and condemned is admitted by various historians, who, nevertheless, have twisted or overlooked the facts, as if Kidd were, in sooth, a legendary character. This blundering, careless treatment is the more surprising because Kidd was made a political issue of such importance as to threaten the overthrow of a Ministry and the Parliamentary censure of the King himself. At the height of the bitter hostility against Somers, the Whig Lord Chancellor of William III, the Kidd affair presented itself as a ready weapon for the use of his political foes.

"About the other patrons of Kidd the chiefs of the opposition cared little," says Macauley.[1] "Bellomont was far removed from the political scene. Romney could not, and Shrewsbury would not play a first part. Orford had resigned his employments. But Somers still held the Great Seal, still presided in the House of Lords, still had constant access to the closet. The retreat of his friends had left him the sole and undisputed head of that party which had, in the late Parliament, been a majority, and which was in the present Parliament outnumbered indeed, disorganized and threatened, but still numerous and respectable. His placid courage rose higher and higher to meet the dangers which threatened him.

"In their eagerness to displace and destroy him, they overreached themselves. Had they been content to accuse him of lending his countenance, with a rashness unbecoming his high place, to an ill-concerted scheme, that large part of mankind which judges of a plan simply by the event would probably have thought the accusation well founded. But the malice which they bore to him was not to be so satisfied. They affected to believe that he had from the first been aware of Kidd's character and designs. The Great Seal had been employed to sanction a piratical expedition. The head of the law had laid down a thousand

SPOOKY TREASURE TROVES

pounds in the hopes of receiving tens of thousands when his accomplices should return laden with the spoils of ruined merchants. It was fortunate for the Chancellor that the calumnies of which he was object were too atrocious to be mischievous.

"And now the time had come at which the hoarded ill-humor of six months was at liberty to explode. On the sixteenth of November the House met.... There were loud complaints that the events of the preceding session had been misrepresented to the public, that emissaries of the Court, in every part of the kingdom, declaimed against the absurd jealousies or still more absurd parsimony which had refused to his Majesty the means of keeping up such an army as might secure the country against invasion. Angry resolutions were passed, declaring it to be the opinion of the House that the best way to establish entire confidence between the King and the Estates would be to put a brand on those evil advisers who had dared to breathe in the royal ear calumnies against a faithful Parliament.

"An address founded on these resolutions was voted; many thought that a violent rupture was inevitable. But William returned an answer so prudent and gentle that malice itself could not prolong the dispute. By this time, indeed, a new dispute had begun. The address had scarcely been moved when the House called for copies of the papers relating to Kidd's expedition. Somers, conscious of his innocence, knew that it was wise as well as right and resolved that there should be no concealment.

"Howe raved like a maniac. 'What is to become of the country, plundered by land, plundered by sea? Our rulers have laid hold of our lands, our woods, our mines, our money. And all this is not enough. We cannot send a cargo to the farthest ends of the earth, but they must send a gang of thieves after it.' Harley and Seymour tried to carry a vote of censure without giving the House time to read the papers. But the general feeling was strongly for a short delay. At length on the sixth of December, the subject was considered in a committee of the whole House. Shower undertook to prove that the letters patent to which Somers had put the Great Seal were illegal. Cowper replied to him with immense applause, and seems to have completely refuted him.

"At length, after a debate which lasted from mid-day till nine at night, and in which all the leading members took part, the committee divided on the question that the letters patent were dishonorable to the King, inconsistent with the laws of nations, contrary to the statutes of the realm, and destructive of property and trade. The Chancellor's enemies had felt confident of victory, and made the resolution so strong in order that it might be impossible for him to retain the Great Seal. They soon found that it would have been wise to propose a gentler censure. Great numbers of their adherents, convinced by Cowper's arguments, or unwilling to put a cruel stigma on a man of whose genius and accomplishments the nation was proud, stole away before the doors were closed. To the general astonishment, there were only one hundred and thirty-three Ayes to one hundred and eighty-nine Noes. That the city of London did not consider Somers as the destroyer, and his enemies as the protectors of trade, was proved on the following morning by the most unequivocal of signs. As soon as the news of the triumph reached the Royal Exchange, the price of stocks went up."

There is a very rare pamphlet which illuminates the matter in much more detail. It was written and published as a defense of Bellomont and his partners and the very length, elaboration, and heat its argument shows how furiously the political pot was boiling while Kidd was imprisoned in London awaiting his trial. This *ex parte* production is entitled "A Full Account of the Actions of the Late Famous Pyrate, Captain Kidd, With the Proceedings against Him and a Vindication of the Right Honourable Richard, Earl of Bellomont, Lord Caloony, late Governor of New England, and other Honourable Persons from the Unjust Reflection; Cast upon Them. By a Person of Quality."[2]

It is herein recorded that the arguments to support the question moved in Parliament were:

"1—That by law the King could not grant the Goods of Pirates, at least, not before conviction.

"2—That the Grant was extravagant, for all Goods of Pirates, taken with or by any persons in any part of the world, were granted away.

"3—Not only the Goods of the Pirates, but all Goods taken with them were granted, which was illegal, because tho' the Goods were taken by Pirates, the rightful Owners have still a Title to them, Piracy working no change of Property.

"5—By this Grant a great Hardship was put upon the Merchants whose Goods might be taken with the Pirates, for they had nowhere to go for Justice. They could not hope for it in the Chancery, the Lord Chancellor being interested; nor at the Board of Admiralty where the Earl of Orford presided; nor from the King, all access to him being by the Duke of Shrewsbury; nor in the Plantations where the Earl of Bellomont was. So the only Judge who the Pirates were, and what goods were theirs, was Captain Kidd himself."

Whatsoever may have been wrong with his contract or his commissions, and Parliament sustained them by vote as already mentioned, Captain Kidd cannot be held blameworthy on this score. And it is absurd to call him a premeditated pirate who sailed from Plymouth with evil purpose in his heart. His credentials and endorsements, his record as a shipmaster, and his repute at home, cannot be set aside. They speak for themselves. Nor is it possible to reconcile the character of the man, as he was known by his deeds up to that time, with the charges laid against him.

It is worth noting that the complaints made against his conduct in the waters

SPOOKY TREASURE TROVES

of the Far East came from the East India Company which denounced and proclaimed him as a pirate with a price on his head. It was a case of the pot calling the kettle black. Although the House of Commons had decided five years before that the old Company should no longer have a monopoly of English trade in Asiatic seas, the merchants of London or Bristol dared not fit out ventures to voyage beyond the Cape of Good Hope, and found it necessary to send their goods in the ships that flew the flag of India House. The private trader still ran grave of being treated as a smuggler, if not as a pirate. "He might, indeed, if he was wronged, apply for redress to the tribunals of his country. But years must elapse before his cause could be heard; his witnesses must be conveyed over fifteen thousand miles of sea; and in the meantime he was a ruined man."[3]

This powerful corporation which ruled the Eastern seas as it pleased, confiscating the ships and goods of private traders, accused Kidd of seizing two ships with their cargoes which belonged to the Great Mogul, and of several petty depredations hardly to be classed as piracy. The case against him was built up around the two vessels known as the *November* and the *Quedah Merchant*. His defense was that on board these prizes he had found French papers, or safe conduct passes made out in the name of the King of France and issued by the French East India Company. He therefore took the ships as lawful commerce of the enemy.

The crews of such trading craft as these comprised men of many nations, Arabs, Lascars, Portuguese, French, Dutch, English, Armenian, and Heaven knows what else. The nationality of the skipper, the mate, the supercargo, or the foremast hands had nothing to do with the ownership of the vessel, or the flag under which she was registered, or chartered. The papers found in her cabin determined whether or not she should be viewed as a prize of war, or permitted to go on her way. In order to protect the ship as far as possible, it was not unusual for the master to obtain two sets of papers, to be used as occasion might require, and it is easily possible that the *Quedah Merchant*, trading with the East India Company, may have taken out French papers, in order to deceive any French privateer or cruiser that might be encountered. Nor did the agents of the East India Company see anything wrong in resorting to such subterfuges.

The corner stone of Kidd's defense and justification was these two French passes, which precious documents he had brought home with him, and it was admitted even by his enemies that the production of them as evidence would go far to clear him of the charges of piracy. That they were in his possession when he landed in New England and that Bellomont sent them to the Lords of Plantations in London is stated in a letter quoted in the preceding chapter. The documents then disappeared, their very existence was denied, and Kidd was called a liar to his face, and his memory damned by historians writing later, for trying to save his neck by means of evidence which he was powerless to exhibit.

SPOOKY TREASURE TROVES

It would appear that these papers were not produced in court because it had been determined that Kidd should be found guilty as a necessary scapegoat. But he told the truth about the French passes, and after remaining among the state papers for more than two centuries, the original of one of them, that found by him aboard the *Quedah Merchant*, was recently discovered in the Public Record Office by the author of this book, and it is herewith photographed in *fac simile*. Its purport has been translated as follows:

FROM THE KING.

WE, FRANCOIS MARTIN ESQUIRE, COUNCILLOR OF THE ROYAL DIRECTOR, Minister of Commerce for the Royal Company of France in the Kingdom of Bengal, the Coast of Coramandel, and other (dependencies). To all those who will see these presents, Greetings:

The following, *Coja Quanesse, Coja Jacob, Armenian; Nacodas*, of the ship *Cara Merchant*, which the Armenian merchant Agapiris Kalender has freighted in Surate from Cohergy ... having declared to us that before their departure from Surate they had taken a passport from the Company which they have presented to us to be dated from the first of January, 1697, signed *Martin* and subscribed *de Grangemont*; that they feared to be molested during the voyage which they had to make from this port to Surate, and alleging that the aforementioned passport is no longer valid, and that for this reason they begged of us urgently to have another sent to them;—For these reasons we recommend and enjoin upon all those under the authority of the Company; we beg the Chiefs of Squadrons and Commanders of Vessels of His Majesty: and we request all the friends and allies of the Crown in nowise to retard the voyage and to render all possible aid and comfort, promising on a similar occasion to do likewise. In testimony of which we have signed these presents, and caused them to be countersigned by the Secretary of the Company, and the seal of his arms placed thereon.

MARTIN.

(Dated Jan. 16, 1698.)

SPOOKY TREASURE TROVES

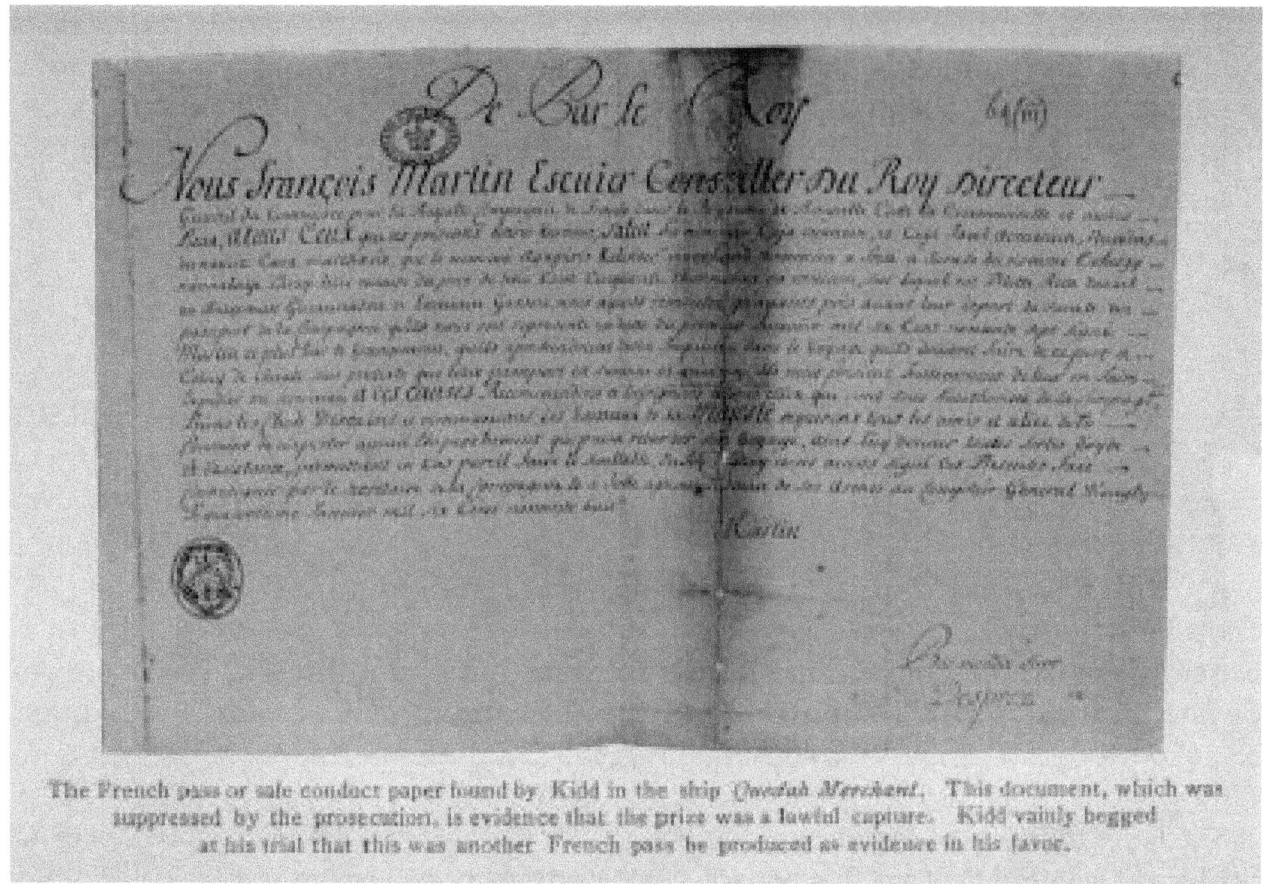

The French pass or safe conduct paper found by Kidd in the ship *Quedah Merchant*. This document, which was suppressed by the prosecution, is evidence that the prize was a lawful capture. Kidd vainly begged at his trial that this was another French pass be produced as evidence in his favor.

It is reasonable to assume that the *Cara Merchant* of the passport, is intended to designate the ship in which the document was found by Kidd. In various reports of the episode, the name of the vessel was spelled *Quidah, Quedah, Queda* and *Quedagh*. The word is taken from the name of a small native state of the Malay Peninsula, and even to-day it is set down in various ways, as *Quedah, Kedda*, or *Kedah*. Other circumstances confirm this supposition and go far to prove that the ship was a lawful prize for an English privateer. During the period between the Revolution and the War of 1812, England confiscated many American merchant vessels in the West Indies under pretexts not a whit more convincing than Kidd's excuse for snapping up the *Quedah Merchant*.

What Kidd himself had to say about this affair is told in his narrative of the voyage as he related it during his preliminary examination while under arrest in Boston. It runs as follows:

SPOOKY TREASURE TROVES

A Narrative of the Voyage of Capt. William Kidd, Commander of the *Adventure Galley*, from London to the East Indies.

That the Journal of the said Capt. Kidd being violently taken from him in the Port of St. Maries in Madagascar; and his life many times being threatened to be taken away from him by 97 of his men that deserted him there, he cannot give that exact Account he otherwise would have done, but as far as his memory will serve, it is as follows, Vizt:

That the said *Adventure Galley* was launched in Castles Yard at Deptford about the 4th. day of December, 1695, and about the latter end of February the said Galley came to ye buoy in the Nore, and about the first day of March following, his men were pressed from him for the Fleet which caused him to stay there about 19 days, and then sailed for the Downs and arrived there about the 8th or 10th day of April 1696, and sailed thence to Plymouth and on the 23rd. day of the said month of April he sailed from Plymouth on his intended Voyage. And some time in the month of May met with a small French Vessel with Salt and Fishing tackle on board, bound for Newfoundland, which he took and made prize of and carried the same into New York about the 4th day of July where she was condemned as lawful prize, and the produce whereof purchased Provisions for the said Galley for her further intended Voyage.

That about the 6th. day of September, 1696, the said Capt. Kidd sailed for the Madeiras in company with one Joyner, Master of a Brigantine belonging to Bermuda, and arrived there about the 8th. day of October following, and thence to Bonavista where they arrived about the 19th. of the said month and took in some Salt and stay'd three or four days and sailed thence to St. Jago and arrived there the 24th, of the said month, where he took in some water and stay'd about 8 or 9 days, and thence sailed for the Cape of Good Hope and in the Latitude of 32, on the 12th day of December, 1696, met with four English men of war whereof Capt. Warren was Commodore and sailed a week in their company, and then parted and sailed to Telere, a port in the Island of Madagascar.

And being there about the 29th day of January, there came in a Sloop belonging to Barbadoes loaded with Rum, Sugar, Powder, and Shott, one French, Master, and Mr. Hatton and Mr. John Batt, merchants, and the said Hatton came on board the said *Galley* and was suddenly taken ill and died in the Cabbin. And about the latter end of February sailed for the Island of Johanna, and the said Sloop keeping company, and arrived thereabout the 18th day of March, where he found four East India merchantmen, outward bound, and watered there all together and stay'd about four days, and from thence about the 22nd day of March sailed for Mehila, an Island ten Leagues distant from Johanna, where he arrived the next morning, and there careened the said *Galley, and about fifty men died there in a*

SPOOKY TREASURE TROVES

week's time.[4]

And about the 25th day of April, 1697, set sail for the coast of India, and came upon the coast of Malabar, in the beginning of the month of September, and went into Carawar upon that coast about the middle of the same month, and watered there. The Gentlemen of the English Factory gave the Narrator an account that the Portugese were fitting out two men of war to take him, and advised him to set out to sea, and to take care of himself from them, and immediately he set sail therefrom about the 22nd of the said month of September. And the next morning, about break of day, saw the said two men-of-war standing for the said *Galley*, and they spoke with him and asked him whence he was, who replied from London, and they returned answer from Goa, and so parted, wishing each other a good Voyage.

And making still along the coast, the Commodore of the said men-of-war kept dogging the said *Galley* at night, waiting an opportunity to board the same, and in the morning without speaking a word fired six great guns at the *Galley*, some whereof went through her and wounded four of his men. And therefore he fired upon him again, and the fight continued all day, and the Narrator had eleven men wounded. The other Portugese men of war lay some distance off, and could not come up with the *Galley*, being calm, else would have likewise assaulted the same. The said fight was sharp and the said Portugese left the said Galley with such satisfaction that the Narrator believes no Portugese will ever attack the King's Colours again, in that part of the World especially.

Afterwards continued upon the said coast till the beginning of the month of November 1697 cruising upon the Cape of Cameroon for Pyrates that frequent that coast. Then he met with Capt. How in the *Loyal Captain*, a Dutch Ship belonging to Madras, bound to Surat whom he examined and finding his pass good, designed freely to let her pass about her affairs. But having two Dutchmen on board, they told the Narrator's men that they had divers Greeks and Armenians on board who had divers precious Stones and other rich goods, which caused his men to be very mutinous, and they got up their Arms, and swore they would take the Ship. The Narrator told them the small arms belonged to the *Galley*, and that he was not come to take any Englishmen or lawful Traders, and that if they attempted any such thing, they should never come on board the *Galley* again, nor have the boat or small arms, for he had no Commission to take any but the King's Enemies and Pyrates and that he would attack them with the *Galley* and drive them into Bombay, (the other Vessel being a Merchantman, and having no guns, they might easily have done it with a few hands).

With all the arguments and menaces he could use, he could scarce restrain them from their unlawful design, but at last prevail'd and with much ado got him clear and let him go about his business. All of which Captain How will attest if

SPOOKY TREASURE TROVES

living.

And about the 18th. or 19th day of the said month of November met with a Moors' Ship of about 200 Tons coming from Surat, bound to the Coast of Malabar, loaded with two horses, Sugar and Cotton, having about 40 Moors on board with a Dutch Pylot, Boatswain, and Gunner, which said Ship the Narrator hailed, and commanded (the Master) on board and with him came 8 or 9 Moors and the said three Dutchmen, who declared it was a Moors'

{109}

ship, and he (the Narrator) demanding their Pass from Surat which they showed and the same was a French Pass which he believed was showed by mistake, for the Pylot swore by Sacrament she was a Prize and staid on board the *Galley* and would not return again on board the Moors' Ship but went in the *Galley* to the port of St. Maries.

And that about the first day of February following, upon the same coast, under French Colours with a designe to decoy, met a Bengali merchantman[5] belonging to Surat, of the burthen of 4 or 500 tons, 10 guns, and he commanded the master on board, and a Frenchman, Inhabitant of Surat and belonging to the French Factory there and Gunner of said ship, came on board as Master, and when he came on board the Narrator caused the English Colours to be hoysted, and the said Master was surprised, and said "You are all English," and asked which was the Captain, whom when he (the Frenchman) saw, he said, "Here is a good prize" and delivered him the French pass.

And that with the said two Prizes, he (the Narrator) sailed for the Port of St. Maries in Madagascar, and sailing thither the *Galley* was so leaky that they feared she would have sunk every hour, and it required eight men every two glasses to keep her free, and they were forced to woold her round with Cables to keep her together, and with much ado carried her into port.... And about the 6th day of May, the lesser Prize was haled into the careening island or key (the other not having arrived), and ransacked and sunk by the mutinous men who threatened the Narrator and the men that would not join with them, to burn and sink the other Ship that they might not go home and tell the news.

And that when he arrived in the said port, there was a Pyrate Ship, called the *Moca Frigat*, at an Anchor, Robert Culliford, Commander thereof, who with his men left the same and ran into the woods, and the Narrator proposed to his men to take the same, having sufficient power and authority so to do, but the mutinous crew told him if he offered the same they would rather fire two guns into him than one into the other; and thereupon 97 deserted and went into the *Moca Frigat*, and sent into the woods for the said Pyrates and brought the said Culliford and his men on board again. And all the time she (the *Moca Frigat*) staid in the said Port, which was for the space of 4 or 5 days, the said deserters, sometimes in great numbers, came on board the *Adventure Galley* and her prize and carried away the great gun, powder, shot, arms, sails, anchors, etc., and what they pleased, and threatened several times to murder the Narrator (as he was informed and advised to take care of himself), which they designed in the night to effect, but was prevented by his locking himself in his Cabbin and securing himself with barricading the same with bales of Goods, and having about forty Small arms besides Pistols ready charged, kept them out. Their wickedness was so great that after they had plundered and ransacked sufficiently, they went four miles off to one Edward Welche's house where his (the Narrator's) chest was lodged, and broke it open and took out 10 ounces of gold, forty pounds of plate, 370 pieces of eight, the Narrator's Journal, and a great many papers that belonged to him, and to the people of New Yorke that fitted him out.

That about the 15th day of June the *Moca Frigate* went away, being manned with about 130 men and forty guns, bound out to take all Nations. Then it was that the Narrator was left with only about 13 men, so that the Moors he had to pump and keep the *Adventure Galley* above water being carried away, she sank in the Harbour, and the Narrator with the said Thirteen men went on board of the *Adventure's* Prize where he was forced to stay five months for a fair wind. In the meantime some Passengers presented themselves that were bound for these parts, which he took on board to help to bring the said *Adventure's* Prize[6] home.

That about the beginning of April 1699, the Narrator arrived at Anguilla in the West Indies and sent his boat on shore where his men heard the News that he and his People were proclaimed Pirates, which put them into such a Consternation that they sought all opportunities to run the Ship on shore upon some reefs or shoal, fearing the Narrator should carry them into some English port.

From Anguilla, they came to St. Thomas where his brother-in-law, Samuel Bradley, was put on shore, being sick, and five more went away and deserted him. There he heard the same News, that the Narrator and his Company were proclaimed Pirates, which incensed the people more and more. From St. Thomas set sail for Mona, an Island between Hispaniola and Porto Rico, where they met with a Sloop called the *St. Anthony*, bound for Antigua from Curacoa, Mr. Henry Bolton, Merchant, and Samuel Wood, Master. The men on board then swore they would bring the ship no farther. The Narrator then sent the said Sloop, *St. Anthony*, to Curacoa for canvas to make sails for the Prize, she being not able to proceed, and she returned in 10 days, and after the canvas came he could not persuade the men to carry her for New England.

Six of the men went and carried their Chests and things on board of two Dutch Sloops bound for Curacoa, and would not so much as heel the Vessel or do anything. The remainder of the men, not being able to bring the *Adventure* Prize to Boston, the Narrator secured her in a good safe harbour in some part of

SPOOKY TREASURE TROVES

Hispaniola and left her in the possession of M. Henry Bolton of Antigua, Merchant, and the Master, and three of the old men, and 15 or 16 of the men that belonged to the said sloop, *St. Anthony*, and a Brigantine belonging to one Burt of Curacoa.

That the Narrator bought the said Sloop, *St. Anthony*, of Mr. Bolton, for the Owners' account, after he had given directions to the said Bolton to be careful of the Ship and lading and persuaded him to stay three months till he returned. And he then made the best of his way for New York where he heard the Earl of Bellomont was, who was principally concerned in the *Adventure Galley*, and hearing his Lordship was at Boston, came thither and has now been 45 days from the said Ship. Further, the Narrator saith that the said ship was left at St. Katharine on the southeast part of Hispaniola, about three Leagues to leeward of the westerly end of Savano. Whilst he lay at Hispaniola he traded with Mr. Henry Bolton of Antigua and Mr. William Burt of Curacoa, Merchants, to the value of Eleven Thousand Two Hundred Pieces of Eight, whereof he received the Sloop *Antonio* at 3000 Ps. of eight, and Four Thousand Two Hundred Ps. of Eight in Bills of Lading drawn by Bolton and Burt upon Messers. Gabriel and Lemont, Merchants, in Curacoa, made payable to Mr. Burt who went himself to Curacoa, and the value of Four Thousand Pieces of Eight more in dust and bar gold. Which gold, with some more traded for at Madagascar, being Fifty pounds weight or upwards in quantity, the Narrator left in custody of Mr. Gardiner of Gardiner's Island, near the eastern end of Long Island, fearing to bring it about by sea.

It is made up in a bagg put into a little box, lockt and nailed, corded about and sealed. The Narrator saith he took no receipt for it of Mr. Gardiner. The gold that was seized at Mr. Campbell's, the Narrator traded for at Madagascar, with what came out of the *Galley*. He saith that he carried in the *Adventure Galley* from New York 154 men, seventy whereof came out of England with him.

Some of his Sloop's company put two bails of Goods on store at Gardiner's Island, being their own property. The Narrator delivered a chest of Goods, Vizt; Muslins, Latches, Romals, and flowered silk unto Mr. Gardiner of Gardiner's Island to be kept there for him. *He put no goods on shore anywhere else*. Several of his company landed their Chests and other goods at several places.

Further saith he delivered a small bail of coarse callicoes unto a Sloopman of Rhode Island that he had employed there. The Gold seized at Mr. Campbell's, the Narrator intended for presents to some that he expected to do him kindness.

Some of his company put their Chests and bails on board a New York Sloop lying at Gardiner's Island.

WM. KIDD.

Presented and taken *die prædict* before his Exc'y and Council Addington, Sec'y.

SPOOKY TREASURE TROVES

More than a year after Kidd had been carried to England with twelve of his crew, he was arraigned for trial at the Old Bailey. Meantime Lord Bellomont had died in Boston. Trials for piracy were common enough, but this accused shipmaster was confronted by such an array of titled big-wigs and court officials as would have been sufficient to try the Lord Chancellor himself. For the government, the Lord Chief Baron, Sir Edward Ward, presided, and with him sat Sir Henry Hatsell, Baron of the Exchequer; Sir Salathiel Lovell, the Recorder of London; Sir John Turton and Sir Henry Gould, Justices of the King's Bench, and Sir John Powell, a Justice of the Common Pleas. As counsel for the prosecution, there was the Solicitor General, Dr. Oxenden; Mr. Knapp, Mr. Coniers, and Mr. Campbell.

For Captain William Kidd, there was no one. By the law of England at that time, a prisoner tried on a criminal charge could employ no counsel and was permitted to have no legal advice, except only when a point of law was directly involved. Kidd had been denied all chance to muster witnesses or assemble documents, and, at that, the court was so fearful of failing to prove the charges of piracy that it was decided to try him first for killing his gunner, William Moore, and convicting him of murder. He would be as conveniently dead if hanged for the one crime as for the other.

Now, it is not impossible that Kidd had clean forgotten that trifling episode of William Moore. For a commander to knock down a seaman guilty of disrespect or disobedience was as commonplace as eating. The offender was lucky if he got off no worse. Discipline in the naval and merchant services was barbarously severe. Sailors died of flogging or keelhauling, or of being triced up by the thumbs for the most trifling misdemeanors. As for Moore, he was a mutineer, and an insolent rogue besides, who had stirred up trouble in the crew, and nothing would have been said to any other skipper than Kidd for shooting him or running him through. However, let the testimony tell its own story.

After the Grand Jury had returned the bill of indictment for murder, the Clerk of Arraignment said:

"William Kidd, hold up thy hand."

With a pluck and persistence which must have had a certain pathetic dignity, Kidd began to object.

"May it please your Lordship, I desire you to permit me to have counsel."

The Recorder. "What would you have counsel for?"

Kidd. "My Lord, I have some matters of law relating to the indictment, and I desire I may have counsel to speak to it."

Dr. Oxenden. "What matter of law can you have?"

Clerk of Arraignment. "How does he know what he is charged with? I have not told him."

The Recorder. "You must let the Court know what these matters of law are before you can have counsel assigned you."

Kidd. "They be matters of law, my Lord."

The Recorder. "Mr. Kidd, do you know what you mean by matters of law?"

Kidd. "I know what I mean. I desire to put off my trial as long as I can, till I can get my evidence ready."

The Recorder: "Mr. Kidd, you had best mention the matter of law you would insist on."

Dr. Oxenden. "It cannot be matter of law to put off your trial, but matter of fact."

Kidd. "I desire your Lordship's favor. I desire that Dr. Oldish and Mr. Lemmon here be heard as to my case (indicating lawyers present in court)."

Clerk of Arraignment. "What can he have counsel for before he has pleaded?"

The Recorder. "Mr. Kidd, the Court tells you it shall be heard what you have to say when you have pleaded to your indictment. If you plead to it, if you will, you may assign matter of law, if you have any, but then you must let the Court know what you would insist on."

Kidd. "I beg your Lordship's patience, till I can procure my papers. I had a couple of French passes which I must make use of, in order to my justification."

The Recorder. "This is not matter of law. You have had long notice of your trial, and might have prepared for it. How long have you had notice of your trial?"

Kidd. "A matter of a fortnight."

Dr. Oxenden. "Can you tell the names of any persons that you would make use of in your defense?"

Kidd. "I sent for them, but I could not have them."

Dr. Oxenden. "Where were they then?"

Kidd. "I brought them to my Lord Bellomont in New England."

The Recorder. "What were their names? You cannot tell without book. Mr. Kidd, the Court sees no reason to put off your trial, therefore you must plead."

Clerk of Arraignment. "William Kidd, hold up thy hand."

Kidd. "I beg your Lordship I may have counsel admitted, and that my trial may be put off, I am not really prepared for it."

The Recorder. "Nor never will, if you could help it."

Dr. Oxenden. "Mr. Kidd, you have had reasonable notice, and you know you must be tried, and therefore you cannot plead you are not ready."

Kidd. "If your Lordships permit those papers to be read, they will justify me. I desire my counsel may be heard."

Mr. Coniers. "We admit of no counsel for him."

SPOOKY TREASURE TROVES

The Recorder. "There is no issue joined, and therefore there can be no counsel assigned. Mr. Kidd, you must plead."

Kidd. "I cannot plead till I have those papers that I insisted upon."

Mr. Lemmon. "He ought to have his papers delivered to him, because they are very material for his defense. He has endeavored to have them, but could not get them."

Mr. Coniers. "You are not to appear for anyone, (Mr. Lemmon) till he pleads, and that the Court assigns you for his counsel."

The Recorder. "They would only put off the trial."

Mr. Coniers. "He must plead to the indictment."

Clerk of Arraignment. "Make silence."

Kidd. "My papers are all seized, and I cannot make my defense without them. I desire my trial may be put off till I can have them."

The Recorder. "The Court is of opinion that they ought not to stay for all your evidence; it may be they will never come. You must plead; and then if you can satisfy the Court that there is a reason to put off the trial, you may."

Kidd. "My Lord, I have business in law, and I desire counsel."

The Recorder. "The course of Courts is, when you have pleaded, the matter of trial is next; if you can then show there is cause to put off the trial, you may, but now the matter is to plead."

Kidd. "It is a hard case when all these things shall be kept from me, and I am forced to plead."

The Recorder. "If he will not plead, there must be judgment."

Kidd. "Would you have me plead and not have my vindication by me?"

Clerk of Arraignment. "Will you plead to the indictment?"

Kidd. "I would beg that I may have my papers for my vindication."

It is very obvious that up to this point Kidd was concerned only with the charges of piracy, and attached no importance to the fact that he had been indicted for the murder of his gunner. Regarding the matter of the French passes, Kidd was desperately in earnest. He knew their importance, nor was he begging for them as a subterfuge to gain time. He had been employed as a privateering commander against the French in the West Indies and on the New England coast, as the documents of the Provincial Government have already shown. It is fair to assume that he knew the rules of the game and the kind of papers necessary to make a prize a lawful capture by the terms of the English privateering commission which he held. But his efforts to introduce this evidence which had been secured by Bellomont and forwarded to the authorities in London, were of no avail. Compelled to plead to the indictment for murder, Kidd swore that he was not guilty, and the trial then proceeded under the direction of Lord Chief Baron Ward. Dr.

Oldish, who sought to be assigned, with Mr. Lemmon, as counsel for the prisoner, was not to be diverted from the main issue, and he boldly struck in.

"My Lord, it is very fit his trial should be delayed for some time because he wants some papers very necessary for his defense. It is very true he is charged with piracies in several ships, but they had French passes when the seizure was made. Now, if there were French passes, it was a lawful seizure."

Mr. Justice Powell. "Have you those passes?"

Kidd. "They were taken from me by my Lord Bellomont, and these passes would be my defense."

Dr. Oldish. "If those ships that he took had French passes, there was just cause of seizure, and it will excuse him from piracy."

Kidd. "They were taken from me by my Lord Bellomont and those passes show there was just cause of seizure. That we will prove as clear as the day."

The Lord Chief Baron. "What ship was that which had the French passes?"

Mr. Lemmon. "The same he was in; the same he is indicted for."

Clerk of Arraignment. "Let all stand aside but Captain Kidd. William Kidd, you are now to be tried on the Bill of Murder; the jury is going to be sworn. If you have any cause of exception, you may speak to them as they come to the Book."

Kidd. "I challenge none. I know nothing to the contrary but they are honest men."

The first witness for the Crown was Joseph Palmer, of the *Adventure Galley* (who had been captured by Bellomont in Rhode Island and who had informed him of the incident of the death of Moore, the gunner). He testified as follows:

"About a fortnight before this accident fell out, Captain Kidd met with a ship on that coast (Malabar) that was called the *Loyal Captain*. And about a fortnight after this, the gunner was grinding a chisel aboard the *Adventure*, on the high seas, near the coast of Malabar in the East Indies."

Mr. Coniers. "What was the gunner's name!"

Palmer. "William Moore. And Captain Kidd came and walked on the deck, and walked by this Moore, and when he came to him, says, 'How could you have put me in a way to take this ship (*Loyal Captain*) and been clear?' 'Sir,' says William Moore, 'I never spoke such a word, nor thought such a thing.' Upon which Captain Kidd called him a lousie dog. And says William Moore, 'If I am a lousie dog, you have made me so. You have brought me to ruin and many more.' Upon him saying this, says Captain Kidd, 'Have I ruined you, ye dog?' and took a bucket bound with iron hoops and struck him on the right side of the head, of which he died next day."

Mr. Coniers. "Tell my Lord what passed next after the blow."

Palmer. "He was let down the gun-room, and the gunner said 'Farewell, Farewell! Captain Kidd has given me my last.' And Captain Kidd stood on the deck and said, 'You're a villain.'"

Robert Bradingham, who had been the surgeon of the *Adventure Galley*, then testified that the wound was small but that the gunner's skull had been fractured.

Mr. Cooper. "Had you any discourse with Captain Kidd after this, about the man's death?"

Bradingham. "Some time after this, about two months, by the coast of Malabar, Captain Kidd said, 'I do not care so much for the death of my gunner, as for other passages of my voyage, for I have good friends in England, who will bring me off for that.'"

With this, the prosecution rested, and the Lord Chief Baron addressed Kidd.

"Then you may make your defense. You are charged with murder, and you have heard the evidence that has been given. What have you to say for yourself?"

Kidd. "I have evidence to prove it is no such thing, if they may be admitted to come hither. My Lord, I will tell you what the case was. I was coming up within a league of the Dutchman (the *Loyal Captain*), and some of my men were making a mutiny about taking her, and my gunner told the people he could put the captain in a way to take the ship and be safe. Says I, 'How will you do that?' The gunner answered, 'We will get the captain and men aboard.' 'And what then?' 'We will go aboard the ship and plunder her and we will have it under their hands that we did not take her.' Says I, 'This is Judas-like. I dare not do such a thing.' Says he, '*We* may do it. We are beggars already.' 'Why,' says I, 'may we take the ship because we are poor?' Upon this a mutiny arose, so I took up a bucket and just threw it at him, and said 'You are a rogue to make such a notion.' This I can prove, my Lord."

Thereupon Kidd called Abel Owens, one of his sailors, and asked him:

"Can you tell which way this bucket was thrown?"

Mr. Justice Powell (to Owens). "What was the provocation for throwing the bucket?"

Owens. "I was in the cook-room, and hearing some difference on the deck, I came out, and the gunner was grinding a chisel on the grind-stone, and the captain and he had some words, and the gunner said to the captain, 'You have brought us to ruin, and we are desolate.' 'And,' says he, (the captain) 'have I brought you to ruin? I have not brought you to ruin. I have not done an ill thing to ruin you; you are a saucy fellow to give me these words.' And then he took up the bucket, and did give him the blow."

Kidd. "Was there a mutiny among the men?"

Owens. "Yes, and the bigger part was for taking the ship, and the captain said, 'You that will take the Dutchman, you are the strongest, you may do what you please. If you will take her, you may take her, but if you go from aboard here, you shall never come aboard again.'"

The Lord Chief Baron. "When was this mutiny you speak of?"

Owens. "When we were at sea, about a month before this man's death."

Kidd. "Call Richard Barlicorn."

(Barlicorn was an apprentice who has been mentioned in the inventory of the Sloop *San Antonio*.)

Kidd. "What was the reason the blow was given to the gunner?"

Barlicorn. "At first, when you met with the ship (*Loyal Captain*) there was a mutiny, and two or three of the Dutchmen came aboard, and some said she was a rich vessel, and they would take her. And the captain (Kidd) said, 'No, I will not take her,' and there was a mutiny in the ship, and the men said, 'If you will not, we will.' And he said, 'If you have a mind, you may, but they that will not, come along with me.'"

Kidd. "Do you think William Moore was one of those that was for taking her?"

Barlicorn. "Yes. And William Moore lay sick a great while before this blow was given, and the doctor said when he visited him, that this blow was not the cause of his death."

The Lord Chief Baron. "Then they must be confronted. Do you hear, Bradingham, what he says?"

Bradingham. "I deny this."

As for this surgeon, Kidd swore that he had been a drunken, useless idler who would lay in the hold for weeks at a time. Seaman Hugh Parrott was then called and asked by Kidd:

"Do you know the reason why I struck Moore?"

Parrott. "Yes, because you did not take the *Loyal Captain*, whereof Captain How was commander."

The Lord Chief Baron. "Was that the reason that he struck Moore, because this ship was not taken?"

Parrott. "I shall tell you how this happened, to the best of my knowledge. My commander fortuned to come up with this Captain How's ship and some were for taking her, and some not. And afterwards there was a little sort of mutiny, and some rose in arms, the greater part; and they said they would take the ship. And the commander was not for it, and so they resolved to go away in the boat and take her. Captain Kidd said, 'If you desert my ship, you shall never come aboard again, and I will force you into Bombay, and I will carry you before some of the Council there.' Inasmuch that my commander stilled them again and they remained on board. And about a fortnight afterwards, there passed some words between this William Moore and my commander, and then, says he (Moore), 'Captain, I could have put you in a way to have taken this ship and been never the worse for it.' He says, (Kidd), 'Would you have had me take this ship? I cannot answer it. They are our friends,' and with that I went off the deck, and I understood afterwards the blow was given, but how I cannot tell."

Kidd. "I have no more to say, but I had all the provocation in the world given me. I had no design to kill him. I had no malice or spleen against him."

The Lord Chief Baron. "That must be left to the jury to consider the evidence that has been given. You make out no such matter."

Kidd. "It was not designedly done, but in my passion, for which I am heartily sorry."

Kidd was permitted to introduce no evidence as to his previous good reputation, and the Court concluded that it had heard enough. Lord Chief Baron Ward thereupon delivered himself of an exceedingly adverse charge to the jury, virtually instructing them to find the prisoner guilty of murder, which was promptly done. Having made sure of sending him to Execution Dock, the Court then proceeded to try him for piracy, which seems to have been a superfluous and unnecessary pother. Kidd declared, when this second trial began:

"It is vain to ask any questions. It is hard that the life of one of the King's subjects should be taken away upon the perjured oaths of such villains as these (Bradingham and Palmer). Because I would not yield to their wishes and turn pirate, they now endeavor to prove I was one. Bradingham is saving his life to take away mine."

The Crown proved the capture of the two ships belonging to the Great Mogul, and an East Indian merchant, representing the merchants, testified as to the value of the lading and the regularity of the ship's papers. Kidd challenged this evidence, and once more pleaded with the Court that he be allowed to bring forward the French passes. He asserted that the *Quedah Merchant* had a French Commission, and that her master was a tavern keeper of Surat. That he told the truth, the accompanying photograph of the said document bears belated witness. The Lord Chief Baron put his finger on the weak point of the case by asking to know why Kidd had not taken the ship to port to be lawfully condemned as a prize, as demanded by the terms of his commission from the King. To this Kidd replied that his crew were mutinous, and the *Adventure Galley* unseaworthy, for which reasons he made for the nearest harbor of Madagascar. There his men, to the number of ninety odd, mutinied and went over to the pirate Culliford in the *Mocha Frigate*. He was left short-handed, his own ship was unfit to take to sea, so he burned her, and transferred to the *Quedah Merchant*, after which he steered straight for Boston to deliver her prize to Lord Bellomont, which he would have done had he not learned in the West Indies that he had been proclaimed a pirate.

SPOOKY TREASURE TROVES

Edward Davis, mariner, confirmed the statement regarding the French passes, in these words:

"I came home a passenger from Madagascar and from thence to Amboyna, and there he (Kidd) sent his boat ashore, and there was one that said Captain Kidd was published a pirate in England, and Captain Kidd gave those passes to him to read. The Captain said they were French passes."

Kidd. "You heard that one, Captain Elms, say they were French passes?"

Davis. "Yes, I heard Captain Elms say they were French passes."

Mr. Baron Hatsell. "Have you any more to say, Captain Kidd?"

Kidd. "I have some papers, but my Lord Bellomont keeps them from me, so that I cannot bring them before the Court!"

Bradingham and other members of the crew admitted that they understood from Kidd that the captured ships were sailing under French passes. Kidd, having been convicted of murder, was now allowed to fetch in witnesses as to his character as a man and a sailor previous to the fatal voyage. One Captain Humphrey swore that he had known Capt. Kidd in the West Indies twelve years before. "You had a general applause," said he, "for what you had done from time to time."

The Lord Chief Baron. "That was before he was turned pirate."

Captain Bond then declared:

"I know you were very useful at the beginning of the war in the West Indies."

Colonel Hewson put the matter more forcibly and made no bones of telling the Court:

"My Lord, he was a mighty man there. He served under my command there. He was sent to me by the order of Colonel Codrington."

The Solicitor General. "How long was this ago?"

Colonel Hewson. "About nine years ago. He was with me in two engagements against the French, and fought as well as any man I ever saw, according to the proportion of his men. We had six Frenchmen (ships) to deal with, and we had only mine and his ship."

Kidd. "Do you think I was a pirate?"

Colonel Hewson. "I knew his men would have gone a-pirating, and he refused it, and his men seized upon his ship; and when he went this last voyage, he consulted with me, and told me they had engaged him in such an expedition. And I told him that he had enough already and might be content with what he had. And he said that was his own inclination, but Lord Bellomont told him if he did not go the voyage there were great men who would stop his brigantine in the river if he did not go."

Thomas Cooper. "I was aboard the *Lyon* in the West Indies and this Captain Kidd brought his ship from a place that belonged to the Dutch and brought her

SPOOKY TREASURE TROVES

into the King's service at the beginning of the war, about ten years ago. And he took service under the Colonel (Hewson), and we fought Monsieur Du Cass a whole day, and I thank God we got the better of him. And Captain Kidd behaved very well in the face of his enemies."

It may be said also for Captain William Kidd that he behaved very well in the face of the formidable battery of legal adversaries.

As a kind of afterthought, the jury found him guilty of piracy along with several of his crew, Nichols Churchill, James How, Gabriel Loiff, Hugh Parrott, Abel Owens, and Darby Mullins. Three of those indicted were set free, Richard Barlicorn, Robert Lumley, and William Jenkins, because they were able to prove themselves to have been bound seamen apprentices, duly indentured to officers of the ship who were responsible for their deeds. Before sentence was passed on him, Kidd said to the Court:

"My Lords, it is a very hard judgment. For my part I am the most innocent person of them all."

Execution Dock long since vanished from old London, but tradition has survived along the waterfront of Wapping to fix the spot, and the worn stone staircase known as the "Pirates' Stairs," still leads down to the river, and down these same steps walked Captain William Kidd. The *Gentleman's Magazine* (London) for 1796 describes the ancient procedure, just as it had befallen Captain Kidd and his men:

"Feb. 4th. This morning, a little after ten o'clock, Colley, Cole, and Blanche, the three sailors convicted of the murder of Captain Little, were brought out of Newgate, and conveyed in solemn procession to Execution Dock, there to receive the punishment awarded by law. On the cart on which they rode was an elevated stage; on this were seated Colley, the principal instigator in the murder, in the middle, and his two wretched instruments, the Spaniard Blanche, and the Mulatto Cole, on each side of him; and behind, on another seat, two executioners.

"Colley seemed in a state resembling that of a man stupidly intoxicated, and scarcely awake, and the two discovered little sensibility on this occasion, nor to the last moment of their existence, did they, as we hear, make any confession. They were turned off about a quarter before twelve in the midst of an immense crowd of spectators. On the way to the place of execution, they were preceded by the Marshall of the Admiralty in his carriage, the Deputy Marshall, bearing the silver oar, and the two City Marshals on horseback, Sheriff's officers, etc. The whole cavalcade was conducted with great solemnity."

John Taylor, "the water poet," who lived in the time of Captain Kidd, wrote these doleful lines, which may serve as a kind of obituary:

"There are inferior Gallowses which bear,(According to the season) twice a year;And there's a kind of waterish tree at WappingWhere sea-thieves or pirates are catched napping."

Kidd's body, covered with tar and hung in chains, was gibbeted on the shore of the reach of the Thames hard by Tilbury Fort, as was the customary manner of displaying dead pirates by way of warning to passing seamen. His treasure was confiscated by the Crown, and what was left of it, after the array of legal gentlemen had been paid their fees, was turned over to Greenwich Hospital by act of Parliament.

Kidd hanging in chains. (*From The Pirates' Own Book*.) "The Pirates' Stairs" leading to the site of Execution Dock at Wapping where Kidd was hanged. The old stone steps are visible beneath the modern iron bridge.

Thus lived and died a man, who, whatever may have been his faults, was unfairly dealt with by his patrons, misused by his rascally crew, and slandered by credulous posterity.

[1] History of England.

[2] Published in 1701.

[3] Macauley.

[4] "From hence putting off to the West Indies, wee were not many dayes at sea, but there beganne among our people such mortalitie as in fewe days there were dead above two or three hundred men. And until some seven or eight dayes after our coming from S. Iago, there had not died any one man of sickness in all

SPOOKY TREASURE TROVES

the fleete; the sickness shewed not his infection wherewith so many were stroken until we were departed thence, and then seazed our people with extreme hot burning and continuall agues, whereof very fewe escaped with life, and yet those for the most part not without great alteration and decay of their wittes and strength for a long time after."—Hakluyt's Voyages.—(A Summarie and True Discourse of Sir Francis Drake's West Indian voyage begun in the Year 1585.)

[5] The *Quedah Merchant*.

[6] The *Quedah Merchant*.

SPOOKY TREASURE TROVES

CHAPTER V
THE WONDROUS FORTUNE OF WILLIAM PHIPS

The flaw in the business of treasure hunting, outside of fiction, is that the persons equipped with the shovels and picks and the ancient charts so seldom find the hidden gold. The energy, credulity, and persistence of these explorers are truly admirable but the results have been singularly shy of dividends the world over. There is genuine satisfaction, therefore, in sounding the name and fame of the man who not only went roving in search of lost treasure but also found and fetched home more of it than any other adventurer known to this kind of quest.

On the coast of Maine, near where the Kennebec flows past Bath into the sea, there is a bit of tide water known as Montsweag Bay, hard by the town of Wiscasset. Into this little bay extends a miniature cape, pleasantly wooded, which is known as Phips Point, and here it was that the most illustrious treasure seeker of them all, William Phips, was born in 1650. The original Pilgrim Fathers, or some of them, were still hale and hearty, the innumerable ship-loads of furniture brought over in the *Mayflower* had not been scattered far from Plymouth, and this country was so young that the "oldest families" of Boston were all brand-new.

James Phips, father of the great William, was a gun-smith who had come over from Bristol in old England to better his fortunes. With the true pioneering spirit he obtained a grant of land and built his log cabin at the furthest outpost of settlement toward the eastward. He cleared his fields, raised some sheep, and betimes repaired the blunderbusses with which Puritan and Pilgrim were wont to pot the aborigine. The first biography of William Phips was written by Cotton Mather, whom the better you know the more heartily you dislike for a canting old bigot who boot-licked men of rank, wealth, or power, and was infernally active in getting a score of hapless men and women hanged for witchcraft in Salem.

Cotton Mather deserves the thanks of all good treasure seekers, however, for having given us the first-hand story of William Phips whom he knew well and extravagantly admired. In fact, after this hero had come sailing home with his treasures and because of these riches was made Sir William Phips and Royal Governor of Massachusetts by Charles II, he had his pew in the old North Church of Boston of which Rev. Cotton Mather was pastor. But this is going ahead too fast, and we must hark back to the humble beginnings. "His faithful mother, yet living," wrote Mather in his very curious *Magnalia Christi Americana*, "had no less than Twenty-six Children, whereof Twenty-one were Sons: but Equivalent to them all was William, one of the youngest, whom his Father dying, was left young with his mother, and with her he lived, keeping ye Sheep in the Wilderness until he was Eighteen Years old."

Then William decided that the care of the farm and the sheep might safely be left to his twenty brothers, and he apprenticed himself to a shipwright who was building on the shore near the settlement those little shallops, pinnaces, and sloops in which our forefathers dared to trade up and down their own coasts and as far as the West Indies, mere cockle-shells manned by seamen of astonishing temerity and hardihood. While at work with hammer and adze, this strapping lump of a lad listened to the yarns of skippers who had voyaged to Jamaica and the Bahamas, dodging French privateers or running afoul of pirates who stripped them of cargo and gear, and perhaps it was then that he first heard of the treasures that had been lost in wrecked galleons, or buried by buccaneers of Hispaniola. At any rate, William Phips wished to see more of the world and to win a chance to go to sea in a ship of his own, wherefore he set out for Boston after he had served his time, "having an accountable impulse upon his mind, persuading him, as he would privately hint unto some of his friends, that he was born to greater matters."

Twenty-two years old, not yet able to read and write, young Phips found work with a ship-carpenter and studied his books as industriously as he plied his trade. Soon he was wooing a "young gentlewoman of good repute, the daughter of one Captain Roger Spencer," and there was no resisting this headstrong suitor. They were married, and shortly after this important event Phips was given a contract to build a ship at a settlement on Sheepscot river, near his old home on the Kennebec, "where having launched the ship," Cotton Mather relates, "he also provided a lading of lumber to bring with him, which would have been to the advantage of all concerned.

"But just as the ship was hardly finished, the barbarous Indians on that river broke forth into an open and cruel war upon the English, and the miserable people, surprised by so sudden a storm of blood, had no refuge from the infidels but the ship now finishing in the harbor. Wherefore he left his intended lading behind him, and instead thereof carried with him his old neighbors and their families, free of all charges, to Boston. So the first thing he did, after he was his own man, was to save his father's house, with the rest of the neighborhood from ruin; but the disappointment which befell him from the loss of his other lading plunged his affairs into greater embarrassment with such as he had employed him. But he was hitherto no more than beginning to make scaffolds for further and higher actions. He would frequently tell the gentlewoman, his wife, that he should yet be Captain of a King's Ship; that he should come to have the command of better men than he was now accounted himself, and that he would be the owner of a fair brick house in the Green Lane of North Boston."[1]

Inasmuch as William Phips would have been a very sorry scoundrel indeed, to run away, for the sake of a cargo of lumber, and leave his old friends and neighbors to be scalped, it seems as Cotton Mather was sounding the timbrel of praise somewhat over-loud, but the parson was a fulsome eulogist, and for reasons of his own he proclaimed this roaring, blustering seafarer and hot-headed royal governor as little lower than the angels. Here and there Mather drew with firm stroke the character of the man, so that we catch glimpses of him as a live and moving figure. "He was of an inclination cutting rather like a hatchet than a razor; he would propose very considerable matters and then so cut through them that no difficulties could put by the edge of his resolution. Being thus of the true temper for doing of great things, he betakes himself to the sea, the right scene for such things."

Sir William Phips, first royal governor of Massachusetts.

Phips had no notion of being a beggarly New England trading skipper, carrying codfish and pine boards to the West Indies and threshing homeward with molasses and niggers in the hold, or coasting to Virginia for tobacco. A man of mettle won prizes by bold strokes and large hazards, and treasure seeking was the game for William. Among the taverns of the Boston water-front he picked up tidings and rumors of many a silver-laden galleon of Spain that had shivered her

SPOOKY TREASURE TROVES

timbers on this or that low-lying reef of the Bahama Passage where there was neither buoy nor lighthouse. Here was a chance to win that "fair brick house in the Green Lane of North Boston" and Phips busied himself with picking up information until he was primed to make a voyage of discovery. Keeping his errand to himself, he steered for the West Indies, probably in a small chartered sloop or brig, and prowled from one key and island to another.

This was in the year 1681, and the waters in which Phips dared to venture were swarming with pirates and buccaneers who would have cut his throat for a doubloon. Morgan had sacked Panama only eleven years before; Tortuga, off the coast of Hayti, was still the haunt of as choice a lot of cutthroats as ever sailed blue water; and men who had been plundering and killing with Pierre le Grande, Bartholomew Portugez and Montbars the Exterminator, were still at their old trade afloat. Mariners had not done talking about the exploit of L'Ollonais who had found three hundred thousand dollars' worth of Spanish treasure hidden on a key off the coast of Cuba. He it was who amused himself by cutting out the hearts of live Spaniards and gnawing these morsels, or slicing off the heads of a whole ship's crew and drinking their blood. A rare one for hunting buried treasure was this fiend of a pirate. When he took Maracaibo, as Esquemeling relates in the story of his own experiences as a buccaneer, "L'Ollonais, who never used to make any great amount of murdering, though in cold blood, ten or twelve Spaniards, drew his cutlass and hacked one to pieces in the presence of all the rest, saying: 'If you do not confess and declare where you have hidden the rest of your goods, I will do the like to all your companions.' At last, amongst these horrible cruelties and inhuman threats, one was found who promised to conduct him and show the place where the rest of the Spaniards were hidden. But those that were fled, having intelligence that one discovered their lurking holes to the Pirates, changed the place, and buried all the remnant of their riches underground; insomuch that the Pirates could not find them out, unless some other person of their own party should reveal them."

From this first voyage undertaken by Phips he escaped with his skin and a certain amount of treasure, "what just served him a little to furnish him for a voyage to England," says Mather. The important fact was that he had found what he sought and knew where there was a vast deal more of it. A large ship, well armed and manned, was needed to bring away the booty, and Captain William Phips intended to find backing in London for the adventure. He crossed the Atlantic in "a vessel not much unlike that which the Dutchmen stamped on their first coin," and no sooner had his stubby, high-pooped ark of a craft cast anchor in the Thames than he was buzzing ashore with his tale of the treasure wreck.

It was no less a person than the king himself whom Phips was bent on enlisting as a partner, and he was not to be driven from Whitehall by lords or flunkies. With bulldog persistence he held to his purpose month after month, until almost a

SPOOKY TREASURE TROVES

year had passed. At length, through the friends he had made at Court, he gained the ear of Charles II, and that gay monarch was pleased to take a fling at treasure hunting as a sporting proposition, with an eye also to a share of the plunder.

He gave Phips a frigate of the king's navy, the *Rose* of eighteen guns and ninety-five men, which had been captured from the Algerine corsairs. As "Captain of a King's Ship," he recruited a crew of all sorts, mostly hard characters, and sailed from London in September, 1683, bound first to Boston, and thence to find the treasure. Alas, for the cloak of piety with which Cotton Mather covered William Phips from head to heels. Other accounts show convincingly that he was a bullying, profane, and godless sea dog, yet honest withal, and as brave as a lion, an excellent man to have at your elbow in a tight pinch, or to be in charge of the quarter-deck in a gale of wind. The real Phips is a more likeable character than the stuffed image that Cotton Mather tried to make of him.

While in Boston harbor in the *Rose*, Captain Phips carried things with a high hand. Another skipper had got wind of the treasure and was about to make sail for the West Indies in a ship called the *Good Intent*. Phips tried to bluff him, then to frighten him, and finally struck a partnership so that the two vessels sailed in company. Refusing to show the Boston magistrates his papers, Phips was haled to court where he abused the bench in language blazing with deep-sea oaths, and was fined several hundred pounds. His sailors got drunk ashore and fought the constables and cracked the heads of peaceable citizens. Staid Boston was glad when the *Rose* frigate and her turbulent company bore away for the West Indies.

There was something wrong with Phip's information or the Spanish wreck had been cleaned of her treasure before he found the place. The *Rose* and the *Good Intent* lay at the edge of a reef somewhere near Nassau for several months, sending down native divers and dredging with such scanty returns that the crew became mutinous and determined on a program very popular in those days. Armed with cutlasses, they charged aft and demanded of Phips that he "join them in running away with the ship to drive a trade of piracy in the South Seas. Captain Phips ... with a most undaunted fortitude, rushed in upon them, and with the blows of his bare hands felled many of them and quelled all the rest."

It became necessary to careen the *Rose* and clean the planking all fouled with tropical growth, and she was beached on "a desolate Spanish island." The men were given shore liberty, all but eight or ten, and the rogues were no sooner out of the ship than "they all entered into an agreement which they signed in a ring (a round-robin), that about seven o'clock that evening they would seize the captain and those eight or ten which they knew to be true to him, and leave them to perish on the island, and so be gone away into the South Seas to seek their fortune.... These knaves, considering that they should want a carpenter with them in their villainous expedition, sent a messenger to fetch unto them the carpenter who was then at work upon the vessel; and unto him they showed their articles; telling him what he must look for if he did not subscribe among them.

"The carpenter, being an honest fellow, did with much importunity prevail for one half hour's time to consider the matter; and returning to work upon the vessel, with a spy by them set upon him, he feigned himself taken with a fit of the collick, for the relief whereof he suddenly ran into the captain in the great cabin for a dram. Where, when he came, his business was only in brief to tell the captain of the horrible distress which he has fallen into; but the captain bid him as briefly return to the rogues in the woods and sign their articles, and leave him to provide for the rest.

"The carpenter was no sooner gone than Captain Phips, calling together the few friends that were left him aboard, whereof the gunner was one, demanded of them whether they would stand by him in this extremity, whereto they replied they would stand by him if he could save them, and he answered, 'By the help of God, he did not fear it.' All their provisions had been carried ashore to a tent made for that purpose, about which they had placed several great guns, to defend it in case of any assault from Spaniards. Wherefore Captain Phips immediately ordered those guns to be silently drawn and turned; and so pulling up the bridge, he charged his great guns aboard and brought them to bear on every side of the tent.

"By this time the army of rebels came out of the woods; but as they drew near to the tent of provisions they saw such a change of circumstances that they cried out, *We are betrayed!* And they were soon confirmed in it when they heard the captain with a stern fury call to them, *Stand off, ye wretches, at your peril*. He quickly cast them into more than ordinary confusion when they saw him ready to fire his great guns upon them.

"And when he had signified unto them his resolve to abandon them unto all the desolation which they had proposed for him, he caused the bridge to be again laid, and his men began to take the provisions on board. When the wretches beheld what was coming upon them, they fell to very humble entreaties; and at last fell down upon their knees protesting that they never had anything against him, except only his unwillingness to go away with the King's ship upon the South Sea design. But upon all other accounts they would choose rather to live and die with him than with any man in the world. However, when they saw how much he was dissatisfied at it, they would insist upon it no more, and humbly begged his pardon. And when he judged that he had kept them on their knees long enough, he having first secured their arms, received them aboard, but he immediately weighed anchor and arriving at Jamaica, turned them off."

This is a very proper incident to have happened in a hunt for hidden treasure, and Cotton Mather tells it well. One forgives Phips for damning the eyes of

SPOOKY TREASURE TROVES

the Boston magistrates, and likely enough they deserved it, when it is recalled that the witchcraft trials were held only a few years later. Having rid himself of the mutineers, Captain Phips shipped other scoundrels in their stead, there being small choice at Jamaica where every other man had been pirating or was planning to go again. His first quest for treasure had been a failure, but he was not the man to quit, and so he filled away for Hispaniola, now Hayti and San Domingo, where every bay and reef had a treasure story of its own.

The small island of Tortuga off that coast had long been the headquarters of the most successful pirates and buccaneers of those seas, and Frederick A. Ober, who knows the West Indies as well as any living man, declares not only that Cuba, the Isle of Pines, Jamaica, and Hispaniola are girdled with Spanish wrecks containing "as yet unrecovered millions and millions in gold and silver," but also that "during the successive occupancies of Tortuga by the various pirate bands great treasure was hidden in the forest, and in the caves with which the island abounds. Now and again the present cultivators of Tortuga find coins of ancient dates, fragments of gold chains, and pieces of quaint jewelry cast up by the waves or revealed by the shifting sands.

"It was not without reason that the only harbor of the buccaneers was called Treasure Cove, nor for nothing that they dug the deep caves deeper, hollowing out lateral tunnels and blasting holes beneath the frowning cliffs. The island now belongs to Hayti, the inhabitants of which have not the requisite sagacity to conduct an intelligent search for the long-buried treasures; and as they resent the intrusion of foreigners, it is probable that the buccaneers' spoils will remain an unknown quantity for many years to come."

Captain William Phips lay at anchor off one of the rude settlements of Hispaniola for some time, and his rough-and-ready address won him friends, among them "a very old Spaniard" who had seen many a galleon pillaged by the pirates. From this informant Phips "fished up a little advice about the true spot where lay the wreck which he had hitherto been seeking ... that it was upon a reef of shoals a few leagues to the northward of Port de la Plata upon Hispaniola, a port so called, it seemed, from the landing of some of a shipwrecked company, with a boat full of plate saved out of their sunken Frigot."

SPOOKY TREASURE TROVES

Map of Hispaniola (Hayti and San Domingo) engraved in 1723, showing the buccaneers at their trade of hunting wild cattle. The galleon due north of Port Plate on the north coast is almost exactly in the place where Phips found his treasure.

Map of Hispaniola (Hayti and San Domingo) engraved in 1723, showing the buccaneers at their trade of hunting wild cattle. The galleon due north of Port Plate on the north coast is almost exactly in the place where Phips found his treasure.

On the very old map of Hispaniola, reproduced herewith, this place is indicated on the north coast as "Port Plate," and due north of it is the spirited drawing of a galleon which happens to be very nearly in the position of the sunken treasure which the old Spaniard described to Captain Phips. The *Rose* frigate sailed in search of the reef and explored it with much care but failed to find the wreck. Phips was confident that he was on the right track, however, and decided to return to England, refit and ship a new crew. The riff-raff which he had picked up at Jamaica in place of the mutineers were hardly the lads to be trusted with a great store of treasure on board.

At about this time, Charles II quit his earthly kingdom and it is to be hoped found another kind of treasure laid up for him. James II needed all his warships, and he promptly took the *Rose* frigate from Captain Phips and set him adrift to shift for himself. A man of less inflexible resolution and courage might have been disheartened, but Phips made a louder noise than ever with his treasure story, and would not budge from London. He was put in jail, somehow got himself out, and stood up to his enemies and silenced them, all the while seeking noble patrons with money to venture on another voyage.

At length, and a year had been spent in this manner, Phips interested the Duke of Albemarle, son of the famous General Monk who had been active in restoring Charles II to the throne of the Stuarts. Several other gentlemen of the Court took shares in the speculation, including a naval man, Sir John Narborough. They put up £2,400 to outfit a ship, and the King was persuaded to grant Phips letters of patent, or a commission as a duly authorized treasure seeker, in return for which favor His Majesty was to receive one-tenth of the booty. To Phips was promised a sixteenth of what he should recover.

This enterprise was conceived in 1686, and was so singularly like the partnership formed ten years later to finance the cruise of Captain Kidd after pirates' plunder that the Earl of Bellomont, Lord Chancellor Somers, the Earl of Shrewsbury, and William III may have been somewhat inspired to undertake this unlucky venture by the dazzling success of the Phips "syndicate."

In a small merchantman called the *James and Mary*, Captain Phips set sail from England in 1686, having another vessel to serve as a tender. Arriving at Port de la Plata, he hewed out a large canoe from a cotton-wood tree, "so large as to carry eight or ten oars," says Cotton Mather, "for the making of which perigua (as they call it), he did, with the same industry that he did everything else, employ his own hand and adze, and endure no little hardship, lying abroad in the woods many nights together." The canoe was used by a gang of native divers quartered on board the tender. For some time they worked along the edge of a reef called the Boilers, guided by the story of that ancient Spaniard, but found nothing to reward their exertions.

This crew was returning to report to Captain Phips when one of the men, staring over the side into the wonderfully clear water, spied a "sea feather" or marine plant of uncommon beauty growing from what appeared to be a rock. An Indian was sent down to fetch it as a souvenir of the bootless quest, that they might, however, carry home something with them. This diver presently bobbed up with the sea feather, and therewithal a surprising story "that he perceived a number of great guns in the watery world, where he had found the feather; the report of which great guns exceedingly astonished the whole company; and at once turned their despondencies for their ill success into assurances that they had now lit upon the true spot of ground which they had been looking for; and they were further confirmed in these assurances when upon further diving, the Indian fetched up a *Sow* as they styled it, or a lump of silver worth perhaps two or three hundred

SPOOKY TREASURE TROVES

pounds. Upon this they prudently buoyed the place, that they might readily find it again; and they went back unto their Captain whom for some while they distressed with nothing but such bad news as they formerly thought they must have carried him. Nevertheless, they so slipped the Sow of silver on one side under the table (where they were now sitting with the Captain, and hearing him express his resolutions to wait still patiently upon the Providence of God under these disappointments), that when he should look on one side, he might see that Odd Thing before him. At last he saw it and cried out with some agony:

"*'What is this? Whence comes this?'* And then with changed countenance they told him how and where they got it. Then said he, '*Thanks be to God! We are made!*' And so away they went, all hands to work; wherein they had this further piece of remarkable prosperity, that whereas if they had first fallen upon that part of the Spanish wreck where the Pieces of Eight had been stowed in bags among the ballast, they had seen more laborious and less enriching times of it. Now, most happily, they first fell upon that room in the wreck where the Bullion had been stored up, and then so prospered in this new fishery that in a little while they had without the loss of any man's life, brought up *Thirty Two Tons* of silver, for it was now come to measuring silver by tons."

While these jolly treasure seekers were hauling up the silver hand over fist, one Adderley, a seaman of the New Providence in the Bahamas, was hired with his vessel to help in the gorgeous salvage operations. Alas, after Adderley had recovered six tons of bullion, the sight of so much treasure was too much for him. He took his share to the Bermudas and led such a gay life with it that he went mad and died after a year or two. Hard-hearted William Phips was a man of another kind, and he drove his crew of divers and wreckers, the sailors keeping busy on deck at hammering from the silver bars a crust of limestone several inches thick from which "they knocked out whole bushels of pieces of eight which were grown thereinto. Besides that incredible treasure of plate in various forms, thus fetched up from seven or eight fathoms under water, there were vast riches of Gold, and Pearls, and Jewels, which they also lit upon: and indeed for a more comprehensive invoice, I must but summarily say, *All that a Spanish frigot was to be enriched withal.*"

At length the little squadron ran short of provisions, and most reluctantly Captain Phips decided to run for England with his precious cargo and return the next year. He swore all his men to secrecy, believing that there was more good fishing at the wreck. During the homeward voyage, his seamen quite naturally yearned for a share of the profits, they having signed on for monthly wages. They were for taking the ship "to be gone and lead a short life and a merry one," but Phips argued them out of this rebellious state of mind, promising every man a share of the silver, and if his employers would not agree to this, to pay them from his own pocket.

SPOOKY TREASURE TROVES

Up the Thames sailed the lucky little merchantman, *James and Mary* in the year of 1687, with three hundred thousand pounds sterling freightage of treasure in her hold, which would amount to a good deal more than a million and a half dollars nowadays. Captain Phips played fair with his seamen, and they fled ashore in the greatest good humor to fling their pieces of eight among the taverns and girls of Wapping, Limehouse, and Rotherhite. The King was given his tenth of the cargo, and a handsome fortune it was. To Phips fell his allotted share of a sixteenth, which set him up with sixteen thousand pounds sterling. The Duke of Albemarle was so much gratified that he sent to that "gentlewoman" Mrs. William Phips, a gold cup worth a thousand pounds. Phips showed himself an honest man in age when sea morals were exceeding lax, and not a penny of the treasure, beyond what was due him, stuck to his fingers. Men of his integrity were not over plentiful in England after the Restoration, and the King liked and trusted this brusque, stalwart sailor from New England. At Windsor Castle he was knighted and now it was Sir William Phips, if you please.

Judge Sewall's diary contains this entry, Friday, October 21, 1687:

"I went to offer my Lady Phips my House by Mr. Moody's and to congratulate her preferment. As to the former, she had bought Sam' Wakefield's House and Ground last night for £350. I gave her a Gazette that related her Husband's Knighthood, which she had not seen before; and wish'd this success might not hinder her passage to a greater and better estate. She gave me a cup of good Beer and thank'd me for my visit."

Sir William would have still another try at the wreck, and this time there was no lack of ships and patronage. A squadron was fitted out in command of Sir John Narborough, and one of the company was the Duke of Albemarle. They made their way to the reef, but the remainder of the treasure had been lifted, and the expedition sailed home empty-handed. Adderley of New Providence had babbled in his cups and one of his men had been bribed to take a party of Bermuda wreckers to the reef. The place was soon swarming with all sorts of craft, some of them from Jamaica and Hispaniola, and they found a large amount of silver before they stripped the wreck clean.

The King offered Sir William a place as one of the Commissioners of the Royal Navy, but he was homesick for New England and desired to be a person of consequence in his own land. His friends obtained for him a patent as High Sheriff of Massachusetts and he returned to Boston after five years' absence "to entertain his Lady with some accomplishment of his predictions; and then built himself a fair brick house in the very place which was foretold."

The "fair brick house" was of two stories with a portico and columns. It stood on the corner of the present Salem Street (then the Green Lane) and Charter Street, so named by Sir William Phips in honor of the new charter under which he became the first provincial or royal governor. There was a lawn and gardens, a watch-house and stables, and a stately row of butternuts. "North Boston" was then the fashionable or "Court end" of the town.

The Puritans and Pilgrims were seething with indignation against the royal government overseas. The original charter under which the Colony of Massachusetts Bay exercised self-government had been annulled, and Charles II was determined to bring all the New England Colonies under the sway of a royal governor. The question of taxation had also begun to simmer a full century before the Revolution. Sir William Phips found his berth of High Sheriff a difficult and turbulent business, and "the infamous Government then rampant there, found a way wholly to put by the execution of his patent; yea, he was like to have had his person assassinated in the face of the sun, before his own door."

This rough ship carpenter and treasure seeker weathered the storm and rose so high in the good graces of the throne that in 1692 he carried to Massachusetts the new charter signed by William III by virtue of which he became the first royal governor of that colony, and as an administrator he was no less interesting than when he was cruising off the coast of Hispaniola. The manners of the quarter-deck he carried to the governor's office. His fists were as ready as his tongue, and his term of two years was enlivened by one lusty quarrel after another. In nowise ashamed of his humble beginnings, he gave a dinner to his old friends of the Boston ship-yard and told these honest artisans that if it were not for his service to the people, he "would be much easier in returning to his broad axe again."

Hawthorne has given a picture of him in the days of his greatness, "a man of strong and sturdy frame, whose face has been roughened by northern tempests, and blackened by the burning sun of the West Indies. He wears an immense periwig flowing down over his shoulders. His coat has a wide embroidery of golden foliage, and his waistcoat likewise is all flowered over and bedizened with gold. His red, rough hands, which have done many a good day's work with the hammer and adze, are half covered by the delicate lace ruffles at his wrists. On a table lies his silver-headed sword, and in a corner of the room stands his gold-headed cane, made of a beautifully polished West India wood."

Cotton Mather helps to complete the presentment by relating that "he was very tall, beyond the common set of men, and thick as well as tall, and strong as well as thick. He was in all respects exceedingly robust, and able to conquer such difficulties of diet and travel as would have killed most men alive. Nor did the fat whereinto he grew very much in his later years, take away the vigor of his motions."

As a fighting seaman and soldier, Sir William Phips saw hard service before he was made royal governor. In 1690 he was in command of an expedition which made a successful raid on the French in Arcadia, captured Port Royal, and con-

SPOOKY TREASURE TROVES

quered the province. Among the English state papers in the Public Record office is his own account of this feat of arms of his expedition against Quebec. "In March, 1690," he wrote, "I sailed with seven ships and seven hundred men, raised by the people of New England, reduced Arcadia in three weeks and returned to Boston. It was then thought well to prosecute a further expedition. 2300 men were raised, with whom and with about thirty ships I sailed from New England on the 10th, August, 1690, but by bad weather and contrary winds did not reach Quebec till October. The frost was already so sharp that it made two inches of ice in a night.

"After summoning Count de Frontenac and receiving a reviling answer, I brought my ships up within musket shot of their cannon and fired with such success that I dismounted several of their largest cannon and beat them from their works in less than twenty-four hours. At the same time 1400 men, who had been landed, defeated a great part of the enemy, and by the account of the prisoners, the city must have been taken in two or three days, but the small-pox and fever increased so fast as to delay the pushing of the siege till the weather became too severe to permit it. On my leaving Quebec, I received several messages from French merchants of the best reputation, saying how uneasy they were under French administration, and how willing they were to be under their Majesties."

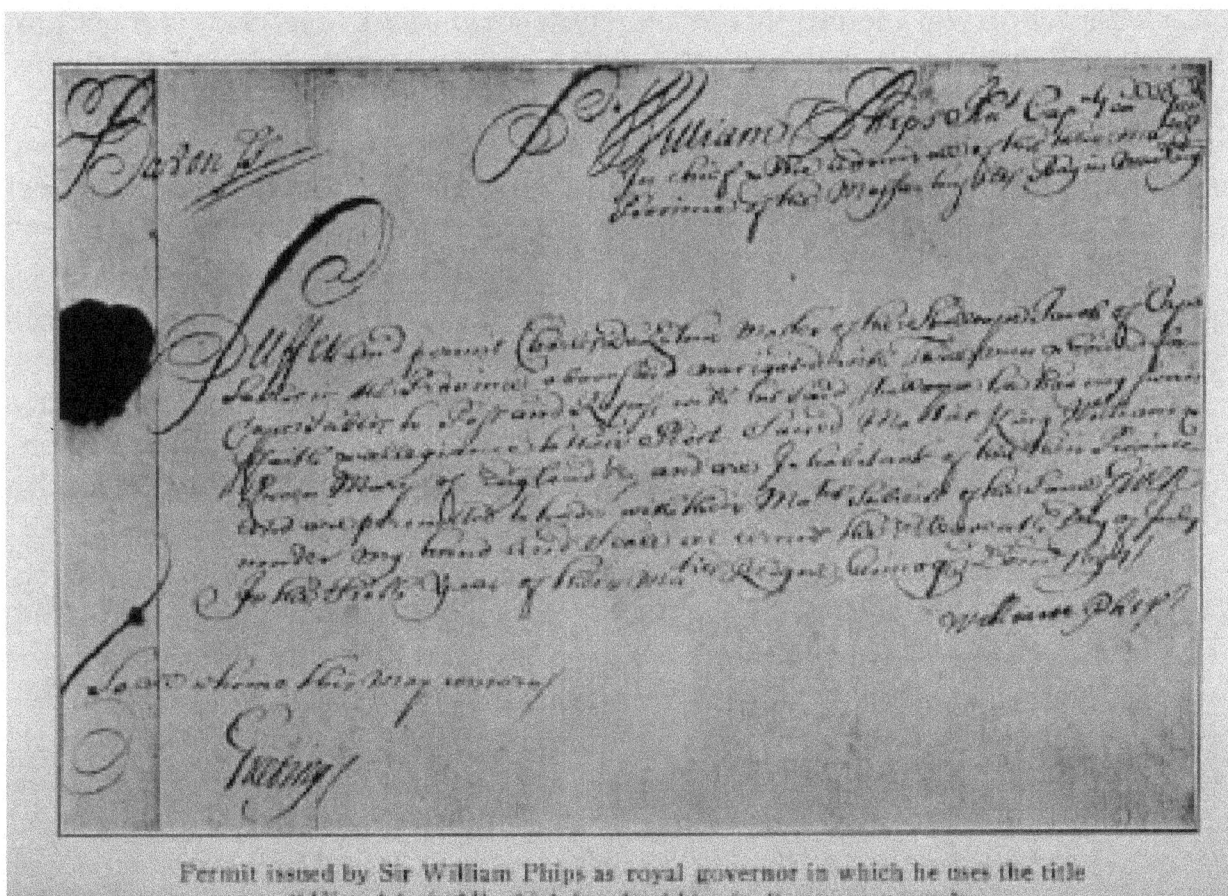

Permit issued by Sir William Phips as royal governor in which he uses the title "Vice Admiral" which involved him in disastrous quarrels.

SPOOKY TREASURE TROVES

In a "Narrative of the Expedition against Quebec," written at the time, is this passage:

"Whilst these things were doing on shore, Sir Wm. Phips with his men of war came close up to ye City. He did acquit himself with ye greatest bravery. I have diligently enquired of those that know it who affirm there was nothing wanting in his Part, either as to Conduct or Courage. He ventured within Pistol shot of their cannon, and soon beat them from thence, and battered ye Town very much. He was for some Hours warmly entertained with their great Guns. The Vessel wherein Sir William commanded had 200 men. It was shot through in a hundred places with shot of twenty-four pound weight; yet through ye wonderful Providence of God, but one man was killed and two mortally wounded in that hot Engagement, which continued ye greatest part of ye night and ye next day several hours."

Another letter written by Sir William Phips, addressed from Boston to William Blathwayt, soon after he was made Governor, shows him in a light even more engaging. The witchcraft frenzy was at its height, and only three weeks before this date, October 12, 1692, fourteen men and women had been hanged in Salem. This letter, as copied from the original document, runs as follows:

"On my arrival I found this Province miserably harrassed by a most horrible witchcraft or possession of devils, which had broken in upon several towns. Some scores of poor people were taken with preternatural torments; some were scalded with brimstone; some had pins stuck into their flesh, others were hurried into fire and water, and some were dragged out of their houses and carried over the tops of trees and hills for many miles together.

"It has been represented to me as much like that of Sweden thirty years ago, and there were many committed to prison on suspicion of witchcraft before my arrival. The loud cries and clamor of the friends of the afflicted, together with the advice of the Deputy Governor and Council, prevailed with me to appoint a Court of Oyer and Terminer to discover what witchcraft might be at the bottom, and whether it were not a possession. The chief judge was the Deputy Governor, and the rest people of the best prudence and figure that could be pitched upon.

"At Salem in Essex County they convicted more than twenty persons of witchcraft, and some of the accused confessed their guilt. The Court, as I understand, began their proceedings with the accusations of the afflicted persons, and then went upon other evidences to strengthen that. I was in the East of the Colony throughout almost the whole of the proceedings, trusting to the Court as the right method of dealing with cases of witchcraft. But when I returned I found many persons in a strange ferment of dissatisfaction which was increased by some hot spirits that blew upon the flame. But on enquiry into the matter, I found that the Devil had taken upon him the name and shape of several persons who were doubtless innocent, for which cause I have now forbidden the committal of any more accused persons.

"And them that have been committed I would shelter from any proceedings wherein the innocent could suffer wrong. I would also await the King's orders in this perplexing affair. I have put a stop to the printing of any discourses on either side that may increase useless disputes, for open contests would mean an unextinguishable flame. I have been grieved to see that some who should have done better services to their Majesties and this Province have so far taken counsel with passion as to declare the precipitancy of these matters.... As soon as I had done fighting the King's enemies, and understood the danger of innocent people through the accusations of the afflicted, I put a stop to the Court proceedings till the King's pleasure should be known."

It was Governor Phips who suppressed the witchcraft persecutions and the special court that had passed so many wicked death sentences was shorn of its powers by his order. Other prisoners were later acquitted, and a hundred and fifty released from jail. No sooner was this burly figure of a man finished with the witchcraft business than he was leading a force of Indian allies against the French. "His birth and youth in the East had rendered him well known to the Indians there," says Cotton Mather, "he had hunted and fished many a weary day in his childhood with them; and when these rude savages had got the story that he had found a ship full of money, and was now become all one a King, they were mightily astonished at it; but when they further understood that he was now become the Governor of New England, it added a further degree of consternation to their astonishment."

He was too strenuous a person, was this astonishing William Phips, to remain tamed and conservative when there was no strong work in hand. With that gold-headed cane of his he cracked the head of the Captain of the *Nonesuch* frigate of the royal navy, and with his hard fists he pounded the Collector of the Port after swearing at him with such oaths as better befitted a buccaneer than the governor of the province. These quarrels arose from a dispute over the authority of Sir William to lay down the law as he pleased. By virtue of his commission as Vice Admiral of the Colony he held that he had the right to judge and condemn naval prizes. The Collector claimed jurisdiction and when he refused to deliver a cargo of plunder brought in by a privateer, the governor blacked his eyes for him.

As for the naval skipper, Captain Short, his experience with the Phips temper was even more disastrous. He refused to lend some of his men to man a cruiser which the governor wished to send after coastwise pirates. When next the twain met, Captain Short was first well threshed, then bundled off to prison, and from there skipped home to England in a merchantman.

Such methods of administration had served admirably well to rule those mutinous dogs of seamen aboard the *Rose* frigate, but they were resented in Boston, and after other altercations, Governor Phips found it necessary to go to England to answer the complaints which had been piling up in the offices of the Lords of the Council of Trade and Plantations. He sailed in his own yacht, a brigantine built in a Boston shipyard, and we may be sure that he was ready to face his accusers with a stout heart.

Hutchinson, in his History of Massachusetts, analyzed the trouble as follows:

"Sir William Phips' rule was short. His conduct when captain of a ship of war is represented very much to his advantage; but further talents were necessary for the good government of a province. He was of a benevolent, friendly disposition; at the same time quick and passionate....

"A vessel arrived from the Bahamas, with a load of fustick, for which no bond had been given. Col. Foster, a merchant of Boston, a member of the Council, and fast friend of the Governor, bought the fustick at such price that he was loth to give up the bargain. The Collector seized the vessel and goods; and upon Foster's representation to the Governor, he interposed. There was at that time no Court of Admiralty. Sir William took a summary way of deciding this case, and sent an order to the Collector to forbear meddling with the goods, and upon his refusal to observe orders, the Governor went to the wharf, and after warm words on both sides, laid hands upon the Collector, but with what degree of violence was controverted by both. The Governor prevailed, and the vessel and goods were taken out of the hands of the Collector.

"There had been a misunderstanding also between the Governor and Captain Short of the *Nonesuch* frigate. In their passage from England a prize was taken; and Short complained that the Governor had deprived him of part of his share or legal interest in her. Whether there were grounds for it does not appear. The captains of men of war stationed in the colonies were in those days required to follow such instructions as the governors gave them relative to their cruises and the protection of the trade of the colonies, and the Governor, by his commission, had power in case of any great crime committed by any of the captains of men of war, to suspend them, and the next officer was to succeed.

"The Governor required Captain Short to order part of the men belonging to the *Nonesuch* upon some service, which I do not find mentioned, probably to some cruiser, there being many picaroons about the eastern coasts, but he refused to do it. This was ill taken by the Governor; and meeting Captain Short in the street, warm words passed, and at length the Governor made use of his cane and broke Short's head. Not content with this, he committed him to prison. The right of a governor to commit by his own warrant had not then been questioned.

"From the prison he removed him to the castle, and from those on board a merchant bound to London, to be delivered to the order of one of their Majesties'

SPOOKY TREASURE TROVES

principal secretaries of state; giving the master a warrant or authority to do so. The vessel, by some accident, put into Portsmouth in New Hampshire. Sir William who seems to have been sensible of some irregularity in these proceedings, went to Portsmouth, required the master of the merchantman to return him the warrant, which he tore to pieces, and then ordered the cabin of the ship to be opened, secured Short's chests, and examined the contents.

"Short was prevented going home in this vessel, and went to New York to take passage from thence for England; but Sir F. Wheeler arriving soon after at Boston, went for him and carried him home with him. The next officer succeeded in the command of the ship, until a new captain arrived from England. Short was restored to the command of as good a ship."

King William refused to depose the famous treasure finder without hearing what he had to say in his defense, and Sir William stoutly swore that those whom he had punished got no more than they deserved. A strong party had been mustered against him, however, and he waged an uphill fight for vindication until Death, the one foe for whom he did not think himself a match, took him by the heels and laid him in a vault beneath the Church of St. Mary Woolnoth, London. A guidebook of that city, published in 1708, contained this description of the memorial placed therein:

"At the east end of the Church of St. Mary Woolnoth, near the northeast angle, is a pretty white marble monument, adorned with an urn between two Cupids, the figure of a ship, and also a boat at sea, with persons in the water; these beheld by a winged eye, all done in basso relieve; also the seven medals, as that of King William and Queen Mary; some with Spanish impressions, as the castle, crossportent, etc. and likewise the figures of a sea quadrant; cross-staff, and this inscription:

"'Near this place is interred the Body of Sir William Phips, knight; who in the year 1687, by his great industry, discovered among the rocks near the Banks of Bahama on the north side of Hispaniola a Spanish plate-ship which had been under water 44 years, out of which he took in gold and silver to the value of £300,000 sterling: and with a fidelity equal to his conduct, brought it all to London, where it was divided between himself and the rest of the adventurers. For which great service he was knighted by his then Majesty, King James the 2nd, and at the request of the principal inhabitants of New England, he accepted of the Government of the Massachusetts, in which he continued up to the time of his death; and discharged his trust with that zeal for the interests of the country, and with so little regard to his own private advantage, that he justly gained the good esteem and affection of the greatest and best part of the inhabitants of that Colony.

"'He died the 18th of February, 1694, and his lady, to perpetuate his memory, hath caused this monument to be erected.'"

SPOOKY TREASURE TROVES

It is far better to know the man as he was, rough-hewn, hasty, unlettered, but simple and honest as daylight, than to accept the false and silly epitaph of Cotton Mather, that "he was a person of so sweet a temper that they who were most intimately acquainted with him would commonly pronounce him the Best Conditioned Gentleman in the World." After he had wrested his fortune from the bottom of the sea in circumstances splendidly romantic, he used the power which his wealth gained for him wholly in the service of the people of his own country.

During his last visit to London, when he had grown tired of being a royal governor, he harked back to his old love, and was planning another treasure voyage. "The Spanish wreck was not the only nor the richest wreck which he knew to be lying under the water. He knew particularly that when the ship which had Governor Bobadilla aboard was cast away, there was, as Peter Martyr says, an entire table of Gold of Three Thousand Three Hundred and Ten Pounds Weight. And supposing himself to have gained sufficient information of the right way to such a wreck, it was his purpose upon his dismission from his Government, once more to have gone upon his old Fishing-Trade, upon a mighty shelf of rocks and bank of sands that lie where he had informed himself."

The oldest existing print of Boston harbor as it appeared in the time of Sir William Phips, showing the kind of ships in which he sailed to find his treasure.

Never was there so haunting a reference to lost treasure as this mention of that gold table that went down with Governor Bobadilla. The words ring like a peal of magic bells. Alas, the pity of it, that Sir William Phips did not live to fit out

SPOOKY TREASURE TROVES

a brave ship and go in quest of this wondrous treasure, for of all men, then or since, he was the man to find it.

Bobadilla was that governor of Hispaniola who was sent from Spain in 1500 by Ferdinand and Isabella to investigate the affairs of the colony as administered by Christopher Columbus. He put Columbus in chains and shipped him home, but the great discoverer found a friendly welcome there, and was sent back for his fourth voyage. He reached Hispaniola on the day that Bobadilla was sailing for Spain, in his turn to give place to a new Governor, Ovando by name. Bobadilla embarked at San Domingo in the largest ship of the fleet on board of which was put an immense amount of gold, the revenue collected for the Crown during his government, which he hoped might ease the disgrace of his recall.

The Spanish historian, Las Casas, besides other old chroniclers, mention this solid mass of virgin gold which Peter Martyr affirmed had been fashioned into a table. This enormous nugget had been found by an Indian woman in a brook on the estate of Francisco de Garay and Miguel Diaz and had been taken by Bobadilla to send to the king. According to Las Casas, it weighed three thousand, six hundred castellanos.

When Bobadilla's fleet weighed anchor, Columbus sent a messenger urging the ships to remain in port because a storm was imminent. The pilots and seamen scoffed at the warning, and the galleons stood out from San Domingo only to meet a tropical hurricane of terrific violence. Off the most easterly point of Hispaniola, Bobadilla's ship went down with all on board. If this galleon carrying the gold table, besides much other treasure, had foundered in deep water, it is unlikely that Sir William Phips would have planned to go in search of her. If, however, the ship had been smashed on a reef, he may have "fished up" information from some other ancient Spaniard as to her exact location.

The secret was buried in his grave and he left no chart to show where he hoped to find that marvelous treasure, and nobody knows the bearings of that "mighty shelf of rock and bank of sands that lie where he had informed himself."

[1] In order to make easier reading, this and the following extracts from Cotton Mather's narrative are somewhat modernized in respect of quaint spelling, punctuation, and the use of capitals, although, of course, the wording is unchanged.

SPOOKY TREASURE TROVES

CHAPTER VI
THE BOLD SEA ROGUE, JOHN QUELCH

The Isles of Shoals, lying within sight of Portsmouth Harbor on the New Hampshire coast, are rich in buried treasure legends and rocky Appledore is distinguished by the ghost of a pirate, "a pale and very dreadful specter," whose neck bears the livid mark of the hangman's noose. This is a ghost in whose case familiarity has bred contempt among the matter-of-fact islanders, for they call him "Old Bab" and employ him to frighten naughty children. Drake's "Nooks and Corners of the New England Coast" narrates in the proper melodramatic manner the best of these traditions.

"Among others to whom it is said these islands were known was the celebrated Captain Teach, or Blackbeard, as he was often called. He is supposed to have buried immense treasure here, some of which has been dug up and appropriated by the islanders. On one of his cruises, while lying off the Scottish coast waiting for a rich trader, he was boarded by a stranger who came off in a small boat from the shore. The visitor demanded to be led before the pirate chief in whose cabin he remained closeted for some time. At length Blackbeard appeared on deck with the stranger whom he introduced as a comrade. The vessel they were expecting soon came in sight, and, after a bloody conflict, became the prize of Blackbeard. The newcomer had shown such bravery that he was given command of the captured merchantman.

"The stranger soon proved himself a pirate leader of great skill and bravery and went cruising off to the southward and the coasts of the Spanish Main. At last after his appetite for wealth had been satiated he sailed back to his native land of Scotland, made a landing, and returned on board with the insensible body of a beautiful young woman in his arms.

"The pirate ship then made sail, crossed the Atlantic, and anchored in the roadstead of the Isles of Shoals. Here the crew passed the time in secreting their riches and in carousing. The commander's portion was buried on an island apart from the rest. He roamed over the isles with his beautiful companion, forgetful, it would seem, of his fearful trade, until one day a sail was seen standing in for the islands. All was now activity on board the pirate; but before getting under way the outlaw carried the maiden to the island where he had buried his treasure, and made her take a fearful oath to guard the spot from mortals until his return, were it not 'til doomsday.

"The strange sail proved to be a warlike vessel in search of the freebooter. A long and desperate battle ensued, in which the cruiser at last silenced her adversary's guns. The vessels were grappled for a last struggle when a terrible explosion strewed the sea with the fragments of both. Stung to madness by defeat, knowing that if taken alive a gibbet awaited him, the rover had fired the magazine, involving friend and foe in a common fate.

"A few mangled wretches succeeded in reaching the islands, only to perish miserably one by one, from hunger and cold. The pirate's mistress remained true to her oath to the last, or until she had succumbed to want and exposure. By report, she has been seen more than once on White Island—a tall shapely figure, wrapped in a long sea cloak, her head and neck uncovered, except by a profusion of golden hair. Her face is described as exquisitely rounded, but pale and still as marble. She takes her stand on the verge of a low, projecting point, gazing fixedly out upon the ocean in an attitude of intense expectation. A forager race of fishermen avouched that her ghost was doomed to haunt those rocks until the last trump shall sound, and that the ancient graves to be found on the islands were tenanted by Blackbeard's men."

It is more probable that whatever treasure may be hidden among the Isles of Shoals was hidden there by the shipmates of a great scamp of a pirate named John Quelch who fills an interesting page in the early history of the Massachusetts Colony. In proof of this assertion is the entry in one of the old records of Salem, written in the year 1704:

"Major Stephen Sewall, Captain John Turner, and 40 volunteers embark in a shallop and Fort Pinnace after Sunset to go in search of some Pirates who sailed from Gloucester in the morning. Major Sewall brought into Salem a Galley, Captain Thomas Lowrimore, on board of which he had captured some Pirates, and some of their Gold at the Isle of Shoals. Major Sewall carries the Pirates to Boston under a strong guard. Captain Quelch and five of his crew are hung. About 13 of the ship's Company remain under sentence of death and several more are cleared."

By no means all of the bloodstained gold of Quelch was recovered by this expedition which went to the Isles of Shoals and it is more likely to be hidden there to this day than anywhere else. Quelch was a bold figure of a pirate worthy to be named in the company of the most dashing of his profession in the era of

SPOOKY TREASURE TROVES

Kidd, Bradish, Bellamy, and Low. His story is worth the telling because it is, in a way, a sequel of the tragedy of Captain Kidd.

In 1703, the brigantine *Charles*, of about eighty tons, owned by leading citizens and merchants of Boston, was fitted out as a privateer to go cruising against the French off the coasts of Arcadia and Newfoundland. On July 13th of that year, her commander, Captain David Plowman, received his commission from Governor Dudley of the province to sail in pursuit of the Queen's enemies and pirates, with other customary instructions. There was some delay in shipping a crew, and on the first of August the *Charles* was riding off Marblehead when Captain Plowman was taken ill. He sent a letter to his owners, stating that he was unable to take the vessel to sea, and suggesting that they come on board next day and "take some speedy care in saving what we can."

The owners went to Marblehead, but the captain was too ill to confer with them. He was able, however, to write again, this time urging them to have the vessel carried to Boston, and the arms and stores landed in order to "prevent embezzlement," and advising against sending the *Charles* on her cruise under a new commander, adding the warning that "it will not do with these people," meaning the crew then on board.

Before the owners could take any measures to safeguard their property, the brigantine had made sail and was standing out to sea, stolen by her crew. The helpless captain was locked in his cabin, and the new Commander on the quarter-deck was John Quelch who had planned and led the mutiny. Instead of turning to the northward, the bow of the *Charles* was pointed for the South Atlantic and the track of the Spanish trade where there was rich pirating. Somewhere in the Gulf Stream, poor Captain Plowman was dragged on deck and tossed overboard by order of Quelch.

A flag was then hoisted, called "Old Roger," described as having "in the middle of it an Anatomy (skeleton) with an Hourglass in one hand, and a dart in the Heart with 3 drops of Blood proceeding from it in the other." When the coast of Brazil was reached, Quelch and his men drove a thriving trade. Between November 15, 1703, and February 17, 1704, they boarded and took nine vessels, of which five were brigantines, and one a large ship carrying twelve guns. All these craft flew the Portugese flag, and Portugal was an ally of England by virtue of a treaty which had been signed at Lisbon on May 16, 1703. What became of the crews of these hapless vessels was not revealed, but the plunder included salt, sugar, rum, beer, rice, flour, cloth, silk, one hundred weight of gold dust, gold and silver coin to the value of a thousand pounds, two negro boys, great guns, small arms, ammunition, sails, and cordage. One of the largest of the brigantines was kept to serve as a tender.

Two weeks after the *Charles* had taken French leave from Marblehead, her owners, surmising that she had been headed toward the West Indies, persuaded Governor Dudley to take action, and letters were sent to officials in various islands instructing them to be on the look-out for the runaway privateer and to seize her crew as pirates. Quelch was a wily rogue, however, and kept clear of all pursuit, nor was anything more heard of the *Charles* until with extraordinary audacity he came sailing back to New England in the following May and dropped anchor off Marblehead. His men quickly scattered alongshore, and gave out the story which he had cooked up for them, that Captain Plowman had died of his illness while at sea, that Quelch had been obliged to take command, and that they had recovered a great deal of treasure from the wreck of a Spanish galleon.

The yarn was fishy, the men talked too much in their cups, and the owners of the *Charles* were not satisfied with Quelch's glib explanation. They laid information against him in writing, and the vessel was searched, the plunder indicating that the lawless crew had been lifting the goods of subjects of the King of Portugal. The first mention of the affair in the *Boston News-Letter* was in the issue for the week of May 15, 1704:

"Arrived at Marblehead, Captain Quelch in the Brigantine that Captain Plowman went out in. Is said to come from New Spain and have made a good Voyage."

Quelch was a good deal more of a man than Captain Kidd who skulked homeward, hiding his treasure, parleying with Governor Bellomont at long range, afraid to come to close quarters. A strutting, swaggering, villain was John Quelch, daring to beard the lion in his den, trusting to his ability to deceive with the authorities. To have run away with a privateer, thrown the captain overboard, filled the hold with loot, and then sailed back to Marblehead was no ordinary achievement. However, this truly artistic piracy was so coldly welcomed that a week after his arrival had been chronicled, he was in jail and the following proclamation issued:

"By the Honourable THOMAS POVEY, Esq., Lieut. Governour and Commander in Chief, for the time being, of Her Majesties Province of the Massachusetts Bay in New England.

A PROCLAMATION

Whereas, John Quelch, late Commander of the Brigantine *Charles* and Company to her belonging, Viz, John Lambert, John Miller, John Clifford, John Dorothy, James Parrot, Charles James, William Whiting, John Pitman, John Templeton, Benjamin Perkins, William Wiles, Richard Lawrance, Erasmus Peterson, John King, Charles King, Isaac Johnson, Nicholas Lawson, Daniel Chevalle, John Way, Thomas Farrington, Matthew Primer, Anthony Holding, William Raynor, John Quittance, John Harwood, William Jones, Denis Carter, Nicholas Richardson, James Austin, James Pattison, Joseph Hutnot, George Pierse, George Norton, Gabriel Davis, John Breck, John Carter, Paul Giddens, Nicholas Dunbar, Richard Thurbar,

SPOOKY TREASURE TROVES

Daniel Chuly, and others; Have lately imported a considerable quantity of Gold dust, and some Bar and Coin'd Gold, which they are Violently suspected to have gotten and obtained by Felony and Piracy from some of Her Majesties Friends and Allies, and have Imported and Shared the same among themselves without any Adjudication or Condemnation thereof to be lawful Prizes; The said Commander and some others being apprehended and in Custody, the rest are absconded and fled from Justice.

"I have therefore thought fit, by and with the advice of Her Majesties Council, strictly to Command and Require all Officers Civil and Military, and others Her Majesties loving Subjects to Apprehend and Seize the said Persons, or any of them, whom they may know or find, and them secure and their Treasure, and bring them before one of the Council, or next Justice of the Peace, in order to their being safely conveyed to Boston, to be Examined and brought to Answer what shall be Objected against them, on Her Majesties behalf.

"And all Her Majesties Subjects, and others, are hereby strictly forbidden to entertain, harbour, or conceal any of the said Persons, or their Treasure, or to convey away, or in any manner further the Escape of any of them, on pain of being proceeded against with utmost Severity of Law, as accessories and partakers with them in their Crime.

Given at the Council Chamber in Boston the 24th Day of May in the Third Year of the Reign of our Sovereign Lady ANNE, by the Grace of GOD of England, Scotland, France, and Ireland, QUEEN, Defender of the Faith, etc. Annoque Domi. 1704.

T. POVEY.

By Order of the Lieut.Governor and Council,Isaac Addington, Secr.GOD Save The QUEEN."

The editor of *The Boston News-Letter*, commenting on the foregoing fulmination, saw fit to qualify his previous mention of Quelch's voyage, and announced under date of May 27:

"Our last gave an Account of Captain Quelch's being said to Arrive from N. Spain, having made a good Voyage, but by the foregoing Proclamation 'tis uncertain whence they came, and too palpably evident they have committed Piracies, either upon her Majesties Subjects or Allies.... William Whiting lyes sick, like to dye, not yet examined. There are two more of them sick at Marble head, and another in Salem Gaol, and James Austin imprisoned at Piscataqua."

SPOOKY TREASURE TROVES

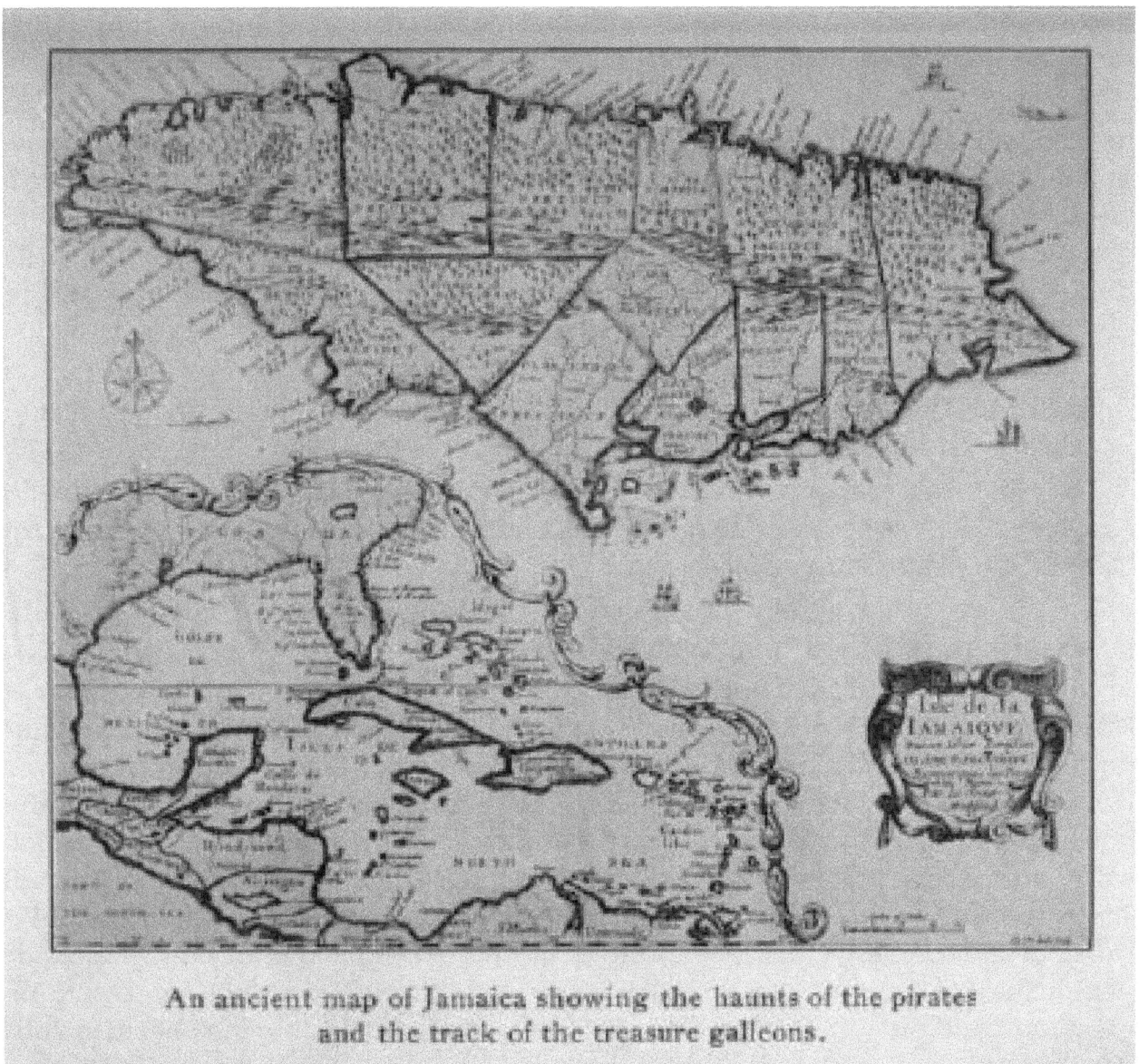

An ancient map of Jamaica showing the haunts of the pirates and the track of the treasure galleons.

As soon as Governor Dudley returned to Boston, a few days later, he issued a proclamation to reinforce that of the Lieutenant Governor, and one paragraph indicated that the case of John Quelch was moving swiftly toward the gallows.

"And it being now made Evident by the Confession of some of the said Persons apprehended and Examined, that the Gold and Treasure by them Imported was robb'd and taken from the Subject of the Crown of Portugal, on which they have also acted divers Villainous Murders, I have thought fit," etc.

It was believed that several of the crew had scampered off with a large amount of the treasure, for Governor Dudley laid great stress on overhauling sundry of them, mentioned by name, "with their Treasure concealed." In his speech at the opening of the General Court on June 1, he stated:

"The last week has discovered a very notorious piracy, committed upon her Majesties Allies, the Portugal, on the coast of Brazil, by Quelch and company, in the *Charles Galley*; for the discovery of which all possible methods have been used, and the severest process against those vile men shall be speedily taken, that the Province be not thereby disparaged, as they have been heretofore; and I hope every good man will do his duty according to the several Proclamations to discover the pirates and their treasure, agreable to the Acts of Parliament in that case made and provided."

Dudley was as energetic in pursuit of the runaway pirates as Bellomont had been, and the *News-Letter* recorded his activities in this wise:

"Warrants are issued forth to seize and apprehend Captain Larimore in the *Larimore Galley*, who is said to have Sailed from Cape Anne with 9 or 11 Pirates of Captain Quelch's Company."

"There is two more of the Pirates seized this week and in Custody viz. Benjamin Perkins, and John Templeton."

"Rhode Island, June 9. The Honorable Samuel Cranston, Esq., Governour of Her Majesties Colony of Rhode Island, etc., Having received a Proclamation Emitted by His Excellency Joseph Dudley, Esq. General and Gov. in Chief in and over Her Majesties Province of the Mass. Bay, etc., for Seizing and Apprehending the late Company of Pirates belonging to the Briganteen *Charles*, of whom John Quelch was Commander, By and with the advice of the Deputy Governour and Council Present, issued forth his further Proclamation to Seize and Apprehend said Pirates, or any of their Treasure, and to bring them before one of the Council, or next Justice of the Peace, in order to be conveyed to the town of Newport, to be examined and proceeded with according to Law. Commanding the Sheriff to Publish this and His Excellencies Proclamation in the Town of New-port, and in other Towns of the Colony. Strictly forbidding all Her Majesties Subjects and others to conceal any of them or their treasure, or convey and further their escape, on pain of being proceeded against with utmost severity of law."

"Marblehead, June 9. The Honorable Samuel Sewall, Nathanael Byfield, and Paul Dudley, Esqrs. came to this place yesterday, in obedience to His Excellency the Governour, his Order for the more effectual discovering and Seizing the Pirates lately belonging to the Briganteen *Charles*, John Quelch Commander, with their Treasure. They made Salem in their way, where Samuel Wakefield the Water Baily informed them of a rumour that two of Quelch's Company were lurking at Cape Anne, waiting for a Passage off the Coast. The Commissioners made out a Warrant to Wakefield to Search for them, and dispatched him away on Wednesday night. And having gain'd intelligence this Morning that a certain number of them well Armed, were at Cape Anne, designing to go off in the *Larimore Galley*, then at Anchor in the Harbour, they immediately sent Men from the several adjacent Towns by Land and Water to prevent their escape, and went thither themselves, to give necessary orders upon the place."

"Gloucester, upon Cape Anne, June 9. The Commissioners for Seizing the Pirates and their Treasure arrived here this day, were advised that the *Larimore Galley* Sail'd in the Morning Eastward, and that a Boat was seen to go off from the head of the Cape, near Snake Island, full of men, supposed to be the Pirates. The Commissioners, seeing the Government mock'd by Captain Larimore and his officers, resolved to send after them. Major Stephen Sewall who attended with a Fishing Shallop, and the Fort Pinnace, offered to go in pursuit of them, and Captain John Turner, Mr. Robert Brisco, Capt. Knight, and several other good men voluntarily accompanied him, to the Number of 42 men who rowed out of the Harbour after Sun-sett, being little Wind."

"Salem, June 11. This afternoon Major Sewall brought into this Port the *Larimore Galley* and Seven Pirates, viz., Erasmus Peterson, Charles James, John Carter, John Pitman, Francis King, Charles King, John King, whom he with his Company Surprized and Seized at the Isles of Sholes the 10th. Instant viz. four of them on Board the *Larimore Galley*, and three on shoar on Starr Island, being assisted by John Hinckes and Thomas Phipps, Esqrs., two of her Majesties Justices of New Hampshire, who were happily there, together with the Justices and the Captain of the Place. He also seized 45 Ounces and Seven Penny weight of Gold of the said Pirates. Captain Thomas Larimore, Joseph Wells, Lieutenant, and Daniel Wormall, Master, and the said Pirates are Secured in our Gaol."

"Gloucester, June 12. Yesterday Major Sewall passed by this place with the *Larimore Galley* and Shallop *Trial* standing for Salem, and having little wind, set our men ashore on the Eastern Point, giving of them notice that William Jones and Peter Roach, two of the Pirates had mistook their way, and were still left at the Cape, with strict charge to search for them, which our Towns People performed very industriously. Being strangers and destitute of all Succours, they surrendered themselves this Afternoon, and were sent to Salem Prison."

"Boston, June 17. On the 13th. Instant, Major Sewall attended with a strong guard brought to Town the above mentioned Pirates and Gold he had seized and gave His Excellency a full Account of his Procedure in Seizing them. The Prisoners were committed to Gaol in order to a Tryal, and the Gold delivered to the Treasurer and Committee appointed to receive the same. The service of Major Sewall and Company was very well Accepted and Rewarded by the Governour.

"His Excellency was pleased on the 13 Currant to open the High Court of Admiralty for trying Capt. John Quelch, late Commander of the Briganteen *Charles*, and Company for Piracy, who were brought to the Barr, and the Articles exhibited against them read. They all pleaded Not Guilty, excepting three, viz. Matthew Primer, John Clifford, and James Parrot, who were reserved for Evidences and are in her Majesties Mercy. The Prisoners moved for Council, and His Excellency assigned them Mr. James Meinzes. The Court was adjourned to the 16th. When met again Capt. Quelch preferr'd a Petition to His Excellency and Honorable Court, craving longer time which was granted till Monday Morning at Nine of the Clock, when said Court is to sit again in order to their Tryal."

Newspaper reporting was primitive in the Year of Our Lord, 1704, and we are denied further information of the merry chase after the fleeing pirates and their treasure. One would like to know more of that adventure at the Isles of Shoals and what the fugitives were doing "on shoar" at Starr Island. The trial of Quelch and his companions was recorded with much more detail because it had certain important and memorable aspects. It will be recalled that Kidd and his men were sent to England for trial by Bellomont for the reason that the colonial laws made no provision for executing the death sentence in the case of a convicted pirate. The difficulties and delays and the large expense incident to the Kidd proceedings were among the considerations which moved Parliament, by an act passed in the reign of William III, to confer upon the Crown authority to issue commissions for the trial of pirates by Courts of Admiralty out of the realm. Such a commission was finally sent to Lord Bellomont for the trial of pirates in Massachusetts, New Hampshire, and Rhode Island. Another document of the same kind, granting him this power for New York, arrived there after his death.

These rights were confirmed by Queen Anne, and in her instructions to Governor Dudley she expressed "her will and pleasure that in all matters relating to the prosecution of pirates, he govern himself according to the act and commission aforesaid." The trial of Quelch was the first to be held by virtue of these authorizations, and therefore the first capital proceedings against pirates in the New England Colonies. A special court was convened, and an imposing tribunal it was, comprising the Governors and Lieutenant Governors of the Provinces of Massachusetts Bay, and New Hampshire, the Judge of Vice Admiralty in each, the Chief Justices of the Superior Court of Judicature, the Secretary of the Province, Members of the Council of Massachusetts Bay, and the Collector of Customs for New England.

The sessions were held in the Star Tavern, on the present Hanover Street of Boston, and Quelch was tried first, "being charged with nine several articles of piracy and murder." He was very expeditiously found guilty and sentenced to death, after which nineteen of his company, in two batches, were dealt the same verdict. From this wholesale punishment only two were excepted, William Whiting, "the witnesses proving no matter of fact upon him, said Whiting being sick all the voyage and not active," and John Templeton, "a servant about fourteen years of age, and not charged with any action." These were acquitted.

SPOOKY TREASURE TROVES

There are preserved only two copies of a broadside published in Boston in July of 1704 which quaintly portrays the strenuous efforts made to save the souls of the condemned pirates who must have been men of uncommonly stout endurance to stand up under the sermons with which they were bombarded. This little pamphlet may serve as a warning to venturesome boys of the twentieth century who yearn to go a-pirating and to bury treasure.

An Account of the Behaviour and Last Dying SPEECHES

Of the Six Pirates that were Executed on Charles River, Boston side, On Fryday, June 30th. 1704. Viz.

Captain John Quelch, John Lambert, Christopher Scudamore, John Miller, Erasmus Peterson, and Peter Roach.

The Ministers of the Town had used more than ordinary Endeavours to Instruct the Prisoners, and bring them to Repentance. There were Sermons Preached in their hearing Every Day; And Prayers daily made with them. And they were Catechised; and they had many occasional Exhortations. And nothing was left that could be done for their Good.

On Fryday, the 30th of June, 1704, Pursuant to Orders in the Dead Warrant, the aforesaid Pirates were guarded from the Prison in Boston by Forty Musketeers, Constables of the Town, the Provost Marshal and his Officers, etc, with two Ministers who took great pains to prepare them for the last Article of their Lives. Being allowed to walk on foot through the Town, to Scarlet's Wharf: where the Silver Oar being carried before them, they went by Water to the Place of Execution being crowded and thronged on all sides by Multitudes of Spectators. The Ministers then spoke to the Malefactors to this Effect:

"We have told you often, yea, we have told you weeping, that you have by Sin undone yourselves; That you were born Sinners; That you have lived Sinners; That your Sins have been many and mighty; and that the Sins for which you are now to Dy, are of no Common aggravation. We have told you that there is a Saviour for Sinners, and we have shewn you how to commit yourselves into his Saving and Healing Hands. We have told you that if He Save you He will give you as hearty Repentance for all your Sins, and we have shewn you how to Express that Repentance. We have told you what Marks of Life must be desired for your Souls, that you may Safely appear before the Judgment Seat of God. Oh! That the means used for your Good may by the Grace of God be made Effectual. We can do no more, but leave you in His Merciful Hands."

When they were gone upon the Stage, and Silence was Commanded, One of the Ministers Prayed as followeth:

"Oh! Thou most Great and Glorious LORD! Thou art a Righteous and a Terrible God. It is a righteous and an Holy Law that thus hast given unto all, but what would soon have done the worst things in the World. Oh! The Free-Grace! Oh! The Riches of that Grace, which has made all the Difference! But now, we cry us. To break that Good Law, and Sin against thy Infinite Majesty can be no little Evil. Thy Word is always True, and very Particular, that Word of thine which has told us and warned us, EVIL PURSUETH SINNERS. We have seen it, we have seen it. We have before our Eyes a dreadful Demonstration of it. Oh! Sanctify unto us, a Sight that has in it so much of the Terror of the Lord!

"Here is a Number of men that have been very great Sinners, and that are to Dy before their Time, for their being wicked overmuch.

"... But now we cry mightily to Heaven, we Lift up our Cries to the God of all Grace, for the Perishing Souls which are just now going to Expire under the Stroke of Justice, before our Eyes. We Mourn, we Mourn, that upon some of them at least, we do unto this minute see no better Symptoms. But, Oh! is there not yet a Room for Sovereign Grace to be display'd, in their Conversion and Salvation? They Perish if they do not now Sincerely turn from Sin to God, and give themselves up to the Lord JESUS CHRIST; They Righteously and Horribly Perish! And yet, without Influences from above, they can do none of those things which must be done if they do not perish. Oh! let us beg it of our God that He would not be so Provoked at their Multiplied and Prodigious Impieties, and at their obstinate Hardness under means of Good formerly afforded them, as to withhold those Influences from them. We cry to thee, O God of all Grace, That thou wouldst not Suffer them to continue in the Gall of Bitterness and Bond of Iniquity, and in the Possession of the Devil. Oh! Knock off the Chains of Death which are upon their Souls; Oh! Snatch the prey out of the Hands of the Terrible.

"... Discover to them, the only Saviour of their Souls. Oh! Dispose them, Oh! Assist them to give the Consent of their Souls unto His Wonderful Proposals. Let them dy Renouncing all Dependence on any Righteousness of their own. Alas, what can they have of their own to Depend upon! As a Token and Effect of their having Accepted the Righteousness of God, Let them heartily Repent of all their Sins against thee, and Abhor and cast up every Morsel of their Iniquity. Oh! Let them not go out of the World raging and raving against the Justice of God and Man. And whatever part of the Satanick Image is yet remaining on their Souls, Oh! Efface it! Let them now dy in such a State and such a Frame as may render them fit to appear before God the Judge of all. What shall plead for them?

"Great GOD grant that all the Spectators may get Good by the horrible Spectacle that is now before them! Let all the People hear and fear, and let no more any such Wickedness be done as has produced this woeful Spectacle. And let all the People beware how they go on in the ways of Sin, and in the paths of the Destroyer, after so Solemn Warnings.

"Oh! but shall our *Sea-faring Tribe* on this Occasion be in a Singular manner affected with the Warnings of God! Lord, May those our dear Bretheren be Saved from the Temptations which do so threaten them! Oh! Let them not Abandon Themselves to Profanity, to Swearing, to Cursing, to Drinking, to Lewdness, to a cursed Forgetfulness of their Maker, and of the End for which He made them! Oh! Let them not be abandoned of God unto those Courses that will hasten them to a Damnation that slumbers not! Oh! Let the men hear the Lord exceedingly, We Pray thee! Let the Condition of the Six or Seven men whom they now see Dying for their Wickedness upon the Sea be Sanctified unto them...."

They then severally Spoke, Viz.

—I—*Captain John Quelch*. The last Words he spoke to one of the Ministers at his going up the Stage were, *I am not afraid of Death. I am not afraid of the Gallows, but I am afraid of what follows; I am afraid of a Great God, and a Judgment to Come*. But he afterwards seem'd to brave it out too much against that fear; also when on the Stage first he pulled off his Hat, and bowed to the Spectators, and not concerned, nor behaving himself so much like a Dying man as some would have done. The Ministers had in the Way to his Execution much desired him to Glorify God at his Death, by bearing a due Testimony against the Sins that had ruined him, and for the ways of Religion which he had much neglected; yet now being called upon to speak what he had to say, it was but this much. *What I have to say is this. I desire to be informed for what I am here. I am Condemned only upon Circumstances. I forgive all the World. So the Lord be Merciful to my Soul*. When *Lambert* was Warning the Spectators to beware of Bad Company, *Quelch* joyning *They should also take care how they brought Money into New England, to be Hanged for it!*

—II—*John Lambert*. He appeared much hardened, and pleaded much on his Innocency; He desired all men to beware of Bad Company; he seem'd in a great Agony near his Execution; he called much and frequently on Christ for Pardon of Sin, that God Almighty would save his innocent Soul; he desired to forgive all the World. His last words were, *Lord, forgive my Soul! Oh, receive me into Eternity! Blessed Name of Christ, receive my Soul*.

—III—*Christopher Scudamore*. He appeared very Penitent since his Condemnation, was very diligent to improve his time going to, and at the place of Execution.

—IV—*John Miller*. He seem'd much concerned, and complained of a great Burden of Sins to answer for; expressing often *Lord, what shall I do to be Saved*!

—V—*Erasmus Peterson*. He cryed of injustice done him, and said *It is very hard for so many lives to be taken away for a little Gold*. He often said his Peace was made with God, and his Soul would be with God, yet extream hard to forgive those he said had wronged him. He told the Executioner, *he was a strong man, and Prayed to be put out of misery as soon as possible*.

—VI—*Peter Roach*. He seem'd little concerned, and said but little or nothing at all. Francis King was also brought to the place of Execution but Repriev'd.

Printed for and Sold by Nicholas Boone, at his Shop near the Old Meeting-House in Boston. 1704.

ADVERTISEMENT.

There is now in the Press and will speedily be Published: The Arraignment, Tryal and Condemnation of Captain John Quelch, and others of his Company etc. for sundry Piracies, Robberies and Murder committed upon the Subjects of the King of Portugal, Her Majesties Allie, on the Coast of Brasil etc. Who upon full Evidence were found guilty at the Court-House in Boston on the 13th of June 1704. With the Arguments of the Queen's Council and Council for the Prisoners, upon the Act for the more effectual Suppression of Piracy. With an account of the Ages of the several Prisoners, and the Places where they were Born.

The *News-Letter* was less inclined to vouch for the pious inclinations of these poor wretches, and gravely stated that "notwithstanding all the great labour and pains taken by the Reverend Ministers of the Town of Boston, ever since they were first Seized and brought to Town, both before and since their Tryal and Condemnation, to instruct, admonish, preach, and pray for them: yet as they had led a wicked and vicious life, so to appearance they dyed very obdurately and impenitently, hardened in their Sins."

Be that as it may, the figure of bold John Quelch on the gallows, bowing to the spectators, hat in hand, was that of no whimpering coward, and one admires him for that grimly sardonic touch of humor as he warned the silent, curious multitude to take care "how they brought money into New England, to be hanged for it." Among these devout and somber Pilgrims and Puritans who Listened to that singularly moving prayer, tremendous in its sincerity, were more than a few who were bringing money into New England by means of trade in rum and negroes, or very quietly buying and selling the merchandise fetched home by pirates who were lucky enough to keep clear of the law. The Massachusetts colonists dearly loved to make public parade of a rogue caught in the act, and to see six pirates hanged at once was a rare holiday indeed.

These only of the number convicted and condemned were hanged. All the others were pardoned a year later by Queene Anne at the recommendation of Governor Dudley, with the exhortation "that as they had now new Lives given them, they should be new men, and be very faithful and diligent in the Service of Her Majesty; who might as easily and justly have ordered their Execution this day as sent their Pardon." As one way of turning pirates to some useful account, these forgiven rogues were promptly drafted into the royal navy as able seamen, and doubtless made excellent food for powder.

SPOOKY TREASURE TROVES

Although a large part of that hundred weight of gold was successfully concealed by Quelch and his comrades, either buried at the Isles of Shoals, or otherwise spirited away, enough of it was recovered to afford a division of the spoils among various officials in a manner so suggestive of petty graft as to warrant the conclusion that piracy was not entirely a maritime trade in Puritan Boston. Every man Jack of them who had anything whatever to do with catching or keeping or hanging Quelch and his fellows poked his fingers into the bag of gold. It seems like very belated muck-raking to fish up the document that tells in detail what became of so much of the Quelch treasure as fell into the greedy hands of the authorities, but here are the tell-tale figures:

"To Stephen North, who kept the Star Tavern in which the trial was held, for entertainment of the Commissioners during the sitting of the Court of Admiralty, and for Witnesses, Twenty-eight pounds, Eleven shillings, and six pence.

"To Lieut. Gov. Usher, Expenses in securing and returning of James Austin's Gold from the Province of New Hampshire, Three pounds, ten shillings.

"To Richard Jesse, Sheriffe of New Hampshire and his Officers and under keeper, for charge of keeping the said Austin, expenses in his sickness, and charge of conveying him into this Province, Nine pounds, five shillings.

"To Mr. James Menzies of Council for the Prisoners on their Tryal, as signed by the Commissioners, Twenty Pounds.

"To Henry Franklyn, Marshal of the Admiralty for the Gibbet, Guards, and execution, Twenty-nine pounds, nineteen shillings. Later forty shillings added to Thomas Barnard for erecting the gibbet.

"To Samuel Wakefield, Deputy Marshal of the Admiralty, for charges in apprehending several of the said Pirates, Four Pounds, five shillings and six pence.

"To Mr. Apthorp and Mr. Jesse, two of the Constables of Boston for their service about apprehending the said Pirates, forty shillings.

"To the Constables of the Several Towns betwixt Bristol and Boston for apprehending and conveying of Christopher Scudamore, two pounds, eighteen shillings.

"To Captain Edward Brattle, charges on a Negro boy imported by the said Pirates, Twenty five shillings.

"To Andrew Belcher, Esq., charges for Clothing of the Witnesses sent to England with Larrimore and Wells, charged as accessories, seven pounds, eighteen shillings.

"To Paul Dudley, Esq., the Queen's Advocate for the prosecution of the said Pirates, preparing the said Tryal for the press, supervising of the same, and for his service relating to Captain Larrimore, in the whole, Thirty-six pounds.

"To Thomas Newton, Esq. of Council for the Queen in the said Tryal, ten pounds.

"To Mr. John Valentine, Register, for his service on the Tryal and for transcribing them to be transmitted to her Majesty's High Court of Admiralty in England, Thirteen pounds.

"To Mr. Sheriffe Dyer, for his service relating to the said Prisoners, Five pounds.

"To Wm. Clarke of Boston, for Casks, shifting and landing the Sugar and other things piratically and feloniously obtained by Captain Quelch and Company, and for storage of them, Thirteen pounds.

"To Daniel Willard, Keeper of the Prison in Boston, toward the charge of feeding and keeping of the said Pirates, Thirty pounds.

"To Andrew Belcher, the Commissary-General, an additional sum of five pounds nine shillings and six pence for necessary clothing supplied to some of the Pirates in prison.

"To Major James Sewall for his pursuit and apprehension of seven of the Pirates, and for the gratification of himself, Captain Turner, and other officers, one hundred and thirty-two pounds, five shillings."

The town and bay of Tobermory, Island of Mull. The treasure galleon is supposed to have gone down in the place indicated by the cross at the right hand side of the photograph.

SPOOKY TREASURE TROVES

The commissioners, Sewall, Byfield and Paul Dudley, received for their expenses and services, twenty-five pounds, seven shillings, and ten pence.

Finally, there were given to the captains of the several companies of militia in the town for Boston, "for their charges and expenses on Guards and Watches on the Pirates during their Imprisonment, Twenty-seven pounds, sixteen shillings, and three pence: to Captain Tuthill, for his assistance to secure and bring about the Vessel and goods from Marblehead, five pounds; to Mr. Jeremiah Allen, the Treasurer's bookkeeper, for his care and service about the said Gold and goods, five pounds; to Constable Apthorp and Jesse, for their services, a further allowance of three pounds."

The amount of the "royal bounty" given the Governor as his share of the pirates' booty, is not recorded. If the belief of those of their contemporaries who best know the Dudleys may be relied on, the fees and emoluments officially awarded them were by no means the extent of the profits from their dealings with the pirates and their treasure. When Cotton Mather quarreled with Governor Dudley a few years later he did not hesitate to intimate this charge pretty broadly in the following passage in his memorial on Dudley's administration:

"There have been odd *Collusions* with the Pyrates of Quelch's Company, of which one instance is, That there was extorted the sum of about Thirty Pounds from some of the crew for liberty to walk at certain times in the prison yard. And this liberty having been allowed for two or three days unto them, they were again confined to their former wretched circumstances."

SPOOKY TREASURE TROVES

CHAPTER VII
THE ARMADA GALLEON OF TOBERMORY BAY

Between the western Highlands of Scotland and the remote, cloudy Hebrides lies the large island of Mull on a sound of that name. Its bold headlands are crowned with the ruins of gray castles that were once the strongholds of the clans of the MacLeans and the MacDonalds. Along these shores and waters one generation after another of kilted fighting men, savage as red Indians, raided and burned and slew in feuds whose memories are crowded with tragedy and romance. Near where Mull is washed by the Atlantic and the Sound opens toward the thoroughfares of the deep-sea shipping is the pleasant town of Tobermory, which in the Gaelic means Mary's Well. The bay that it faces is singularly beautiful, almost landlocked, and of a depth sufficient to shelter a fleet.

Into this Bay of Tobermory there sailed one day a great galleon of Spain, belonging to that mighty Armada which had been shattered and driven in frantic flight by English seamen with hearts of oak under Drake, Hawkins, Howard, Seymour, and Martin Frobisher, names to make the blood beat faster even now. The year was 1588, in the reign of Elizabeth, long, long, ago. This fugitive galleon, aforetime so tall and stately and ornate, was racked and leaking, her painted sails in tatters, her Spanish sailors sick, weary, starved, after escaping from the English Channel and faring far northward around the stormy Orkneys. Many of her sister ships had crashed ashore on the Irish coast while the surviving remnant of this magnificent flotilla wallowed forlornly home. Seeking provisions, repairs, respite from the terrors of the implacable ocean the galleon *Florencia* dropped anchor in Tobermory Bay, and there she laid her bones.

With her, it is said, was lost a great store of treasure in gold and plate, and ever since 1641, for more than two and a half centuries, the search for these riches has been carried on at intervals. More than likely, if you should go in one of Donald MacBrayne's steamers through the Sound of Mull next summer, and a delightful excursion it is, you would find an up-to-date suction dredge and a corps of divers,

SPOOKY TREASURE TROVES

employed by the latest syndicate to finance the treasure hunt, ransacking the mud of Tobermory Bay in the hope of finding the Spanish gold of the *Florencia*. Many thousands have been vainly spent in the quest, but the lure of lost treasure has a fascination of its own, and after all the failure of Scotch and English seekers, American enterprise and capital have now taken hold of this romantic task.

With the history of the *Florencia* galleon and her treasure is intimately interwoven the stirring chronicle of the deeds of the MacLeans of Mull and the MacDonalds of Islay and Skye. Out of the echoing past, the fanfare of Spanish trumpets is mingled with the skirl of the pipes, and the rapier of Toledo flashes beside the claymore of the Highlanders. The story really begins long before the doomed galleon sought refuge in Tobermory Bay. There were island chieftains of the Clan MacLean, busy at cutting the throats of their enemies, as far remote in time as the thirteenth century, but their turbulent pedigrees need not concern our narrative until the warlike figure of Lachlan Mo'r MacLean, "Big Lachlan," steps into its pages in the year of 1576.

It was then that he came of age and set out from the Court of James VI at Edinburgh, where he had been brought up, to claim his inherited estates of Mull. His wicked step-father, Hector, met him in the castle of Duart whose stout walls and battlements still loom not far from Tobermory and tried to set him aside with false and foolish words. The astute youth perceived that if he were to come into his own, he must be up and doing, wherefore he speedily mustered friends and led them into Castle Duart by night. They carried this scheming step-father to the island of Coll and there beheaded him, which made Lachlan's title clear to the lands of his ancestors.

The next to mistake the mettle of young Lachlan Mo'r was no less than Colin Campbell, sixth Earl of Argyll, head of a family very powerful in the Highlands even to this day. He was for seizing the estate by force after plotting to no purpose, and Angus MacDonald of Dunyweg was persuaded to help him with several hundred fighting men. Thus began the feud between the MacLeans and MacDonalds which a few years later was to involve that great galleon *Florencia* of the Armada. Argyll and his force wasted the lands of Lachlan with fire and sword, and besieged one of his strongholds with twelve hundred followers.

War thus begun was waged without mercy, and one bloody episode followed on the heels of another. At the head of his clansmen, Lachlan swept into Argyle's country and made him cry quits. This was a large achievement, and the spirited young Lord of Duart was hailed as a Highland chief worthy of the king's favor. He went to court, was flattered by the great men there, and became the hero of as pretty and gallant a romance as heart could wish. The king arranged that he should marry the daughter of the powerful Earl of Athol, and Lachlan could not say his sovereign nay. The contract arranged, he started for Mull to make ready for the wedding, but chanced to visit on the way William Cunningham, Earl of Glencairn, at his castle overlooking the Clyde.

Cards were played to while away the evening, and Lachlan's partner was one of the daughters of the host. It so happened that the game was changed and the players again cut for partners. At this another daughter, the fair Margaret Cunningham, whispered to her sister that if the handsome Highland chief had been *her* partner, "she would not have hazarded the loss of him by cutting anew." Lachlan overheard the compliment, as perhaps he was meant to do, and so far as he was concerned hearts were trumps from that moment. He wooed and won Margaret Cunningham and married her forthwith. The king was greatly offended but what cared this happy man! He carried his bride to Duart and laughed at his foes.

The quiet life at home was not for him, however. Soon he was playing the game of the sword with the MacDonalds of Islay until a truce was patched by means of a marriage between the clans. There was peace for a time, but the trouble blazed anew over the matter of some lifted cattle, and they were at it again hammer-and-tongs. The royal policy seems to have been to permit these Highland gamecocks to fight each other so long as they were fairly well matched. In this case the various MacDonalds combined in such numbers against Lachlan MacLean that the king interfered and persuaded them to seek terms of reconciliation. Accordingly the Lord of the MacDonalds journeyed to Duart Castle with his retinue of bare-legged gentlemen and was hospitably received. Lachlan was canny as well as braw, and he clinched the terms of peace by first locking the visitors in a room whose walls were some twenty feet thick, and then holding as hostages the two young sons of Angus MacDonald.

The high-tempered MacDonald was naturally more exasperated than pacified, and he turned the tables when Lachlan soon after went to Islay to receive performance of the promises made touching certain lands in dispute. The Highland code of honor was peculiar in that treachery appears to have been a weapon used without scruple. The MacDonalds swore that not a MacLean should suffer harm, but no sooner had Lachlan and his clansmen and servants arrived than they were attacked at night by a large force. The party would have been put to the sword, but that Lachlan rushed into the midst of the foe holding aloft one of MacDonald's sons as a shield.

This caused postponement of the slaughter, MacDonald offering quarter if his child should be delivered to him. The MacLeans were disarmed and bound, except two young men who had distinguished themselves by laying many a MacDonald low in the heather. These were beheaded at once, and beginning next morning two MacLeans were led out and executed each day in the presence of their own chief until no more than Lachlan and his uncle were left. They were

SPOOKY TREASURE TROVES

spared only because the sanguinary Angus MacDonald fell from his horse and was badly hurt before he could finish his program.

Duart Castle, chief stronghold of the MacLeans.

Ardnamurchan Castle, seat of the MacIans and the MacDonalds.

SPOOKY TREASURE TROVES

It would be tiresome to relate much more of this ensanguined, interminable game of give and take which was the chief business of the Highland clans in that century. The clan of the MacIans whose seat was at Ardnamurchan Castle on Mull later sided actively with the MacDonalds and the feud became three-cornered. Lachlan Mo'r MacLean was no petty warrior, and his men were numbered by the thousand when he was in the prime of his power. Once he fell upon the island of Islay and put to the sword as many as five hundred of his foes, "all the men capable of bearing arms belonging to the Clan-donald," says an old account. Angus himself was chased into his castle and forced to give over half of Islay to Lachlan to save his skin.

Now, indeed, was there a mustering of the MacDonalds from near and far to invade Mull. They gathered under the chiefs of Kintyre, Skye and Islay, with the lesser clans under MacNeil of Gigha, the MacAllisters of Loupe, and the MacPhees of Colonsay. Bold Lachlan Mo'r MacLean was outnumbered, but a singular stroke of luck enabled him to win a decisive battle. That MacDonald who was called the Red Knight of Sleat, was much disturbed and shaken by a dream in which a voice chanted a very doleful prophecy of which this is a sample:

"Dire are the deeds the fates have doomed on thee!Defeated by the sons of Gillean the invading host shall be.On thee, Gearna-Dubh,[1] streams of blood shall flow;And the bold Red Knight shall die ere a sword is sheathed."

This message caused the Red Knight to sound the retreat soon after the fray began, and his example spread panic among the force which broke and ran for their boats, and the best MacDonald was he who first reached the beach. The claymores of the MacLeans hewed them down without mercy and their heads were chopped off and thrown into a well which has since borne a Gaelic name descriptive of the event. It would seem that these clans must have exterminated each other by this time, but the bleak moors and rocky slopes of these western islands bore a wonderful crop of fighting men, and soon the MacLeans were invading the coast of Lorn and spreading havoc among the MacDonalds with great slaughter.

Lachlan found time also to seek vengeance on the MacIans for daring to meddle in his affairs. John MacIan, chief of that smaller clan which owed fealty to the MacDonalds, had been a suitor for the hand of Lachlan Mo'r MacLean's mother, who was a sister of the Earl of Carlyle, and had a fortune in her own right. Now the MacIan renewed his attentions, and Lachlan looked on grimly, aware that the motive was greed of gold and lands. His mother gave her consent but her two-fisted son made no objection until the MacIan came to Mull to claim his bride. The marriage was performed in the presence of Lachlan and his most distinguished retainers, and there was a feast and much roaring conviviality. In the evening, the company being hot with wine, a rash MacIan brought up the matter of the recent feud and a pretty quarrel was brewed in a twinkling.

SPOOKY TREASURE TROVES

Several of the MacIans boasted that their chief had wed "the old lady" for the sake of her wealth. "Drunkards ever tell the truth," flung back a MacLean with which he plunged a dirk into the heart of the tactless guest. Instantly the swords were flashing, and hardly a MacIan came alive out of the banqueting hall. Lachlan missed this mêlée, for some reason or other, but coming on the scene a little later he quoted in the Gaelic a proverb which means, "If the fox rushes upon the hounds he must expect to be torn." His followers took it that he felt no sorrow at the fate of the MacIans, and forthwith they rushed into the chamber of the bridegroom, dragged him forth, and would have dispatched him, but the lamentations of Lachlan's mother for once moved her rugged son to pity, and he contented himself with throwing the chief of the MacIans into the dungeon of Duart Castle.

This happened in the summer of 1588, and affairs were in this wise when the galleon *Florencia* came sailing into Tobermory Bay. Her captain, Don Pareira, was a fiery sea-fighter whom misfortune had not tamed. These savage Highlanders were barbarians in his eyes, and he would waste no courtesy on them. There were several hundred Spanish soldiers in the galleon, of the great army of troops which had been sent in the Armada to invade England, and Captain Pareira thought himself in a position to demand what he wanted. He sent a boat ashore with a message to Lachlan Mo'r MacLean at his castle at Duart, asking that provisions be furnished him, and adding that in case of refusal or delay he should take them by force. To this Lachlan sent back the haughty reply that "the wants of the distressed strangers should be attended to after the captain of the Spanish ship had been taught a lesson in courteous behavior. In order that the lesson might be taught him as speedily as possible, he was invited to land and supply his wants by the forcible means of which he boasted. It was not the custom of the Chief of the MacLeans to pay attention to the demands of a threatening and insolent beggar."

At this it may be presumed that Captain Pareira swore a few rounds of crackling oaths in his beard as he strode his high-pooped quarter-deck. His men who had gone ashore reported that the MacLean was an ill man to trifle with and that he had best be let alone. Already the clan was gathering to repel a landing force from the galleon. The captain of the battered *Florencia* took wiser counsel with himself and perceived that he had threatened over hastily. Pocketing his pride, he assured the ruffled Lachlan of Castle Duart that he would pay with gold for whatever supplies might be granted him.

Lachlan had other fish to fry, for the MacDonalds, exceedingly wroth at the scurvy treatment dealt that luckless bridegroom and ally, the chief of the MacIans, were up in arms and making ready to avenge the black insult. In need of men to defend himself, Lachlan MacLean struck a bargain with the captain of the galleon. If Pareira should lend him a hundred soldiers from the *Florencia* he would consider this service as part payment for the supplies and assistance desired.

SPOOKY TREASURE TROVES

Away marched the contingent from the galleon in company with the MacLean clansmen, and laid siege to the MacIan castle of Mingarry after ravaging the small islands of Rum and Eigg. Lachlan Mo'r was carrying all before him, burning, killing, plundering both MacDonalds and MacIans, when Captain Pareira sent him word that the *Florencia* was ready to sail, and he should like to have his soldiers returned. To this MacLean replied that the account between them had not been wholly squared. There was the matter of payment promised in addition to the loan of the soldiers. The people of Tobermory and thereabouts had sent grain and cattle aboard the galleon, and they must have their money before sailing day.

Captain Pareira promised that every satisfaction should be given before he left the country, and again requested that his hundred *soldadoes* be marched back to their ship.

This Lachlan was willing to do, but still suspecting the commander of the galleon as a wily bird, he detained three of the officers of the troops as hostages to assure final settlement. Then he sent on board the *Florencia* young Donald Glas, son of the MacLean of Morvern, to collect what was due and adjust the affair. No sooner had he set foot on deck, than he was disarmed and bundled below by order of Pareira who considered that two could play at holding that form of collateral known as hostages.

Now ensued a dead-lock. Lachlan MacLean refused to yield up his brace of Spanish officers unless the demands of his people were paid in full, while Captain Pareira kept Donald Glas locked in a cabin and swore to carry him to sea. The tragedy which followed is told in the traditions of Mull to this day. When Donald Glas learned that he was kidnapped in the galleon, he resolved to wreak dreadful revenge for the treachery dealt his kinsmen. On the morning when the *Florencia* weighed anchor, an attendant who had been confined with him was sent on shore and Donald sent word of his fell intention to the chief of the clan.

Overnight Donald Glas had discovered that only a bulkhead separated his cabin from the powder magazine of the galleon, and by some means, which tradition omits to explain, he cut a hole through the planking and laid a train ready for the match. Just before the *Florencia* weighed anchor he was fetched on deck for a moment to take his last sight of the heathery hills of Mull and Morvern. Then the captive was thrust back into his cabin, and with her great, gay banners trailing from aloft, the galleon made sail and began slowly to move away from the shore of Tobermory Bay.

It was then that Donald Glas, true MacLean was he, fired his train of powder, and bang! the magazine exploded. The galleon was torn asunder with terrific violence, and the bodies of her soldiers and mariners were flung far over the bay and even upon the shore. So complete was the destruction that only three of the several hundred Spaniards escaped alive. The *Florencia* had vanished in a manner truly epic, and proud were the MacLeans of the deed of young Donald Glas who gave his life for the honor of his clan.

One of the surviving traditions is that a dog belonging to Captain Pareira was hurled ashore alive. The faithful creature, when it had recovered from its hurts, refused to leave that part of the strand nearest the wreck, and continued to howl most piteously by day and night as long as it existed, which was more than a year. The Spanish officers, who had remained as hostages in the hands of Lachlan Mo'r MacLean were set at liberty by that sometimes courteous chief, and were permitted to proceed to Edinburgh where they lodged complaint with the king touching the destruction of their galleon. The matter of Captain Pareira having been disposed of in this explosive fashion, Lachlan MacLean returned to his main business of harrying the MacDonalds, and so fiercely and destructively was the feud conducted thereafter, that King James thought it time to interfere, lest he should have no subjects left in the Western Highlands. The warring chiefs were summoned to Edinburgh and imprisoned and fined, after which they made their peace with the king and returned to their island realms. The affair of the *Florencia* was named in the charges brought against MacLean. In the official records of Holyrood Palace, seat of the Scottish kings, is this information, laid before the Privy Council on January 3rd, 1591:

That in the preceding October, Lachlan MacLean "accompanied with a great number of thieves, broken men and ... of clans, besides the number of one hundred Spaniards, came to the properties of His Majesty, Canna, Rum, Eigg and the Isle of Elenole, and after they had wracked and spoiled the said islands, they treasonably raised fire, and in maist barbarous, shameful and cruel manner, burnt the same island, with the men, women and children there, not sparing the youths and infants; and at the same time past came to the Castle of Ardnamurchan, besieged the same, and lay about the said castle three days, using in the meantime all kinds of hostilities and force, both by fire and sword.... The like barbarous and shameful cruelty has seldom been heard of among Christians in any kingdom or age."

On the 20th of March, 1588, King James "granted a remission to Lachlan MacLean of Duart for the cruel murder of certain inhabitants of the islands of Rum, Canna, and Eigg," but from the remission was excepted the "plotting or felonious burning and flaming up, by sulphurous powder, of a Spanish ship and of the men and provisions in her, near the island of Mull."

Swift and tragic as was the fate of Captain Pareira and his ship's company, it was perhaps more merciful than that which befell the great squadron of galleons of the Armada that were cast on the coast of Ireland, on the rocks of Clare and Kerry, in Galway Bay, and along the shores of Sligo and Donegal. More than thirty ships perished in this way, and of the eight thousand half-drowned wretches who struggled ashore no more than a handful escaped slaughter at the hands of the

SPOOKY TREASURE TROVES

wild Irish who knocked them on the head with battle-axes or stripped them naked and left them to die of the cold. Many were Spanish gentlemen, richly clad, with gold chains and rings, and the common sailors and soldiers had each a bag of ducats lashed to his wrist when he landed through the surf. They were slain for their treasure, and on one sand strip of Sligo an English officer counted eleven hundred bodies.

In a letter to Queen Elizabeth, Sir E. Bingham, Governor of Ulster, wrote of the wreckage of twelve Armada ships which he knew of, "the men of which ships did all perish in the sea save the number of eleven hundred or upwards which we put to the sword; amongst whom there were divers gentlemen of quality and service, as captains, masters of ships, lieutenants, ensign bearers, other inferior officers and young gentlemen to the number of some fifty.... which being spared from the sword till orders must be had from the Lord Deputy how to proceed against them, I had special directions sent me to see them executed as the rest were, only reserving alive one Don Luis de Cordova, and a young gentleman, his nephew, till your Highness's pleasure be known."

Alas, Elizabeth could not find it in her heart to spare even these two luckless gentlemen of Spain, and one judges those rude Highlanders less harshly for their bloodthirsty feuds at learning that the great Queen herself "ordered their immediate execution when she received the letter, and it was duly carried out."

Defeat of the Spanish Armada. From the painting by P. de Loutherbourg.

SPOOKY TREASURE TROVES

Froude, in his essay "The Defeat of the Armada," comes to the defense of Elizabeth, or at least he pleads extenuating circumstances.

"Most pitiful of all was the fate of those who fell into the hands of the English garrisons of Galway and Mayo. Galleons had found their way into Galway Bay,—one of them had reached Galway itself,—the crews half dead with famine and offering a cask of wine for a cask of water. The Galway townsmen were humane, and tried to feed and care for them. Most were too far gone to be revived, and died of exhaustion. Some might have recovered, but recovered they would be a danger to the State. The English in the West of Ireland were but a handful in the midst of a sullen, half-conquered population. The ashes of the Desmond rebellion were still smoking, and Dr. Sanders and his Legatine Commission were fresh in immediate memory. The defeat of the Armada in the Channel could only have been vaguely heard of.

"All that the English officers could have accurately known must have been that an enormous expedition had been sent to England by Philip to restore the Pope; and Spaniards, they found, were landing in thousands in the midst of them with arms and money; distressed for the moment, but sure, if allowed time to get their strength again, to set Connaught in a blaze. They had no fortresses to hold so many prisoners, no means of feeding them, no more to spare to escort them to Dublin. They were responsible to the Queen's Government for the safety to the country. The Spaniards had not come on any errand of mercy to her or hers. The stern order went out to kill them all wherever they might be found, and two thousand or more were shot, hanged, or put to the sword. Dreadful! Yes, but war itself is dreadful, and has its own necessities."

A quaint recital of the fate of these fleeing galleons is to be found in a history published by order of Oliver Cromwell, with the title of "Old England Forever, or Spanish Cruelty Displayed." One chapter runs as follows:

"Here followeth a particular Account of the Miserable Condition of the Spanish Fleet, fled to the North of Scotland, and scattered, for many Weeks, on the Sea-Coasts of Ireland. Written October 19, 1588.

"About the Beginning of August, the Fleet was, by Tempest, driven beyond the Isles of Orkney, the Place being above 60 Leagues North Latitude (as already mentioned) a very unaccustomed climate for the Young Gallants of Spain, who did never before feel Storms on the Sea nor cold weather in August. And about those Northern Islands their Mariners and Soldiers died daily by Multitudes, as by their Bodies cast on land did appear. And after twenty Days or more, having passed their Time in great Miseries, they being desirous to return Home to Spain, sailed very far Southward into the Ocean to recover Spain.

"But the Almighty, who always avenges the Cause of his afflicted People who put their Confidence in Him, and brings down his Enemies who exalt themselves to the Heavens, order'd the Winds to be violently contrarious to this proud Navy, that it was with Force dissevered on the High Seas to the West of Ireland; and so a great number of them were driven into divers dangerous Bays, and upon Rocks, all along the West and North Parts of Ireland, in sundry Places distant above an hundred Miles asunder, and there cast away, some sunk, some broken, some run on sands, and some were burned by the Spaniards themselves.

"As in the North Part of Ireland, towards Scotland, between the two Rivers of Lough-foile and Lough-sivelly, nine were driven on Shore, and many of them broke, and the Spaniards forced to come to Land for Succor among the Wild Irish.

"In another Place, twenty miles South West from thence, in a Bay called Borreys, twenty Miles Northward from Galloway, belonging to the Earl of Ormond, one special great Ship of 1000 Tons, with 50 Brass Pieces, and four Cannons was sunk, and all the People drowned, saving 16, who by their Apparel, as it is advertized out of Ireland, seemed to be Persons of Great Distinction.

"Then to come more to the Southward, thirty Miles upon the coast of Thomond, North from the River of Shannon, two or three more perished, whereof one was burned by the Spaniards themselves, and so driven to the Shore. Another was of San Sebastian, wherein were 300 men, who were also all drowned, saving 60; a third Ship, with all her Lading was cast away at a Place called Breckan.

"In another Place, opposite Sir Tirlogh O'Brien's House, there was another great Ship lost, supposed to be a Galleass. The Losses above mentioned were betwixt the 5th, and 10th of September; as was advertized from sundry Places out of Ireland. So as by accompt. from the 21st of July, when this Navy was first beaten by the Navy of England, until the 10th of September, being the space of Seven Weeks, and more, it is very probable that the said Navy had never had one good Day or Night."

That much treasure of gold and jewels and plate went down in these lost galleons was the opinion of Scotch and Irish tradition, but these stories gained the greatest credence in the case of the *Florencia* of Tobermory Bay. She was said to have contained the paymaster's chests of the Armada, and to have carried to the bottom thirty million ducats of money, and the church plate of fabulous richness. It is certain that the *Florencia* was one of the largest galleons of the Armada and that she never returned to Spain. Her armament comprised fifty-two guns, and her company numbered 400 soldiers and eighty-six sailors. It is probable that this was the *Florencia* belonging to the Duke of Tuscany, which was refitting at Santander in September, 1587, concerning which Lord Ashley wrote to Walsingham, after the destruction of the Armada, that she was commanded by a grandee of the first rank who was always "served on silver."

While even now the most painstaking investigation is unable to find definite information regarding the amount of treasure lost in the galleon of Tobermory

SPOOKY TREASURE TROVES

Bay, that she contained a vast amount of riches was believed as early as a half century after her destruction. The papers of the great house of Argyll record the beginning of the search almost as far away as 1640. Of these fascinating documents, the first is the grant to the Marquis of Argyll and his heirs by the Duke of Lennox and Richmond, Lord High Admiral, with consent of King Charles the First, of all rights and ownership in the wreck of the *Florencia* and her treasure. The deed of gift is dated from the Court of St. Theobold's, February 5th, 1641 and "proceeds upon the narrative that in the year 1588, when the great Spanish Armada was sent from Spain towards England and Scotland, and was dispersed by the mercie of God, there were divers ships and other vessels of the Armada, with ornaments, munition, goods, and gear, which were thought to be of great worth, cast away, and sunk to the sea ground on the coast of Mull, near Tobermory, in the Scots seas, where they lay, and still lie as lost; and that the Marquis of Argyll, near whose bounds the ships were lost, having taken notice thereof, and made inquiries therefor, and having heard some doukers[2] and other experts in such matters state that they consider it possible to recover some of the ships and their valuables, was moved to take and to cause pains to be taken thereupon at his own charges and hazard.

"For this reason, the Great Admiral, with the King's consent, gives, grants, and disposes to the Marquis the said ships, ornaments, munition, etc. of the Spanish Armada, and the entire profit that might follow, or that he had already obtained therefrom, with full power to the Marquis, his doukers, seamen, and others to search for the ships, and intromit with them, providing the Marquis were accountable and made prompt payment to the Duke of Lennox and Richmond of a hundredth part of the ships, etc. with deduction of the expenses incurred for their recovery, *pro rata*."

In these words the Crown assigned the treasure of the *Florencia* to the house of Argyll as part of its admiralty rights along that coast where marched the family estates. In 1665, the ninth Earl of Argyll, son of him who had obtained ownership of the galleon, employed an expert diver and wrecker by the name of James Mauld to search for the treasure of ducats and plate. It was an attractive speculation for that notable "douker" who was promised four-fifths of all the "gold, silver, metal, goods, etc." recovered and incidentally the Earl bound himself "that the same James Mauld shall not be molested in his work, and that his workmen shall have peaceable living in these parts during their stay, and traveling through the Highlands and Isles, and shall be free from all robberies, thefts, etc. so far as the said Earl can prevent the same. The said contract provides further lodging houses for the workmen at the usual rates, and is fixed to endure for three years after March 1, 1666."

These divers easily found the hull of the galleon, and they made a chart showing its exact bearings by landmarks on two sides of the bay. This ancient

SPOOKY TREASURE TROVES

chart of the "Spanish wrack" as it is labeled, is owned by the present Duke of Argyll, and has been used by the modern treasure seekers who are unable even with its aid to find the remains of the *Florencia*, so deeply have her timbers sunk in the tide-swept silt of the bay. The interest of the ninth Earl of Argyll in exploring the galleon was diverted by Monmouth's Rebellion in which luckless adventure he became an active leader. He was made prisoner and suffered the loss of his head which abruptly snuffled out his romantic activities as a seeker after lost treasure.

He left among his papers a memorandum concerning the galleon, under date of 1677, which states that "the Spanish wrackship was reputed to have been the *Admiral of Florence*, one of the Armada of 1588, a ship of fifty-six guns, with 30,000,000 of money on board. It was burned and so blown up that two men standing upon the cabin were cast safe on shore. It lay in a very good road, landlocked betwixt a little island and a bay in the Isle of Mull, a place where vessels ordinarily anchored free of any violent tide, with hardly any stream, a clean, hard channel, with a little sand on the top, and little or no mud in most places about, upon ten fathoms at high water and about eight at ground ebb.

"The fore part of the ship above water was quite burned, so that from the mizzen mast to the foreship, no deck was left. The hull was full of sand and the Earl caused it to be searched a little without finding anything but a great deal of cannon ball about the main mast, and some kettles, and tankers of copper, and such like in other places. Over the hindship, where the cabin was, there was a heap of great timber which it would be difficult to remove, but under this is the *main expectation*.

"The deck under the cabin was thought to be entire. The cannon lay generally at some yards distance from the ship, from two to twenty. The Earl's father had the gift of the ship, and attempted the recovery of it, but from want of skilled workmen he did not succeed. In 1666, the Laird of Melgum (James Mauld), who had learned the art of the (diving) bell in Sweden and had made a considerable fortune by it, entered into a contract with the Earl for three years by which Melgum was to be at all the charge, and to give the Earl the fifth part of what was brought up. He wrought only three months, and most of the time was spent in mending his bells and sending for material he needed, so that he raised only two brass cannon of a large calibre, but very badly fortified, and a great iron gun.

"After this, being invited to England, he wrought no more, thinking his trade a secret, and that the Spanish ship would wait for him. On the expiring of the contract, the Earl undertook the work alone and without the aid of any one who had ever seen diving, recovered six cannon, one of which weighed near six hundred weight. The Earl afterwards entered into a contract with a German who undertook great things, and talked of bringing a vessel of forty guns, but instead brought only a yacht and recovered only one anchor, going away soon after, taking his gold with him and leaving some debt behind.

"The contract with the German has expired, and the Earl is provided with a vessel, bells, ropes, and tongs, and with men to work by direction, yet, although he is confident in his own understanding of the art of diving with the bell, he is willing to enter into a contract. He will dispone (grant) the vessel for three years, provided the contractor should keep four skilled men to work in seasonable weather from May 1 to October 1. The Earl will furnish a ship of 60 or 70 tons with twelve seamen, and give his partner a fifth part of the proceeds. If a Crown were found it was to be exempted from the division and presented to his Majesty....

"It is concluded that if the money expected be fallen upon, the fifth part will quickly pay all expenses, and reward the ingenious artist, and if that fail, the cannon will certainly repay the charges."

There are also preserved articles of agreement, dated December 18th, 1676, by which the Earl makes over a three-year concession to John Saint Clare, minister at Ormistoun in Scotland, "for himself and as taking burden for his father," to search the wreck on shares, the Earl reserving "one-third part of what should be recovered during the first year, and one-half of what should be recovered during the last two years." It is also provided that "if the Saint Clares were disturbed during the first year, so as not to be able to work or raise the wreck without damage to their persons (by reason of the unsettled state of the country), the contract should be regarded as not taking effect for a year. The Earl binds himself to produce before November 1, 1676, his right to the ship, under the Great Seal of Scotland, at Edinburgh, and to deliver a copy of it to the Saint Clares. John Saint Clare, younger, binds himself to repair with all skill for its recovery, and for the recovery of the valuables, during the space of three years, and to make true account and payment of the shares above reserved to the Earl and his heirs, etc. Lastly, both parties oblige themselves faithfully to observe all the articles of agreement under the liquidated penalty of 2,000 marks, Scots."

The Saint Clares, or Sinclairs, as the name is spelled in other documents of the same tenor, assigned their rights and contract to one Hans Albricht von Treibelen, who was probably that German referred to by the Earl as taking his gold with him and leaving his debts behind. This document contains a fascinating mention of "all that might be found in the water and about the ship, as gold, silver, bullion, jewels, etc." and sets forth a new scheme of division of the spoils. Now there appears Captain Adolpho E. Smith as a partner of Hans Albricht von Treibelen, and one finds another parchment executed by the Earl who appears to have thought that these "doukers" would bear watching, for they are enjoined "immediately on the recovery of the wreck to deliver on the spot to the Earl's factors or servants who are daily to attend the work and to be witnesses of what is recovered.... Should the work be impeded by the violence of the country people, it is provided that the term of the contract might be lengthened."

The repeated references to molestation by the inhabitants round about were aimed at the Clan MacLean. The great Lachlan M'or had long since closed his stormy career, and, wrapped in his plaid, his bones were smouldering in a grave by Duart Castle. His kinsmen had good memories, however, and there was that debt for provisions which had been left owing by Captain Pareira of the *Florencia* some eighty years before. It might seem that young Donald Glas had squared the account when he blew the galleon and her crew to kingdom come, but the MacLeans were men to nurse the embers of a feud and set the sparks to flying at the next opportunity. They held it that theirs was the first right to the wreck, and cared not a rap for any documentary rights that might have been granted to the Campbells (the clan of the Earls of Argyll), by the Great Admiral of Scotland.

Hector MacLean, brother of Lachlan MacLean of Castle Torloisk, near Tobermory, rallied a force and drove the divers from the wreck. Then, in order that there might be no doubt about the views of the MacLeans, they built a small fort overlooking the bay and the scene of the wreck, the ruins of which still survive. There a detachment was posted with orders to make it hot for any interlopers who might try to find the sunken treasure without first consulting the MacLeans.

This interference found its way into the Courts at Edinburgh in the form of a petition of grievances suffered by Captain Adolpho E. Smith. He swore before a notary that John MacLean, of Kinlochalan, and John MacLean, a servitor to Lachlan MacLean of Torloisk, "had convocated six or seven score of armed men, and he had exhibited to them a royal warrant bearing his Majesty's protection and free liberty to Captain Smith and his servants to work at the wreck-ship at Tobermory, and prohibiting any of his Majesty's subjects from interrupting them. Captain Smith then required the MacLeans to dissipate the armed men, part of whom were in a fort or trench at Tobermory, newly built by them for interrupting the work, and the rest in the place or houses adjacent,—as John MacLean of Kinlochalan acknowledged,—and in his Majesty's name required them to give him and his men liberty to prosecute their work at the wreck.

"Upon this Kinlochalan answered that the men in arms were not commanded by him but by Hector MacLean, brother of Lachlan MacLean of Torloisk, and others; and he declared that not only would Captain Smith and his men be hindered, but that the men in arms would shoot guns, muskets and pistols at them, should any of them offer to duck or work at the wreck. Whereupon Captain Smith took this instrument, protesting against the aforesaid MacLeans and their accomplices, at Tobermory in Mull, 7 September, 1678." The militant and tenacious MacLeans struck terror to the heart of Captain Adolpho Smith, according to another official document called a "notorial instrument at the instance of William Campbell, skip-

SPOOKY TREASURE TROVES

per to the Earl of Argyll's frigate, called *Anna of Argyll*. This worthy sea dog, it appears, as procurator for the Earl," had compeared, desired, and required Captain Adolpho E. Smith and his men to duck and work at the wreckship and to conform to the minutes of contract betwixt the Earl and him, otherwise to give the bells, sinks, and other instruments necessary for ducking to William Campbell, and the men on board the Earl's frigate, who would duck them without any regard to the threatenings of the MacLeans.

"Notwithstanding this, Captain Smith and his men refused to duck and work, or to give over the bells, etc., necessary for the work to William Campbell who thereupon, as procurator for the Earl of Argyll asked and took instruments and protested against Captain Smith for cost, skaith, and damage conform to the contract. The instrument was taken by Donald McKellar, notary public, at and aboard the yacht belonging to Captain Adolpho E. Smith, lying in the Bay of Tobermory in Mull, 7 September, 1678."

The wreck of the galleon was fought over about this time, not only by the mettlesome MacLeans but also by the Duke of York as Lord High Admiral of Scotland and the Isles, succeeding in that office the Duke of Lennox. He challenged the rights of the house of Argyll to the *Florencia* and her treasure and instituted legal proceedings in due form which were decided in favor of the defendant, thereby confirming for all time the possession of the wreck, which belongs to the present Duke of Argyll. The verdict read in part as follows:

"The rights, reasons, and allegations of the parties, and the gifts and ratifications therein referred to, produced by Archibald, Earl of Argyll, being at length heard and seen, the Lords of Council and Session assoilzied the said Archibald Earl of Argyll from the hail points and articles of the summons libelled or precept intended and pursued against him at the instance of said William Aikman, Procurator-Fiscal of the Admiralty, before said Lord High Admiral and his deputies, and decreed and declared him quit and free thereof in all time coming. Dated 27th, July, 1677."

There comes into the story, during the lifetime of the ninth Earl, the figure of Sir William Sacheverall, Governor of the Isle of Man, who was interested as a partner in one of the several concessions granted. He had left an account of his voyage to Mull in the year 1672, printed shortly after the event, in which he not only records sundry efforts to fish up the treasure but gives also a lively and vivid picture of the primitive Highlander on his native heather.

"About twelve o'clock," he wrote, "we made the Sound of Mull. We saluted the Castle of Duart with five guns, and they returned three. I sent in my pinnace for the boats, and things you had left there; and in the evening we cast anchor in the Bay of Tauber Murry, which for its bigness, is one of the finest and fastest in the world. The mouth of it is almost shut up with a little woody island call'd the Calve, the opening to the South not passable for small boats at low-water, and that to the North barely Musquet-shot over. To the Landward, it is surrounded with high Mountains cover'd with woods, pleasantly intermixed with rocks, and three or four Cascades of water which throw themselves from the top of the Mountain with a pleasure that is astonishing, all of which together make one of the oddest and most charming Prospects I ever saw.

"Italy itself, with all the assistance of Art, can hardly afford anything more beautiful and diverting; especially when the weather was clear and serene, to see the Divers sinking three-score foot under water and stay sometimes above an hour, and at last returning with the spoils of the Ocean; whether it were Plate, or Money, it convinced us of the Riches and Splendor of the once thought *Invincible Armada*. This rais'd a variety of Ideas, in a Soul as fond of Novelty as mine. Sometimes I reflected with horror on the danger of the British Nation, sometimes with Pleasure on that generous Courage and Conduct that sav'd a sinking State; and sometimes of so great an Enterprize baffled and lost, by accidents unthought of and unforseen....

"The first week the weather was pleasant, but spent in fitting our Engines, which proved very well, and every way suited to the design; and our Divers outdid all examples of this nature. But with the Dog-Days the autumnal rains usually begin in these parts, and for six weeks we had scarce a good day. The whole frame of Nature seem'd inhospitable, bleak, stormy, rainy, windy, so that our Divers could not bear the cold, and despairing to see any amendment of weather I resolved on a journey across the Isle of Mull, to the so much celebrated Il-Columb-Kill,[3] in English St. Columb's Church....

"The first four miles we saw but few houses, but cross'd a wild desert country, with a pleasant mixture of Woods and Mountains. Every man and thing I met seem'd a Novelty. I thought myself entering upon a new Scene of Nature, but Nature rough and unpolished, in her undress. I observed the men to be large bodied, stout, subtile, active, patient of cold and hunger. There appeared in all their actions a certain generous air of freedom, and contempt of those trifles, Luxury and Ambition, which we so servilely creep after. They bound their appetites by their necessities and their happiness consists not in having much, but in coveting little.

"The Women seem to have the same sentiments as the men; tho' their Habits were mean, and they had not our sort of breeding, yet in many of them there was a natural Beauty, and a graceful Modesty which never fails of attracting. The usual outward habit of both sexes is the Plaid; the women's much finer, the colours more lively, and the squares larger than the men's, and put me in mind of the ancient Picts. This serves them for a Veil and covers both head and body. The men wear theirs after another manner; when designed for ornament it is loose and

SPOOKY TREASURE TROVES

flowing, like the mantles our painters give their Heroes.

"Their thighs are bare, with brawny Muscles; a thin brogue on the foot, a short buskin of various colours on the leg, tied above the calf with a strip'd pair of garters. On each side of a large Shot-pouch hangs a Pistol and a Dagger; a round Target on their backs, a blue Bonnet on their heads, in one hand a broadsword, and a musket in the other. Perhaps no nation goes better arm'd, and I assure you they will handle them with bravery and dexterity, especially the Sword and Target, as our veteran Regiments found to their cost at Killie Crankie."

Although Sir William Sacheverall, he of the facile pen and the romantic temper, brought no Spanish treasure to light, he helped us to see those fighting MacLeans and MacDonalds as they were in their glory, and his description was written almost two and a half centuries ago.

The "Spanish wrack" was handed down from one chief of the Campbell clan to another, as part of the estate, until in 1740, John, the second Duke of Argyll, decided to try his luck, and employed a diving bell, by which means a magnificent bronze cannon was recovered. It has since been kept at Inverary Castle, the seat of the Dukes of Argyll, as an heirloom greatly esteemed. This elaborately wrought piece of ordnance, almost eleven feet in length, bears the arms of Francis I of France (for whom it was cast at Fontainebleau) and the fleur-de-lis. It was probably captured from Francis at the battle of Pavia during his invasion of Italy, and the Spanish records state that several of such cannon were put on a vessel contributed to the Armada by the state of Tuscany. At the same time a large number of gold and silver coins were found by the divers, and the treasure seeking was thereby freshly encouraged. Modern experts in wrecking and salvage have agreed that the crude apparatus of those earlier centuries was inadequate to combat the difficulties of exploring a wreck of the type of the *Florencia* galleon, built as she was of great timbers of the iron-like African oak which to-day is found to be staunch and unrotted after a submersion of more than three hundred years.

The diving bells of those times were dangerous and clumsy, and easily capsized. The men worked from inside them by thrusting out hooks and tong-like appliances, and dared venture no deeper than eight fathoms, or less than fifty feet. In other words, the treasure might be in the galleon, but it was impossible to find and bring it up. For another century and more, the *Florencia* was left undisturbed until about forty years ago, the present Duke of Argyll, then Marquis of Lorne, considered it his family duty to investigate the bottom of Tobermory Bay, his curiosity being pricked at finding the ancient chart, and other documents already quoted, among the archives stored in Inverary Castle. More for sport than for profit, he sent down a diver who found a few coins, pieces of oak, and a brass stanchion, after which the owner bothered his head no more about these phantom riches for some time.

SPOOKY TREASURE TROVES

In 1903, or three hundred and fifteen years after the *Florencia* found her grave in Tobermory Bay, a number of gentlemen of Glasgow, rashly speculative for Scots, formed a company and subscribed a good many thousand dollars to equip and maintain a treasure-seeking expedition by modern methods. The Duke of Argyll, like his ancestors before him, was ready to grant permission to search the wreck of the galleon for a term of years, conditioned upon a fair division of the spoils. He let them have the chart, without which no treasure hunt deserves the name, and all the family papers dealing with the *Florencia*. In charge of the operations was placed Captain William Burns of Glasgow, a hard-headed and vastly experienced wrecker who had handled many important salvage enterprises for the marine underwriters in seas near and far.

The contrast between this twentieth century syndicate with its steam dredges and electric lights, and that primitive age when the MacLeans were harassing Captain Adolpho Smith from their fort beside the bay, is fairly astonishing. The gentlemen of Glasgow were not moved by sentiment, however, and soon Captain Burns was spending their money in a preliminary survey of the waters and the sands where the galleon was supposed to be. Although the ancient chart was explicit in its bearings, and these were made when men were living who had seen a part of the wreck above tide, locating the *Florencia* proved to be a baffling puzzle. During the first season, 1903, divers and lighters were employed in this work of searching, but the salvage consisted of no more than another bronze cannon loaded with a stone ball, several swords, scabbards, and blunderbusses, a gold ring, and some fifty doubloons bearing the names of Ferdinand and Isabella, and Don Carlos.

Two years later, in 1905, the work was fairly begun with a costly equipment. The bottom of the bay was photographed and a mound of sand revealed, which, it was concluded, covered the surviving part of the galleon. Digging into this bank, the divers found many curious trophies, among them more arms and munition, bottles or canteens, boarding pikes, copper powder pans, and other small furniture, much corroded and encrusted. It was surmised that the vessel lay with her stern cocked up, and that in this end, indicated by the swelling of the sand bank, the treasure was hidden.

Powerful suction pumps worked by steam were set going to clear away this bank, and they bored into it steadily for three weeks while the divers dug shafts to clear away obstructions. At length, a massive silver candlestick was fetched up, and the sand pumps clanked more industriously than ever. At the end of the summer, about one hundred square feet of the bank had been removed, but the whereabouts of the galleon was by no means certain.

As soon as the weather became favorable in the following spring, Captain Burns and his crew returned to the quest with more men and machinery than be-

SPOOKY TREASURE TROVES

fore. It was really impossible that such a business as this could be carried on without some touch of the fantastic and the picturesque. There now intrudes a Mr. Cossar, employed as "the famous expert, who, by means of delicate apparatus can indicate where metal or wood is buried in any quantity underground," and he spent the summer taking observations and buoying the bay with floats or markers. At these places boring was carried on means of steel rods to a depth of one hundred and forty feet, while the dredges were busy exploring the vicinity of the sand bank.

The area thoroughly explored was increased to eight acres in 1906, in water from seven to fourteen fathoms deep. That famous expert, Mr. Cossar, and his delicate apparatus were reinforced by Mr. John Stears of Yorkshire, one of the most notable diviners of England. He operated with no more apparatus than a hawthorn twig and professed to be able to locate precious metals no matter how many fathoms deep, and more than this, *mirabile dictu*, to tell you whether it was gold, or silver, or copper that made his inspired twig twist and bend in his fingers. Mr. Stears was taken as seriously as Mr. Cossar had been, and the findings of one confirmed the verdicts of the other. The powerful salvage steamer *Breamer* with a large crew searched where the diviner told them to go, and several pieces of silver plate were recovered amid the excitement of all hands.

The *Breamer* continued work in 1907, but during the next year the waters of Tobermory Bay were unvexed by the treasure-seekers. Then the syndicate went into its pockets for more cash, got its second wind, so to speak, and wrapped its operations in a cloud of secrecy, quite the proper dodge for a venture of this kind. A new and taciturn crew was hired for the *Breamer*, and whatever was found under water was hidden from prying eyes. The additional funds raised amounted to $15,000, and Captain Burns was told to obtain the best equipment possible. It was reported in the autumn of that year that "Mr. Cossar, the mineral expert, by whose skill the scope of the operations was more or less controlled, had broken down in health owing to the severe strain, and had gone home to recruit," but John Stears of Yorkshire with his hawthorn twig was still finding treasure which refused to be found by divers.

The five-year concession from the Duke of Argyll had expired and was renewed by a syndicate organized in London, the manager a Col. K. M. Foss, an American, who appeared in Tobermory and conveyed an impression of cocksure Yankee hustle. He announced that his agents were making historical researches in the libraries and museums of Europe and had already convinced him that the lost galleon was crammed with treasure; that the chart relied on in past searches was all wrong, and expressed his surprise that the extensive salvage operations of recent years should have failed to locate the exact position of the wreck. In a word, Scotchmen might know a thing or two, but your up-to-date Yankee was the man to crack the nut of the lost *Florencia* and deftly extract the kernel.

SPOOKY TREASURE TROVES

The appearance of this Colonel Foss in this storied landscape of Tobermory Bay has a certain humorous aspect. He hardly seems to belong in the *ensemble* of the search for the treasure galleon which has been carried on for centuries.

Diving to find the treasure galleon in Tobermory Bay.
(Photographed in 1909.)

The salvage steamer *Brenner* equipped with suction dredge, removing a sandbank from the supposed location of the Florencia galleon in 1909.

SPOOKY TREASURE TROVES

This entertaining American may perhaps have unearthed information hitherto unknown, but the fact is worth some stress that all previous investigations had failed to prove beyond doubt that the *Florencia* bore from Spain the thirty millions of money reputed to have been stowed in her lazarette. An ancient document known as "The Confession of Gregorie de Sotomeya of Melgaco in Portugal" contains a list of the treasure ships of the Armada. He was with the fleet in the galleon *Neustra Senora del Rosario*, commanded by Dom Pedro de Valdes, and he goes on to say:

"To the sixth question concerning what treasure there was in the fleet, I say there was great stories of money and plate which came in the galleon wherein the Duke of Medina was (*The San Martin*), and in the ship of Dom Pedro de Valdez which was taken, and in the Admiral of the galleons (*The San Lorenzo*), and in the Galley Royal (*The Capitana Royale*), and in the Vice Admiral wherein was Juan Martinez de Ricalde (*The Santa Anna*), and in the Vice Admiral whereof was General Diego (*The San Christobel*), and in the Vice Admiral of the pinnaces (*N. S. de Pilar de Targoza*), and in the Vice-Admiral of the hulks (*The Gran Grifon*), and in a Venitian ship in which came General Don Alonzo de Leyna. The report goeth that this ship brought great stores of treasure, for that there came in her the Prince of Ascoli, and many other noblemen. This is all I know touching the treasure."

The name of the *Florencia* does not appear herein, yet the report of her vast riches was current in the Western Highlands no more than one lifetime after the year of the Armada. That men of solid business station and considerable capital can be found to-day to charter wrecking steamers, divers, dredges, and what not to continue this enterprise proves that romance is not wholly dead.

In the town of Tobermory, the busy, mysterious parties of treasure seekers, as they come year after year with their impressive flotilla of apparatus, furnish endless diversion and conjecture. The people will tell you, in the broad English of the Highlander, and in the Gaelic, even more musical, as it survives among the Western Islands, the legend of the beautiful Spanish princess who came in the *Florencia*, and was wooed and won by a bold MacLean, and they will show you the old mill whose timbers, still staunchly standing, were taken from the wreck of the galleon. In Mull, and oftener among the islands further seaward and toward the Irish coast, are to be found black-eyed and black-haired men and women, not of the pure Celtic race, in whose blood is the distant strain bequeathed by those ancestors who married shipwrecked Spanish sailors of the Armada, and perhaps among them are descendants of these two or three seamen who were hurled ashore alive when the *Florencia* was destroyed by the hand of young Donald Glas MacLean.

In quaint Tobermory whose main street nestles along the edge of the bay, the ancient foemen, MacLeans and MacDonalds, tend their shops side by side,

SPOOKY TREASURE TROVES

and it seems as if almost every other signboard bore one of these clan names. If you would hear the best talk of the galleon and her treasure, it is wise to seek the tiny grocery and ship chandlery of Captain Coll MacDonald, a gentle white-bearded man, so slight of stature and mild of mien and speech that you are surprised to learn that for many years he was master of a great white-winged clipper ship of the famous City Line of Glasgow, in the days when this distinction meant something. Now he has come back to spend his latter days in this tranquil harbor and to spin yarns of many seas.

Scabbards, flasks, cannon balls, and small objects recovered from the sunken Armada galleon.

Stone cannon balls and breech-block of a breech loading gun fished up from the wreck of the Florencia galleon.

Scabbards, flasks, cannon balls, and small objects recovered from the sunken Armada galleon. Stone cannon balls and breech-block of a breech loading gun fished up from the wreck of the Florencia galleon.

"The scour of the tide has settled the wreck of the galleon many feet in the sand," he told me. "I can show you on a chart what the old bearings were, as they were handed down from one generation to the next, but Captain Burns is not sure that he has yet found her. The money is there, I have no doubt. There was a bark in the bay not long ago, and when she pulled up anchor a Spanish doubloon was sticking to one fluke. Mr. Stears, the Yorkshireman with the divining rod, did some wonderful things, but the

SPOOKY TREASURE TROVES

treasure was not found. To test him, bags of silver and gold and copper money were buoyed under water in the bay, with no marks to show. It was done by night and he was kept away. He went out in a boat next morning and was rowed around a bit, and wherever the metal was hid under water, his twig told him, without a mistake. More than that, he knew what kind of metal it was under the water."

"And how was that!" I asked of Captain Coll MacDonald.

"He would hold a piece of gold money in each hand when the twig began to twist and dip. If the gold was under the water, the twig would pull with a very strong pull, so that he knew. If it was undecided like, he would hold silver money, and the twig told him the proper message. I watched him working many a time, and it was very wonderful."

"But he did not find the treasure," I ventured to observe.

"Ah, lad, it was no fault of his," returned the old gentleman. "The Spanish gold is scattered far and wide over the bottom of the bay, I have no doubt. Donald Glas MacLean did a very thorough job when he blew the galleon to hell."

The present Duke of Argyll, brother-in-law of the late King Edward, bears among the many and noble and resonant titles that are his by inheritance, several which recall the earlier pages of the history of the Clan Campbell, the brave days of the feudal Highlands, and the ancient rights in the Armada Galleon of Tobermory Bay. He is Baron Inverary, Mull, Morvern, and Tiry; twenty-ninth Baron of Lochow, with the Celtic title of the Cailean Mo'r, chief of the Clan Campbell, from Sir Colin Campbell, knighted in 1286; Admiral of the Western Coast and Islands, Marquis of Lorne and Kintye; Keeper of the Great Seal of Scotland and of the Castles of Dunstaffnage, Dunoon and Carvick, Hereditary High Sheriff of the County of Argyll.

He once explained how the ownership of the *Florencia* galleon came to his family by means of the ancient grant already quoted. The Campbells held the admiralty rights of the coast of Mull at the time of the Armada, and any wreck was lawfully theirs for this reason. The document was simply a formal confirmation of these rights. The *Florencia* was flotsam and jetsam to be taken by whatever chiefs held the rights of admiralty. A case involving the salmon fishing rights of a Scottish river was recently decided by virtue of a charter of admiralty rights granted by Robert the Bruce, who ruled and fought six hundred years ago.

In order to complete the documentary links of this true story of the Armada galleon, it may be of interest to quote from a letter recently received by the author from the present Duke of Argyll, in which he says:

The galleon was the ship furnished by Tuscany as her contribution to the Armada. She was called the *Florencia*, or *City of Florence*, and was commanded by Captain Pereira, a Portugese, and had a crew largely Portugese on board. We have found specimens of his plate with the Pereira arms engraved on the plate

SPOOKY TREASURE TROVES

border. She carried breech loading guns on her upper deck, and you will see one of them at the Blue Coat School now removed from London to the suburbs.

On the lower deck were some guns got from Francis I at the Battle of Pavia. I have a very fine one at Inverary Castle, got from the wreck in 1740. Diving with a diving bell was commenced in 1670 and discontinued on account of civil troubles. Pereira foolishly took part in local clan disputes, helping the MacLeans of Mull against the MacDonalds. One of the MacDonalds, when a prisoner on board, is said to have blown up the vessel as she was warping out of harbor.

I found an old plan and located the "Spanish wrack" from the plan, but only sent a man down once from a yacht.

There was little obtained during the last divings, cannon balls, timber, a few pieces of plate, small articles—about 70 dollars, etc.

Yours faithfully,   ARGYLL.

Kensington Palace, April 25,—1910."

[1] A cliff which was the key to the position held by the MacLeans.
[2] Divers.
[3] Iona.

SPOOKY TREASURE TROVES

CHAPTER VIII
THE LOST PLATE FLEET OF VIGO

No treasure yarn is the real thing unless it glitters with ducats, ingots, and pieces of eight, which means that in the brave days when riches were quickest won with cutlass, boarding pike, and carronade, it was Spain that furnished the best hunting afloat. For three centuries her galleons and treasure fleets were harried and despoiled of wealth that staggers the imagination, and their wreckage littered every ocean. English sea rovers captured many millions of gold and silver, and pirates took their fat shares in the West Indies, along the coasts of America from the Spanish Main to Lima and Panama, and across the Pacific to Manila. And to-day, the quests of the treasure seekers are mostly inspired by hopes of finding some of the vanished wealth of Spain that was hidden or sunk in the age of the Conquistadores and the Viceroys.

Of all the argosies of Spain, the richest were those plate fleets which each year carried to Cadiz and Seville the cargoes of bullion from the mines of Peru, and Mexico, and the greatest treasure ever lost since the world began was that which filled the holds of the fleet of galleons that sailed from Cartagena, Porto Bello, and Vera Cruz in the year 1702. What distinguishes this treasure story from all others is that it is not befogged in legend and confused by mystery and uncertainty. And while ships' companies are roaming the Seven Seas to find what small pickings the pirates and buccaneers may have lifted in their time, the most marvelous Spanish treasure of them all is no farther away than a harbor on the other side of the Atlantic.

At the bottom of Vigo Bay, on the coast of Spain, lies that fleet of galleons and one hundred millions of dollars in gold ingots and silver bars. This estimate is smaller than the documentary evidence vouches for. In fact, twenty-eight million pounds sterling is the accepted amount, but one hundred million dollars has a sufficiently large and impressive sound, and it is wise to be conservative to the verge of caution in dealing with lost treasure which has been made so much more the theme of fiction than a question of veracity. After escaping the perils of buccaneer and privateer and frigate, this treasure fleet went down in a home port, amid smoke and flame and the thunder of guns manned by English and Dutch tars under that doughty admiral of Queen Anne, Sir George Rooke. It was the deadliest blow ever dealt the mighty commerce of Spain during those centuries when her ruthless grasp was squeezing the New World of its riches.

There, indeed, is the prize for the treasure seeker of to-day who dreams of doubloons and pieces of eight. Nor could pirate hoard have a more blood-stained, adventurous history than these millions upon millions, lapped by the tides of Vigo Bay, which were won by the sword and lost in battle. During these last two hundred years many efforts have been made to recover the freightage of this fleet, but the bulk of the treasure is still untouched, and it awaits the man with the cash and the ingenuity to evolve the right salvage equipment. At work now in Vigo Bay is the latest of these explorers, an Italian, Pino by name, inventor of a submarine boat, a system of raising wreck, and a wonderful machine called a hydroscope for seeing and working at the bottom of the sea.

With Pino it is a business affair operated by means of a concession from the Spanish government, but he is something more than an inventor. He is a poet, he has the artistic temperament, and when he talks of his plans it is in words like these:

"I have found means to disclose to human eyes the things hidden in the being of the furious waves of the infinite ocean, and how to recover them. Mine is the simple key with which to open to man the mysterious virgin temples of the nymphs and sirens who, by their sweet singing, draw men to see and to take their endless treasures."

This interesting Pino is no dreamer, however, and he has enlisted ample capital with which to build costly machinery and charter yachts and steamers. With him is associated Carlo L. Iberti, and there is an ideal pattern of a treasure seeker for you, a man of immense enthusiasm, of indefatigable industry, dreaming, thinking, living in the story of the galleons of Vigo Bay. It was he who secured the concession from Madrid, it was he who as he says, "was flying from province to province, from country to country, from archives to archives, from library to library, ever studying, copying, and acquiring all documents relating to Vigo. I had made up my mind to find out all that was to be known about the treasure. And I believe I have succeeded."

Never was there such a prospectus as Iberti wrote to awaken the interest of investors in the undertaking of Pino. It was a historical work bristling with data, authorities, references, from French, Spanish, and English sources. It was convincing, final, positively superb. One blinked at reading it, as if dazzled by the sight of mountains of gold, and moreover every word of it was true. As a text for

SPOOKY TREASURE TROVES

this narrative, his summary, the peroration, so to speak, fairly hits one between the eyes:

"As the total quantity of treasure which arrived at Vigo in 1702 amounted to 126,470,600 pesos, or £27,493,609, there is not the least doubt that the treasure in gold and silver still lying in the galleons of Vigo Bay amounts to as much as 113,396,085 pieces of eight, or £24,651,323, after deducting the treasure unloaded before the battle, the booty taken by the victors, and that recovered by explorers. That would have been the value of the treasure two hundred years ago. Today, its value would be greater, at a moderate estimate of £28,000,000. Such is the sum which we who are interested in the recovery of the treasure have set our hearts on winning from the sea."

Sir George Rooke, commanding the British fleet at the battle of Vigo Bay.

After this, the hoards of the most notorious and hard-working pirates seem picayune, trifling, shabby, the small change of the age of buried treasure. Why Signor Iberti is so cock-sure of his figures, and how that wondrous treasure fleet was lost in Vigo Bay is a story worth telling if there be any merit in high adventures, hard fighting, and the tang of salty seas in the days when the world was young. No more than nine years after the first voyage of Columbus, galleons laden with treasure were winging it from the West

Sir George Rooke, commanding the British fleet at the battle of Vigo Bay.

SPOOKY TREASURE TROVES

Indies to Spain, and this golden stream was flowing year by year until the time of the American Revolution. The total was to be counted not in millions but in billions, and this prodigious looting of the New World gave to Spain such wealth and power that her centuries of greatness were literally builded upon foundations of ingots and silver bars.

Before Sir Francis Drake sailed into the Caribbean, the Dutch and English had been playing at the great game of galleon hunting, but their exploits had been no more than vexations, and the security of the plate fleets was not seriously menaced until "El Draque" spread terror and destruction down one coast of the Americas and up the other, from Nombre de Dios to Panama. Heaven alone knows how many great galleons he shattered and plundered, but from the *San Felipe* and the *Cacafuego* he took two million dollars in treasure, and he numbered his other prizes by the score. Martin Frobisher carried the huge East India galleon *Madre de Dios* by boarding in the face of tremendous odds, the blood running from her scuppers, and was rewarded with $1,250,000 worth of precious stones, ebony, ivory, and Turkish carpets.

During the period of the English Commonwealth, Admiral Stayner pounded to pieces a West Indian treasure fleet of eight sail, and from one of them took two millions in silver, while Blake fought his way into the harbor of Teneriffe and destroyed another splendid argosy under the guns of the forts. It is recorded that thirty-eight wagons were required to carry the gold and jewels thus obtained from Portsmouth to London. The records of the British Admiralty have preserved a memorandum of the prize money distributed to the officers and men of the *Active* and *Favorite* from the treasures taken in the *Hermione* galleon off Cadiz in 1762, and it is a document to make a modern mariner sigh for the days of his forefathers. Here is treasure finding as it used to flourish:

    The Admiral and the Commander of the Fleet.... $324,815
    The Captain of the _Active_..................... 332,265
    Each of three Commissioned Officers........... 65,000
    " " Eight Warrant Officers................ 21,600
    " " Twenty Officers....................... 9,030
    " " 150 Seamen and Marines................ 2,425
    The Captain of the _Favorite_.................. 324,360
    Each of 2 Commissioned Officers............... 64,870
    " " 77 Warrant Officers................... 30,268
    " " 15 Petty Officers..................... 9,000
    " " 100 Seamen and Marines................ 2,420

In 1702 it happened that no treasure fleet had returned to Spain for three years, and the gold and silver and costly merchandise were piling up at Cartagena and Porto Bello and Vera Cruz waiting for shipment. Spain was torn with strife over the royal succession, and inasmuch as the king claimed as his own one-fifth of all the treasure coming from the New World, the West India Company and the officials of the treasury kept the galleons away until it should be known who had the better right to the cargoes. Moreover, the high seas were perilous for the passage of treasure ships, what with the havoc wrought by the cursed English men-of-war and privateers, not to mention the buccaneers of San Domingo and the Windward Islands who had a trick of storming aboard a galleon from any crazy little craft that would float a handful of them.

Timidly the galleons delayed until a fleet of French men-of-war was sent out to convey them home, and at length this richest argosy that ever furrowed blue water, freighted with three years' treasure from the mines, made its leisurely way into mid-ocean by way of the Azores, bound to the home port of Cadiz. There were forty sail in all, seventeen of the plate fleet, under Don Manuel de Velasco, and twenty-three French ships-of-the-line and frigates obeying the Admiral's pennant of the Count of Chateaurenaud.

The news came to Queen Anne that this fleet had departed from the Spanish Main, and a squadron of twenty-seven British war vessels, commanded by the famous Sir Cloudesley Shovel, was fitted out to intercept and attack it. The manoeuvres of the hunted galleons and their convoy wear an aspect grimly humorous as pictured in the letters and narratives of that time. One of these explains that "the fleet was performing its voyage always with the fear that the enemy was lying in wait for it; the King of France also was in continual anxiety on the same account, and urged by these forebodings he sent dispatches in different vessels so that the fleet might avoid the threatened danger. One of the dispatch boats met it on the open sea, and gave it notice of the enemy's armada being over against Cadiz, upon which warning the commander called a council of war in the ship *Capitana* to consider and fix upon the port which they ought to make for. At this meeting various views were expressed, for the French held that the fleet would be more secure in the ports of France, and especially in that of Rochelle. Of the same opinion were many of the Spaniards, who were looking not to the interests of individuals, but to the public good.

"And yet there were also seen the ill-consequences that might arise from the treasure not being conveyed to its proper destination and the possibility of the Most Christian King's finding some pretext which would endanger its safety."

Which is to say that if "His Most Christian Majesty," Louis XIV of France, who was safe-guarding the treasure, should once entice it into one of his own ports, he was likely to keep it there. And so the courteous Spanish captains and the equally polite French captains eyed one another suspiciously in the cabin of the galleon

SPOOKY TREASURE TROVES

and held council until it was decided to seek refuge in Vigo Bay on the coast of Gallicia, thereby both dodging the English and remaining at a sufficient distance from France to spoil any designs which might be prompted by the greed of "His Most Christian Majesty."

The Royal Sovereign, one of Admiral Sir George Rooke's line-of-battle ships, engaged at Vigo Bay.

The Royal Sovereign, one of Admiral Sir George Rooke's line-of-battle ships, engaged at Vigo Bay.

SPOOKY TREASURE TROVES

Without mishap, the treasure fleet and the convoy anchored in the sheltered, narrow stretch of Vigo harbor, and preparations for standing off an English attack were begun at once. The forts were manned, the militia called out, and a great chain boom stretched across the entrance of the inner roadstead. This was all very well in its way, but so incredible a comedy of blundering, stupid delay ensued that although for one whole month the galleons lay unmolested, the treasure was not unloaded and carried to safety ashore. In a letter from Brussels, printed in the *London Postman* of November 10, 1702, the grave results of this Spanish procrastination were indicated in these words:

"The last advices from Spain and Paris have caused great consternation here. The treasure and other goods brought by the said fleet are of such consequence to Spain, and in particular to this province, that most of our traders are ruined if this fleet is taken and destroyed."

While the English and their allies, the Dutch, were making ready to take this treasure fleet bottled up in Vigo Bay, the officials of Spain were so entangled in red tape that there seemed to be no way of unloading the galleons. A Spanish writer of that era thus describes the lamentable state of affairs:

"The commerce of Cadiz maintained that nothing could be disembarked in Gallicia,—that to unload the fleet was their privilege, and that the ships ought to be kept safe in the harbor of Vigo, without discharging their cargoes, till the enemies were gone away. In addition to this, the settlement of the matter in the Council of the Indies was not so speedy as the emergency demanded,—both through the slowness and prudence natural to the Spaniard, and through the diversity of opinions on the subject."

Don Modesto Lafuento, a later Spanish historian, gravely explains that "as the arrival of the fleet at this port was unexpected and contrary to the usual custom, there was no officer to be found who could examine merchandise for the payment of duties, without which no disembarkation could be lawfully made. When notice of this was at length sent to the Court, much discussion arose there as to who should be sent. They fixed upon Don Juan de Larrea, but this councillor was in no hurry about setting out on his journey, and spent a long time in making it, and when he arrived he occupied himself with discussion about the disposition of the goods that had come in the fleet. This gave the opportunity for the Anglo-Dutch fleet, which had notice of everything, to set out and arrive in the waters of Vigo before the disembarkation was effected."

Surely never was so much treasure so foolishly endangered, and although a small part of it was taken ashore, notwithstanding the asinine proceedings of the government and Don Juan de Larrea, the English *Post* newspaper of November 2, asserted that "the Spaniards, being informed that the enemy's fleet was returned

SPOOKY TREASURE TROVES

home, sent aboard a great quantity of their plate which they had carried to land for fear of them."

Admiral Sir Cloudesley Shovel had missed finding the treasure fleet at sea, but a lucky chance favored another sterling English commander, Sir George Rooke. He was homeward bound from a disastrous attempt to take Cadiz, in which affair the Duke of Ormond had led the troops engaged. One of his ships, the *Pembroke*, was detached from the fleet and while calling at Lagos Bay for water, the chaplain became friendly with a gentleman of the port who passed him word that the galleons and the French fleet were safe at Vigo. This talkative informant proved to be a messenger from Lisbon, sent by the German minister with dispatches for the treasure fleet which he had first sought in vain at Cadiz.

The chaplain carried the rare tidings to Captain Hardy of the *Pembroke* who instantly made sail to find Sir George Rooke and the English fleet, which was jogging along toward England. The admiral was "extream glad," says an old account, and "imparted the same immediately to the Dutch Admiral, declaring it his opinion that they should go directly to Vigo." The Dutchman and his tars joyfully agreed, and Dalrymple, in his memoirs, relates that "at the sound of treasure from the South Seas, dejection and animosity ceased, and those who a few days before would not speak when they met, now embraced and felicitated each other, etc. All the difficulties that had appeared to be mountainous at Cadiz, dwindled into mole-hills at Vigo.

"The gunners agreed that their bombs would reach the town and the shipping; the engineers, that lodgments and works could easily be made; the soldiers, that there was no danger in landing; the seamen that the passage of the Narrows could easily be forced, notwithstanding all the defenses and obstructions; and the pilots, that the depth of water was everywhere sufficient, and the anchorage safe. Rooke's gout incommoded him no longer; he went from ship to ship, even in the night time, and became civil,—and the Duke of Ormond, with his father's generosity, his brother's and his own, forgot all that was past."

These were the sentiments of men who had no more rations left aboard ship than two biscuits per day, whose fleet was leaky, battered, and unseaworthy after the hard fighting at Cadiz, and who were going to attack a powerful array of French vessels, protected by numerous forts and obstructions, and supported by the seventeen galleons which in armament and crews were as formidable as men-of-war. At a council of flag officers called by Sir George Rooke, it was resolved:

"That, considering the attempting and destroying these ships would be of the greatest advantage and honor to her Majesty and her allies, and very much tend to the reducing of the power of France, the fleet should make the best of its way to the port of Vigo, and insult them immediately with the whole line in case there was room enough for it, and if not, by such detachment as might render the

SPOOKY TREASURE TROVES

attack most effective."

In naval history no swifter and more deadly "insult" was ever administered than that which befell when Sir George Rooke, his gout forgotten, appeared before Vigo and lost no time in coming to close quarters. He called a council of the general land and sea officers who concluded that "in regard the whole fleet could not without being in danger of being in a huddle, attempt the ships and galleons where they were, a detachment of fifteen English and ten Dutch ships of the line of battle with all the fire ships should be sent to use their best endeavors to take or destroy the aforesaid ships of the enemy, and the frigates and bomb vessels should follow the rear of the fleet, and the great ships move after them to go in if there should be occasion."

Next morning the Duke of Ormond landed two thousand British infantry to take the forts and destroy the landward end of the boom, made of chain cables and spars which blocked the channel. These errands were accomplished with so much spirit and determination that the Grenadiers fairly chased the Spanish garrisons out of their works. Rooke did not wait for the finish of this task, but flew the signal to get under way, Vice Admiral Hopson leading in the *Torbay*. British and Dutch together, the wind blowing half a gale behind them, surged toward the inner harbor, stopped not for the boom but cut a way through it, and became engaged with the French men-of-war at close range. The hostile fleets were so jammed together that it was not a battle of broadsides. A Spanish chronicler related that "they fought with fires of inhuman contrivance, hand grenades, fireballs, and lumps of burning pitch."

Within one-half hour after the English and Dutch had gained entrance to the bay, its surface was an inferno of blazing galleons and men-of-war. Some of the French ships were carried with the cutlass and boarding pike, but fire was the chief weapon used by both sides. The flaming vessels drifted against each other, some of them set purposely alight and filled with explosives. When the galleons tried to move further up the bay, British troops on shore raked them with musketry, and prevented the attempts to put some of the treasure on land. The lofty treasure ships, their huge citadels rising fore and aft, and gay with carving and gilt, burned like so much tinder.

The English had no desire to destroy these golden prizes, and as soon as the French fleet had been annihilated, every ship burned, sunk, captured, or driven ashore, heroic efforts were made to save the galleons still unharmed, "whereupon Don Manuel de Velasco, who was not wanting in courage, but only in good fortune, ordered them to be set on fire.... The enemy saw the greater part of the treasure sunk in the sea. Many perished seeking for riches in the middle of the flames; these, with those who fell in the battle, were 800 English and Dutch; 500 were wounded, and one English three-decker was burnt. Nevertheless, they took thirteen French and Spanish ships, seven of which were men-of-war, and six merchantmen, besides some others much damaged and half-burnt. There fell 2000 Spaniards and French, few escaped unwounded.

"The day after the bloody battle, they sent down into the water a great many divers, but with little result, for the artillery of the city hindered them. So setting to work to embark their people, and covering their masts with flags and streamers, they celebrated their victory with flutes and fifes. Thus they steered for their own ports, leaving that country full of sadness and terror."

It was a prodigiously destructive naval engagement, the costliest in point of material losses that history records. The victors got much booty to take home to England and the Netherlands, and were handsomely rewarded for their pains. Sir George Rooke carried to London the galleon *Tauro* which had escaped burning, and she had a mighty freight of bullion in her hold. Of this ship the *Post Boy* newspaper made mention, January 19, 1703:

"There was found in the galleon unloaded last week abundance of wrought plate, pieces of eight, and other valuable commodities, and so much that 'tis computed the whole cargo is worth £200,000."

All records of that time and event agree, however, that the treasure saved by the allied fleet was no more than a small part of what was lost by the wholesale destruction of the galleons, and chiefly interesting to the present day are the most reliable estimates of the amount of gold and silver that still rests embedded in the tidal silt of Vigo Bay. There were sunk in water too deep to be explored by the engineers of that century eleven French men-of-war, and at least a round dozen of treasure laden galleons. The French fleet carried no small amount of gold and silver which had been entrusted to the Admiral and his officers by merchants of the West Indies. As for the galleons, the English *Post* of November 13, 1702, stated:

"Three Spanish officers belonging to the galleons, one of whom was the Admiral of the Assogna ships, are brought over who report that the effects that were on board amounted to nine millions sterling, and that the Spaniards, for want of mules to carry the plate into the country, had broke the bulk of very few ships before the English forced the boom."

The amount of the treasure is greatly underestimated in the foregoing assertion, for the annual voyage of the plate fleet had carried to Spain an average lading worth from thirty to forty million dollars, and this doomed flota bore the accumulated treasure of three years. Not more than ten million dollars in bullion and merchandise could have been looted by the Dutch and English victors, according to the most reliable official records. Our enthusiastic friend, Signor Don Carlos Iberti, he who had been "flying from province to province," in behalf of the latest treasure company of Vigo Bay, dug deep into the musty records of the "Account Books of the Ministry of Finance, of the Colonies, of the Royal Treasury,

SPOOKY TREASURE TROVES

of the Commercio of Cadiz, of the Council of the West Indies," and so on, and can tell you to the last peso how much gold and silver was sent from the mines of America in the treasure fleets, and precisely the value of the shipments entrusted to the magnificent flota of 1702. A score of English authorities might be quoted to confirm what has been said of the vastness of this lost treasure. The event was the sensation of the time in Europe, and many pens were busy chronicling in divers tongues the details of the catastrophe and the results thereof. In a letter from Madrid which reached England a few days after the event, the writer lamented:

"Yesterday an express arrived from Vigo with the melancholy news that the English and Dutch fleets came before that place the 22nd past and having made themselves masters of the mouth of the river, in less than two hours took and burnt all the French men-of-war and galleons in the harbour. We have much greater reason to deplore our misfortune in silence and tears than to give you a particular account of this unspeakable loss, which will hasten the utter ruin of this our monarchy.

"The inhabitants of this place, not being able to re-collect themselves from their consternation, have shut up their houses and shops for fear of being plundered by the common people who exclaim publicly against the government, and particularly against Cardinal Porto Carrero and others of the Council, who not being content with the free gift of three millions offered to the king out of the galleons, besides an *indulto* of two millions, hindered the landing of the plate at Vigo before the enemy arrived there. But the Cardinal laid the blame upon the Consultat of Seville, who, mistrusting the French, would not suffer them to carry the galleons to Brest or Port Lewis, but gave orders that they should sail back from Vigo to Cadiz after the English and Dutch fleets were returned home. 'Tis said that only three of the galleons put their cargo ashore before the arrival of the enemy."

The news was a most bitter pill for His Christian Majesty, Louis XIV of France, and put him and his court "into a mighty consternation." He was quoted as saying that "there was not one-tenth part of the plate and merchandise landed from on board the fleet. This is the most facetious piece of news that could come to the enemies of France and Spain."

All the records lay stress on the immense value of the treasure lost, one that "the Spanish galleons were coming from Mexico overladen with riches," another that "vast wealth in gold, silver, and merchandise was lost in that terrible battle of Vigo," a third that "this was the richest flota that ever came into Europe." It is extraordinary that most of this treasure has remained untouched for more than two centuries at the bottom of Vigo Bay. The records of the Spanish government contain almost complete memoranda of every concession granted to searching parties, and of the valuables recovered, which total to date is no more than a million and a half of dollars.

SPOOKY TREASURE TROVES

Soon after the battle, Spain began to fish for her lost galleons and in that same year of 1702, the official newspaper of Madrid recorded that "we are instructed from Vigo that they are proceeding with success in the raising of the precious burden belonging to the *Capitana*, and *Almiranta* of the Flota." For some reason or other, the task was shortly abandoned, and the work turned over to private enterprise and companies which were granted special charters, the Crown demanding as much as ninety-five per cent. of all the treasure recovered. During the half century following the loss of the fleet, as many as thirty of these concessions were granted, but most of them accomplished nothing. The first treasure hunter to achieve results worth mention was a Frenchman, Alexandre Goubert, who went to work in 1728, and after prodigious exertion succeeded in dragging almost ashore a hulk which turned out to be no galleon but one of the men-of-war of his own country, at which there was much merriment in "perfidious Albion." This disgusted M. Goubert and he was heard of no more.

An Englishman, William Evans, tried a diving bell of his own invention in the same century, and raised many plates of silver, but a Spanish concessionaire, jealous of this good fortune, persuaded his government that it was in bad taste to let history repeat itself by giving the English another fling at the treasure. In 1825, time having softened these poignant memories, a Scotchman was permitted to work in the bay, and local tradition affirms that he found much gold and silver, outwitting the officials at Madrid who demanded eighty per cent. of his findings. The inspectors posted to keep watch of his operations he made comfortably drunk, bundled them ashore, clapped sail on his brigantine, and vanished with his booty. Later a castle was built near Perth in Scotland, and given the name of Dollar House. Here the Scotchman aforesaid "lived happily ever afterwards" for all that is known to the contrary.

Through the eighteenth century French, English, and Spanish exploring parties were intriguing, quarreling, buying one another out, now and then finding some treasure, and locating the positions of most of the galleons. In 1822, American treasure hunters invaded the bay, organized as the International Submarine Company, and hailing from Philadelphia. Nothing worth mention was done until these adventurous gentlemen after a good deal of bickering, made a fresh start under the name of the Vigo Bay Treasure Company. Their affairs dragged along for a half century or so, during which they lifted one galleon from the bottom but the weight of mud in her hull broke her to small bits. A Spanish war-vessel watched the operations, by night and day, the government being somewhat sensitive and suspicious ever since the flight of that Scotchman and his brigantine.

At last the American company was unable to get a renewal of its long drawn out concession, and for some time the galleons were left alone. It was in 1904, that Signor Don Carlos Iberti obtained the "Royal Decree of Concession" for the Pino Company, Limited, of Genoa, and now indeed there was to be treasure seeking in earnest.

"Until recently the search for the treasure in the Bay of Vigo seemed only an Utopian mania," cried Iberti. "Those who set about the arduous enterprise were taken for mad scientists, rascals, or deceivers of innocent speculators. But for my part I shall always admire those bands of adventurers who sought to recover this treasure, from the first day after the battle until the present time."

Framework of an "elevator" devised by Pino for raising the galleons in Vigo Bay. An "elevator" with air bags inflated. Photographed in Vigo Bay. (*By permission of The World's Work, London.*)

Pino's first invention was a submarine boat which was tested with brilliant success before putting it into service at Vigo Bay. For the preliminary work of treasure finding, he perfected his hydroscope, a kind of sea telescope consisting of a floating platform from which depend a series of tubes ending in a chamber equipped with electric lamps, lenses and reflectors, like so many gigantic eyes through which the observer is able to view the illuminated bottom of bay or ocean.

To lift the galleons bodily is Pino's plan, and he has devised what he calls "elevators" or clusters of great bags of waterproofed canvas each capable of raising forty tons in the water when pumped full of air. These are placed in the hull of the sunken ship or attached outside, and when made buoyant by means of powerful air pumps, exert a lifting force easily comprehended. In addition, this inge-

SPOOKY TREASURE TROVES

nious Italian engineer, who has made a science of treasure seeking, makes use of metal arms capable of embracing a rotting, flimsy hull, huge tongs which are operated by a floating equipment of sufficient engine power to lift whatever is made fast to. The Japanese government successfully employed his submarine inventions in raising the Russian war ships sunk at Port Arthur.

Already one of the Spanish galleons has been brought to the surface of Vigo Bay, but she happened to have been laden with costly merchandise instead of plate, and her cargo was long since ruined by water and corrosion. The list of articles recovered during the searches of recent years is a fascinating catalogue to show that the story of the lost fleet is a true romance of history. I quote Iberti who dwells with so much joyous enthusiasm over "the anchors, including that of the *Misericordia*, of Santa Cruz, guns of different caliber, wood of various kinds, thirty gun carriages, wheels, mortars, silver spoons, mariner's compasses, enormous cables, innumerable balls and bombs, statuettes of inlaid gold, magnificently engraved pipe holders, Mexican porcelain, tortas, or plates of silver, some weighing as much as eighty pounds; gold pieces stamped by the Royal Mint of Mexico and ingots from Peru."

Cannon of the treasure galleons recovered by Pino from the bottom of Vigo Bay.

Hydroscope invented by Pino for exploring the sea bottom and successfully used in finding the galleons of Vigo Bay.
(By permission of *The World's Work, London.*)

SPOOKY TREASURE TROVES

The latest of the concession held by Pino and his company whose shareholders have invested large sums of real money, is an unusual document in that bona-fide treasure seeking seems so incongruous an industry in this twentieth century. It bears the signature of His Excellency Don Jose Ferrandiz, Minister of the Royal Navy, and was granted on August 24, 1907, to be in force until 1915. The wording runs thus:

"With this date, I say to the Director General of the Mercantile Marine as follows:

"Most Excellent Sir,—Having taken into consideration the petition presented by the Italian subject, Don Carlos Iberti, representing Cav. Don Jose Pino, inventor of the hydroscope apparatus for seeing, photographing, and recovering objects sunk to the bottom of the sea, in which petition he explains that he obtained a Concession for the term of eight years to exploit what there is in the Bay of Vigo appertaining to the galleons which came from America, which Concession was published in the *Gaceta Official* of the 5th of January, 1904; that he was at the Bay of Vigo from the month of April until the end of the said year, carrying on dredging operations; but unforeseen difficulties prevented them from effecting a real and direct exploitation, so that the work accomplished was only preliminary, as that of seeing, examining, and studying the difficulties of the submarine bed, and the conditions in which the submerged galleons are; that having obtained all these data necessary for undertaking the work for recovery, in accord with the Commander of the Marine at Vigo, and other gentlemen who constitute the Council of Inspection, they suspended the operations in order to study and construct new apparatus, more powerful and more adapted to this kind of operation, and they returned to Italy with the intention of going again to Vigo as soon as they had finished the new appliances with which to complete the work of recovery; that they have already spent large sums there, the greater part of which have gone to benefit the inhabitants of Vigo; that in view of all this that has been put forward he prays for an extension on the same terms in which the Concession was granted:

"Considering, that by granting him the solicited extension, the State interests would not be prejudiced, on the condition of its receiving 20 per cent. of all that is recovered, irrespective of the artistic and historic value of the objects recovered:

"*His Majesty the King* in accord with what has been proposed by the Council of Ministers, has deigned to grant the solicited extension on the same conditions which were already put in the concession, which are:—

"First,—The Concessionaire shall utilize for all manual labor which shall be necessary, the small craft of the locality and sailors of the maritime department.

"Second,—The work once commenced shall be carried on without interruption unless there shall be justifiable cause to hinder it.

"Third,—He undertakes to give to the State 20 per cent. of the value of the objects recovered.

"Fourth,—In fulfilment of what has been established by Art. 351 of the Civil Code, if any objects of interest to science or art or of any historic value should be extracted, they shall be given to the State, if it requires, and the State will pay the fair price, which will be fixed by experts, taking into account the expenses of their recovery.

"Which by Royal Decree I have the pleasure to announce to you for your knowledge and satisfaction. May God preserve you for many years."

This long-winded proclamation seems faintly to echo of another and far distant day "appertaining to the galleons which came from America," that day on which the news of the catastrophe was received in the palace of Madrid. Gabriel de Savoy, the child queen, then only fourteen years old and wed to Philip V, heard the tidings of the battle of Vigo Bay, "on the day and hour which was fixed upon for her to go in public to give thanks to the Virgin of Atocha for the triumphs of the king, and to place in that temple the banners captured from the enemy in Italy. This wise lady lamented bitterly such fatal news, but not wishing to discourage and afflict her people, she put on courage, and resolving to go forth presented herself with so serene a countenance as to impose upon all, who were astonished at her courage, and the ceremony was performed as if nothing had happened."

Vigo to-day is a pretty and thriving town of 30,000 people, with a large trade by sea, and fertile fields stretching between bay and mountain. Round about are the ancient forts and castles which were stormed and battered by the grenadiers of the Duke of Ormond and the guns of the British and Dutch ships under Sir George Rooke. Vigo won a melancholy renown on that terrific day so long ago, and its blue waters have a haunting interest even now, recalling the glory of the age of the galleons and the wild romance of their voyaging from the Spanish Main. Perhaps the ingenious Don Jose Pino, with his modern machinery, may find the greatest treasure ever lost, certain as he is that "in dim green depths rot ingot-laden ships, with gold doubloons that from the drowned hand fell." At any rate, there is treasure-trove in the very story of that fight in Vigo Bay, in the contrast between the timid, blundering, procrastinating Spanish, afraid to leave their gold and silver in the galleons, yet afraid to unload it; and the instant decision of the English admiral who cared not a rap for the odds. His business it was to smash the French fleet and destroy the plate ships, and he went about it like the ready, indomitable sea dog that he was.

Among the English state papers is the manuscript log-book of the captain of the Torbay, flag ship of Vice Admiral Hopson who led the attack. This is how a fighting seaman of the old school disposed of so momentous and severe a naval action as that of Vigo Bay, as if it were no more than a common-place item in the

SPOOKY TREASURE TROVES

day's work:

"This 24 hours little wind, the latter part much rain and dirty weather. Yesterday about 3 in the afternoon we anchored before Vigo Town in 15 fathoms water. This morning Vice Admiral Hopson hoisted the red flag at our fore-topmast head in order to go ahead of the fleet to defeat the French and Spanish galleons which lay up the river. About noon we weighed, having sent our soldiers on there to engage the forts which opposed our coming. We being come near, the forts fired at us.

"About one o'clock, coming across the forts which were on each side the harbor, they fired smartly at us, and we fired our guns at both sides of them again, and went past and broke the boom which crossed the river to hinder our passage so that 4 and 5 men-of-war engaged us at once, but soon deserted, firing and burnt their ships. They sent a fireship which set us on fire."

It was a very simple business, to hear the captain of the *Torbay* tell it, but the golden empire of Spain was shaken from Cadiz to Panama, and gouty, dauntless Sir George Rooke helped mightily to hasten the end which was finally brought about by another admiral, George Dewey by name, in that Manila Bay whence the treasure galleons of the East Indies *flota* had crossed the Pacific to add their wealth to the glittering cargoes gathered by the Viceroys of Mexico and Peru.

SPOOKY TREASURE TROVES

CHAPTER IX
THE PIRATES' HOARD OF TRINIDAD

Of all the freebooters' treasure for which search is still made by means of curious information having to do with charts and other plausible records, the most famous are those buried on Cocos Islands in the Pacific and on the rocky islet of Trinidad in the South Atlantic. These places are thousands of miles apart, the former off the coast of Costa Rica, the latter several hundred miles from the nearest land of Brazil and not to be confused with the better known British colony of Trinidad in the Leeward Islands group of the West Indies.

Each of these treasures is of immense value, to be reckoned in millions of dollars, and their stories are closely interwoven because the plunder came from the same source at about the same time. Both narratives are colored by piracy, bloodshed and mystery, that of Cocos Island perhaps the more luridly romantic of the two by reason of an earlier association with the English buccaneers of Dampier's crew. Each island has been dug over and ransacked at frequent intervals during the last century, and it is safe to predict that expeditions will be fitting out for Cocos or Trinidad for many years to come.

The history of these notable treasures is a knotty skein to disentangle. Athwart its picturesque pages marches a numerous company of bold and imaginative liars, every man of them ready to swear on a stack of Bibles that his is the only true, unvarnished version of the events which caused the gold and jewels and plate to be hidden. However, when all the fable and fancy are winnowed out, the facts remaining are enough to make any red-blooded adventurer yearn to charter a rakish schooner and muster a crew of kindred spirits.

During the last days of Spanish rule on the west coast of South America, the wealthiest city left of that vast domain won by the Conquistadores and held by the Viceroys, was Lima, the capital of Peru. Founded in 1535 by Francisco Pizarro, it was the seat of the government of South America for centuries. The Viceregal court was maintained in magnificent state, and the Archbishop of Lima was the

SPOOKY TREASURE TROVES

most powerful prelate of the continent. Here the religious orders and the Inquisition had their centers. Of the almost incredible amount of gold and silver taken from the mines of the country, much remained in Lima to pile up fortunes for the grandees and officials, or to be fashioned into massy ornaments for the palaces, residences, churches, and for the great cathedral which still stands to proclaim the grandeur that was Spain's in the olden days.

Lima Cathedral

When Bolivar, the Liberator, succeeded in driving the Spanish out of Venezuela, and in 1819 set up the free republic of Colombia, the ruling class of Peru took alarm which increased to panic as soon as it was known that the revolutionary forces were organizing to march south and assault Lima itself. There was a great running to and fro among the wealthy Spanish merchants, the holders of fat positions under the Viceroy, and the gilded idlers who swaggered and ruffled it on riches won by the swords of their two-fisted ancestors. It was feared that the rebels of Bolivar and San Martin would loot the city, and confiscate the treasure,

SPOOKY TREASURE TROVES

both public and private, which consisted of bullion, plate, jewels, and coined gold.

Precious property to the value of six million sterling was hurried into the fortress of Lima for safe keeping and after the capture of the city by the army of liberation, Lord Dundonald, the English Admiral in command of the Chilian fleet assisting the revolutionists, offered to let the Spanish governor depart with two-thirds of this treasure if he would surrender the remainder and give up the fortifications without a fight. The Peruvian liberator, San Martin, set these terms aside, however, and allowed the Spanish garrison to evacuate the place, carrying away the six million sterling. This immense treasure was soon scattered far and wide, by sea and land. It was only part of the riches dispersed by the conquest of San Martin and his patriots. The people of Lima, hoping to send their fortunes safe home to Spain before the plundering invaders should make a clean sweep, put their valuables on board all manner of sailing vessels which happened to be in harbor, and a fugitive fleet of merchantmen steered out from the hostile coast of Peru, the holds piled with gold and silver, the cabins crammed with officials of the state and church and other residents of rank and station. At the same time there was sent to sea the treasure of the great cathedral of Lima, all its jeweled chalices, monstrances, and vestments, the solid gold candle-sticks and shrines, the vast store of precious furniture and ornaments, which had made this one of the richest religious edifices of the world.

There had not been so much dazzling booty afloat at one time since the galleon plate fleets were in their heyday during the sixteenth and seventeenth centuries. In 1820 there were no more of those great buccaneers and gentlemen adventurers who had singed the beard of the King of Spain in the wake of Francis Drake. They had sailed and fought and plundered for glory as well as gain, or for revenge as much as for doubloons. Their successors as sea rovers were pirates of low degree, base wretches of a sordid commercialism who preyed on honest merchant skippers of all flags, and had little taste for fighting at close quarters. The older race of sea rogues had been wolves; the pirates of the early nineteenth century were jackals.

Many a one of these gentry got wind of the fabulous treasure that had been sent afloat from Lima, and there is no doubt that much of it failed to reach Spain. While in some instances, these fleeing ships were boarded and scuttled by pirate craft, in others the lust of gold was too strong for the seamen to whom the rare cargoes had been entrusted, and they rose and took the riches away from their hapless passengers. It has been believed by one treasure seeking expedition after another, even to this day, that Captain Thompson of the British trading brig, *Mary Dear* received on board in the harbor of Lima as much as twelve million dollars' worth of gold and silver, and that he and his crew, after killing the Spanish owners, sailed north in the Pacific and buried the booty on Cocos Island.

SPOOKY TREASURE TROVES

Captain Thompson somehow escaped and joined a famous pirate of that time, Benito Bonito, who accumulated a large treasure which he also buried on Cocos Island. The British Admiralty records show that Bonito was overhauled in his turn by the frigate *Espiegle* and that rather than be hanged in chains, he very handsomely blew out his brains on his own deck.

This same treasure of Lima, or part of it, furnished the foundation of the story belonging to the volcanic islet of Trinidad in the South Atlantic. One version of this is that the pirates who chose this hiding-place had been the crew of a fast English schooner in the slave trade. While at sea they disposed of their captain by the unpleasant method of pinning him to the mainmast with a boarding pike through his vitals. Then the black flag was hoisted and with a new skipper they stood to the southward, finding a great amount of plunder in a Portuguese ship which had on board a "Jew diamond dealer" among other valuable items. After taking an East Indiaman, and other tempting craft, they buried the total proceeds on the desolate, uninhabited island of Trinidad, intending to return for it before the end of the cruise.

Unfortunately, for the successful pirates, they ran afoul of a heavily armed and manned merchant vessel which shot away their rudder, tumbled their spars about their rascally ears, boarded them with great spirit and determination, and clapped the shackles on the twenty gentlemen of fortune who had survived the engagement. These were carried into Havana and turned over to the Spanish authorities who gleefully hanged nineteen, not twenty, mark you, for one had to make a marvelous escape in order to hand down the secret of the treasure to posterity. This survivor died in bed in England at a very great age, so the story runs, and of course he had a chart to set the next generation to digging.

The earlier statements of this narrative may be cast aside as worthless. The real, true pirate of Trinidad was not in the slave schooner which captured the "Jew diamond dealer" of the Portuguese ship. An odd confusion of facts caused the mistake. While Benito Bonito was harrying the Spanish shipping of the Pacific and burying his treasure on Cocos Island, there was on the Atlantic a bloodthirsty pirate by the name of Benito de Soto. He was a Spaniard who sailed out of Buenos Aires in the year 1827, bound to Africa to smuggle a cargo of slaves. The crew was composed of French, Spanish, and Portuguese desperadoes, and led by the mate and De Soto they marooned the captain and ran away with the ship on a pirate voyage. They plundered and burned and slaughtered without mercy, their most nefarious exploit being the capture of the British merchant ship *Morning Star*, bound from Ceylon to England in 1828, and carrying as passengers several army officers and their wives and twenty-five invalided soldiers. After the most fiendish conduct, De Soto and his crew, drove the survivors into the hold of the *Morning Star*, and fastened the hatches, leaving the vessel to founder, for they had taken care to bore numerous auger holes in her bottom. By a miracle of good fortune,

SPOOKY TREASURE TROVES

the prisoners forced the hatches and were taken off next day by a passing vessel.

Benito de Soto met his end as the result of being wrecked in his own ship off the Spanish coast. He was caught in Gibraltar and hanged by the English Governor. An army officer who saw him turned off related that he was a very proper figure of a pirate, "there was no driveling fears upon him,—he walked firmly at the tail of the fatal cart, gazing sometimes at his coffin, sometimes at the crucifix which he held in his hand. This he frequently pressed to his lips, repeated the prayers spoken in his ear by the attendant clergyman, and seemed regardless of everything but the world to come. The gallows was erected beside the water, and fronting neutral ground. He mounted the cart as firmly as he had walked behind it, and held up his face to Heaven and the beating rain, calm, resigned, but unshaken; and finding the halter too high for his neck, he boldly stepped upon his coffin, and placed his head in the noose. Then watching the first turn of the wheels, he murmured, 'farewell, all,' and leaned forward to facilitate his fall ... The black boy was acquitted at Cadiz, but the men who had fled to the Caracas, as well as those arrested after the wreck, were convicted, executed, their limbs severed and hung on iron hooks, as a warning to all other pirates."

This Benito, who died so much better than he had lived, was not hanged at Havana, it will be perceived, and the version of the Trinidad treasure story already outlined is apparently a hodgepodge of the careers of Benito de Soto, and of Benito of Cocos Island, with a flavor of fact in so far as it refers to the twenty pirates who were carried to Cuba to be strung up, or garroted. The Spanish archives of that island record that this gang was executed and that they had been found guilty of plundering ships sailing from Lima shortly after the city had been entered by the revolutionists. Their association with the island of Trinidad is explained herewith as it was told to E. F. Knight, an Englishman, who organized and commanded an expedition which sailed in search of the treasure in 1889.

There was at that time near Newcastle, England, a retired sea captain who had been in command of an East Indiaman engaged in the opium trade in the years 1848 to 1850. "The China seas were then infested by pirates," said Mr. Knight's informant, "so that his vessel carried a few guns and a larger crew than is usual in these days. He had four quarter-masters, one of whom was a foreigner. The captain was not sure of his nationality but thought he was a Finn. On board the vessel the man went under the name of 'The Pirate' because of a deep scar across his cheek which gave him a somewhat sinister appearance. He was a reserved man, better educated than the ordinary sailor, and possessing a good knowledge of navigation.

"The captain took a liking to him, and showed him kindness on various occasions. This man was attacked by dysentery on the voyage from China to Bombay, and by the time the vessel reached port he was so ill, in spite of the captain's

SPOOKY TREASURE TROVES

nursing, that he had to be taken to the hospital. He gradually sank, and when he found that he was dying he told the captain, who frequently visited him, that he felt very grateful for the kind treatment given him, and that he would prove his gratitude by revealing a secret which might make his captain one of the richest men in England. He then asked the skipper to go to his chest and take out from it a parcel. This contained a piece of old tarpaulin with a plan of an island of Trinidad upon it.

"The dying soldier told him that at the spot indicated, that is at the base of the mountain known as Sugar Loaf, there was an immense treasure buried, consisting principally of gold and silver plate and ornaments, the plunder of Peruvian churches which certain pirates had concealed there in the year 1821. Much of this plate, he said, came from the cathedral of Lima, having been carried away from there during the war of independence, when the Spaniards were escaping the country and that among other riches were several massive gold candle-sticks.

"He further stated that he was the only survivor of the pirates, as all the others had been captured by the Spaniards and executed in Cuba some years before, and consequently it was probable that no one but himself knew the secret. He then gave the captain instructions as to the exact position of the treasure in the bay under the Sugar Loaf, and enjoined him to go there and search for it, as it was almost certain that it had not been removed."

Mr. Knight, who was a young barrister of London, investigated this story with much diligence, and discovered that the captain aforesaid had sent his son to Trinidad in 1880 to try to identify the marks shown on the old pirate's tarpaulin chart. He landed from a sailing ship, did no digging for lack of equipment, but reported that the place tallied exactly with the description, although a great landslide of reddish earth had covered the place where the treasure was hid. This evidence was so convincing that in 1885 an expedition was organized among several adventurous gentlemen of South Shields who chartered a bark of six hundred tons, the *Aurea*, and fitted her at a large outlay with surf boats, picks, shovels, timber, blasting powder, and other stores. This party found the island almost inaccessible because of the wild, rock-bound coast, the huge breakers which beat about it from all sides, and the lack of harbors and safe anchorage. After immense difficulty, eight men were landed, with a slender store of provisions and a few of the tools. The dismal aspect of the island, the armies of huge land crabs which tried to devour them, the burning heat, and the hard labor without enough food or water, soon disheartened this band of treasure seekers, and they dug no more than a small trench before courage and strength forsook them. Signaling to their ships, they were taken off, worn out and ill, and thus ended the efforts of the expedition.

In the same year, an American skipper chartered a French sailing vessel in

SPOOKY TREASURE TROVES

Rio Janeiro, and sailed for Trinidad with four Portuguese sailors to do his digging for him. They were ashore several days, but found no treasure, and vanished from the story after this brief fling with the dice of fortune. Now, Knight was of different stuff from these other explorers. He was a first-class amateur seaman who had sailed his yacht *Falcon* to South America in 1880, and was both experienced and capable afloat and ashore. While bound from Montevideo to Bahia he had touched at Trinidad, curious to see this remote islet so seldom visited. This was before he heard the buried treasure story. Therefore when he became acquainted, several years later, with the chart and information left by the old pirate, he was able to verify the details of his own knowledge, and he roundly affirmed:

"In the first place, his carefully prepared plan of the island, the minute directions he gave as to the best landing, and his description of the features of the bay on whose shores the treasure was concealed, prove beyond doubt to myself and others who know Trinidad, that he, or if not himself some informant of his, had landed on this so rarely visited islet; and not only landed but passed some time on it, and carefully surveyed the approaches to the bay, so as to be able to point out the dangers and show the safest passage through the reefs. This information could not have been obtained from any pilot-book. The landing recommended by previous visitors is at the other side of the island. This bay is described by them as inaccessible, and the indications on the Admiralty chart are completely erroneous.

"And beyond this, the quartermaster must have been acquainted with what was taking place in two other distant portions of the world during the year of his professed landing on the desert island. He knew of the escape of pirates with the cathedral plate of Lima. He was also aware that, shortly afterwards, there were hanged in Cuba the crew of a vessel that had committed acts of piracy on the Peruvian coast.

"It is scarcely credible that an ordinary seaman,—even allowing that he was superior in education to the average of his fellows,—could have pieced these facts together so ingeniously into this plausible story."

This argument has merit and it was persuasive enough to cause Knight to buy the staunch cutter *Alerte*, muster a company of gentlemen volunteers, ship a crew, and up anchor from Southampton for Trinidad.

There was never a better found treasure expedition than this in the *Alerte*. The nine partners, each of whom put up one hundred pounds toward the expenses, were chosen from one hundred and fifty eager applicants. Articles of agreement provided that one-twentieth of the treasure recovered was to be received by each adventurer and he in turn bound himself to work hard and obey orders. In the equipment was a drilling apparatus for boring through earth and rock, an hydraulic jack for lifting huge bowlders, portable forge and anvil, iron wheel-barrows,

SPOOKY TREASURE TROVES

crow-bars, shovels and picks galore, a water distilling plant, a rapid fire gun, and a full complement of repeating rifles and revolvers.

A few days before the *Alerte* was ready to sail from Southampton an elderly naval officer boarded the cutter and was kind enough to inform Mr. Knight of another buried treasure which he might look for on his route to Trinidad. The story had been hidden for many years among the documents of the Admiralty, and as a matter of government record, it is, of course, perfectly authentic. In 1813, the Secretary of the Admiralty instructed Sir Richard Bickerton, commanding at Portsmouth, to send in the first King's ship touching at Madeira a seaman who had given information concerning a hidden treasure, in order that the truth of his story might be tested.

The Admiralty order was entrusted to Captain Hercules Robinson of the *Prometheus* and in his report he states that "after being introduced to the foreign seaman referred to in the above letter, and reading the notes which had been taken of his information, he charged him to tell no person what he knew or what was his business, that he was to mess with the captain's coxswain, and that no duty would be required of him. To this the man replied that that was all he desired, that he was willing to give his time, and would ask no remuneration for his intelligence."

While the *Prometheus* was anchored at Funchal, Madeira, Captain Robinson closely questioned the mysterious seaman whose name was Christian Cruse. He declared that he had been in a hospital ill of yellow fever, several years before, and with him was a shipmate, a Spaniard, who died of the same malady. Before his death he told Cruse that in 1804 he had been in a Spanish ship, from South America to Cadiz, with two millions of silver in chests. When nearing the coast of Spain, they were signaled by a neutral vessel that England had declared war and that Cadiz was blockaded. Rather than risk capture by the British fleet, and unwilling to run all the way back to South America, the captain resolved to try to gain the nearest of the West Indies and save his treasure.

Passing to the southward of Madeira, a cluster of small, uninhabited islands, called the Salvages, was sighted. Thereupon the crew decided that it was foolishness to continue the voyage. The captain was accordingly stabbed to death with a dirk, and the ship steered to an anchorage. The chests of Spanish dollars were landed in a small bay, a deep trench dug in the sand above highwater mark, and the treasure snugly buried, the body of the captain deposited in a box on top of it. The mutineers then sought the Spanish Main where they intended to burn their ship, buy a small vessel under British colors, and return to carry off the two million dollars.

Near Tobago they suffered shipwreck because of poor navigation and only two were saved. One died ashore, and the other was the Spanish seaman who made the dying declaration to Christian Cruse in the hospital at Vera Cruz.

SPOOKY TREASURE TROVES

Captain Hercules Robinson was a seasoned officer of His Majesty's navy, used to taking sailors' yarns with a grain of salt, but that he was convinced of the good faith of Christian Cruse and of the truth of the narrative is shown by his interesting comments, as he wrote them down a century ago:

"May Cruse not have had some interested object in fabricating this story? Why did he not tell it before? Is not the cold-blooded murder inconceivable barbarity, and the burying the body over the treasure too dramatic and buccaneer-like? Or might not the Spaniard have lied from love of lying and mystifying his simple shipmate, or might he not have been raving?

"As to the first difficulty, I have the strongest conviction of the honesty of Christian Cruse, and I think I could hardly be grossly deceived as to his character, and his disclaiming any reward unless the discovery was made, went to confirm my belief that he was an honest man. And then as to his withholding the information for four or five years, be it remembered that the war with Denmark might have truly shut him out from any intercourse with England. Next as to the wantonness and indifference with which the murder was perpetrated, I am afraid there is no great improbability in this. I have witnessed a disregard of human life in matters of promotion in our service, etc., which makes the conduct of these Spaniards under vehement temptation, and when they could do as they pleased, sufficiently intelligible.

"But certainly the coffin over the treasure looked somewhat theatrical and gave it the air of Sadler's Wells, or a novel, rather than matter of fact. I enquired, therefore, from Christian Cruse why the body of the captain was thus buried, and he replied that he understood the object was, that in case any person should find the marks of their proceedings and dig to discover what they had been about, they might come to the body and go no further."

After further reflection, Captain Robinson convinced himself that the Spanish seaman had been clear-headed when he made his confession to Cruse, and that it would have been beyond him deliberately to invent the statement as fiction. The *Prometheus* was headed for the Salvages, and arriving off the largest of these islands, a bay was found and a level white patch of beach above high water mark situated as had been described to Christian Cruse. Fifty sailors were sent ashore to dig with shovels and boarding pikes, making the sand fly in the hope of winning the reward of a hundred dollars offered to the man who found the murdered captain's coffin.

The search lasted only one day because the anchorage was unsafe and Captain Robinson was under orders to return to Madeira. Arriving there, other orders recalled his ship to England for emergency duty and the treasure hunt was abandoned. So far as known, no other attempt had been made to find the chests of dollars until Mr. Knight decided to act on the information and explore the Sal-

SPOOKY TREASURE TROVES

vages in passing.

Of this little group of islands it was decided by the company of the *Alerte* that the one called the Great Piton most closely answered the description given Christian Cruse by the Spanish pirate. A bay was found with a strip of white sand above high-water mark, and Mr. Knight and his shipmates pitched a camp nearby and had the most sanguine expectations of bringing to light the rude coffin of the murdered captain.

A series of trenches was opened up after a systematic plan, and some crumbling bones discovered, but the ship's surgeon refused to swear that they had belonged to a human being. The trouble was that the surface of the place had been considerably changed by the action of waves and weather, which made the Admiralty charts of a century before very misleading. The destination of the *Alerte* was Trinidad, after all, and the visit to the Salvages was only an incident, so the search was abandoned after four days. In all probability, the treasure of the Salvages is still in its hiding-place, and any adventurous young gentlemen seeking a field of operations will do well to consult for themselves the documentary evidence of Captain Hercules Robinson and Christian Cruse, as filed among the records of the British Admiralty Office.

Trinidad is a much more difficult island to explore than any of the Salvages group. In fact, this forbidding mass of volcanic rock is a little bit of inferno. It is sometimes impossible to make a landing through the surf for weeks at a time, and when a boat makes the attempt in the most favorable circumstances, the venture is a hazard of life and death. As a vivid summary of the aspect of this lonely treasure island, I quote from Mr. Knight, because he is the only man who has ever described Trinidad at first hand:

"As we neared it, the features of this extraordinary place could gradually be distinguished. The north side, that which faced us, is the most barren and desolate portion of the island, and appears to be utterly inaccessible. Here the mountains rise sheer from the boiling surf,—fantastically shaped of volcanic rock; cloven by frightful ravines; lowering in perpendicular precipices; in places overhanging threateningly, and, where the mountains have been shaken to pieces by the fires and earthquakes of volcanic action, huge landslips slope steeply in the yawning ravines,—landslips of black and red volcanic debris, and loose rocks large as houses, ready on the slightest disturbance to roll down, crashing, into the abysses below. On the summit of the island there floats almost constantly, even on the clearest day, a wreath of dense vapor, never still, but rolling and twisting into strange shapes as the wind eddies among the crags. And above this cloud-wreath rise mighty pinnacles of coal-black rock, like the spires of some gigantic Gothic cathedral piercing the blue southern sky. It would be impossible to convey in words a just idea of the mystery of Trinidad. The very coloring seemed unearthly,

SPOOKY TREASURE TROVES

in places dismal black, and in others the fire-consumed crags are of strange metallic hues, vermilion red and copper yellow. When one lands on its shores, this uncanny impression is enhanced. It bears all the appearances of being an accursed spot, whereupon no creatures can live, save the hideous land-crabs and foul and cruel sea birds."

An ideal place, this, for pirates to bury treasure, you will agree, and good for nothing else under Heaven. The South Atlantic Directory, the shipmaster's guide, states that "the surf is often incredibly great, and has been seen to break over a bluff which is two hundred feet high." Trinidad was first visited by Halley, the astronomer, after whom the famous comet was named, who called there in 1700 when he was a captain in the Royal Navy. Captain Amos Delano, the Yankee pioneer in the Far Eastern trade, made a call in 1803, prompted by curiosity, but as a rule mariners have given the island a wide berth, now and then touching there when in need of water or fresh meat in the shape of turtles.

At one time the Portuguese attempted to found a settlement on Trinidad, probably before the forests had been killed by some kind of volcanic upheaval. The ruins of their stone huts are still to be seen as humble memorials of a great race of explorers and colonists in the golden age of that nation.

With tremendous exertion, the party from the *Alerte* was landed with its tools and stores, and headquarters established close to the ravine which was believed to be the hiding-place of the treasure as indicated by the chart and information of the Finn quartermaster with the scar across his cheek. It was found that there had been no actual landslide, but the ravine was choked with large bowlders which at various times had fallen from the cliffs above. These were packed together by the red earth silting and washing during the rainy season when the ravines were flooded.

Along the whole of the windward coast were found innumerable fragments of wreckage, spars, timbers, barrels. From the position of the island, in the belt of the southeast trade winds, many derelict vessels must have been driven ashore. Some of this immense accumulation of stuff may have lain there for centuries, or ever since vessels first doubled the Cape of Good Hope. Here and there were the gaunt rows of ribs to show where a ship had been stranded bodily, and doubtless much valuable property in silver and gold, in bars, ingots, and doubloons, lies buried in the shattered hulks of these old Dutch East Indiamen, and galleons from Peru.

As particular landmarks near the ravine, the pirate had mentioned three cairns which he and his comrades had heaped up. Sure enough, the previous treasure seekers of the *Aurea* expedition from England had found the three cairns, but foolishly demolished them on the chance that gold might be buried underneath. Mr. Knight could find traces of only one of them, and he discovered also a

SPOOKY TREASURE TROVES

water-jar, a broken wheel-barrow and other tools to show where the others had been digging. The crew of the *Alerte* were confident that they were at the right place, and they set to work with the most admirable zeal and fortitude, enduring hardships cheerfully, and during the three months of their labors on Trinidad, removing earth and rock literally by the thousands of tons, until the ravine was scooped out to a depth of from eight to twenty feet.

Their vessel had to anchor far off shore, and once forsook them for a fourteen hundred mile voyage to Bahia to get provisions. These London lawyers and other gentlemen unused to toil with the hands became as tough and rough and disreputable to see as the pirates who had been there aforetime. In costume of shirt, trousers, and belt, they became ragged and stained from head to foot with the soil, and presented a uniform, dirty, brownish, yellow appearance like so many Brazilian convicts. Their surf boat was wrecked or upset at almost every attempt to land or to go off to the *Alerte*, and when they were not fishing one another out of the surf, they were diving to recover their submerged and scattered stores. Their leader, Mr. Knight, paid them a tribute of which they must have been proud:

"They had toiled hard and had kept up their spirits all the while and what is really wonderful under circumstances so calculated to try the temper and wear out the patience, they had got on exceedingly well with each other, and there had been no quarreling or ill feeling of any sort."

At length the melancholy verdict was agreed upon in council. All the bright dreams of carrying home a fortune for every adventurer were reluctantly dismissed. The men were worn to the bone, and it was becoming more and more difficult to maintain communication with the *Alerte*. The prodigious excavation was abandoned, and Mr. Knight indulged himself in a soliloquy as he surveyed the "great trenches, the piled-up mounds of earth, the uprooted rocks, with broken wheelbarrows and blocks, worn-out tools, and other relics of our three months strewn over the ground; and it was sad to think that all the energy of these men had been spent in vain. They well deserved to succeed, and all the more so because they bore their disappointment with so much pluck and cheerfulness."

But, in truth, the expedition had not been in vain. The toilers had been paid in richer stuff than gold. They had lived the true romance, nor could a man of spirit and imagination wish for anything more to his taste than to be encamped on a desert island, with the surf shouting in his ears, the sea birds crying, all hands up with daybreak to dig for buried treasure whose bearings were found on a tarpaulin chart that had belonged to a pirate with a deep scar across his cheek. How it would have delighted the heart of Robert Louis Stevenson to be one of this company of the *Alerte* at Trinidad! The gallant little vessel, only sixty-four feet long she was, filled away for the West Indies, homeward bound, while the men aboard amused themselves by wondering how many nations might have laid claim to the treasure, had it been found;—England which hoisted its flag on Trinidad in 1770; Portugal because Portuguese from Brazil made a settlement there in 1750; Brazil, because the island lay off her coast; Spain, to whom the treasure had belonged, and Peru from whose cathedral it was taken, and lastly the Roman Church.

In conclusion, Mr. Knight, to whose fascinating narrative, "The Cruise of the *Alerte*," I am indebted for the foregoing information, sums it up like a true soldier of fortune:

"Well, indeed, it was for us that we had not found the pirates' gold; for we seemed happy enough as we were, and if possessed of this hoard, our lives would of a certainty have become a burden to us. We should be too precious to be comfortable. We should degenerate into miserable, fearsome hypochondriacs, careful of our means of transit, dreadfully anxious about what we ate or drank, miserably cautious about everything. 'Better far, no doubt,' exclaimed these cheerful philosophers, 'to remain the careless, happy paupers that we are.'

"'Do you still believe in the existence of the treasure?' is a question that has been often put to me since my return. Knowing all I do, I have very little doubt that the story of the Finn quartermaster is substantially true,—that the treasures of Lima were hidden on Trinidad; but whether they have been taken away, or whether they are still there and we failed to find them because we were not in possession of one link of the directions, I am unable to say."

In later years, E. F. Knight became a war correspondent, and lost an arm in the Boer campaign. I met him at Key West during the Spanish war in which he represented *The London Times* and found him to be a solid, well-ballasted man who knew what he was about and not at all one to have gone treasure seeking without excellent reasons. That he was adventurous in his unassuming way he proved by landing on the Cuban coast near Havana in order to interview the Spanish Captain-General. A newspaper dispatch boat ran close in shore, the skipper risking being blown out of water by the batteries of Morro Castle, and Knight was transferred to a tiny flat-bottomed skiff of the tonnage of a bath-tub. Equipped with a note-book, revolver, water bottle, and a small package of sandwiches, he said good-by in his very placid manner, and was seen to be standing on his head in the surf a few minutes later. He scrambled ashore, probably recalling to mind a similar style of landing on the coast of Trinidad, and vanished in the jungle. That he ran grave danger of being potted for an *Americano* by the first Spanish patrol he encountered appeared to give him no concern whatever. It was easy to perceive that he must have been the right kind of man to lead a treasure-hunting expedition.

Since the *Alerte* sailed on her dashing quest in 1889, the pirates' gold of Trinidad has figured in an adventure even more fantastic. Many readers will doubtless remember the career of the late Baron James Harden-Hickey who attempted

SPOOKY TREASURE TROVES

to establish a kingdom of his own on the islet of Trinidad. He belonged in another age than this and he was laughed at rather more than he deserved. Duelist, editor, *boulevardier*, fond of the tinsel and trappings of life, he married the daughter of John H. Flagler of the Standard Oil Company and with funds from this excessively commercial source created a throne, a court, and a kingdom. He had seen the island of Trinidad from a British merchant ship in which he went round the Horn in 1888, and the fact that this was a derelict bit of real estate, to which no nation thought it worth while to lay formal claim, appealed to his active imagination.

A would-be king has difficulty in finding a stray kingdom nowadays, and Harden-Hickey bothered his head not in the least over the problem of populating this god-forsaken jumble of volcanic rock and ashes. Ere long he blossomed forth most gorgeously in Paris and New York as King James I of the Principality of Trinidad. There was a royal cabinet, a Minister of Foreign Affairs, a Chancellerie, and uniforms, court costumes, and regalia designed by the king himself. Most dazzling of all the equipment was the Order of the Insignia of the Cross of Trinidad, a patent and decoration of nobility to be bestowed on those deemed worthy of the signal honor.

The newspapers bombarded King James I with gibes and jeers, but he took himself with immense, even tragic seriousness, and issued a prospectus of the settlement of his kingdom, inviting an aristocracy of intellect and good breeding to comprise the ruling class, while the hard work was to be done by hired menials. He mustered on paper some kind of a list of resources of Trinidad, although he was hard put to name anything very tangible, and laid special stress on the buried treasure. It was to be dug up by the subjects and, if found, to be divided among the patriots who had bought the securities issued by the royal treasury. Surely a pirates' treasure was never before gravely offered among the assets of a kingdom, but King James had no sense of humor, and the lost treasure was as real to him as any other of his marvelous dreams.

Some work was actually done at Trinidad, building material landed, a vessel chartered to run from Brazil, and a few misguided colonists recruited, when in 1895 the British Government ruthlessly knocked the Principality of Trinidad into a cocked hat and toppled over the throne of King James I. The island was wanted as a cable landing or relay station, and a naval officer raised the red ensign to proclaim annexation by reason of Halley's discovery in 1700. At this Brazil set up a protest on the ground that her Portuguese had been the original settlers. While the diplomats of these two powers were politely locking horns over the question of ownership, that unfortunate monarch, King James I of the Principality of Trinidad, Baron Harden-Hickey of the Holy Roman Empire, perceived that his realm had been pulled out from under him, so to speak. Whichever nation won the dispute it meant no comfort for him. Trinidad was no longer a derelict island and he was a

SPOOKY TREASURE TROVES

king without a kingdom.

He surrendered not one jot or tittle of his rights, and to his Minister of Foreign Affairs he solemnly bequeathed the succession and the claim to proprietorship. And among these rights and privileges was the royal interest in the buried treasure. Harden-Hickey, when he could no longer live a king, died as he thought befitting a gentleman, by his own hand. It seems a pity that he could not have been left alone to play at being king, and to find the pirates' gold.

SPOOKY TREASURE TROVES

CHAPTER X
THE LURE OF COCOS ISLAND

It will be recalled that Lord Bellomont, in writing to his government of the seizure of Kidd and his treasure, made mention of "a Pirate committed who goes by the name of Captain Davis, that came passenger with Kidd from Madagascar. I suppose him to be that Captain Davis that Dampier and Wafer speak of in their printed relations of Voyages, for an extraordinary stout[1] man; but let him be as stout as he will, here he is a prisoner, and shall be forthcoming upon the order I receive from England concerning him."

If Bellomont was right in this surmise, then he had swept into his drag-net one of the most famous and successful buccaneers of the seventeenth century, a man who must have regarded the alleged misdeeds of Kidd as much ado about nothing. Very likely it was this same Captain Edward Davis who may have been at the East Indies on some lawful business of his own, but he had no cause for anxiety at being captured by Bellomont as a suspicious character. He had honorably retired in 1688 from his trade of looting Spanish galleons and treasure towns, in which year the king's pardon was offered all buccaneers who would quit that way of life and claim the benefit of the proclamation.

It is known that he was afterwards in England, where he dwelt in quietness and security. William Dampier mentions him always with peculiar respect. "Though a buccaneer, he was a man of much sterling worth, being an excellent commander, courageous, never rash, and endued in a superior degree with prudence, moderation, and steadiness, qualities in which the buccaneers generally have been most deficient. His character is not stained with acts of cruelty; on the contrary, wherever he commanded, he restrained the ferocity of his companions. It is no small testimony to his abilities that the whole of the buccaneers in the South Sea during his time, in every enterprise wherein he bore part, voluntarily placed themselves under his guidance, and paid him obedience as their leader; and no symptom occurs of their having at any time wavered in this respect or shown inclination to set up a rival authority.[2]

During the Kidd proceedings, the Crown officers made out no case against Edward Davis, and he appears at the trial only as a witness in Kidd's behalf. He testified in corroboration of the fact that Kidd had brought home the two French passes taken out of his captures, and his experienced mind was quick to recognize the importance of the documents as a sound defense against the charges of piracy.

Curiously enough, the name of Captain Edward Davis has since been linked with a buried treasure story, that of Cocos Island in the Pacific. Certain it is that he and his comrades took great spoils along the Spanish coasts of South America and the Isthmus, and that he used Cocos Island as a convenient base for careening ship and recuperating the health of his hard-fighting, careless crew. Wafer has given the following description of this popular resort for treasure seekers of modern times:

"The middle of Cocos Island is a steep hill, surrounded with a plain declining to the sea. This plain is thick set with cocoanut trees; but what contributes greatly to the pleasure of the place is that a great many springs of clear and sweet water, rising to the top of the hill, are there gathered as in a deep large basin or pond, and the water having no channel, it overflows the verge of its basin in several places, and runs trickling down in pleasant streams. In some places of its overflowing, the rocky side of the hill being more perpendicular and hanging over the plain beneath, the water pours down in a cataract, so as to leave a dry space under the spout, and form a kind of arch of water. The freshness which the falling water gives the air in this hot climate makes this a delightful place.

"We did not spare the cocoa-nuts. One day, some of our men being minded to make themselves merry went ashore and cut down a great many cocoa-nut trees, from which they gathered the fruit, and drew about twenty gallons of the milk. They then sat down and drank healths to the King and Queen, and drank an excessive quantity; yet it did not end in drunkenness; but this liquor so chilled and benumbed their nerves that they could neither go nor stand. Nor could they return on board without the help of those who had not been partakers of the frolic, nor did they recover under four or five days' time."[3]

Captain Edward Davis had found this delectable islet during a singularly adventurous voyage. The English buccaneers and the French *filibustiers* who had long cruised in the West Indies, were driven from their haunts by the vigorous activity of the European governments, and in 1683 an expedition was organized to go pirating against the Spaniards in the Pacific, or the "South Sea." Dampier was of this number, also Captain John Cook, Captain Edward Davis, and Lionel Wafer who wrote the journal of the voyage. The scheme was hatched on the coast of Hispaniola, and after taking two prizes, French vessels, to Virginia to be sold, the company seventy strong, and most of them old hands at this game, stood out from the Chesapeake in an eighteen-gun ship called the *Revenge*.

Off the coast of Guinea they found a large Danish ship which better suited their purpose, wherefore she was carried by boarding. They christened her the *Batchelor's Delight*, and abandoned their old vessel which was burned, "that she might tell no tales." In February of 1684, they rounded Cape Horn and made for the island of Juan Fernandez, which several of the company had previously visited with Watling. Then sailing northward, the ship visited the Galapagos Islands to catch turtle, and bore away for Cocos which was missed because of adverse winds and faulty navigation. On this stretch of the voyage, the *Batchelor's Delight* passed what was known as the Isle of Plate, or Drake's Island, in latitude 2 min. 42 sec. S., which has an alluring lost treasure story of its own. Says Esquemeling:

"This island received its name from Sir Francis Drake and his famous actions, for here it is reported by tradition that he made the dividend or sharing of that quantity of plate which he took in the Armada of this sea, distributing it to each man of his company by whole bowls full. The Spaniards affirm to this day that he took at that time twelve score tons of plate, and sixteen bowls of coined money a man, his number being then forty-five men in all. Insomuch that they were forced to heave much of it overboard, because his ship could not carry it all. Hence was this island called by the Spaniards themselves the Isle of Plate, from this great dividend, and by us Drake's Isle."[4]

The mainland of South America, or New Spain, was sighted near Cape Blanco, where Captain John Cook died, and Edward Davis, then quartermaster, was elected commander. He cruised for some time along the coast, learning among other interesting news that at Point Saint Elena, "many years before a rich Spanish ship was driven ashore for want of wind to work her, that immediately after she struck she heeled off to seaward and sank in seven or eight fathoms of water, and that no one ever attempted to fish for her because there falls in here a great high sea."[5]

In the bay of Guayaquil, on the coast of Peru, Davis and Swan, who had joined him in a small ship called the *Cygnet*, captured four vessels, three of which had cargoes of negroes. Most of them were let go, to the great disappointment of Dampier who was filled with a mighty scheme of treasure finding which he outlined in these words:

"Never was put into the hands of men a greater opportunity to enrich themselves. We had 1000 negroes, all lusty young men and women, and we had 200 tons of flour stored up at the Galapagos Islands. With these negroes we might have gone and settled at Santa Maria on the Isthmus of Darien, and have employed them in getting gold out of the mines there. All the Indians living in that neighborhood were mortal enemies to the Spaniards, were flushed by successes against them, and for several years had been fast friends of the privateers. Add to which, we should have had the North Sea open to us, and in a short time should have received assistance from all parts of the West Indies. Many thousands of buccaneers from Jamaica and the French islands would have flocked to us; and we should have been an overmatch for all the force the Spaniards could have brought out of Peru against us."

Soon after this, the little squadron blockaded the Bay of Panama for several weeks, plundering whatever shipping came their way. There they were joined by two hundred Frenchmen and eighty Englishmen, old buccaneers who had crossed the Isthmus of Darien to have a fling in the South Seas. Presently another party of two hundred and sixty-four sea rovers under French command were added to the fleet, besides a strong force of Englishmen led by one Townley. Davis was made commander-in-chief of this formidable combination of ten ships and nine hundred and sixty men, of which the flagship was the *Batchelor's Delight*. They laid in wait for the annual treasure fleet sent by the Viceroy of Peru to Panama and found it, but were beaten off because Davis' confederates lacked his eagerness for fighting at close quarters.

Turning his attention to the mainland, Davis sacked and burned the city of Leon on the lake of Nicaragua. There one of the free-booters killed "was a stout, grey-headed old man of the name of Swan, aged about eighty-four years, who had served under Cromwell, and had ever since made privateering or buccaneering his occupation. This veteran would not be dissuaded from going on the enterprise against Leon; but his strength failed in the march, and after being left on the road he was found by the Spaniards, who endeavored to make him their prisoner; but he refused to surrender, and fired his musket amongst them, having in reserve a pistol still charged; on which he was shot dead."[6]

After this, the force scattered in small bands to plunder on their own account, Davis keeping together the best of the men whom he took to Cocos Island where a considerable stay was made. Thence he ravaged the coast of Peru, capturing many vessels and taking many towns. With booty amounting to five thousand pieces of eight for every man, Davis sailed to Juan Fernandez to refit, intending to proceed from there to the West Indies, but before the ships and men were ready for the long voyage around Cape Horn, many of the buccaneers had lost all their gold at dice, and they could not endure to quit the South Sea empty handed. Their luckier comrades sailed for the West Indies with Captain Knight, while they chose to remain and try their fortune afresh with Captain Davis, in the *Batchelor's Delight*. They soon fell in with a large party of French and English buccaneers who had formerly cruised with them, and were now engaged in trying to take the rich city of Guayaquil. They were making sorry business of it, however, and in sore need of such a capable leader as Davis. He finished the task with neatness and dispatch and shared in the gorgeous plunder of gold and silver and jewels,

SPOOKY TREASURE TROVES

reckoned by one of the Frenchmen in his account of the episode at fifteen hundred thousand livres.

Davis was now satisfied to leave the Pacific, but whether he went first to Cocos Island to bury any treasure, history saith not, although tradition roundly affirms that he did. That he and many of his fellow buccaneers frequently resorted to the Galapagos group, as well as tarrying at Cocos, is a matter of record. Of the former islands, Captain Colnet who touched there in 1793, wrote:[7]

"This isle appears to have been a favorite resort of the buccaneers as we found seats made by them of stone and earth, and a considerable number of broken jars scattered about, and some whole, in which the Peruvian wine and liquors of the country are preserved. We also found daggers, nails and other implements. The watering-place of the buccaneers was at this time entirely dried up, and there was only found a small rivulet between two hills, running into the sea, the northernmost of which hills forms the south point of Fresh Water Bay. There is plenty of wood, but that near the shore is not large enough for other use than firewood."

The buccaneers of other voyages than these may have landed at Cocos Island to leave their treasure. Heaven knows they found plenty of it in those waters. There was Captain Bartholomew Sharp, for example, with whom Dampier had sailed several years before. He took a Guayaquil ship called the *San Pedro* off Panama, and aboard her found nearly forty thousand pieces of eight, besides silver, silver bars and ingots of gold, and a little later captured the tall galleon *Rosario*, the richest prize ever boarded by the buccaneers. She had many chests of pieces of eight, and a quantity of wine and brandy. Down in her hold, bar upon bar, "were 700 pigs of plate," rough silver from the mines, not yet made ready for the Lima mint. The pirates thought this crude silver was tin, and so left it where it lay, in the hold of the *Rosario*, "which we turned away loose into the sea,"[8] with the precious stuff aboard her. One pig of the seven hundred was taken aboard the *Trinity* of Captain Sharp "to make bullets of." About two-thirds of it was "melted and squandered," but a fragment remained when the ship touched at Antigua, homeward bound, and was given to a "Bristol man" in exchange for a drink of rum. He sold it in England for seventy-five pounds sterling.

"Thus," says Basil Ringrose, "we parted with the richest booty we got on the whole voyage." Captain Bartholomew Sharp may have been thinking of something else than the cargo of silver, for aboard the *Rosario* was a woman, "the beautifullest Creature that his Eyes had ever beheld," while Ringrose calls her "the most beautiful woman that I ever saw in the South Seas."

Of these wild crews that flung away their lives and their treasure to enrich romance and tradition, it has been said:

"They were of that old breed of rover whose port lay always a little farther on; a little beyond the sky-line. Their concern was not to preserve life, but rather to squander it away; to fling it, like so much oil, into the fire, for the pleasure of going up in a blaze. If they lived riotously, let it be urged in their favor that at least they lived. They lived their vision. They were ready to die for what they believed to be worth doing. We think them terrible. Life itself is terrible. But life was not terrible to them, for they were comrades; and comrades and brothers-in-arms are stronger than life. Those who live at home at ease may condemn them. The old buccaneers were happier than they. The buccaneers had comrades and the strength to lead their own lives."[9]

This stout old breed had long since vanished when Cocos Island once more became the theater of buried treasure legend. The versions of this latter story agree in the essential particular that it was Captain Thompson of the merchant brig *Mary Dear* who stole the twelve million dollars' worth of plate, jewels, and gold coin which had been entrusted to him by the Spanish residents of Lima in 1820, and buried them on Cocos Island. Then, after he had joined the crew of the pirate, Benito Bonito, and somehow managed to escape alive when that enterprising gentleman came to grief, he tried to return to Cocos Island to recover the fabulous treasure.

The account of his later wanderings and adventures, as handed down in its most trustworthy form, has been the inspiration of several modern treasure-seeking expeditions. It is related that a native of Newfoundland, Keating by name, while sailing from England in 1844, met a man of middle age, "handsome in appearance and having about him something of an air of mystery which had an attraction of its own." This was, of course, none other than Captain Thompson of the *Mary Dear*. He became friendly with Keating and when they landed at Newfoundland, the latter asked him to accept the hospitality of his home. The stranger, who appeared anxious to avoid public notice, remained for some time with Keating, and wishing to make some return for his kindness, at length confided that he was one of the two survivors of Benito Bonito's crew, and possessed a secret which would make them immensely rich. If Keating could persuade one of the merchants of Newfoundland to fit out a vessel, they would sail to the Pacific and fetch home enough treasure to buy the whole island.

Keating believed the strange tale and passed it on to a ship-owner who agreed to furnish a vessel provided one Captain Bogue should go in command of the expedition. While preparations were under way, Thompson was inconsiderate enough to die, but it goes without saying that he left a map carefully marked with crosses and bearings. Keating and Bogue set sail with this precious document, and after a long and tedious voyage into the Pacific, they cast anchor off Cocos Island.

There the brace of adventurers were rowed ashore, leaving the vessel in charge of the mate. Captain Thompson's directions were found to be accurate, and a cave was discovered and in it a dazzling store of treasure to make an honest sailor-man rub his eyes and stagger in his tracks. Keating and Bogue decided that the secret must be withheld from the crew at all hazards, but their excitement betrayed them and all hands clamored that they must be given shares of the booty. Keating protested that a division should not be made until they had returned to their home port and the owner of the ship had been given the greater part which belonged to him by rights.

A mutiny flared up, and the mate and the men went ashore, leaving Keating and Bogue marooned on board, but the search was bootless for lack of directions. They returned to the ship in a very savage temper indeed and swore to kill the two leaders unless they should tell them how to find the cave. Promising to show the way on the morrow, Keating and Bogue slipped ashore in a whale-boat that night, planning to take all the treasure they could carry and hoping to find opportunity to secrete it on shipboard.

This program was spoiled by a tragedy. While trying to get back to the ship through the heavy surf that roared on the beach, the boat was upset. Bogue, heavily ballasted with treasure, went to the bottom like a plummet and was seen no more. Keating clung to the water-logged boat which was caught in a current and carried to sea. Two days later he was picked up, exhausted almost unto death, by a Spanish schooner which put him ashore on the coast of Costa Rica. Thence he made his way overland to the Atlantic, and worked his passage home to Newfoundland in a trading vessel. His ship returned with never a doubloon among the mutinous crew.

This experience seemed to have snuffed out the ardor of Keating for treasure-seeking, and it was as much as twenty years later that he confided the tale to a townsman named Nicholas Fitzgerald. They talked about fitting out another ship, but Keating up and died in the midst of the scheming. He had married a very young wife, and she set great store by the chart and directions preserved as a heritage from Captain Thompson. In 1894 she struck a partnership with a Captain Hackett and they organized an expedition which sailed for Cocos Island in a small brig called the *Aurora*. This adventure amounted to nothing. There was dissension on board, the voyage was longer than expected, provisions fell short, and the *Aurora* jogged homeward without sighting the treasure island.

Meanwhile other explorers had been busy. A German, Von Bremer, spent several thousand dollars in excavating and tunneling, but found no reward. The tales of treasure also fired the brain of a remarkable person named Gissler, who took up his solitary residence on Cocos Island more than twenty years ago where he has since reigned with the title and authority of governor of the same, by virtue of a commission duly signed, sealed, and delivered by the republic of Costa Rica. As a persistent and industrious treasure-hunter, this tropical hermit is unique.

He was visited in 1896 by Captain Shrapnel of H.M.S. *Haughty* who had heard the stories of Thompson and Benito Bonito along the coastwise ports. By way of giving his blue-jackets something to do, he landed a party three hundred strong on Cocos Island whose landscape they vainly blasted and otherwise disarranged for several days, but without success. The Admiralty lacked imagination and reprimanded Captain Shrapnel for his enterprising break in the dull routine of duty. It was decreed that no more naval vessels were to touch at Cocos Island on any pretext whatever.

This by no means discouraged Captain Shrapnel who waited until it was permissible for him to apply for leave of absence. In England he found gentlemen adventurers sufficient to finance an expedition which sailed in the *Lytton* in 1903. Of this party was Hervey de Montmorency, whose account of the venture includes the following information:

Treasure-seekers digging on Cocos Island.

Christian Cruse, the hermit treasure-seeker of Cocos Island.

"On the ninth of August, at four o'clock in the morning, every treasure-seeker was on deck straining his eyes to penetrate the mist and darkness; then as the sun rose, the gray mass on the horizon turned to green, and Cocos Island, with its lofty wooded peak, its abrupt, cliff-like shores, its innumerable cascades of sparkling water, was displayed to eager and admiring eyes.

"The anchor was dropped in the little bay, and at the splash, flocks of birds rose screaming and circling overhead. The sandy beach on which the seekers landed is strewn with boulders, on each of which is carved the name and business of some vessel which has called at Cocos. Some of the dates carry one back to Nelson's time; and all sorts of ships seem to have visited the lonely little island, while many a boulder testified to blighted hopes and fruitless errands after treasure.

"Captain Shrapnel's party set to work with the highest expectation. No previous expedition had been so well furnished with clues. Once on the right track, it seemed impossible that they should fail. They searched for ten days, encouraged now by the finding of the broken arm of a battered cross brought from some Peruvian church, again by a glimpse into what promised falsely to be a treasure cave; but all blasting, digging, and damming of streams proved useless. Captain Shrapnel at last called a council of war, and declared his opinion that the search was hopeless; landslips, previous excavations, and the torrential rains of this tropical region had so entirely altered the face of the island that clues and directions were of little avail, nor did their agreement with the owners of the *Lytton* permit of a longer stay on Cocos.

"We did not leave the island, however, without paying a visit to its governor, Gissler, whose little settlement is on Wafer Bay. Rounding the headland from Chatham Bay, we came into the quiet little nook where he has made his home, and he at once waded out in the surf to greet the visitors,—a tall, bronzed man, with a long, gray heard reaching below his waist, and deep-set eyes which gazed with obvious suspicion. Gissler had learned to distrust the coming of strangers, who have paid small regard to his rights, pillaging his crops, killing his livestock, and even making free with his home.

"Reassured by Captain Shrapnel's party that he had nothing to fear from them, he invited them to his house and clearing, and told them of his long and lonely hunt for the pirate's treasure. When he first went to live on Cocos, he found many traces of the freebooters. There were traces of their old camps, with thirty-two stone steps leading to a cave, old fire-places, rusty pots and arms, and empty bottles to mark the scene of their carousing. He had found only one gold coin, a doubloon of the time of Charles III of Spain, bearing the date of 1788."

In 1901, a company was formed in Vancouver, with a capital of $10,000, to fit out an expedition for Cocos Island. Gissler got wind of this project and formally addressed the government of Costa Rica in these written words:

"Allow me to inform you that no company with any such intent would have the right to land on Cocos Island, as I hold a concession from the authorities of Costa Rica in regard to the said treasure, in which concession the Costa Rica government has an interest. Certainly anything that might be undertaken by such a company from Vancouver would amount to naught without my consent."

SPOOKY TREASURE TROVES

This protest was paid due heed, but two years later, an Englishman, Claude Robert Guiness, persuaded the officials of Costa Rica to listen kindly to his plea, and he was granted the right to explore the island for two years. Gissler stood by his guns, drew up a list of grievances, and sailed for the mainland in a small boat to assert his rights to his kingdom. At that time, a wealthy British naval officer, Lord Fitzwilliam, was bound out to Cocos Island in his own steam yacht with a costly equipment of machinery and a heavy crew to find the treasure. He found poor Gissler in a Costa Rican port, became interested in his wrongs, and promptly supported his claims. An English nobleman with surplus wealth is a person to wield influence in the councils of a Central American republic and Gissler was pacified and given a renewal of his documentary rights as governor and population of Cocos Island.

Lord Fitzwilliam took him on board the yacht and in this dignified fashion Gissler returned to this kingdom. He earned his passage by telling his own version of the treasure, as he had culled and revised it from various sources, and his bill of particulars was something to gloat over, including as it did such dazzling bits of narrative as this:

"Besides the treasure buried by Captain Thompson, there was vast wealth left on Cocos by Benito Bonito himself. He captured a treasure galleon off the coast of Peru and took two other vessels laden with riches sent out from Mexico at the outbreak of the revolution against the Spaniards. On Cocos he buried three hundred thousand pounds' weight of silver and silver dollars, in a sandstone cave in the side of the mountain. Then he laid kegs of powder on top of the cave and blew away the face of the cliff. In another excavation he placed gold bricks, 733 of them, four by three inches in size, and two inches thick, and 273 gold-hilted swords, inlaid with jewels. On a bit of land in the little river, he buried several iron kettles filled with gold coin."

Lord Fitzwilliam and his yacht arrived at Cocos in December of 1904, and the party of laborers fell to with prodigious zest. While they were making the dirt fly, another English expedition, commanded by Arnold Gray, hove in sight, and proceeded to begin excavating at inconveniently close range. In fact, both parties were cocksure that the lost cave was located in one spot beneath a great mass of debris that had tumbled down from the overhanging height. The inevitable result was that a pretty quarrel arose. Neither force would yield its ground. Inasmuch as both were using dynamite rather lavishly, treasure hunting became as dangerous as war. When the rival expeditions were not dodging the rocks that were sent hurtling by the blasting, they were using bad language, the one accusing the other of effacing its landmarks and playing hob with its clues.

The climax was a pitched battle in which heads were broken and considerable blood spilt. It is almost needless to observe that no treasure was found. Lord

SPOOKY TREASURE TROVES

Fitzwilliam sailed home in his yacht and found that the news of his escapade had aroused the displeasure of the naval authorities, after which he lost all zest for finding buried treasure.

Since then, hardly a year has passed but an expedition or two for Cocos Island has been in the wind. In 1906, a company organized in Seattle issued an elaborate printed prospectus, offering shares in a venture to sail in a retired pilot schooner, and recounting all the old tales of Captain Thompson, Benito Bonito, and Keating. At about the same time, a wealthy woman of Boston, after a summer visit to Newfoundland, was seized with enthusiasm for a romantic speculation and talked of finding a ship and crew. San Francisco has beheld more than one schooner slide out through the Golden Gate in quest of Cocos Island.

To enumerate these ventures and describe them in detail would make a tiresome catalogue of the names of vessels and adventurous men with the treasure bee in their bonnets. Charts and genuine information are no longer necessary to one of these expeditions. Cocos Island is under such a spell as has set a multitude to digging for the treasure of Captain Kidd. The gold is there, this is taken for granted, and no questions are asked. The island was long a haunt of buccaneers and pirates, this much is certain, and who ever heard of a true pirate of romance who knew his business that did not employ his spare time in "a-burying of his treasure?"

[1] Strong, or robust.

[2] *History of the Buccaneers of America*, by Captain James Burney (1816).

[3] *Voyage and Description*, etc., by Lionel Wafer, London (1699).

[4] "The Buccaneers of America," by John Esquemeling (Published, 1684).

[5] Dampier. To search for this wreck with a view to recover the treasure in her was one of the objects of an expedition from England to the South Sea a few years later than the voyage of Davis.

[6] "History of the Buccaneers of America," by Captain James Burney (1816).

[7] Colnet's "Voyage to the Pacific."

[8] Esquemeling.

[9] "On the Spanish Main," by John Masefield.

SPOOKY TREASURE TROVES

CHAPTER XI
THE MYSTERY OF THE LUTINE FRIGATE

Harbored in the stately edifice of the Royal Exchange, down in the heart of London City, is that ancient and powerful corporation known to seafaring men the world over as Lloyd's. Its chief business is the underwriting of maritime insurance risks and its word is law wherever fly the house-flags of merchant shipping. More than two hundred years ago, one Edward Lloyd kept a coffeehouse in Tower Street, a thoroughfare between Wapping and the Thames side of the city, and because of its convenient situation the place became a popular resort for sea captains, underwriters, and insurance brokers who discussed such important matters as arrivals in port, wrecks, missing ships, and rumors of war.

In time Lloyd's coffeehouse was recognized as a sort of unofficial headquarters for this special variety of insurance speculation, and the gentlemen most active there drifted into a loosely formed organization for the purpose of making the business less hazardous. In 1773, this association of underwriters moved into the Royal Exchange, taking the name of Lloyd's, and later appointed a governing body or committee to control the more adventurous spirits who were fond of gambling on the chances of war, on the length of Napoleon's life, and who would undertake to insure a man against the risk of twins in his family. From this beginning grew the vastly influential and highly organized Lloyd's of the present day which is something more than a corporation. It is also an aggregation of individual underwriters and brokers carrying on business, each for his own personal profit and on the strength of his good name and resources. As a corporation, Lloyd's has no financial liability in the event of the failure of any of its members or subscribers.

All that Lloyd's does, in its corporate capacity, is to permit the admission only of men of stability and sound repute by means of stringent tests, and to exact a money guarantee or deposit from its members in the sum of £5000 or £6000, together with entrance fees of £400, and annual fees of twenty guineas. These payments form what may be called a reserve fund, and the individual underwriter writes his own policies. If the risk is heavier than he wishes to assume he divides it among his fellows.

There are few more interesting places in London than Lloyd's, encrusted as it is with the barnacles of conservative tradition, and hedged about with all the exclusiveness of a club. The entrance is guarded by a burly porter gorgeously arrayed in the scarlet robes and gold-banded hat of a by-gone century. Having run the gauntlet of this dragon, one is likely to seek the underwriter's room where hundreds of members and their clerks are quartered at rows of little desks or "boxes," every man of them with his hat clapped on his head as decreed by ancient custom.

There is always a crowd of them around the "Arrival Book" and the "Loss Book" in which are posted the movements of vessels in every port of the world, and the wrecks that number three thousand every year. The famous "Captains' Room" where the mariners used to gather and swap briny yarns is now used for the prosaic purposes of luncheon and for the auction sales of ships.

In the two large and handsome rooms used by the secretary and by the committee of Lloyd's are many interesting relics of the earlier history of this body. Here is the oldest policy known to the annals of maritime insurance, a faded document issued on January 20, 1680, for £1200 on a ship, the *Golden Fleece*, and her cargo, on a voyage from Lisbon to Venice, at £4 per cent. premium. Hanging on these walls are also a policy written on the life of Napoleon, and an autograph letter from the Duke of Wellington as Warden of the Cinque Ports.

The most conspicuous furnishings of the Committee Room are a huge table, highly polished, of dark wood, a magnificently carved arm chair, and a ship's bell. The table bears a silver plate inscribed as follows:

H.B.M. Ship *La Lutine*. 32 Gun Frigate Commanded by Captain Lancelot Skynner, R.N. Sailed from Yarmouth Roads On the morning of the 9th October, 1799 with a large amount of specie on board, And was wrecked off the Island of Vlieland the same night, When all on board were lost except one man.

The rudder of which this table was made and the rudder chain and the bell which the table supports, were recovered from the wreck of the ill-fated vessel, in the year 1859, together with a part of the specie, which is now in custody of The Committee for managing the affairs of Lloyd's."

The chair has a similar inscription, and these pieces of furniture serve to remind the visitor that Lloyd's has a lost treasure story of its own. The flavor of piracy is lacking, true enough, but the tragedy of the *Lutine* frigate possessed mystery and romance nevertheless, and is worthy of a place in such a book as this. As the owner of a treasure lost more than a century ago, the corporation of Lloyd's still considers the frigate a possible asset, and as recently as May 31, 1910, Captain E. F. Inglefield, the Secretary of Lloyd's wrote the author as follows:

SPOOKY TREASURE TROVES

"Various attempts have been made, with the sanction of Lloyd's, to recover further treasure, but it was not until 1886, when steam suction dredgers were first employed, that any results worthy of notice were obtained. A number of coins and other relics to the value of about £700 were obtained.

"In 1886, also, two guns were recovered from the wreck, one of which, after being suitably mounted on a naval gun carriage, was presented by Lloyd's to the Corporation of London and has been placed in the Museum at the Guildhall. The other was graciously accepted by Her Late Majesty Queen Victoria, and was forwarded to Windsor Castle.

"In 1891, a few coins of small value were recovered. Since that date, operations have been continued at various times by salvors under agreement with Lloyd's, but nothing of intrinsic value has since been obtained. In 1896, a cannon which was afterwards presented to H. M. Queen Wilhelmina of Holland by the Committee of Lloyds, was found together with some small pieces of the wreck, etc.

"In 1898, some timber weighing about two hundred weight was recovered from the wreck, and was presented to the Liverpool Underwriters' Association, whose Chairman, Mr. S. Cross, had a chair made from the wood, which he presented to that Association.

"A company which was formed for the purpose of continuing operations has made efforts at various times, but the site is extremely exposed and owing to bad weather, it has often been found impossible to continue dredging operations for more than a few days each year. I trust the above information may be of service to you, but I may add that I understand that it is this year intended to operate with some new apparatus."

Some light was thrown on this latest enterprise by the publication of the following in a recent issue of *Lloyd's Weekly Newspaper* of London:

"SEA TREASURE GETTER.
NOVEL MACHINE TO BE USED FOR RAISING SUNKEN WEALTH.

"An extraordinary machine was towed to the mouth of the River Colne, off Brightlingsea, and anchored on Thursday. It is to be used in a final attempt to recover £500,000 treasure of gold, in coins and bars, which is said to have gone down in H. M. S. *Lutine* in 1797 near the island of Terschelling, off the coast of Holland.

"A portion of the treasure has been recovered, but the ordinary dredging plant is now useless, as the vessel has sunk into the sand. The new device is a great steel tube nearly 100 ft. in length, and wide enough to allow a man to walk erect down its centre. At one end is a metal chamber provided with windows and doors, and at the other a medley of giant hooks and other tackle.

SPOOKY TREASURE TROVES

"The apparatus has just been completed, after years of work, by Messers. Forrest and Co., shipbuilders, in their Wyvenhoe yard. One end of the tube, it is explained, will be clamped to the side of a steamship or barge. The other end, by means of water-ballast tanks, will be sunk until it touches the bottom. Then, by means of compressed air, all the water will be forced from the tube and also from the chamber at the bottom of it, which will be flush upon the bed of the sea.

"Divers will walk down a stairway in the centre of the tube until they reach the submerged chamber. Here they will don their diving costumes, and, opening a series of water-tight doors, will step out into the water. Engineers will be stationed in the chamber, and, following the instructions of the divers, who will communicate with them by means of portable telephones, they will operate the mechanism of two powerful suction pumps, or dredges, which are fitted to the sides of the tube.

"These dredges, it is hoped, will suck away the sand around the sides of the heavy chamber until it gradually sinks by its own weight right down on to the deck of the wrecked ship. Then the divers, making their way from the chamber to the deck of the ship, and thence to the hold, will be able to transfer the treasure from the ship to the chamber by easy stages."

How Lloyd's happens to own a treasure frigate of the English navy, lost more than a century ago, is explained in the following narrative, many of the facts of which were found in "The History of Lloyd's and of Marine Insurance in Great Britain," by Frederick Martin, a work now out of print.[1]

On October 19,1799, the *Gentleman's Magazine* of London contained this news:

"Intelligence was this day received at the Admiralty from Admiral Mitchell, communicating the total loss of *La Lutine*, of 32 guns, Captain Skynner, on the outward bank of the Fly Island Passage, on the night of the 9th inst., in a heavy gale at N.N.W. *La Lutine*, had on the same morning, sailed from Yarmouth Roads with several passengers, and an immense quantity of treasure for the Texel; but a strong lee-tide rendered every effort of Captain Skynner to avoid the threatened danger unavailable, and it was alike impossible during the night to receive any assistance, either from the *Arrow*, Captain Portlock, which was in company, or from the shore, from whence several showts were in readiness to go to her. When the dawn broke, *La Lutine* was in vain looked for; she had gone to pieces, and all on board unfortunately perished, except two men who were picked up, and one of whom has since died from the fatigue he has encountered. The survivor is Mr. Shabrack, a notary public. In the annals of our naval history there has scarcely ever happened a loss attended with so much calamity, both of a public as well as a private nature."

In almost all the accounts of the wreck of the *Lutine* it is stated as a fact that the frigate was bound to the Texel, and that the bullion and treasure she carried, and which was lost in her, was designed for the payment of the British forces in the Netherlands. Both statements are without foundation, as proved by a careful search in the archives of the Admiralty. These official records show that the *Lutine* was under orders to sail, not to the Texel, but to the river Elbe, her destination being Hamburg, and that the treasure on board was not the property of the British government, but of a number of London merchants connected with Lloyd's, and that the business of sending the coin and bullion was purely commercial.

The records wholly fail to explain how it happened that, sailing for the mouth of the Elbe, the *Lutine* commanded by an able and experienced officer, and in all respects well manned and found, came to be driven, within eighteen hours after leaving Yarmouth Roads, upon the dangerous shoals of the Zuyder Zee, far out of her course, even when every allowance is made for the strength of a northwesterly gale.

Another mystery of the voyage of this thirty-two gun frigate of the royal navy is her employment as a mere packet, carrying cash and bullion for the benefit of private individuals. The officer responsible for sending the *Lutine* on this unusual errand was Admiral Lord Duncan who "received a pressing invitation from some merchants to convey a quantity of bullion." It was his first intention to dispatch a cutter, but the treasure given in his care was swelled by larger amounts until its total value was £1,175,000 or more than five and a half million dollars. The admiral thereupon discarded the cutter and selected instead the swift and staunch *Lutine* frigate, one of the best vessels of his fleet. On October 9, he wrote to the Admiralty from on board his flagship, the *Kent*, in Yarmouth Roads:

"The merchants interested in making remittances to the continent for the support of their credit, having made application to me for a King's ship to carry over a considerable sum of money, on account of there being no Packet for that purpose, I have complied with their request, and ordered the *Lutine* to Cuxhaven with the same, together with the mails lying there for want of conveyance; directing Captain Skynner to proceed to Stromness immediately after doing so, to take under his protection the Hudson's Bay's ships and see them in safety to the Nore." When this letter was written, the *Lutine* had already sailed, and before Lord Duncan's communication reached the Lords of the Admiralty, the splendid treasure laden frigate had laid her bones on the sand banks of Holland.

Admiral Duncan appears to have escaped all censure for this disaster which followed his action taken without consultation and without waiting for the approval of his superiors. The merchants of London were powerful enough to command the services of the navy, and English credit was needed on the continent to buttress English arms and statesmanship. With her millions of treasure and hundreds of lives, the *Lutine* drove straight toward as fatal a coast to shipping as can be found anywhere in the world.

It is a coast which is neither sea nor land, strewn with wrecks, and with somber memories even more tragic. Where is now the entrance of the Zuyder Zee was unbroken terra firma until the thirteenth century when a terrible hurricane piled the North Sea through the isthmus separating it from the large lake called Vlies by the natives. A wide channel was cut by this inroad, and in 1287 the North Sea scoured for itself a second inlet at the cost of a hundred thousand human lives. Ever since then, the channels have been multiplying and shifting until what was once the coast line has become a maze of islands and sand-banks, the Texel, Vlieland, Terschelling, Ameland, and hundreds of lesser ones which confuse even the mariners born and bred among them.

With a wind which should have enabled him to give this perilous shore a wide berth and to keep to his course up the North Sea, Captain Skynner plunged into a death-trap from which there was no escape. The sole survivor could give no coherent account, and he died while on the way to England before his shattered nerves had mended. There was no more frigate, and as for the hundreds of drowned sailors, they had been obliterated as a day's work in the business of a great navy, so the Admiralty left the mourning to their kinfolk and bestirred itself about that five and a half million dollars' worth of treasure which the sea could not harm. Vice-Admiral Mitchell was informed by letter that "their lordships feel great concern at this very unfortunate accident" and he was directed to take such measures as might be practicable for recovering the stores of the *Lutine*, as well as the property on board, "being for the benefit of the persons to whom it belongs."

The underwriters of Lloyd's with an eye to salvage, were even more prompt than the Admiralty in sending agents to the scene of the wreck. The greater part of the immense amount of coin and bullion had been fully insured, a transaction which indicates the stability and ample resources of this association as far away in time as 1799. The loss was paid in full and with such promptitude that only two weeks after the disaster, the Committee for managing the concerns of Lloyd's addressed a letter to the Secretary of the Admiralty in which was requested "the favor of Mr. Nepean to lay before the Lords Commissioners of the Admiralty the information that a sum of money, equal to that unfortunately lost in the *Lutine*, is going off this night for Hambro, and they trust their Lordships will direct such steps as they think expedient for its protection to be taken."

The request was granted somewhat grudgingly. Apparently the Admiralty regretted the employment of one of its frigates as a merchantman. Admiral Lord Duncan was directed to send a convoy this time, but was told also "to let them know that their lordships have done so in this particular case; but that they must not expect the packets can again be convoyed." With this letter ends all reference to the *Lutine* and her treasure in the correspondence preserved in the Record

SPOOKY TREASURE TROVES

Office of the Admiralty.

Having paid their losses, like the good sportsmen that they were, the underwriters of Lloyd's thereby clinched their right to the ownership of the treasure, provided they could find it. The situation was complicated because England was at that time at war with the Netherlands whose government claimed the wreck as a prize, although inconsistently refusing to let it be adjudicated by a prize court. On this account, Lloyd's could make no attempt to fish for the treasure, which delay was very much to the benefit of the sturdy Dutch fishermen of the islands at the mouth of the Zuyder Zee. The sands and the surf held a golden harvest. The wreck of the *Lutine* was partly exposed at low ebb tide, and a channel ran close to the side of the ship.

The clumsy fishing boats or "showts" swarmed to the place and never was there such easy wealth for honest Dutchmen. Their government soon put a watch on them and took two-thirds of the findings, giving the fishermen the remainder. They toiled in good weather for a year and a half, and recovered treasure to the amount of eighty-three thousand pounds sterling. The official inventory reads like the hoard of a buccaneer, including as it does such romantic items as:

58 bars of gold, weight 646 lbs. 23 ounces.35 bars of silver, weight, 1,758 lbs. 8 ounces.41,697 Spanish silver pistoles.179 Spanish gold pistoles.81 Double Louis d'or.138 Single Louis d'or.4 English guineas.

At the end of the year 1801 the fishermen quit their task, thinking they had found all the treasure. For a dozen years the Dutch forgot the melancholy fragments of the *Lutine*, while the sailors of the desolate islands guarding the Zuyder Zee began to weave superstitious legends around the "gold wreck." In the midst of the crowded events of the great war against Napoleon, England found no time to remember the *Lutine*, and her memory was kept alive only by the kinfolk of the drowned officers and sailors.

After Napoleon had been finally disposed of, the treasure was recalled to public notice by an ingenious gentleman of the Netherlands, Pierre Eschauzier, a sort of lord of the manor under the government, holding the post of "Opper Strand vonder," or "Upper Strand finder," who lived at Terschelling and took a lively interest in the wreck. After a great deal of investigation and cogitation, he arrived at the conclusion that the greater part of the treasure dispatched from England in the *Lutine* was still hidden among her timbers. His argument was based on the fact that the bars of silver and gold already recovered were stamped with certain numbers and letters indicating series or sequences, and that thus far these were very incomplete.

For instance, among the gold bars previously found, were thirteen marked with the letters *NB*, in three separate lots; the first numbered from 58 to 64; the second from 86 to 90; and the third from 87 to 89. Other gold bars with different letters and a variety of numbers went to prove that there were a hundred numbers to each letter, which would yield a total of six hundred gold bars, of which only thirty-one had been recovered in the years 1800 and 1801.

The government of the Netherlands was duly impressed by the calculations of Mr. Eschauzier who had proved himself such an astute "Upper Strand finder," and he was granted a sum by royal decree from the public exchequer to equip a salvage expedition. Alas, the pretty theory was thwarted by the implacable sands which had buried the wreck. For seven years this indefatigable treasure seeker dredged and dug, and found no more than a few gold coin. Then he decided to try a diving bell, King Willem I having bestowed upon him a more favorable privilege by the terms of which the salvage company was to have one-half of the treasure recovered.

The diving bell was no luckier than the dredges had been. In fact, by this time the unstable sands had so concealed the wreck that it could not be found. After vainly groping for several months, the luckless "Upper Strand finder" confessed himself beaten, and there was nothing to show for an expenditure of five thousand pounds sterling. These operations had made some noise in London, however, and the underwriters of Lloyd's remembered that they had an interest in the wreck of the *Lutine* frigate. If there was still treasure to be sought for, it belonged to them, and the government of the Netherlands had no claim upon it, either in law or equity.

The fact that royal decrees had been granting to Dutchmen that which did not belong to them at all, aroused indignation at Lloyd's, whose managing committee was moved to address the English government in the matter. After a good deal of diplomatic palaver with The Hague, that government made over its half share of the treasure reserved under the treaty with "the Upper Strand finder" to the "British claimants." In May 6, 1823, Mr. F. Conyngham, Secretary of the English Foreign Office, communicated this pleasing news to Mr. William Bell, chairman of the committee of Lloyd's in the following letter:

"*Sir*:

"With reference to the several applications which have been made to His Majesty's Government to interfere with that of the Netherlands on behalf of the underwriters, and others, claiming to be allowed to recover certain property still supposed to remain on board of the *Lutine* Frigate, lost off the coast of Holland in 1799, I am directed by Mr. Secretary Canning to acquaint you, for the information of the parties concerned, that after much negotiation His Netherlands' Majesty has expressed his willingness to cede to the British claimants the whole of that moiety of the said property which by His Netherlands' Majesty's decree of the 14th. September, 1821, was reserved for the use of his said Majesty. The other moiety was, by the same decree, granted in the nature of salvage to a private company of his own subjects, who undertook to recover the cargo at their own expense. It has been stipulated that the British claimants shall be at liberty to concert with the said company as to the best mode of effecting that recovery. Considering the difficulties which the negotiation has experienced from disputed points of law, and making due allowance for the engagements formed with the Dutch company, who have been recognized as salvors by the Dutch law, and would have a right to have all services rewarded in the Courts of Holland for the property which may be saved by their exertions, Mr. Canning apprehends that it may be advisable for the claimants in this country to agree to the offer now made. The season for operation is now before them, and no hope could be reasonably entertained that a renewal of the negotiation would bring the matter to a more reasonable close."

It will be observed that diplomacy had obtained for Lloyd's only a half-interest in its own wreck. The other fifty per cent. still belonged to Mr. Eschauzier's company, as King Willem was particular to make clear in his decree, dated from Het Loo, which went on to say: "By our Minister of Foreign Affairs, we have offered to the King of Great Britain to cede to his Majesty all that which by our decree of the 14th of September, 1821, was reserved to the Netherlands in the bottom in question and the cargo therein, doing so solely as a proof of our friendly feeling towards the Kingdom of Great Britain, and in nowise from a conviction of the right of England to any portion of the said cargo....

"We have been pleased and thought fit:

"1. To cede to His Majesty of Great Britain all that which by our decree of the 4th September, 1821, was reserved in favor of the kingdom relative to the cargo of the frigate *Lutine*.

"2. To instruct our minister of inland affairs and the maritime department—Water Staat—to give notice of this our decree, as well as of the cession made on the part of His Majesty of Great Britain to the Society of Lloyd's, to our chancellor of state, governor of North Holland, and to the other authorities concerned, as well as to the participators in the undertaking of 1821 in the Netherlands, and to inform them likewise that an English agent will ere long wait upon them, in order to make all such arrangements with them as may be deemed advisable for the furtherance of their mutual interests. And our Ministers for Inland Affairs and the Maritime Department are charged with the carrying out of this decree."

The members of Lloyd's were hardly better off with the gift of one-half a wreck than they had been with no wreck at all. Before undertaking any salvage operations they must come to some kind of an understanding with the "Upper Strand Finder" and his partners, with respect to expenses and profits. The Dutch, with proverbial caution, were reluctant to scrape acquaintance with the English owners, convinced that in some matter or other, this new ownership in the trea-

SPOOKY TREASURE TROVES

sure had been unfairly extorted from their government at the Hague. It was not until 1830, that friendly relations were established, and in the meantime Mr. Eschauzier had died, leaving his share in the treasure among his legacies.

Then negotiations were interrupted by the political events which caused the separation of Belgium from Holland. The people of the Netherlands heartily hated England for her leading part in this partition, and not even the allurement of fishing gold out of the sea could persuade the Dutch adventurers to have anything to do with Lloyd's or anything that smacked of the perfidious English. For a quarter of a century, the wreck of the *Lutine* was undisturbed. Then, in 1846, two enterprising English divers in need of work, Hill and Downs by name, conceived an audacious scheme to enrich themselves. They drew up a petition to the King of the Netherlands, asking that they be permitted to pick up as much gold as they could lay hands on among the timbers of the *Lutine*. Surprising as was this request, it was not refused. According to custom, the petition was carefully examined at The Hague, and the discovery was gravely announced that there was no legal obstacle in the way of the divers, or anyone else, who cared to seek for the *Lutine's* treasure.

One of the articles of a new code of maritime law, passed by the States General of the Netherlands in 1838, provided that the salvage of vessels wrecked "on the outer banks of the coast," was thrown open to all persons, under stipulated conditions, and that the wreck of the *Lutine* came within this act. The government formally notified Hill and Downs that while the right of salvage could not be granted to any particular person, the ground was free on condition that "one-half of all that might be found must be given up to Lloyd's."

The divers may have found some other employment by this time, for they appeared not at the wreck, but the publication of the proceedings awoke the old Dutch company formed by the "Upper Strand Finder" and they opened negotiations with the committee of Lloyd's. No one concerned seemed to be in a hurry to find the several million dollars remaining in the *Lutine* and nine more years dragged past before a working agreement was signed between the two parties. The Dutch company undertook to carry on the work of salvage, paying over one-half the gross proceeds to Lloyd's.

It was in 1857 that the Dutch went to work, and after a month of exploration the Secretary of Lloyd's received this pleasing information from his agent at the Texel:

"I feel most happy to inform you that the new efforts to save the value out of the *Lutine* have not been without success. Yesterday there was recovered by means of divers and pincers, 13 silver coins, being Spanish piastres, 1 gold Louis d'or, 5 brass hoops and casks, and a quantity of cannon and shot.

"Considering the value of the saved objects, it may not be of much signifi-

SPOOKY TREASURE TROVES

cation; but the salvage itself is of very great importance, as it proves two facts, namely, first, that the wreck of the *Lutine* has really been found, and secondly, that there is specie still in the wreck. As soon as anything more is picked up, I will inform you immediately thereof. Be assured, I have taken the necessary steps to secure the interests of Lloyd's committee, as owners of the treasure, which we hope may entirely be saved."

A little later, the wreck was found to be very little scattered and its precise location was determined. The news of the discovered "gold wreck" spread among the fishermen of the Zuyder Zee and the German Ocean and they winged it to the scene until "there were sixty-eight large and well manned boats in the immediate neighborhood looking for plunder." At this threatening mobilization, the Dutch government thought it wise to send a gunboat with a party of soldiers on board.

In the summer of 1858, the divers brought to the surface the bell of the frigate, which now rests in the committee room of Lloyd's with the other relics. The *Lutine* had been one of the crack ships of the French navy and was captured by Admiral Duncan, he who sent her to her doom. The bell bears on its bronze side the royal crown and arms of Bourbon, and on the rim the name of "Saint Jean" under whose protection the ship and her crew had been placed when she was launched as a fighting frigate of His Majesty, Louis XVI of France.

The treasure seeking was continued for several years, whenever the treacherous sea permitted, until, at length, a great gale out of the northwest closed the channel near the wreck and covered her deeper under the sands. The work was finally abandoned by these salvors in 1861. They had forwarded to England for the benefit of Lloyd's a total amount of £22,162, to show that the undertaking had been worth while. In the Act of Incorporation of Lloyd's granted by Parliament in 1871, the treasure recovered, as well as that still left in the wreck, was carefully referred to, and it was stated that "the Society may from time to time do, or join in doing all such lawful things as they think expedient, with a view to further salving from the wreck of the *Lutine*."

It seems rather extraordinary that the exact amount of the treasure lost in the frigate should be a matter of conjecture, and that the records of Lloyd's throw no light on this point. The explanation is that only part of the precious cargo was insured by the underwriters then doing business in the Royal Exchange building, and that a large amount of gold coin and bullion was hastily forwarded to the *Lutine* by divers bankers and merchants shortly before sailing. The records of these consignments were, of course, scattered and have long since been lost.

The total amount lost has been quite accurately calculated by employing the system of accounting devised by the "Upper Strand Finder." His theory was verified by later undertakings at the wreck, and the sequences of letters and numbers stamped upon the gold and silver bars were found to run in regular order, so that it has been latterly assumed that, in all, one thousand of these were in the ship's hold. The figures accepted by the Dutch partners in the enterprise, and endorsed by Mr. John Mavor Hill, the agent of Lloyd's at Amsterdam, were as follows:

    Salvage in the years 1800 and 1801 .... £ 55,770
        "   "   "   " 1857 and 1858 39,203
        "   "   "   " 1859 to 1861 4,920

    Total salvage .... £ 99,893

Total treasure estimated to have been lost £1,175,000

Treasure remaining in the wreck £1,076,107

It is plausible to assume, therefore, that more than five million dollars in gold and silver are still buried in the sands of the island beach at the entrance of the Zuyder Zee, and that at any time strong gales and shifting currents may once more uncover the bones of the ill-fated *Lutine* frigate. The members of Lloyd's are daily reminded, by the presence of the massive oaken table and chair and the silent ship's bell in the Committee Room, of the princely fortune that is theirs, if they can find it. The story is a romance of maritime insurance, and the end has not yet been written, for with modern equipment and ingenuity those gold and silver bars, Spanish pistoles, and Louis d'or may some day be carried up the staircase of Lloyd's to enrich a corporation of the twentieth century.

[1] "The particulars concerning the *Lutine* which you have obtained from Martin's 'History of Lloyd's,' can, I think, be considered as accurate, as I believe Mr. Martin had full means of access to any documents which were available at Lloyd's or elsewhere in connection with this matter." (Note from Captain Inglefield, Secretary of Lloyd's, to the author.)

SPOOKY TREASURE TROVES

CHAPTER XII
THE TOILERS OF THE THETIS

The *Lutine* was not the only treasure-laden frigate lost by the British navy. The circumstances of the wreck of the *Thetis* in 1830 are notable, not so much for the gold and silver that went down in her, as for the heroic courage and bulldog persistence of the men who toiled to recover the treasure. Their battle against odds was an epic in the annals of salvage. They were treasure-seekers whose deeds, forgotten by this generation, and grudgingly rewarded by their own, were highly worthy of the best traditions of their flag and their race.

On the morning of December 4th of the year mentioned, the forty-six gun frigate *Thetis*, with a complement of three hundred men, sailed from Rio Janeiro, homeward bound. As a favor to various merchants of the South American coast who were fearful of the pirates that still lurked in the West Indies, her captain had taken on board for consignment to London, a total amount of $810,000 in gold and silver bars. During the evening of the second night at sea, the ship was running at ten and a half knots, with studding-sails set, and plenty of offing, by the reckoning of the deck officers. The lookout stationed on the cat-head had no more than bellowed "Breakers under the bow!" when his comrade echoed it with, "Rocks above the mast-head."

An instant later, the soaring bowsprit of the frigate splintered with a tremendous crash against the sheer cliffs of Cape Frio. The charging vessel fetched up all standing. Her hull had not touched bottom and there was nothing to check her enormous momentum. In a twinkling, literally in the space of a few seconds, her three masts were ripped out and fell on deck with all their hamper, killing and wounding many of the crew. Instead of that most beautiful sight in all the world, a ship under full sail and running free, there was a helpless hulk pounding out her life against the perpendicular wall of rock. The catastrophe befell so suddenly that when Captain Burgess rushed from his cabin at the warning shout, the masts tumbled just as he reached the quarterdeck.

SPOOKY TREASURE TROVES

"No description can realize the awful state of the ill-fated ship and all on board at this appalling moment; the night was rainy and so dark that it was impossible to ascertain their position, beyond the fact of their being repeatedly driven with tremendous force against cliffs of a stupendous height above them, and consequently inaccessible, and not offering the slightest chance of escape; the upper deck of the ship, the only part in which exertion could be useful, was completely choked up with masts, sails, and rigging, which presented obstacles that rendered unavailing every attempt at active exertion; while the ears of all, who were of course using their utmost endeavors for the general safety, were pierced by the cries of the dying and wounded for the assistance which the imperious calls of duty forbade them to give. Nothing but inevitable destruction presented itself to all on board; and their perfectly helpless state rendered all deliberation useless; and indeed there was no choice of measures, no point on which to offer an opinion, and they could only await such means as Providence might present."[1]

As by a miracle, the bowsprit and yard-arms had so checked the speed of the frigate, acting as a sort of buffer, that her hull was not smashed like an eggshell but was found to be fairly tight. All of the boats had been smashed by the falling spars, and the wretched company could only hang fast and pray that the wreck might float until daylight. But the hammering seas soon caused her to leak through yawning seams, and despairing of keeping her from sinking, a few of the crew managed to reach a shelving projection of rock about twenty feet above the deck. It was a forlorn hope, so perilous to attempt that many of those who scrambled for a foothold fell between the ship and the cliff and were drowned or crushed to death.

Presently the hulk swung away from the face of the cliff and was driven a distance of a third of a mile along the coast and into a tiny cove or notch in the bold headlands of Cape Frio. Here she remained, now sinking very fast. The party who had succeeded in making a landing on the ledge clawed their way to the rescue, following the drifting ship, and with the hardihood and agility of British tars of the old breed, they made their way down the declivity like so many cats and succeeded in making fast to a rope thrown by their comrades on board. By this means, several men had been hauled to safety when the dying frigate lurched wildly and parted the hawser.

It was discovered that she now rested on the bottom. Part of the port bulwark, the hammock-nettings, the taffrail, and the stumps of the masts remained above water, and to these the crew clung while the surf roared over their heads and threatened to tear them away. The situation was now hopeless, indeed, but all left alive on board were saved by the daring and strength of one man, Boatswain Geach. He fought his way through the breakers to the stump of the bowsprit, lashed himself there, and succeeded in passing a line to his comrades on shore. A strong rope was then hauled up and one by one the men on board were slung to safety

SPOOKY TREASURE TROVES

upon the cliffs. Almost all the survivors were dreadfully bruised and lacerated.

When the news reached Rio Janeiro, the British sloop-of-war *Lightning* was in that port, and her commander, Captain Thomas Dickinson, was the sort of man who likes nothing better than to lead a forlorn hope and grapple with difficulties. Said he:

"The consternation occasioned by the dreadful catastrophe was not confined to naval persons, but was universally felt at Rio, particularly among mercantile people, since from the tenor of the letter, and the description given by the officer who brought it, the ship and everything she contained were considered as totally lost. The event became a matter of general conversation; but while everyone deplored it, I did not hear of any who seemed disposed to venture on an attempt to recover the property, all appearing to consider the case as perfectly hopeless.... Here was an undertaking which, if successful, would assuredly lead to professional reputation and fortune, but which everyone whom I addressed on the subject thought must fail. Still, the scarcity of the opportunities of obtaining distinction and credit, by an extraordinary act of duty, which present themselves to officers in these piping times of peace, offered a consideration which prevailed, and I determined on making the attempt, if I could get orders from the Commander-in-Chief to that effect."

The admiral of the station proceeded to Cape Frio with a squadron of five vessels, and after a careful study of the situation of the wreck concluded that it would be futile to try to recover any of the sunken treasure. In the face of this verdict, Captain Dickinson felt reluctant to press his own views, but the bee in his bonnet would not be denied. "Actuated, however, by the same feelings which had at first prompted me to hazard the attempt, and having a natural repugnance to receding after having, during my inquiries, disclosed my views very freely, I was resolved to persevere. During the absence of the Commander-in-Chief, I constantly employed myself in inquiring for any persons likely to assist me, searching for implements, and obtaining all the information within my reach, and devised several instruments of minor importance which appeared likely to be useful. On his return from Cape Frio, I showed these to him, of the whole of which he approved."

Captain Dickinson could find no diving bell in Rio, so this versatile officer proceeded to make one, and an extraordinary contrivance it was for men to risk their lives in at the bottom of the sea. From H.M.S. *Warspite*, one of the squadron in harbor, he obtained two iron water tanks. These were turned over to an English mechanic named Moore, formerly employed by the Brazilian government, who was assisted by the carpenter of the *Lightning*. Between them they fashioned the water tanks into something that looked like a diving bell. These capable artisans then built an air pump, and now they were shy of hose through which to force air

SPOOKY TREASURE TROVES

to the submerged toilers.

"Being unable to find a workman in Rio Janeiro who would undertake to make an air-tight hose," explains Captain Dickinson, "there appeared for a time to be a stop to my preparations; but recollecting that there was a Truscott's pump on board the *Lightning*, I attempted to render the hoses belonging to it fit for the purpose, and to my great delight succeeded, by first beating them hard with a broad-faced hammer to render the texture as close as possible, then giving them a good coat of Stockholm tar, afterwards parceling them well with new canvas saturated with the same material, and finally serving them with three-yarn spun-yarns, made of new yarns and well twisted.

"Having thus surmounted without assistance the two most formidable difficulties that had yet presented themselves, I entertained a hope that my own resources would prove equally available on future occasions; and hence my confidence in ultimate success increased, in the event of the stores and treasure still remaining where the ship was lost. My officers and crew likewise now began to feel a great interest in all that was doing; and their conduct and expressions afforded me a happy presage that their future exertions would fulfill my most sanguine expectations.... I could not but feel that the same encouragement was not afforded by some from whom I had most reason to expect both it and assistance; for although I had now been for six weeks engaged in work, drudging on in the double capacity of carpenter and blacksmith, I had not a single voluntary offer by them of any article that might be useful to me. Nor was the kindness of my friends very encouraging; for they almost universally endeavored to dissuade me from venturing on an enterprise which everyone considered hopeless; to all of which remonstrances my only reply was, that my mind was made up, and that I should not withdraw from it."

The *Lightning* sailed to begin operations at Cape Frio on the 24th of January, 1831, with a Brazilian launch in tow, "and *La Seine*, French frigate, in company, going to visit the place as a matter of curiosity." At the scene of the wreck were found the sloop of war *Algerine*, a schooner as tender, and a complement from the *Warspite*, which were engaged in saving such stores and spars as had drifted ashore. The theater of Captain Dickinson's ambition as a treasure-seeker was hostile and forbidding, a coast on which it seemed impossible to tarry except in the most favorable weather. As he describes it, "the island of Cape Frio is about three miles long and one in breadth, is the southeastern extremity of Brazil, and separated from the mainland by a narrow strait or gut about four hundred feet broad, having very deep water in it, and through which, the land on each side being very high, the wind constantly rushes in heavy gusts, and a rapid current runs. This island is entirely mountainous, and nearly covered with an almost impenetrable forest, and the whole coast on the sea side of it is formed by precipitous cliffs, washed by very deep water close to the shore; and on the harbor side, with the exception of a sandy bay, is very steep and rugged."

The little notch in the seaward cliffs, into which the frigate had been driven, was named Thetis Cove by Captain Dickinson who explored it vainly for traces of the wrecked hull. Either she had been washed out into deep water, or had entirely broken up. Two months had passed since the disaster, and the only way of trying to find the remains of the vessel was by means of sounding with a hand-lead until the diving bell could be rigged. The depth of water ranged from thirty-six to seventy feet at the base of the cliffs.

This cove was an extraordinarily difficult place to work in, there being no beach and the ramparts of rock towering straight from the water to heights of from one hundred to two hundred feet. Said Captain Dickinson:

"On viewing this terrific place, with the knowledge that at the time of the shipwreck the wind was from the southward, I was struck with astonishment, and it appeared quite a mystery that so great a number of lives could have been saved; and indeed it will never cease to be so, for that part at which the crew landed is so difficult of access, that (even in fine weather), after being placed by a boat on the rock at the base, it required considerable strength and agility, with the assistance of a man-rope, to climb the precipitous face of the cliff; and I am certain that in the hour of extreme peril, when excess of exertion was called forth, there must have been a most extraordinary display of it by a few for the benefit of the whole."

Now, this make-shift diving bell of his had to be suspended from something in order to be raised and lowered, but neither his own ship, the Lightning, nor any of the other vessels of the salvage fleet could be anchored in the cove to serve the purpose because of the grave danger of being caught on a lee shore. At first Captain Dickinson planned to stretch a cable between the cliffs on either side of the cove but this was found to be impracticable. Thereupon he proceeded to fashion a huge derrick from which the diving bell should hang like a sinker at the end of a fishing-rod. There was no timber on the cape that was fit to be worked up by the ship carpenters, but these worthies, Mr. Batt of the *Warspite* and Mr. Daniel Jones of the *Lightning*, were not to be daunted by such a trifling matter as this. If a derrick was needed, they were the men to make it out of nothing.

What they did was to assemble the broken masts and spars that had drifted ashore from the wreck of the *Thetis* and patch them together into one immense derrick arm which with its gear weighed as much as forty tons. It was a masterpiece of ingenuity and seamanship of the old-fashioned school, such as can no longer be found in navies. This breed of handy man at sea belonged with the vanished age of masts and canvas and "wooden walls."

"Our encampment and the adjacent parts of the island now presented a bustling, and, I flattered myself, a rather interesting scene," wrote the commander. "There were parties of carpenters building the derrick, making, carrying to the selected situations, and placing the securities for supporting and working it. Riggers were preparing the gear for it, sawyers cutting wood for various purposes, rope-makers making lashing and seizing stuff from the pieces of cable crept[2] up from the bottom, and two sets of blacksmiths at their forges; those of the *Warspite* making hoops, bolts, and nails, from various articles which had been crept up; and those of the *Lightning* reducing the large diving bell and constructing a smaller one; five gangs of excavators leveling platforms on the heights above the cove, cutting roads to lead to them, and fixing bolts in numerous parts of the faces of the cliffs; some were employed in felling trees and cutting grass for the huts while others were building and thatching them; water carriers were passing to and from the pool with breakers of water; and the officers were attending to the different parties assigned to them for their immediate guidance."

When ready to be placed in position, this derrick, built of odds and ends, was an enormous spar one hundred and fifty-eight feet long. To support it over the water, elaborate devices had to be rigged from the cliff overhead, and the whole story of this achievement, as related by Captain Dickinson, reads like such a masterful, almost titanic battle against odds that it seems worth while quoting at some length:

"We had by this time taken off thirteen feet of the peak of the northeast cliff, and thereby made a platform of eighty feet by sixty. On this was placed the *Lightning's* capstan and four crabs[3] formed of the heels of the *Thetis's* topmasts, the *Lightning's* bower and stream anchors, and the store anchor, to which was shackled the chain splicing-tails and several lengths of the *Thetis's* chain stream cable which we had recovered, extending several fathoms over the cliff to attach the standing parts of the topping-lifts and guy-topping-lifts to, and preserve them from chafing against the rocks. There were also eight large bollards[4] placed in proper positions for other securities. Four other platforms, each large enough for working a crab, were made at appropriate parts for using the guys and guy-topping lifts. The roads and paths had been cut, extending from our encampment to those platforms, and from the one to the other of them together amounted to the length of nearly a mile and a half. The zig-zag path down the cliff was finished, and at those parts of the main cliff which were inaccessible in this manner, rope-ladders were substituted, and thus a communication was formed with the cove at the point where the derrick was to be stepped.

"All this being done, the large hawsers were rove through the blocks, their purchases lashed to them, and partially overhauled over the cliffs. The getting the before-mentioned heavy articles up was most distressingly laborious, for they were obliged to be carried a greater part of the distance where the surface was covered with a deep loose sand, and to this cause may be mainly attributed a complaint of the heart which subsequently attacked several of the people.

SPOOKY TREASURE TROVES

"The derrick, which was now composed of twenty-two pieces united by a great number of dowels and bolts, thirty-four hoops, and numerous wooldings[5] of four-inch ropes, was finished on the evening of the 7th, and the clothing fitted on, and I now had arrived at a point which required much foresight and pre-arrangement, namely, the preparation for erecting it; and it was necessary to weigh with coolness and circumspection the mode by which this was to be done.

"A party of about sixty of our best hands were employed in getting the *Lightning's* chain and hempen stream cables and large hawsers passed over and around the faces of the cliffs, and the purchases were sufficiently overhauled to admit of their reaching the derrick, and the falls brought to the capstan and crabs, ready for heaving it up. All who are well acquainted with the character and manners of sailors know that it is no easy matter to rid them of their habitual heedlessness. I endeavored to impress them with the need of caution, and the almost universal answer I got was 'Never fear, sir,' which from the fearless and careless manner in which it was expressed, was by no means calculated to remove my apprehensions for their safety.

"The task we had now in hand was one of much danger. The parties working over the cliffs were some of them slung in bights of rope, some supported by man-ropes, some assisting each other by joining hands, and others holding by the uncertain tenure of a tuft of grass or a twig, while loose fragments of rock, being disturbed by the gear and by the men who were working on the upper part, were precipitated amidst those below, while the sharp crags lacerated the hands and feet and rendered dodging these dangers extremely difficult. However, by great attention on the part of the officers, and by promptitude in giving aid when required, this very arduous part of our work was performed, which I sincerely believe could not have been accomplished by any men in the world but British seamen; the only accidents being some cuts in the hands and feet, and bruises from falling stones.

"All the gear being prepared, in the evening I arranged the distribution of my officers with their particular parties at the capstan, crabs, purchases, etc. The smallness of the number of hands sent from the *Warspite* rendered it necessary that I should have every working man from the *Lightning*; and on this occasion she was left with only a few convalescents to take care of her, and even the young gentlemen[6] were obliged to give their aid at the capstan. On the morning of the 9th, the derrick was launched without casualty, and while the boats were towing it to the cove, all gear was got ready to be attached to it the moment it arrived at the proper position, according to the plan I had given.

"It had to be towed for a distance of about a mile, subject to the influence of a strong current running westward through the gut, at once exposing us to the two-fold danger of being driven to sea or against the rocks. In apprehension of accident from one or the other of these causes, I had taken the precaution of placing bolts at several points of the rocks, so that in case of necessity a warp might be made fast. However, the derrick reached the cove without disaster, and as everything depended on promptitude of action, I had all the gear fitted to go with toggles, which so much facilitated the rigging that in one hour and a half after its arrival, everything was in place and the *Lightning's* chain stream cable being made fast to the heel of the derrick, ready for heaving up, I left the further management in the cove to Mr. Chatfield, and placed myself upon the main cliff.

"I then gave the order to heave round, and everyone was on the alert; but we had scarcely brought any considerable strain on the gear when a report came to me that the heel of the derrick was displaced and driven into a chasm at the foot of the cliff, an accident which for this time put an end to further efforts. I had no alternative but to cast everything off in a hurry, and if possible return to the harbor with the derrick; but this had become exceedingly doubtful, for the wind was much increased since morning, and the current more rapid. We repeatedly succeeded in towing the derrick into the gut, and were as often driven back; till at length we were compelled to make it fast to the rock outside until a small anchor and some grapnels were laid out, by which means it was finally warped into the harbor, and by half-past eleven at night moored near the *Adelaide*. Undismayed by this failure, by seven o'clock of the following morning, we were again in the cove with the derrick.

"The vast weight, the great height of the purchases, the number of them, and the great distances they were apart, made united effort impossible, but at the close of the day I had the satisfaction of seeing this huge spar in the place assigned for it, and the head of it hove ten feet above the water. On the 11th, we were again at our purchases, and the head of the derrick was raised to the angle I had intended, being about fifty feet above the surface of the sea.

"During the operation of erecting the derrick, it showed great pliability, the result of being composed of so many pieces, which obliged us to get numerous additional guys on; and having thus secured it, we returned to our encampment, all hands greatly fatigued by three days of the most harassing exertion, from half-past four in the morning until late at night. On looking down from the precipice on this enormous machine, with all its necessary rigging, it became a matter of astonishment to myself, and I believe to everyone else who saw it, that with the small means we had, we could have succeeded in such a situation. It has been my lot to witness many circumstances in which there was cause for great solicitude, but never one wherein such general anxiety was manifested as on this occasion. If any one thing had given way, it must have been fatal to the whole—a general crash would have been inevitable."

Meanwhile, Captain Dickinson had found time to devise a small diving bell, made from another water tank, which could be operated from spars and tackle set up on board a launch. This was employed for exploring the bottom of the cove in order to find where the treasure was. The bell held two men, and there were plenty of volunteers to risk their lives in the first descent in this little iron pot. The trip was disastrous, and the commander described it as follows:

"The water happened to be particularly clear, which gave me an indistinct sight of the bell at the depth of eight fathoms, and I had been watching it with breathless anxiety for a long time, when suddenly a small line of air bubbles rose from about the middle of the hose. I instantly gave the word to the men in the launch to make ready to haul away, but the two men in the bell made no signal to be pulled up. The agitation of the sea became greater every minute, and there was a rise and fall of eight or ten feet of surf against the cliffs. The danger was increasing, and I was about to order the bell to be raised when an immense column of air came bursting up from it. It had been driven violently against the rocks, thrown on its side, and filled with water.

"The next moment I saw the two men emerge from the bell and swim to the surface. Heans had been entangled in the signal line, but he managed to release himself, and Dewar bobbed up a few seconds later. They were too exhausted to say much, but Heans called to his partner, 'Never mind, mate, we haven't done with the damn thing yet.'"

These plucky seamen went down again and discovered considerable wreckage of the lost frigate. A Brazilian colonel, with a gang of native Indian divers now appeared on the scene with a great deal of brag about their ability to find the treasure without any apparatus. They proved to be pestering nuisances who accomplished nothing and were sent about their business after several futile attempts under water. They furnished one jest, however, which helped to lighten the toil. The bell was being lowered when one of these natives, or *caboclos*, slid over the side of the boat and disappeared in the green depths. In a few seconds, the signal came from the bell to hoist up. Fearing trouble, the helpers hoisted lustily, and as the bell approached the surface, something of a brownish hue was seen hanging to its bottom which was presently discovered to be the *caboclo* who had tried to enter the bell. The men mistook him for an evil spirit or some kind of a sea monster and kicked him back into the water outside, and he could only hang on by the foot-rail, with his head inside the bell.

The first encouraging tidings was signaled from the small diving bell on March 27th, when a bit of board floated up from the submerged men with these words written upon it: "Be careful in lowering the bell to a foot, for we are now over some dollars." Soon they came up, from seven fathoms down, with their caps full of silver dollars and some gold. Captain Dickinson decided to push the search night and day, and the boats were therefore equipped with torches. It was a spirited and romantic scene as he describes it.

"Thetis Cove would have supplied a fine subject for an artist. The red glare cast from the torches on every projection of the stupendous cliffs rendered the deep shadows of their fissures and indentations more conspicuous. The rushing of roaring sea into the deep chasms produced a succession of reports like those of cannon; and the assembled boats, flashing in and out of the gloom were kept in constant motion by the long swell. The experiment succeeded to admiration, and we continued taking up treasure until two o'clock of the morning of the first of April, when we were glad to retire; having obtained in the whole by this attempt, 6326 dollars, 36 pounds, 10 ounces of Plata pina, 5 pounds, 4 ounces of old silver, 243 pounds, 8 ounces of silver in bars, and 4 pounds, 8 ounces of gold. After a little rest we were again at our employment by half-past five, and proceeded very prosperously for some hours, and then had to desist because of a dangerous shift of wind."

As soon as the larger bell and the giant derrick could be put in service, the happy task of fishing up treasure was carried on at a great pace. Unlike many other such expeditions, nothing was done at haphazard. The toilers under water "were first to go to the outermost dollar, or other article of gold they could discover, and to place a pig of ballast, with a bright tally board fast to it, against and on the inner side of the nearest fixed rock they could find. From this they were then to proceed to take up all that lay immediately on the surface of the bottom, but not to remove anything else until all that was visible was obtained. This being done, they were to return to the place first searched and passing over the same ground, remove the small rocks and other articles, one by one, and progressively take up what might be recovered by such removal, but not on any account to dig without express orders from me."

Life in the camp on Cape Frio had no holiday flavor, and while there was continual danger afloat, there were troubles and hardships on shore. "In addition to our sufferings from the wind and rain penetrating our flimsy huts, we were attacked by myriads of tormentors in the shape of ants, mosquitoes, fleas, and worst of all, jiggers. Many of the people frequently had their eyes entirely closed from the stings of the mosquitoes. At night swarms of fleas assailed us in our beds, while by day it afforded a kind of amusement to pull up the leg of one's trousers and see them take flight like a flock of sparrows from a corn-stack, while there might be a hundred congregated inside the stocking. Those little insidious devils, the jiggers, penetrated the skin in almost all parts of the body, forming a round ball and causing sores which, being irritated by the sand, became most painful and troublesome ulcers, and produced lameness to half of our number at a time.

"Snakes were so numerous that the thatching and almost every nook of our huts was infested with them. They were often found in the peoples' hammocks and clothes, and several were caught on board the ship. On one occasion, my clerk's assistant was writing in his hut when a rustling in the overhanging growth caused him to look up and discover a huge snake, its head extending several feet inside the hole that served as a window. He alarmed the camp, and muskets, cutlasses, sticks, and every other weapon were caught up. The snake escaped, but I received numerous reports of his extraordinary dimensions. My steward insisted that it was as big around as his thigh, the sentry said it was as big as the *Lightning's* bower cable, and as to length the statements varied between twenty and thirty feet. At another time, Mr. Button, the boatswain, went into the store, in which there was no window, to get a piece of rope. Going in from the glare of the sun, the place appeared dark to him, and he laid hold of what he thought was a length of rope, pulled lustily at it, and was not undeceived until it was dragged out into the light. Then he was horror-struck to find he had hold of a large snake."

In May, Captain Dickinson was able to send to England in H.M.S. *Eden*, treasure to the handsome amount of $130,000 in bullion and specie, and had every promise of recovering most of the remainder of the precious cargo. Then a terrific storm swept the cove, totally demolished the derrick, carried the large diving bell to the bottom, and made hash of the whole equipment devised with such immense toil and pains. Was he discouraged? Not a bit of it. He straightway set his men at work to construct new apparatus with which he fetched up more gold and silver, to the value of half a million dollars before he forsook the task. First let him tell you in his own words of that tragic storm and its results.

"At one o'clock of the morning of May 19th, it blew a perfect gale, the cove was in a far more disturbed state than I had ever seen it before, the seas rolled up the cliff to an astonishing height, and by daylight the cove was in a state of awful commotion. The spray was driven so wildly that while standing on the main platform, at an elevation of 155 feet, I was completely wet and could scarcely resist it. The waves struck the derrick with steadily increasing force, and I watched it with all the distressing feelings that a father would evince toward a favorite child when in a situation of great danger. By six o'clock the wind threw the waves obliquely against the southeast cliff, and caused them to sweep along its whole length until opposed by the opposite cliff from which as each wave recoiled it was met by the following one, and thus accumulated, they rose in one vast heap under the derrick stage, beat it from under the bell, and washed away the air-pump, air-hoses, and semaphore. The stage was suspended at a height of thirty-eight feet above the surface of the sea in ordinary weather, from which circumstances an idea may be formed of the furious agitation of the cove.

"Nine o'clock arrived, and I had been watching for fourteen hours. The constant concussions had caused the gear of the derrick to stretch, and every blow from the sea caused it to swing and buckle to an alarming degree. Nothing more could possibly be done to save it, and I saw plainly that unless the gale soon ceased its destruction was inevitable. I therefore left an officer on watch, and quitted the cliff to go to my hut and arrange my parties for the work to be put in hand after the catastrophe. Presently he came down to meet me, and reported that a stupendous roller had struck the derrick on its side, and broke it off twenty feet from the heel. Thus in one crash was destroyed the child of my hopes, and in a very short time the derrick was dashed into six pieces, forming, with the complicated gear, one confused mass of wreckage."

Before the storm had subsided, the indefatigable seamen, blacksmiths, and carpenters were solving the problem afresh, just as if there had not been a clean sweep of their weary months of effort. This time it was a new scheme for a suspension cable that had occurred to Captain Dickinson. While this work was in progress he made another diving bell from a water-tank, and succeeded in finding his air pump at the bottom of the cove. Two men were drowned in the surf at this stage of operations, the only fatalities suffered by the heroic company. The diving bell was successfully slung from the suspended cable after a vast deal of ingenious and daring engineering, and by means of it much treasure was recovered, although the contrivance yawed fearfully under water and more than once capsized and spilled its crew who fought their gasping way to the surface.

Thetis Cove in calm weather, showing salvage operations.

Thetis Cove during the storm which wrecked the salvage equipment. (From lithographs made in 1836.)

After fourteen months of incessant toil, the men and officers worn to the bone and ravaged by fever and dysentery, they had found almost six hundred thousand dollars in bullion and specie, or three-fourths of the total amount lost in the *Thetis*. It had been magnificently successful salvage, achieved in the face of odds that would have disheartened a less resourceful and courageous commander

SPOOKY TREASURE TROVES

than Captain Thomas Dickinson. He appears to have been the man in a thousand for the undertaking. Then occurred an inexplicable sort of a disappointment, an act of such gross injustice to him that it can be explained only on the theory of favoritism at naval headquarters. Captain Dickinson had a grievance and he describes the beginning of his troubles in this fashion:

"On the 7th and 8th of March, some more treasure was found in a part from which we had removed several guns, and here I had determined to have a thorough examination by digging, feeling assured that here would be found all the remaining treasure that could be obtained. Our labors were drawing to a close, but while I was enjoying the pleasing anticipation of a speedy and successful termination of the enterprise, on the 6th I was surprised by the arrival of His Majesty's sloop *Algerine*, with orders from the Commander-in-Chief to me to resign the charge to Commander the Honorable J. F. F. de Roos of that sloop. It appears that the Admiralty had been led to think that no more property could be rescued, and therefore ordered my removal. I could not but feel this a most mortifying circumstance. I had been the only person who had come forward to attempt the recovery of the large property which was considered to be irretrievably lost; I had devised the whole of the methods by which a very large portion of it was recovered; I had endured peril, sickness, toil, and privation during more than a year; and the work was now reduced to a mere plaything compared with what it had been, and yet I was not allowed to put the finishing hand to it. Notwithstanding this, the deep interest I felt in the undertaking remained unabated, and I was determined that nothing should be wanting on my part to ensure a successful termination of it."

Quite courteously, Captain Dickinson explained in detail to Commander the Honorable J. F. F. de Roos the plant and the operations, and even left for him to fish up a large quantity of treasure already located and which could be scooped up from the diving bell without difficulty. "With a feeling which I thought would be appreciated by a brother officer, I did not attempt to bring up this treasure, but left it for the benefit of our successors, observing at the time that the world should not say that I had left them nothing to do but the labor of removing rocks and rubbish."

The amount subsequently recovered by the *Algerine* was $161,500, so that by Captain Dickinson's efforts, and the use of his plans and equipment, all but one-sixteenth of the lost treasure was restored to its owners, and of this he himself had raised by far the greater part. When he returned to England and learned that salvage was to be awarded to the officers and men who had been engaged in the work, he naturally regarded himself as the principal salvor. The Admiralty, in its inscrutable wisdom, chose to think otherwise, and the underwriters of Lloyd's, taking their cue from this exalted quarter, regarded poor Captain Dickinson with the cold and fishy eye of disfavor. The case was argued in the Court of Admiralty, and the agents of Admiral Baker, he who had been in command of the squadron at

SPOOKY TREASURE TROVES

Rio, set up the claim that he was the principal salvor, although the fact was plain that he had nothing whatever to do with recovering the treasure from the *Thetis*, and not even visited Cape Frio during the year of active operations.

The judge could not stomach such a high-handed claim as this, and his decision set aside the admiral in favor of Captain Dickinson and the crew of the *Lightning*. The salvage award, however, amounting to £17,000, was decreed as due also to the company of the *Algerine*, numbering almost four hundred men, which left small pickings for Captain Dickinson and his heroes. This was so obviously unfair that he appealed to the Judicial Committee of the Privy Council, which increased the award by the sum of £12,000, in which Commander the Honorable J. F. F. de Roos and his belated treasure seekers were not entitled to share. The influential committee of Lloyd's thought that Captain Dickinson should not have been so bumptious in defending his rights, and because he disagreed with their opinions, they ignored him in a set of resolutions which speak for themselves:

"1st. A vote of thanks to Admiral Sir Thomas Baker, for his zeal and exertions.

"2nd. The same to Captain de Roos, of the *Algerine*, and a grant of £2,000 to himself, his officers, and crew, being the amount they would have received had they been parties to the appeal.

"3rd. To mark the sense of the meeting of Captain de Roos's conduct, they further voted to this officer a piece of plate to the value of one hundred guineas."

In other words, an unimportant naval captain deserved this censure because he had not been content to take what was graciously flung at him by Lloyd's and the Admiralty, but had stood up for his rights as long as he had a shot in the locker. There is something almost comic in the figure cut by Commander the Honorable J. F. F de Roos, who reaped the reward of another man's labors and received the formal thanks of Lloyd's as the chief treasure finder of the *Thetis* frigate. Captain Thomas Dickinson was a dogged and aggressive sort of person, not in the least afraid of giving offense in high places, and had he not been of this stamp of man he would never have fought that winning fight against obstacles amid the hostile cliffs and waters of desolate Cape Frio. He shows his mettle in a fine outburst of protest, the provocation for which was a sentence in a letter published in a London newspaper while his case was under discussion: "Had Captain Dickinson relied on the liberality of Lloyd's Coffee House, *he would not have been a poorer man.*"

This was like a spark in a magazine, and the captain of the *Lightning* flings back in retort:

"Here, then we arrive at the development of the real feelings of the Underwriters; here is exposed the head and front of my offending. Rely on the liberality of Lloyd's Coffee House!! So that because I would not abandon my duty to my officers and crew, or separate my interests from theirs, and place myself and them at the mercy of the Underwriters, therefore the enterprise and the services of fourteen months, besides the rescue of nearly six hundred thousand dollars, are to be considered as utterly unworthy of mention. Can it be necessary, in order to entitle a British officer to honorable mention in Lloyd's Coffee House that he should abandon a right, and succumbing to the feet of its mighty Committee, accept a donation, doled out with all the ostentation of a gratuitous liberality, in place of that reward which legally took precedence even of the ownership of the property rescued!!"

[1] The matter quoted in this chapter is from the privately printed account by Captain Dickinson (London, 1836), entitled, "A Narrative of the Operations for the Recovery of the Public Stores and Treasure sunk in H.M.S. *Thetis*, at Cape Frio on the coast of Brazil, on the Fifth December, 1830, to which is prefixed a Concise Account of the Loss of that Ship."

[2] Dredged.

[3] Portable machines used as capstans.

[4] Strong pieces of timber placed vertically in the ground for fastening ropes to.

[5] Wrappings. Captain Kidd uses this old word in his own narrative. See page 109. [Transcriber's note: the words "woolding" or "wooldings" appear nowhere else in this text.]

[6] Midshipmen.

SPOOKY TREASURE TROVES

CHAPTER XIII
THE QUEST OF EL DORADO

In our time the golden word *Eldorado* has come to mean the goal of unattained desires, the magic country of dreams that forever lies just beyond the horizon. Its literal significance has been lost in the mists of the centuries since when one deluded band of adventurers after another was exploring unknown regions of the New World in quest of the treasure city hidden somewhere in the remote interior of South America. Thousands of lives and millions of money were vainly squandered in these pilgrimages, but they left behind them one of the most singularly romantic chapters in the whole history of conquest and discovery.

The legend of El Dorado was at first inspired by the tales of a wonderful and veritable *dorado*, or gilded man, king of a tribe of Indians dwelling, at the time of the Spanish conquest, upon the lofty tableland of Bogotá, in what is now the republic of Colombia. Later investigations have accepted it as true that such a personage existed and that the ceremonies concerning which reports were current early in the sixteenth century took place at the sacred lake of Guatavia. There lived on this plateau, in what is still known as the province of Cundinamarca, small village communities of the Muysca Indians, somewhat civilized and surrounded on all sides by debased and savage tribes. They worshiped the sun and moon, performed human sacrifices, and adored striking natural objects, as was the custom in Peru.

The numerous lakes of the region were holy places, each regarded as the home of a particular divinity to which gold and emeralds were offered by throwing them into the water. Elsewhere than at Guatavita jewels and objects wrought of gold have been discovered in the process of draining these little lakes. Guatavita, however, is most famous of all because here originated the story of "*el hombre dorado.*" This sheet of water is a few miles north of the capital city of Santa Fé de Bogotá, more than nine thousand feet above sea level, in the heart of the Cordilleras. Near the lake is still the village called Guatavita.

In 1490 the inhabitants were an independent tribe with a ruling chief. They had among them a legend that the wife of one of the earlier chiefs had thrown

SPOOKY TREASURE TROVES

herself into the lake in order to escape punishment and that her spirit survived as the goddess of the place. To worship her came the people of other communities of the region, bringing their gold and precious stones to cast into the water, and Guatavita was famed for its religious pilgrimages. Whenever a new chief, or king, of Guatavita was chosen, an imposing ceremonial was observed by way of coronation. All the men marched to the lake in procession, at the head a great party wailing, the bodies nude and painted with ocher as a sign of deep mourning. Behind them were groups richly decorated with gold and emeralds, their heads adorned with feathers, cloaks of jaguar skins hanging from their shoulders. Many uttered joyful cries or blew on trumpets and conch-shells. Then came the priests in long black robes decorated with white crosses. At the rear of the procession were the nobles escorting the newly-elected chief who rode upon a barrow hung with disks of gold.

His naked body was anointed with resinous gums and covered with gold dust so that he shone like a living statue of gold. This was the gilded man, El Dorado, whose fame traveled to the coast of the Caribbean. At the shore of the lake, he and his escort stepped upon a balsa, or raft made of rushes, and moved slowly out to the middle. There the gilded one plunged into the deep water and washed off his precious covering, while with shouts and music the assembled throng threw their offerings of gold and jewels into the lake. Then the worshipers returned to the village for dancing and feasting.[1] In the last decade of the fifteenth century, or while Columbus was making his voyages, the tribe of Guatavita was conquered by a stronger community of the Muysca race, and the new rulers, being of a thriftier mind, made an end of the extravagant ceremony of el dorado. It is therefore assumed that the gilded man had ceased to be, full thirty years before the Spaniards first heard of him at the coast.

Humboldt became interested in the legend during his South America travels and reported:

"I have examined from a geographical point of view the expeditions on the Orinoco, and in a western and southern direction in the eastern side of the Andes, before the tradition of El Dorado was spread among the conquerors. This tradition had its origin in the kingdom of Quito where Luiz Daza, in 1535, met with an Indian of New Granada who had been sent by his prince, the Zipa of Bogotá, or the Caique of Tunja, to demand assistance from Atahuahalpa, the last Inca of Peru. This ambassador boasted, as was usual, of the wealth of his country; but what particularly fixed the attention of the Spaniards who were assembled with Daza was the history of a lord who, his body covered with gold dust, went into a lake amid the mountains.

"As no historical remembrance attaches itself to any other mountain lake in this vicinity, I suppose the reference to be made to the sacred lake of Guatavita, in

SPOOKY TREASURE TROVES

the plains of the Bogotá, into which the gilded lord was made to enter. On the banks of this lake I saw the remains of a staircase, hewn in the rock, and used for the ceremonies of ablution. The Indians told me that powder of gold and golden vessels were thrown into this lake as a sacrifice to the *Adoratorio* de Guatavita. Vestiges are still found of a breach made by the Spaniards in order to drain the lake.... The ambassador of Bogotá, whom Daza met in the kingdom of Quito, had spoken of a country situated towards the east."

The latter reference means that the legend had spread from coast to coast. On the Pacific, the *conquistadores* of Pizarro were for a time too busily engaged in looting the enormous treasures of the last Inca of Peru to pay much heed to the lure of golden legends beckoning them further inland. The first attempt to go in search of the gilded man and his kingdom was made, not by a Spaniard, but by a German, Ambrosius Dalfinger, who was in command of a colony of his countrymen settled on the shore of the Gulf of Venezuela, a large tract of that region having been leased by Spain to a German company. He pushed inland to the westward as far as the Rio Magdalena, treated the natives with horrible barbarity, and was driven back after losing most of his men.

A few years later, and the legend was magnified into a wondrous description of a golden city. In 1538, there marched from the Atlantic coast, Gonzalo Ximenes de Quesada, surnamed *El Conquistador*, to find the El Dorado. At the head of six hundred and twenty-five foot-soldiers and eighty-five mailed horsemen, he made his perilous way up the Rio Magdalena, through fever-cursed swamps and tribes of hostile natives, enduring hardships almost incredible until at length he came to the lofty plateau of Bogotá, and the former home of the real gilded man. More than five hundred of his men had died on the journey of hunger, illness, and exposure. He found rich cities and great stores of gold and jewels, but failed to discover the El Dorado of his dreams.

Many stories were afloat of other treasures to be wrested from the Muysca chiefs, but Quesada, having no more than a handful of fighting men, feared to go campaigning until he had made his position secure. He therefore established a base and laid the foundations of the present city of Bogotá. One of his scouting parties brought back tidings of a tribe of very war-like women in the south who had much gold, and in this way was the myth of the Amazons linked with the El Dorado as early as 1538.

Now occurred as dramatic a coincidence as could be imagined. To Quesada there appeared a Spanish force commanded by Sebastian de Belalcazar, the conqueror of Quito, who had come all the way from the Pacific coast, after hearing from an Indian of New Granada the story of the gilded man. No sooner had this expedition arrived than it was reported to Quesada that white men with horses were coming from the east. This third company of pilgrims in quest of El Dorado

SPOOKY TREASURE TROVES

proved to be Nicholas Federmann and his hard-bitted Germans from the colony in Venezuela who had followed the trail made by Dalfinger and then plunged into the wilderness beyond his furthest outpost.

Thus these three daring expeditions, Quesada from the north, Belalcazar from the south, and Federmann from the east, met face to face on the hitherto unknown plateau of Cundinamarca. None had been aware of the others' march in search of this goal, and each had believed himself to be the discoverer of this country. They were ready to fly at one another's throats, for there could be no amity when gold was the prize at stake. Curiously enough the three forces were evenly matched in fighting strength, each with about one hundred and sixty men. One might think that the two Spanish parties would have united to drive the Germans from the home of El Dorado, but greed stifled all natural ties and emotions.

A conflict was averted by the tact and sagacity of Quesada and the priests of the expeditions who acted as a committee of arbitration. It was finally agreed among the leaders that the several claims should be submitted to the Spanish Court, and Quesada, Belalcazar, and Federmann set out for Spain to appear in person, leaving their forces in possession of the disputed territory. The command of the Spanish troops was turned over to Hernan Perez de Quesada, the cruel and greedy brother of the leader, who fortified himself at Bogotá and proceeded to rob the Muysca people of the last ounce of gold that could be extorted by means of torture and all manner of unspeakable wickedness. In 1540 he tried to drain the lake of Guatavita, tempted by the stories of the vast treasures of gold and jewels that, for centuries, had been thrown into the water by the worshipers, but he recovered valuables only to the amount of four thousand ducats. It was the remains of his drainage tunnel which Humboldt found and made note of.

With the conquest of this region was obtained the last great store of gold discovered by the plundering Spaniards in South America. These explorers finished when [Transcriber's note: what?] Pizarro had begun in Peru. To convey the treasure from Bogotá to the coast of the Carribean a road was built through the mountains, much of it cut as a narrow shelf in solid rock, winding and dipping in a dizzy route to connect with the upper reaches of navigation on the Rio Magdalena. This was the famous *El Camino Real*, or "King's Highway" which is still used as one of the roads by which the capital of Colombia, Santa Fé de Bogotá is reached by the traveler of the twentieth century. It was to intercept one of these treasure trains that Amyas Leigh and his doughty comrades of "Westward Ho!" lay in wait, and the fiction of Kingsley will better serve to portray the time and place than the facts as the old historians strung them together.

"Bidding farewell once and forever to the green ocean of the eastern plains, they have crossed the Cordillera; they have taken a longing glance at the city of Santa Fé, lying in the midst of rich gardens on its lofty mountain plateau, and have

SPOOKY TREASURE TROVES

seen, as was to be expected, that it was far too large for any attempt of theirs. But they have not altogether thrown away their time. Their Indian lad has discovered that a gold-train is going down from Santa Fé toward the Magdalena; and they are waiting for it beside the miserable rut that serves for a road, encamped in a forest of oaks which would make them almost fancy themselves back in Europe were it not for the tree-ferns which form the undergrowth; and were it not for the deep gorges opening at their very feet; in which while their brows are swept by the cool breezes of a temperate zone, they can see far below, dim through their everlasting vapor bath of rank, hot steam, the mighty forms and gorgeous colors of the tropic forest.

"... At last, up from beneath there was a sharp crack and a loud cry. The crack was neither the snapping of a branch, nor the tapping of a woodpecker; the cry was neither the scream of a parrot, nor the howl of a monkey.

"'That was a whip's crack,' said Yeo, 'and a woman's wail. They are close here, lads!'

"'A woman's? Do they drive women in their gangs?' asked Amyas. 'Why not, the brutes? There they are, sir. Did you see their basnets glitter?'

"'Men!' said Amyas in a low voice. 'I trust you all not to shoot till I do. Then give them one arrow, out swords, and at them! Pass the word along.'

"Up they came, slowly, and all hearts beat loud at their coming. First, about twenty soldiers, only one half of whom were on foot; the other half being borne, incredible as it may seem, each in a chair on the back of a single Indian, while those who marched had consigned their heaviest armor and their arquebuses into the hands of attendant slaves, who were each pricked on at will by the pikes of the soldiers behind them.... Last of this troop came some inferior officer also in his chair, who as he went slowly up the hill, with his face turned toward the gang which followed, drew every other second the cigar from his lips to inspirit them with those pious ejaculations ... which earned for the pious Spaniards of the sixteenth century the uncharitable imputation of being the most abominable swearers in Europe.

"... A line of Indians, Negroes, and Zamboes, naked, emaciated, scarred with whips and fetters, and chained together by their left wrists, toiled upwards, panting and perspiring under the burden of a basket held up by a strap which passed across their foreheads. Yeo's sneer was but too just; there were not only old men and youths among them, but women; slender young girls, mothers with children running at their knee; and at the sight, a low murmur of indignation rose from the ambushed Englishmen, worthy of the free and righteous hearts of those days, when Raleigh could appeal to man and God, on the ground of a common humanity, in behalf of the outraged heathens of the New World.

"But the first forty, so Amyas counted, bore on their backs a burden which made all, perhaps, but him and Yeo, forget even the wretches who bore it. Each basket contained a square package of carefully corded hide; the look whereof friend Amyas knew full well.

"'What's in they, Captain?'

"'Gold!' And at that magic word all eyes were strained greedily forward, and such a rustle followed that Amyas, in the very face of detection, had to whisper:

"'Be men, be men, or you will spoil all yet.'"

The muskets and long-bows of the stout Englishmen avenged the wrongs of this pitiable caravan, although there was no help for a vast multitude of Indians who were put to death with devilish torments by their conquerors. But the legend of the El Dorado still survived and it spread like an avenging spirit. "Transplanted by the over-excited imagination of the white man, the vision appeared like a mirage enticing, deceiving and leading men to destruction, on the banks of the Orinoco, and the Amazon, in Omagua and Parime." The conquest of Bogotá made them believe that the gilded man and his golden kingdom were somewhere just beyond. The licentiate, Juan de Castellanos, wrote a poem which was published in 1589, telling of the legend as it had existed in Quito in the days of the *Conquistadores.*

"When with that folk came Annasco,Benalcazar learned from a strangerThen living in the city of Quito,But who called Bogotá his home,Of a land there rich in golden treasure,Rich in emeralds glistening the rock.. . . . . A chief was there, who stripped of vesture,Covered with golden dust from crown to toe,Sailed with offerings to the gods upon a lakeBorne by the waves upon a fragile raft,The dark flood to brighten with golden light."[2]

Another and more imaginative version of the story was told to Oviedo[3] by divers Spaniards whom he met in San Domingo. They had heard from Indians in Quito that the great lord, El Dorado, always went about covered with powdered gold, because he thought this kind of garment more beautiful and distinguished than any decorations of beaten gold. The lesser chiefs were in the habit of adorning themselves likewise, but were not so lavish as the king who put on his gold dust every morning and washed it off at night. He first anointed himself with a fragrant liquid gum, to which the gold dust adhered so evenly that he resembled a brilliant piece of artfully hammered gold metal.

For more than half a century, the mad quest continued, and always there came tragedy and disaster. The German colony of Venezuela was wiped out because of these futile expeditions into the interior. Gonzalo Pizarro, brother of the great Francisco, set out to find the city of legend, and returned after two years, in such dreadful plight that the survivors of the party looked more like wild animals than men, "so that one could no longer recognize them." Pedro de Urzua started from Bogotá to find a "golden city of the sun," and his expedition founded the town of Pampluna. In 1560 the same leader was appointed "governor of Omagua and El Dorado," and he set out to find his domain by way of the Amazon. Urzua was murdered by Lope de Aguirre who treacherously conspired against him, and Aguirre descended the great river and finally reached Venezuela after one of the maddest piratical cruises ever recorded. Guimilla, in a "History of the Oronoke," says:

"I find it (El Dorado) related with such an exact description of the country, as the missionaries of my province and myself have recognized, that I cannot doubt it. I have seen in the jurisdiction of Varinas, in the mountains of Pedrarca, in 1721, the brass halberd which Urzua took with him in his expedition. I have been acquainted with Don Joseph Cabarte who directed for thirty years the missions of Agrico and the Oronoke, the countries traversed by Urzua, and he appeared to be fully persuaded that that was the route to El Dorado."

Meanwhile the myth had assumed new forms. On the southwestern tributaries of the Amazon were the fabled districts of Enim and Paytiti said to have been founded by Incas who had fled from Peru and to have surpassed ancient Cuzco in splendor. North of the Amazon the supposed city of El Dorado moved eastward until in Raleigh's time it was situated in Guiana beside Lake Parima. This lake remained on English maps until the explorations of Schomburgh in the nineteenth century proved that it was nothing more than a pond in a vast swamp. The emerald mountain of Espirito Santo and the Martyrios gold mine, long sought for in Western Brazil recalled the El Dorado myth; while far to the southward in the plains of the Argentine the city of Cæsar, with silver walls and houses was another alluring and persistent phantom. It was said to have been founded by shipwrecked Spanish sailors, and even late in the eighteenth century expeditions were sent in search for it.

It was not until 1582 that the Spanish ceased to pursue the fatal phantom city of El Dorado and Southey's History of the Brazils is authority for the statement that these "expeditions cost Spain more than all the treasures she had received from her South American possessions." There is more meaning than appears on the surface in the Spanish proverb, "Happiness is only to be found in El Dorado which no one yet has been able to reach."

Alas, that Sir Walter Raleigh should have been lured to seek in Guiana the fabled El Dorado which had now become the splendid city of Manoa built on the shores of a vast inland lake of salt water. It was in this guise that he heard the transplanted and exaggerated story of the gilded man. His own narrative, as included in Hakluyt's Voyages, is entitled:[4]

"The discovery of the large, rich and beautiful Empire of Guiana, with a relation of the great and golden city of Manoa (which the Spaniards call El Dorado) and the provinces of Emeria, Aromaia, Amapaia, and other countries, with their rivers adjoining. Performed in the year 1595 by Sir Walter Raleigh, Knight, Captain of Her Majesty's Guard, Lord Warden of the Stanneries, and Her Highness' Lieutenant General of the County of Cornwall."

It was while touching at the island of Trinidad, outward bound, that Raleigh had the misfortune to learn the story of a picturesque liar by the name of Juan Martinez, a derelict Spanish seaman, who had sailed with the explorer Diego de Ordas in 1531. "The relation of this Martinez (who was the first that discovered Manoa) his success and end are to be seen in the Chancery of Saint Juan de Puerto Rico," writes Raleigh, "whereof Berreo had a copy, which appeared to be the greatest encouragement as well to Berreo as to others that formerly attempted the discovery and conquest. Orellana, after he failed of the discovery of Guiana by the said river of the Amazon, passed into Spain, and there obtained a patent of the king for the invasion and conquest, but died by sea about the Islands, and his fleet severed by tempest, the action for that time proceeded not. Diego Ordas followed the enterprise, and departed Spain with six hundred soldiers and thirty horse, who arriving on the coast of Guiana, was slain in mutiny, with the most part of such as favored him, as also of the rebellious part, insomuch as his ships perished, and few or none returned, neither was it certainly known what became of the said Ordas until Berreo found the anchor of his ship in the river of Orinoco; but it was supposed, and so it is written by Lopez that he perished on the seas, and of other writers diversely conceived and reported.

Sir Walter Raleigh.

"And hereof it came that Martinez entered so far within the land and arrived at that city of Inca, the Emperor; for it chanced that while Ordas with his army rested at the port of Morequito (who was either the first or second that attempted Guiana) by some negligence the whole store of powder provided for the service was set on fire; and Martinez having the chief charge[5] was condemned by the General Ordas to be executed forthwith. Martinez, being much favored by the soldiers, had all the means possible procured for his life; but it could not be obtained in other sort than this; That he should be set into a canoe alone without

Sir Walter Raleigh.

any victuals, only with his arms, and so turned loose into the great river.

"But it pleased God that the canoe was carried down the stream and that certain of the Guianians met it the same evening; and having not at any time seen any Christian, nor any man of that color, they carried Martinez into the land to be wondered at, and so from town to town, until he came to the great city of Manoa, the seat and residence of Inca, the Emperor. The emperor after he had beheld him, knew him to be a Christian (for it was not long before that his brethren Guascar and Atabalipa[6] were vanished [Transcriber's note: vanquished?] by the Spaniards in Peru) and caused him to be lodged in his palace and well entertained. He lived seven months in Manoa, but was not suffered to wander into the country anywhere. He was also brought thither all the way blindfold, led by the Indians, until he came to the entrance of Manoa itself, and was fourteen or fifteen days in the passage. He avowed at his death that he entered the city at noon, and then they uncovered his face, and that he traveled all that day till night through the city and the next day from sun rising to sun setting ere he came to the palace of Inca.

"After that Martinez had lived seven months in Manoa, and began to understand the language of the country, Inca asked him whether he desired to return into his own country, or would willingly abide with him. But Martinez not desirous to stay, obtained the favor of Inca to depart; with whom he sent divers Guianians to conduct him to the river of Orinoco, all laden with as much gold as they could carry, which he gave to Martinez at his departure. But when he was arrived near the river's side, the borderers which are called Orenoqueponi robbed him and his Guianians of all the treasure (the borderers being at that time at war, which Inca had not conquered) save only of two great bottles of gourds, which were filled with beads of gold curiously wrought, which those Orenoqueponi thought had been no other thing than his drink or meat, or grain for food, with which Martinez had liberty to pass.

"And so in canoes he fell down from the river of Orinoco to Trinidad and from thence to Margarita, and also to Saint Juan de Puerto Eico, where remaining a long time for passage into Spain, he died. In the time of his extreme sickness, and when he was without hope of life, receiving the Sacrament at the hands of his confessor, he delivered these things, with the relation of his travels, and also called for his calabazas or gourds of the gold beads which he gave to the church and friars to be prayed for.

"This Martinez was he that christened the city of Manoa by the name of El Dorado, and as Berreo informed me, upon this occasion; Those Guianians, and also the borderers, and all others in that tract which I have seen, are marvelous great drunkards; in which vice, I think no nation can compare with them; and at the times of their solemn feasts when the emperor carouseth with his captains, tributaries, and governors the manner is thus:

SPOOKY TREASURE TROVES

"All those that pledge him are first stripped naked, and their bodies anointed all over with a kind of white balsam (by them called *curca*) of which there is great plenty, and yet very dear amongst them, and it is of all other the most precious, whereof we have had good experience. When they are anointed all over, certain servants of the emperor, having prepared gold made into fine powder, blow it through hollow canes upon their naked bodies, until they be all shining from the foot to the head: and in this sort they sit drinking by twenties, and hundreds, and continue in drunkenness sometimes six or seven days together.

"The same is also confirmed by a letter written into Spain, which was intercepted, which Mr. Robert Dudley told me he had seen. Upon this sight, and for the abundance of gold which he saw in the city, the images of gold in their temples, the plates, armors, and shields of gold which they used in the wars, he called it El Dorado."

After mentioning in detail the several ill-fated expeditions of the Spanish to find the El Dorado, Raleigh reviews the mass of evidence in favor of the existence of the hidden and magnificent city, and as gravely relates the current reports of other wonders as prodigious as this. He it was who carried back to Europe the story of the Amazons, "being very desirous to understand the truth of those warlike women, because of some it is believed, of others not. And although I digress from my purpose, yet I will set down that which hath been delivered me for truth of those women, and I spake with a caique or lord of the people, that told me he had been in the river and beyond it.... They are said to be very cruel and bloodthirsty, especially to such as offer to invade their territories. These Amazons have likewise great stores of these plates of gold which they recover chiefly by exchange for a kind of green stones." That the natures of these stern ladies had a softer side is prettily indicated by Raleigh in the statement that in the month of April "all kings of the border assemble, and queens of the Amazons; and after the queens have chosen, the rest cast lots for their Valentines. This one month they feast, dance, and drink of their wines in abundance; and the moon being done, they all depart to their own provinces."

Among the perils that beset the road to El Dorado was a terrible nation of men with no heads upon their shoulders. Raleigh did not happen to encounter them during his voyage up the Orinoco, but nevertheless he took pains to set down in his narrative, "which though it may be thought a mere fable, yet for mine part I am resolved it is true, because every child in the provinces of Arromaia and Canuri affirm the same. They are called Ewaipanoma; they are reported to have their eyes in their shoulders, and their mouths in the middle of their breasts and that a long train of hair groweth backward between their shoulders.[7] The son of Topiawari, which I brought with me into England told me that they are the most mighty men of all the land, and use bows, arrows, and clubs thrice as big as any of Guiana, or of the Orinoco, and that one of the Iwarawakeri took a prisoner of them the year before our arrival there, and brought him into the borders of Aromaia, his father's country. And farther when I seemed to doubt of it, he told me that it was no wonder among them, but that they were as great a nation, and as common as any other in all the provinces, and had of late years slain many hundreds of his father's people: but it was not my chance to hear of them until I was come away, and if I had but spoken but one word of it while I was there, I might have brought one of them with me to put the matter out of doubt. Such a nation was written of by Mandeville[8] whose reports were holden for fables many years, and yet since the East Indies were discovered, we find his relations true of all things as heretofore were held incredible. Whether it be true or no, the matter is not great, neither can there be any profit in the imagination. For my own part, I saw them not, but I am resolved that so many people did not all combine or forethink to make the report.

"When I came to Cumana in the West Indies, afterwards by chance I spake with a Spaniard dwelling not far from thence, a man of great travel, and after he knew that I had been in Guiana, and so far directly west as Caroli, the first question he asked me was, whether I had seen any of the Ewaipanoma, which are those without heads: who being esteemed a most honest man of his word, and in all things else, told me he had seen many of them."

That Sir Walter Raleigh, the finest flower of manhood that blossomed in his age, should have believed these and other wonders does not belittle his fame. He lived and fought and sailed in a world that had not been explored and mapped and charted and photographed and written about until all the romance and mystery were driven out of it. The globe had not shrunk to a globule around which excursionists whiz in forty days on a coupon ticket. Men truly great, endowed with the courage and resourcefulness of epic heroes, and the simple faith of little children, were voyaging into unknown seas to find strange lands, ready to die, and right cheerfully, for God and their King. Sir Walter Raleigh was bound up, heart and soul, in winning Guiana as a great empire for England, and when his enemies at home scouted his reports and accused him of trying to deceive the nation with his tales of El Dorado, he replied with convincing sincerity and pathos:

"A strange fancy it had been in me, to have persuaded my own son whom I have lost, and to have persuaded my wife to have adventured the eight thousand pounds which his Majesty gave them for Shelborne, and when that was spent, to persuade my wife to sell her house at Mitcham in hope of enriching them by the mines of Guiana, if I myself had not seen them with my own eyes! For being old and weakly, thirteen years in prison, and not used to the air, to travel and to watching, it being ten to one that I should ever have returned,—and of which, by reason of my violent sickness, and the long continuance thereof, no man had any hope, what madness would have made me undertake the journey, but the assurance of

SPOOKY TREASURE TROVES

this mine."[9]

He was referring here to his fourth and last voyage in quest of El Dorado. Elizabeth was dead, and James I bore Raleigh no good will. After the long imprisonment, for thirteen years under suspended sentence of death, he was permitted to leave the Tower and embark with a fleet of thirteen ships in 1617, it being particularly enjoined that he should engage in no hostilities with his dearest enemy, Spain. It is generally believed that King James hoped and expected that such a clash of interests as was almost inevitable in the attempt to plant the English flag in Guiana would give him a pretext to send Raleigh to the headman's block. It was on this voyage that Raleigh lost his eldest son, besides several of his ships, and utterly failed in the high-hearted purpose of setting up a kingdom whose capital city should be that splendid lost city of Manoa. He was unable to avoid battles with the insolent Spanish, it was in one of these that his son was killed, and when he returned to England, the price was exacted and paid. Sir Walter Raleigh was executed in the palace yard, Westminster, and thus perished one who brought great glory to England by land and sea.

Concerning El Dorado, Raleigh had given credence to no more than was believed in his time by the Spanish of every port from San Marta on the Caribbean to Quito on the Pacific. The old chronicles are full of it. One instance, chosen almost at random from many of the same kind is quoted by De Pons in his History of Caraccas.[10]

"When the wild Indian appeared before the Spanish governor of Guiana, Don Manuel Centurion of Angostura, he was assailed with questions which he answered with as much perspicuity and precision as could be expected from one whose most intelligible language consisted in signs. He, however, succeeded in making them understand that there was on the border of Lake Parima a city whose inhabitants were civilized and regularly disciplined to war. He boasted a great deal of the beauty of its buildings, the neatness of its streets, the regularity of its squares, and the riches of its people. According to him, the roofs of its principal houses were either of gold or silver. The high-priest, instead of pontifical robes, rubbed his whole body with the fat of the turtle; then they blew upon it some gold dust, so as to cover his whole body with it. In this attire, he performed the religious ceremonies. The Indian sketched on a table with a bit of charcoal the city of which he had given a description.

"His ingenuity seduced the governor. He asked him to serve as a guide to some Spaniards he wished to send on this discovery, to which the Indian consented. Sixty Spaniards offered themselves for the undertaking, and among others Don Antonio Santos. They set off and traveled nearly five hundred leagues to the south, through the most frightful roads. Hunger, the swamps, the woods, the precipices, the heat, the rains, destroyed almost all. When those who survived thought themselves four or five days' journey from the capital city and hoped to reach the end of all their troubles, and the object of their desires, the Indian disappeared in the night.

"This event dismayed the Spaniards. They knew not where they were. By degrees they all perished but Santos to whom it occurred to disguise himself as an Indian. He threw off his clothes, covered his whole body with red paint, and introduced himself among them by his knowledge of many of their languages. He was a long time among them, until at length he fell within the power of the Portugese established on the banks of the Rio Negro. They embarked him on the river Amazon and after a very long detention, sent him back to his country."

In this very brief survey of the growth and results of the El Dorado legend, there is no room even to mention many of the most dramatic and disastrous expeditions which it inspired through the sixteenth century. It was, in truth, the greatest lost treasure story that the world has ever known. The age of those splendid adventurers has vanished, exploration has proved that the golden city hidden in Guiana was a myth, but now and again investigation has harked back to the source of the tradition of the gilded man, at the mountain lake of Guatavita on the lofty tableland of Bogotá. Hernan de Quesada, first to try to drain the lake, was followed a few years later by Antonio de Sepulveda who recovered treasure from the bottom to the amount of more than one hundred thousand dollars, besides a magnificent emerald which was sold at Madrid.

Professor Liborio Zerda, of the University of Colombia at Bogotá, has published his results of an exhaustive study of the legend and the evidence to show that the ceremonies of the gilded man were once performed at Guatavita. He describes a group of figures beaten out of raw gold which was recovered from the lake and is now in the museum of that city. It represents the chief and attendants upon a *balsa*, or raft, and is considered to be a striking confirmation of the tradition.

"Undoubtedly this piece represents the religious ceremony which Zamora has described," writes Professor Zerda, "with the caique of Guatavita surrounded by Indian priests, on the raft which was taken on the day of the ceremony to the middle of the lake. It may be, as some persons believe, that Siecha lagune, and not the present Guatavita, was the place of the *dorado* ceremony, and consequently the ancient Guatavita. But everything seems to indicate that there was really once a *dorado* at Bogotá."

Zamora, who wrote in the seventeenth century, recorded that the Indians believed the spirit of the lake had built a magnificent palace beneath the water where she dwelt and demanded offerings of gold and jewels, which belief spread over all the nation of the Muysca and also among strangers "who all, stricken by this wonderful occurrence, came to offer their gifts by many different routes, of which even to-day some signs remain. In the center of the lake they threw their offerings with ridiculous and vain ceremonies."

In 1823, Captain Charles Stuart Cochran of the English navy was traveling in Colombia and he became keenly interested in the lake of Guatavita and the chances of recovering the lost treasure by means of a drainage project. He delved into the old Spanish records, assembled the traditions that were still alive among the Indians and was convinced that a fabulous accumulation of gold awaited the enterprise of modern engineers. One of the ancient accounts, so he discovered, related that to escape the cruel persecution of the Spanish conquerors the wealthy natives threw their gold into the lake, and that the last caique cast therein the burdens of fifty men laden with gold dust and nuggets.

Captain Cochran did not succeed in finding the funds needed to undertake the tempting task, but his information was preserved, and made some stir in England and France. It was reserved for twentieth century treasure seekers to attack the sacred lake of Guatavita, and to capitalize the venture as a joint stock company with headquarters in London and a glittering prospectus offering investors an opportunity of obtaining shares in a prospective hoard of gold and jewels worth something like a billion dollars. A concession was obtained from the government of Colombia, and work begun in 1903.

As an engineering problem, draining the lake seemed practicable and comparatively inexpensive. It is a deep, transparent pool, hardly more than a thousand feet wide, almost circular, and set like a jewel in a cup-like depression near the top of a cone-shaped peak, several hundred feet above the nearby plateau. The tunnel therefore had only to pierce the hill-side to enter the lake and let the water flow out to the plain below. It was estimated that the shaft had to be driven a distance of eleven hundred feet.

A small village of huts was built to shelter the engineers and laborers, and rock drilling machinery set up not far from the still visible remains of one of the shafts dug by the Spanish treasure seekers of the fifteenth century. No serious obstacles were encountered until the tunnel had tapped the bottom of the lake and the water began to run off through carefully regulated sluices. Then, as the surface lowered, and the submerged mud was exposed to the air, it solidified in a cement-like substance which was almost impossible to penetrate. The treasure must have sunk many feet deep in this mud during four or five centuries, and the workmen found it so baffling that operations were suspended. The promoters of the enterprise found this unexpected obstacle so much more than they had bargained for that they had to abandon it for lack of resources. In their turn they had been thwarted by the spirit of the gilded man, and the treasure of El Dorado is still beyond the grasp of its eager pursuers.

[1] The performance of these ceremonies is vouched for by Lucas Fernandez

SPOOKY TREASURE TROVES

Piedrahita, Bishop of Panama; Pedro Simon, and other early Spanish historians, translated and quoted by A. F. Bandelier in his work, "The Gilded Man (El Dorado)." This version agrees with that described in the volume written by the modern historian, Dr. Liborio Zerda, professor of the University of Colombia, *El Dorado, Estudio Historico, Ethnografico, Y Arqueologico*.

[2] Translated by A. F. Bandelier.

[3] Oviedo, or Oviedo y Valdéz, royal histriographer, who witnessed the first return of Columbus to Spain in 1493. He was later a treasury officer at Darien, governor of Cartagena, and *alcaide* of the fort at Santo Domingo. He wrote the first general account of the discoveries in America, and it has remained a standard authority. His principal work is *Historia natural y general de las Indias* in fifty books.

[4] For the convenience of the reader the spelling has been modernized in this and the following extracts from Hakluyt.

[5] Martinez was the gunner or officer "who had charge of the munitions."

[6] Commonly spelled Huascar and Atalualpa.

[7] "Her father loved me, oft invited me, Still questioned me the story of my lifeFrom year to year, the battles, sieges, fortunes,That I have pass'd.I ran it through, even from my boyish daysTo the very moment that he bade me tell it:Wherein I spake of most disastrous chances,Of moving incidents by flood and field,Of hair-breadth 'scapes i' the imminent deadly breachOf being taken by the insolent foe,And sold to slavery,'of my redemption thence,And portance in my travel's history:Wherein of antres vast and deserts idle,Rough quarries, rocks, and hills whose head touch heaven,It was my hint to speak,—such was the process;And of the Cannibals that each other eat,The Anthropophagi, and men whose headsDo grow beneath their shoulders. This to hearWould Desdemona seriously incline."—Shakespeare. (*The Tragedy of Othello, the Moor of Venice*.)

[8] The date of the first English edition of Sir John Mandeville's book of travels was 1499. According to his own account he discovered this and other wonders in the kingdom of Ethiopia. The book was widely read, very popular in several languages, and was one of the earliest printed books, being published in Germany about 1475. Recent investigations have shown that almost the whole of the matter was cribbed from other authors, and that as a genuine explorer, Sir John Mandeville was the Dr. Frederick Cook of his age.

[9] Cayley's *Life of Raleigh*.

[10] Translation of J. A. Van Heuvel in his "*El Dorado*. Being a Narrative of the Circumstances which gave rise to reports in the Sixteenth Century of the Existence of a Rich and Splendid City in South America." (1844.)

SPOOKY TREASURE TROVES

CHAPTER XIV
THE WIZARDRY OF THE DIVINING ROD

Washington Irving was so thoroughly versed in the lore of buried treasure that the necromancy of the divining rod, as a potent aid to this kind of industry, had received his studious attention. For many centuries, the magic wand of hazel, or various other woods, has been used, and implicitly believed in, as a guide to the whereabouts of secrets hidden underground, whether of running water, veins of metal, or buried treasure. There is nothing far-fetched, or contrary to the fact, in the lively picture of Dr. Knipperhausen, that experienced magician, who helped Wolfert Webber seek the treasure concealed by pirates on the Manhattan Island of the Knickerbocker Dutch of the "Tales of a Traveler."

"He had passed some years of his youth among the Harz mountains of Germany, and had derived much valuable instruction from the miners, touching the mode of seeking treasure buried in the earth. He had prosecuted his studies also under a traveling sage who united the mysteries of medicine with magic and legerdemain. His mind therefore had become stored with all kinds of mystic lore; he had dabbled a little in astrology, alchemy, divination; knew how to detect stolen money, and to tell where springs of water lay hidden; in a word, by the dark nature of his knowledge he had acquired the name of the High-German-Doctor, which is pretty nearly equivalent to that of necromancer.

"The doctor had often heard rumors of treasure being buried in various parts of the island, and had long been anxious to get on the traces of it. No sooner were Wolfert's waking and sleeping vagaries confided to him, than he beheld in them confirmed symptoms of a case of money digging, and lost no time in probing it to the bottom. Wolfert had long been sorely oppressed in mind by the golden secret, and as a family physician is a kind of father confessor, he was glad of any opportunity of unburdening himself. So far from curing, the doctor caught the malady from his patient. The circumstances unfolded to him awakened all his cupidity; he had not a doubt of money being buried somewhere in the neighborhood of the mysterious crosses and offered to join Wolfert in the search.

"He informed him that much secrecy and caution must be observed in enterprises of this kind; that money is only to be digged for at night; with certain forms and ceremonies, and burning of drugs; the repeating of mystic words, and above all, that the seekers must first be provided with a divining rod, which had the wonderful property of pointing to the very spot on the surface of the earth under which treasure lay hidden. As the doctor had given much of his mind to these matters, he charged himself with all the necessary preparations, and, as the quarter of the moon was propitious, he undertook to have the divining rod ready by a certain night.

"Wolfert's heart leaped with joy at having met with so learned and able a coadjutor. Everything went on secretly, but swimmingly. The doctor had many consultations with his patient, and the good woman of the household lauded the comforting effect of his visits. In the meantime the wonderful divining rod, that great key to nature's secrets, was duly prepared.

"The following note was found appended to this passage in the handwriting of Mr. Knickerbocker. 'There has been much written against the divining rod by those light minds who are ever ready to scoff at the mysteries of nature; but I fully join with Dr. Knipperhausen in giving it my faith. I shall not insist upon its efficacy in discovering the concealment of stolen goods, the boundary stones of fields, the traces of robbers and murderers, or even the existence of subterranean springs and streams of water; albeit, I think these properties not to be readily discredited; but of its potency in discovering veins of precious metal, and hidden sums of money and jewels, I have not the least doubt. Some said that the rod turned only in the hands of persons who had been born in particular months of the year; hence astrologers had recourse to planetary influences when they would procure a talisman. Others declared that the properties of the rod were either an effect of chance or the fraud of the holder, or the work of the devil....'"

The worthy and learned Mr. Knickerbocker might have gone on to quote authorities by the dozen. This weighty argument of his is not delivered with a wink to the reader. He is engaged in no solemn foolery. If one desires to find pirates' gold, it is really essential to believe in the divining rod and devoutly obey its magic messages. This is proven to the hilt by that very scholarly Abbé Le Lorrain de Vallemont of France whose exhaustive volume was published in 1693 with the title of *La Physique Occulte*, or "Treatise on the Divining Rod and its Uses for the Discovery of Springs of Water, Metallic Veins, Hidden Treasure, Thieves, and Escaped Murderers." In his preface he politely sneers at those scholars who consider the study of the divining rod as an idle pursuit and shows proper vexation toward the ignorance and prejudice which are hostile to such researches.

The author then indicates that the action of the divining rod is to be explained by the theory of Corpuscular Philosophy,[1] and by way of concrete argument, refers to the most famous case in the ancient annals of this art.

Methods of manipulating the diving rod to find buried treasure.
(From La Physique Occulte, first edition, 1596.)

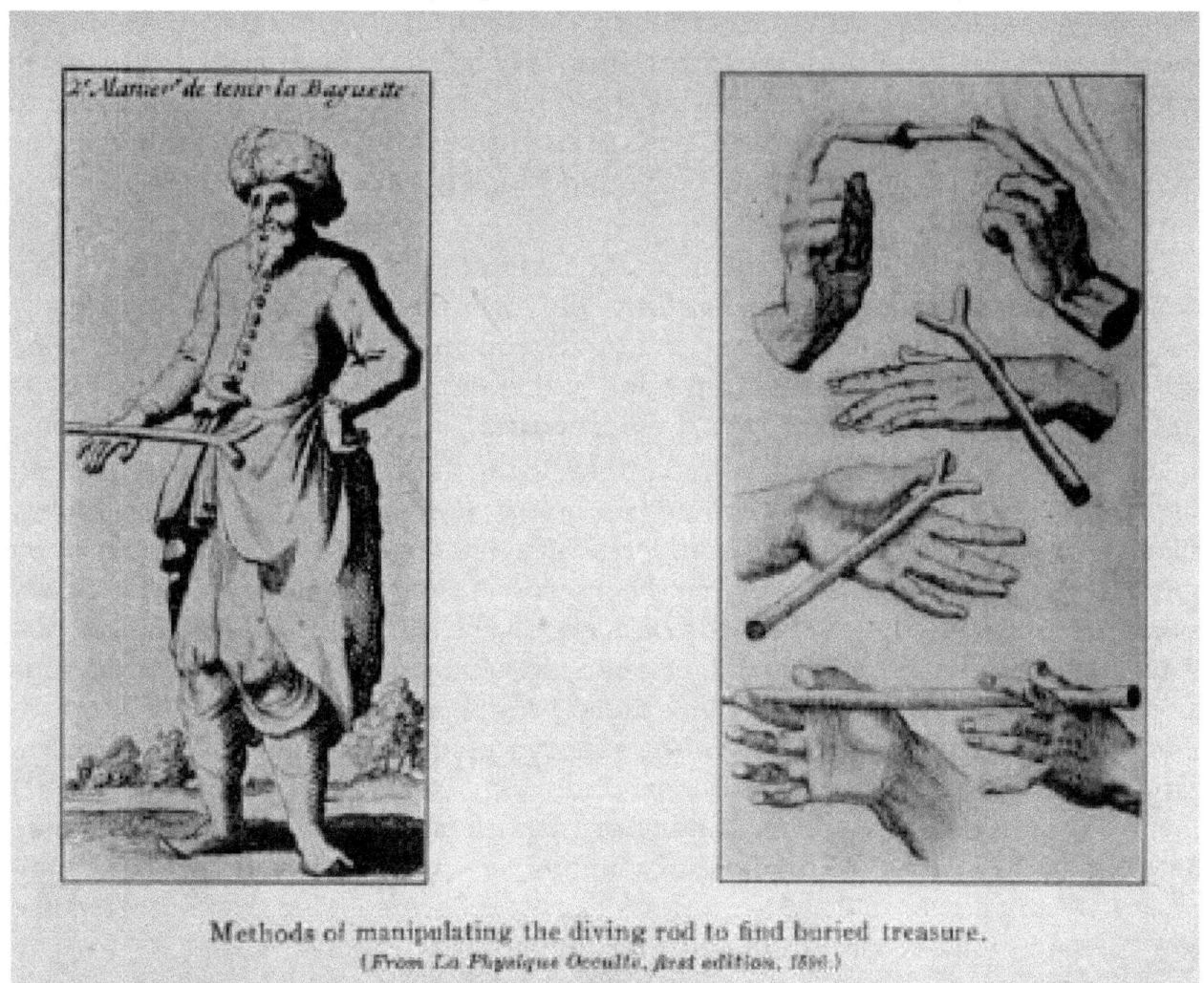

Methods of manipulating the diving rod to find buried treasure.
(From La Physique Occulte, first edition, 1596.)

"It seems to me that my work would have been incomplete, had I not *seen* Jacques Aymar, and that the objection might have been raised that I had only argued about statements not generally accepted. This now famous man came to Paris on January 21st, 1693. I saw him two or three hours a day for nearly a month, and my readers may rest assured that during that time I examined him very closely. It is a positive fact that the divining rod turned in his hands in the direction of springs of water, precious metals, thieves, and escaped murderers. He does not know why. If he knew the physical cause, and had sufficient intellect to reason about it, I am convinced that, whenever he undertook an experiment he would succeed. But a peasant who can neither read nor write will know still less about *atmosphere, volume, motion of corpuscles distributed in the air, etc.* He is still more ignorant as to how these *corpuscles* can be disturbed and cease to produce the motion and dip of the rod. Neither is he capable of recognizing how essential to success it is for him to know whether he is in a fit condition to be susceptible to the action of the *corpuscles* which are thrown off from the objects toward which the rod inclines."

"I do not deny that there are cheats who profess belief in the rod, and put it to too many uses, just as quacks, with a good remedy for a special ailment, hold themselves up to contempt by wishing to palm it off as a cure-all. To this I add that people will be found who, endowed with greater and more delicate sensibility, will possess still more abundantly than he (Jacques Aymar) the faculty of discovering springs of water, metallic veins, and hidden treasure, as well as thieves and escaped murderers. We have already received tidings from Lyons of a youth of eighteen, who surpasses by a long way Jacques Aymar. And anyone can see in Paris to-day, at the residence of Mons. Geoffrey, late sheriff of that city, a young man who discovers gold buried underground by experiencing violent tremors the moment that he walks over it."

M. de Vallemont has no sympathy for those credulous students of natural philosophy who have brought the science into disrepute. They will scoff at the divining rod and yet swallow the grossest frauds without so much as blinking. He proceeds to give an illustration, and it will bear translating because surely it unfolds a unique yarn of buried treasure and has all the charm of novelty.

"Upon this subject there is nothing more entertaining than that which took place at the end of the last century, with regard to a boy who journeyed through several towns exhibiting a golden tooth which he declared had grown in the usual way.

"In the year 1595, towards Easter, a rumor spread that there was in the village of Weildorst in Silesia, Bohemia, a child seven years of age who had lost all his teeth, and that in the place of the last molar a gold tooth had appeared. No story ever created such a stir. Scholars took it up. In a short time, doctors and philosophers came forward to gain knowledge and to pass judgment, as though it were a case worthy of their consideration. The first to distinguish himself was *Jacobus Horstius*, Professor of Medicine in the University of Helmstad. This doctor, in a paper which he caused to be printed, demonstrated that this golden tooth was partly a work of nature and partly miraculous; and he declared that in whatever light one viewed it, it was manifestly a consolation sent from above to the Christians of Bohemia, on whom the Turks were then inflicting the worst barbarities.

"*Martinus Rulandus* published simultaneously with Horstius the story of the golden tooth. It is true that two years later *Johannes Ingolsteterus* refuted the story of Rulandus, but the latter in the same year, 1597, not in the least discouraged, defended his work against the attacks of Ingolsteterus.

SPOOKY TREASURE TROVES

"*Andreas Libavius* then entered the lists, and published a book in which he recounted what had been said for and against the golden tooth. This gave rise to great disputes concerning a matter which ultimately proved to be a somewhat clumsy deception. The child was taken to Breslau, where everybody hastened to see so wonderful a novelty. They brought him before a number of doctors, assembled in great perplexity to examine the famous golden tooth. Amongst them was *Christophorus Rhumbaumius*, a professor of medicine, who was most anxious to see before believing.

"First of all, a goldsmith, wishing to satisfy himself that the tooth was of gold, applied to it his touch-stone, and the line left on the stone appeared, to the naked eye, to be in real gold, but on the application of aqua fortis to this line, every trace disappeared, and a part of the swindle was exposed. Christophorus Khumbaumius, an intelligent and skillful man, on examining the tooth more closely, perceived in it a little hole, and, inserting a probe, found that it was simply a sheet of copper probably washed with gold. He could with ease have removed the copper covering had not the trickster, who was taking the child from town to town, opposed it, complaining bitterly of the injury that was being done him by thus depriving him of the chance of taking money from the curious and the credulous.

"The swindler and child disappeared, and no one knows to this day exactly what became of them. But because learned men have been duped now and then, that is no reason for perpetual doubt.... and although the story of the golden tooth be false, we should be wrong capriciously to reject that of the hazel rod which has become so famous."

Having extinguished the skeptics, as one snuffs a candle, by means of this admirable tale of the golden tooth, the learned author asserts that "it must denote great ignorance of France, and even of books, never to have heard of the divining rod. For I can say with certainty that I have met quite by chance, both in Paris and the provinces, more than fifty persons who have used this simple instrument in order to find water, precious metals and hidden treasure, and in whose hands it has actually turned. 'It is more reasonable,' says Father Malebranche, 'to believe one man who says, *I have seen*, than a million others who talk at random.'

"It is somewhat difficult to determine exactly the period at which the divining rod first came into use. I have discovered no reference to it by writers previous to the middle of the Fifteenth century. It is frequently referred to in the Testament de Basile Valentin, a Benedictine monk who flourished about 1490,[2] and I observe that he speaks of it in a way which might lead one to suppose that the use of this rod was known before that period.

"Might we venture to advance the theory that the Divine Rod was known and used nearly two thousand years ago?[3] Are we to count for naught Cicero's illusion to divination by means of the rod, at the end of the first book of his 'De

SPOOKY TREASURE TROVES

Officiis,' 'If all that we need for our nourishment and clothing comes to us, as people say, by means of some divine rod, then each of us should relinquish public affairs and devote all his time to the study.'

"Varro, according to Vetranius Maurus, left a satire called 'Virgula Divina,' which was often quoted by Nonius Marcellus in his book entitled *de Proprietate sermonum*. But what serves to convince me that Cicero had in his mind the hazel twig, and that it was known at that period, is the passage he quotes from Ennius, in the first half of his 'De Divinatione,' in which the poet, scoffing at those who for a drachma profess to teach the art of discovering hidden treasure, says to them, 'I will give it you with pleasure, but it will be paid out of the treasure found according to your method.'"

And so this seventeenth century Frenchman, his manner as wise as a treeful of owls, drones along from one musty authority to another in defense of the mystic powers of the divining rod. He marshals them in batteries of heavy artillery—names of scholars and alleged scientists who made a great noise in their far-off times when the world was younger and more given to wonderment. The discussions that raged among those Dry-as-dusts have interest to-day because the doctrine of the divining rod is still vigorously alive and its rites are practiced in every civilized country. Call it what you will, a curiously surviving superstition or a natural mystery, the "dowser" with his forked twig of hazel or willow still commands a large following of believers and his services are sought, in hundreds of instances every year, to discover springs of water and hidden treasure. Learned societies have not done with debating the case, and the literature of the phenomenon is in process of making. No one, however, has contributed more formidable ammunition than M. de Vallemont, who could discharge such broadsides as this:

"Father Roberti, who writes in the strongest terms against the divining rod, nevertheless admits, in the heat of the conflict, that the indications on which the most scholarly of men set to work to discover mineral soil are all more or less unreliable, and result in endless mistakes.

"'What!' says this Jesuit father, 'is it possible that people are willing to attribute greater knowledge and judgment to a rough and lifeless piece of wood than to hundreds of enlightened men? They survey fields, mountains and valleys, devoting scrupulous attention to everything that comes under their notice; not a trace of metal do they discover; and if they happen to suspect that there might be such a thing at a certain spot, they confess that their surmise may be quite unfounded, and that every day they learn to their sorrow, after infinite labor and suspense, that their signs are altogether deceptive.

"'Such a one as Goclenius,[4] however, armed with his fork, will wander over the same ground, and led by that instrument, clearer-sighted than the wisest of men, will infallibly come to a standstill over treasures hidden in the earth. Exca-

SPOOKY TREASURE TROVES

vations will be made at the spot indicated and the treasures will be laid bare. *My dear reader, do you wish me to speak candidly? It is the Devil who is guiding Goclenius.'"*

In this emphatic statement of the devout French priest of two centuries ago is to be traced the still lingering superstition of an infernal partnership in buried treasure. It is to be found in scores of coastwise legends of pirates' gold (no Kidd story is properly decorated without its guardian demon or menacing ghost), and the divining rod, handed down from an age of witchcraft, necromancy, and black magic, deserves a place in the kit of every well-equipped treasure seeker. Sober, hard-headed Scotchmen from Glasgow employ a Yorkshire "dowser" to search for the treasure lost in the *Florencia* galleon in Tobermory Bay, and he shows them, and they are convinced, that he can tell whether it be gold, or silver, or copper, which exerts its occult influence over his divining rod.[5] This happens in the year 1906, mind you, but our ardent investigator, M. de Vallemont, was writing two hundred years before:

"But, with the divining rod, it is possible to distinguish what metal is contained in the mine towards which the rod inclines. For if a gold coin be placed in each hand, the rod will only turn in the direction of gold, because it becomes impregnated with the *corpuscles* or minute particles of gold. If silver be treated in the same way, the rod will only dip towards silver. This, at any rate, is what we are told by those who pride themselves on their successful use of the rod."

John Stears, the expert diviner, who was recently employed at Tobermory Bay, is more frequently retained to search for water than for lost treasure. This is his vocation and he takes it seriously enough, as his own words indicate:[6]

"The power is not in the rod, but in the user, the rod acting as an indicator, and rising when over a stream. By moving the arms as I proceed, I can keep on the edge of an underground stream, for the apex descends when the rod is not over the stream. I have several times followed a line of water down to the shore, being rowed out in the bay, and found the water boiling up mixed with land weeds. At such a spot there is no movement of the rod except over the course of the stream. It is almost impossible to describe the sensation caused whilst using the rod; it is sometimes like a current of electricity going through the arms and legs. On raising one foot from the ground the rod descends. The effect produced when walking is that the rod has the appearance of a fishing rod when the fish is hooked,— the rod seems alive. Move it clear of the line of water and down it goes.

"Very few people have the gift of finding water or minerals, and not many rods will do, but those that have thorns on them are all right. In the tropics I used acacia, and in southern Europe the holly or orange. The use of the rod is exhausting. If I have been at it a few hours, the power gradually gets less. A rest and some sandwiches produce fresh power, and I can start again.

SPOOKY TREASURE TROVES

"I think the friction of the water against the rock underground must cause some electric current, for if the person using the rod stands on a piece of glass, india-rubber, or other insulating material, all power leaves him.

"In Cashmere, the rod is used before a well is sunk, and when the French army went to Tonkin, they used the rod for finding drinking water at their camps, as they feared the wells were poisoned."

If the divining rod is able to fathom the secrets of underground water channels, it must be as potent in the case of buried treasure. Several years ago, the claims of the modern "dowsers" were investigated by no less an authority than Professor W. F. Barrett, holding the chair of Experimental Physics in the Royal College of Science for Ireland. The results were presented to the Society of Psychical Research and published in two volumes of its proceedings. He said in his introductory pages:

"At first sight, few subjects appear to be so unworthy of serious notice and so utterly beneath scientific investigation as that of the divining rod. To most men of science, the reported achievements of the diviner are on a par with the rogueries of Sir Walter Scott's 'Dousterswivel.' That anyone with the smallest scientific training should think it worth his while to devote a considerable amount of time and labor to an enquiry into the alleged evidence on behalf of the 'rod' will appear to my scientific friends about as sensible as if he spent his time investigating fortune-telling or any other relic of superstitious folly. Nor was my own prejudice against the subject any less than that of others. For I confess that it was with great reluctance, and even repugnance, that some six years ago, yielding to the earnest request of the Council of the Society for Psychical Research, I began an investigation of the matter, hoping, however, in my ignorance, that a few weeks work would enable me to relegate it 'to a limbo, large and broad, since called the Paradise of Fools.'" In the summing-up of his exhaustive investigations, Professor Barrett committed himself to these conclusions:

"1. That the twisting of the forked twig, or so-called divining rod, is due to involuntary muscular action on the part of the dowser.

"2. That this is the result of an ideo-motor action; any idea or suggestion, whether conscious, or sub-conscious, that is associated in the dowser's mind with the twisting of the twig, will cause it to turn apparently spontaneously in his hands.

"3. Hence the divining rod has been used in the search for all sorts of things, from criminals to water, its action being precisely similar to the '*pendule explorateur*,' i.e., a small suspended ball or ring depending by a thread from the hand.

"4. Dismissing, therefore, the mere twisting of the forked rod, the question at issue is, how is the suggestion derived by the dowser that starts this involuntary muscular action? Here the answer is a very complex and difficult one.

SPOOKY TREASURE TROVES

"5. Careful and critical examination shows that certain dowsers (not all in whose hands the twig turns) have a genuine facility or faculty for finding underground water beyond that possessed by ordinary well-sinkers.

"Part of this success is due (1st) to shrewd observation and the conscious and unconscious detection of the surface signs of underground water. (2nd) A residue, say ten per cent or fifteen per cent of their successes cannot be so explained, nor can these be accounted for by chance nor lucky hits, the proportion being larger than the doctrine of probabilities would account for.

"This residue no known scientific explanation can account for. Personally, I believe the explanation will be found in some faculty akin to clairvoyance; but as the science of to-day does not recognize such a faculty, I prefer to leave the explanation to future inquirers, and to throw on the skeptic the task of disproving my assertions, and giving his own explanations."

This unexplained residue, "akin to clairvoyance," as admitted by a scientist of to-day who wears a top-hat and rides in taxi-cabs, clothes the divining rod in the same alluring mystery which so puzzled those childlike and credulous observers of remote and misty centuries. The Abbé de Vallemont, writing in 1697, found the problem hardly more difficult to explain than does this Professor of Experimental Physics in the Royal College of Science. The wise men of the seventeenth century strove hard to comprehend the "unexplained residue," each after his own fashion.

Michael Mayerus, in his book entitled *Verum Inventum, hoc est, Munera Germanæ*, claimed that the world was indebted to Germany for the invention of gunpowder, and stated that the first wood-charcoal used in its manufacture, mixed with sulphur and saltpeter, was made from the hazel tree. This lead him to refer to the sympathy existing between hazel wood and metals, and to add that for this reason the divining rod was made of this particular wood, which was peculiarly adapted to the discovery of hidden gold and silver.

Philip Melanchthon, 1497-1560, famously learned in Natural Philosophy and Theology, discoursed on Sympathy, of which he recognized six degrees in Nature, and in the second of these he named that sympathy or affinity which is found to exist between plants and minerals. He used as an illustration the forked hazel twig employed by those who search after gold, silver, and other precious metals. He attributed the movement of the rod to the metallic juices which nourish the hazel tree in the soil, and he was therefore convinced that its peculiar manifestations were wholly sympathetic and according to natural law.

Neuheusius spoke of the divining rod as a marvel from the bounteous hands of Nature, and exhorted men to use it in the search for mineral wealth and concealed treasure. Enchanted with this insignificant-looking instrument, he exclaimed: "What shall I say now concerning the Divine Rod, which is but a simple

SPOOKY TREASURE TROVES

hazel twig, and yet possesses the power of divination in the discovery of metals, be that power derived from mutual sympathy, from some secret astral influence, or from some still more powerful source. Let us take courage and use this salutary rod, so that, after having withdrawn the metals from the abode of the dead, we may seek in the metals themselves some such faculty for divination as we find in the hazel."

Rudolph Glauber, who made many experiments with the rod, had this to say of it: "Metallic veins can also be discovered by means of the hazel rod. It is used for that purpose, and I speak after long experience. Melt the metals under a certain constellation, and make a ball of them pierced through the middle; thrust into the hole thus formed a young sprig of hazel, of the same year, with no branches. Carry this rod straight in front of you over the places where metals are believed to be, and when the rod dips and the ball inclines towards the soil, you may rest assured that metal lies beneath. *And as this method is based on natural law, it should undoubtedly be used in preference to any other.*"

Egidius Gustman, supposedly a Rosicrucian friar, and author of a work entitled *La Revelation de la Divine Majeste*, devoted a chapter to the study of the question "whether hazel rods may be used without sin in the search for metals." He reached the conclusion that there could be nothing unchristian in their employment for the discovery of gold and silver, provided neither words, ceremonies, nor enchantments be called into requisition, and that it be done "in the fear and under the eyes of God."

M. de Vallemont quotes as his final authority the Abbé Gallet, Grand Penitentiary of the Church of Carpentras. He considers that the Abbé's high position in the church, and his deep knowledge of physics and mathematics, should lend great weight to his opinion concerning the divining rod. He therefore requests a mutual friend to put to the Abbé this question, "Is not the inclination of the rod due to sleight of hand or something in which the Devil may play a part?" The Abbé returns a long reply in Latin, which de Vallemont is pleased to translate and print in his book. It opens thus:

"Monsieur l'Abbé Gallet declares in his own hand that the rod turns in the direction of water and of metals; that he has used it several times with admirable success in order to find water-courses and hidden treasure, and that he is far from agreeing with those who maintain that there is in it any trickery or diabolical influence."

William Cookworthy, who flourished in England about 1750, was a famous exponent of the divining rod, and he laid down a most elaborate schedule of directions for its use in finding hidden treasure or veins of gold or silver. In conclusion, he sagely observed:[7]

"I would remark that 'tis plain a person may be very easily deceived in making experiments with this instrument, there being, in metallic countries, vast quantities of attracting stones scattered through the earth. The attractions of springs continually occurring; and even about town, bits of iron, pins, etc. may easily be the means of deceiving the unwary. For as quantity makes no alteration in the strength, but only in the wideness of the attraction, a pin under one foot would stop the attraction of any quantity of every other sort, but gold, which might be under the other.... Whoever, therefore, will make experiments need be very cautious in exploring the ground, and be sure not to be too anxious, for which reason I would advise him, in case of debates, not to be too warm and lay wagers on the success, but, unruffled, leave the unbelievers to their infidelity, and permit time and Providence to convince people of the reality of the thing."

If one would know how to fashion the divining rod to give most surely the magic results, he has only to consult "The Shepherd's Calendar and Countryman's Companion" in which it is affirmed:

"Cut a hazel wand forked at the upper end like a Y. Peel off the rind and dry it in a moderate heat; then steep it in the juice of wake-robin or night-shade, and cut the single lower end sharp, and where you suppose any rich mine or treasure is near, place a piece of the same metal you conceive is hid in the earth to the tip of one of the forks by a hair or very fine silk or thread, and do the like to the other end. Pitch the sharp single end lightly to the ground at the going down of the sun, the moon being at the increase, and in the morning at sunrise, by a natural sympathy, you will find the metal inclining, as it were, pointing to the place where the other is hid."

According to the author of the modern book, "The Divining Rod and its Uses,"[8] "it is curious to note that about one hundred years ago there was considerable excitement in the north of England owing to the remarkable powers possessed by a lady of quality in the district, this being no other than Judith Noel, afterwards Lady Milbank, the mother of Lady Byron. Miss Noel discovered her marvelous faculty when a mere girl, yet so afraid was she of being ridiculed that she would not publicly declare it, thinking she might be called a witch, or that she would not get a husband. Lady Milbank afterwards overcame her prejudice and used the rod on many occasions with considerable success."

About 1880, a certain Madame Caillavah of Paris was at the height of her fame as a high-priestess of the divining rod, and her pretensions with respect to finding buried treasure quite set France by the ears. She was besought to discover, among other hoards, the twelve golden effigies taken from the Saint Chapelle during the Revolution and hidden underground for safe-keeping; the treasure of King Stanislaus, buried outside the gates of Nancy; and the vast accumulations of the Petits Pères, or Begging Friars. The French Government took Madame seriously and permitted her to operate by means of an agreement which

SPOOKY TREASURE TROVES

should insure a proper division of the spoils. There could be no better authority for the singular exploits of Madame Caillavah than the columns of *The London Times* which stated in the issue of October 6th, 1882:

"A certain Madame Caillavah, who in spite of a long experience does not yet bring the credentials of success, is said to be exploring the pavement of St. Denis[9] in search of buried treasures. The French Government likes partnerships, conventions, and co-dominions, and it insists on what almost amounts to the lion's share of the spoil. Nevertheless, a good many people have been found to invest largely in the enterprise, which will cost something if it comes to actual digging. The investigation itself is not in the nature of an excavation, nor is it with the spade or the pickax, unless, indeed, it should turn out that it is a veritable gold mine under St. Denis, when the royal monuments may be thankful if even dynamite be not freely resorted to.

"The divining rod is to lead the way.... At the beginning of this century France was one vast field of buried treasure. The silver coin was so bulky that £200 of our money would be a hundredweight to carry, and £1,000 would be a cartload. So it was buried in the hope of a speedy return. The fugitive owners perished or died in exile. Their successors on the spot came upon one hoard after another, and said nothing about it. That they did find the money and put it in circulation, there could be no doubt, for it was impossible to take a handful of silver forty years ago without one or two pieces showing a green rust in place of a white luster. This was the result of long interment, and calculations were made as to the likely total of the exhumation.

"But one then heard nothing of the divining rod, not at least in cities, in cathedrals, among the sepulchers of kings, and in the department of State. Our first wish is that the experiment may be quite successful. It would be so very surprising; quite a new sensation, much wanted in these days. But there would be something more than a passing sensation. Even a moderate success would discover to us a means of support and a mode of existence far easier and pleasanter than any yet known. We should only have to walk about, very slowly with the orthodox rod, properly held and handled, keeping our attention duly fixed on the desirableness of a little more money, and we should find it springing up, as it were, from the ground before us....

"The French Minister of Fine Arts need not be deterred,—nay, it is plain he is not deterred,—by the scruples that interrupted the investigations of the great Linné and stopped him on the very threshold of verification. On one of his travels his secretary brought him a divining wand, with an account of its powers. Linné hid a purse containing one hundred ducats under a *ranunculus*[10] in the garden. He then took a number of witnesses who experimented with the wand all over the ground, but without success. Indeed, they trod the ground so completely that Linné could not find where he had buried the purse.

"They then brought in the 'man with the wand' and he immediately pointed out the right direction, and then the very spot where the money lay. Linné's remark was that another experiment would convert him to the wand. But he resolved not to be converted, and therefore did not repeat the experiment. Possibly feeling that it was neither science nor religion, he would have nothing to do with any other conceivable alternative."

In *The London Times* of November 3rd, 1882, there was published under the head of "Foreign Intelligence," the following dispatch which may be regarded as a tragic sequel of the foregoing paragraphs:

"The titular Archbishop of Lepanto, who is the head of the Chapter of St. Denis, has addressed a remonstrance to the Government against the renewed divining rod experiments on which Madame Caillavah is insisting under her compact with the State for a division of the spoils. He dwells on the absurdity of the theory that on the Revolutionary seizure of 1793 the Benedictines could have concealed a portion of their treasures, of which printed lists existed and the most valuable of which were notoriously confiscated.

"As to the notion of an earlier secretion of treasures, the memory of which had perished, he urges that St. Denis having belonged to the Benedictines from its very erection, no motive for secretion existed and had there been any, the tradition or record of it would have been preserved, while at least four successive reconstructions would certainly have brought any such treasure to light. The mob of 1793, moreover, actually ransacked the vaults, after the removal of the bodies, for the very purpose of discovering such secret hoards. St. Denis, in short, is the very last place in the world for treasure-trove, and as for the central crypt, which the sorceress claims to break into, it was rifled in 1793 when it contained fifty-three bodies which left no vacant space.

"The Archbishop need scarcely have troubled himself with this demonstration. Public ridicule has made an end of the project, and even if Madame Caillavah carried out her threat of a lawsuit, no tribunal would hold her entitled to carry on excavations *ad libitum*, with a risk, perhaps, of herself and her workmen being buried under the ruins of the finest of French cathedrals. In debating the Fine Arts Department estimates, M. Delattre, Deputy for St. Denis, animadverted on the divining rod experiments in the cathedral. M. Tirard replied that the Government had had no share in this ridiculous business. The treaty with the sorceress was concluded in January, 1881, by an official who had since been superannuated, but was not acted upon till she could deposit two hundred francs guarantee, and as soon as he himself heard of the experiments he put a peremptory stop to them.

"It is important here to observe that it afterwards transpired that the object of Madame Caillavah's lawsuit was not so much to obtain damages for any breach of contract as to vindicate her private and public character and her professional reputation as a so-called 'diviner' from the odium, scorn, and defamation which the repudiation of the treaty so universally entailed. The sad result of all this was that the unfortunate and sensitive lady was not able to withstand the opprobrium that was heaped upon her, nor 'the ridicule that made an end of her project.' This maligned and misunderstood lady (who, as expressly stated, 'had no doubt brought a good pedigree with her') after a few months of sorrow, and conscious of her rectitude, at length succumbed and, as reported, ultimately died of a 'broken heart.'"

[1] "*Corpuscular philosophy*, that which attempts to account for the phenomena of nature, by the motion, figure, rest, position, etc., of the minute particles of matter."—*Webster's Dictionary*.

[2] Andrew Lang writes in a chapter on the divining rod in *Custom and Myth*:

"The great authority for the modern history of the divining rod is a work published by M. Chevreul in Paris in 1854. M. Chevreul, probably with truth, regarded the wand as much on a par with the turning tables which, in 1854, attracted a good deal of attention.... M. Chevreul could find no earlier book on the twig than the *Testament du Frere*, Basile Valentin, a holy man who flourished (the twig) about 1413, but whose treatise is possibly apocryphal. According to Basile Valentin, the twig was regarded with awe by ignorant laboring men, which is still true."

[3] "And Jacob took him rods of green poplar, and of the hazel and chestnut tree; and pilled white strakes in them, and made the white appear which was in the rods.

"And he set the rods which he had pilled before the flocks in the gutters in the watering troughs when the flocks came to drink, that they should conceive when they came to drink." (Genesis xxx, 37-38.)

"And the Lord said unto Moses, Go on before the people, and take with thee of the elders of Israel; and thy rod, wherewith thou smotest the river, take in thy hand, and go.

"Behold, I will stand before thee there upon the rock in Horeb; and thou shalt smite the rock, and there shall come water out of it, that the people may drink. And Moses did so in the sight of the elders of Israel." (Exodus xvii, 5-6.)

[4] Goclenius was a diviner who also professed to make "magnetic cures."

[5] See chapter 9, p. 218.

[6] Quoted from the volume, *Water Divining* (London, 1902).

[7] The Gentleman's Magazine (London, 1752).

[8] By Young and Robertson (London, 1894).

[9] For centuries the home of the Benedictine Order.

[10] In plain English, flowers of the buttercup family.

SPOOKY TREASURE TROVES

CHAPTER XV
SUNDRY PIRATES AND THEIR BOOTY

"Seven years were gone and over, Wild Roger came again,He spoke of forays and of frays upon the Spanish Main,And he had stores of gold galore, and silks and satins fine,And flasks and casks of Malvoisie, and precious Gascon wine;Rich booties had he brought, he said, across the Western wave.But Roger was the same man still,—he scorned his brother's prayers—He called his crew, away he flew, and on those foreign shores,Got killed in some outlandish place,—they called it the Eyesores."(*Ingoldsby Legends.*)

The popular delusion that pirates found nothing better to do with their plunder than to bury it, like so many thrifty depositors in savings banks, clashes with what is known of the habits and temperaments of many of the most industrious rovers under the black flag. By way of a concluding survey of the matter, let us briefly examine the careers of divers pirates of sorts and try to ascertain what they did with their gold and whether it be plausible to assume that they had any of it left to bury. Of course, romance and legend are up in arms at the presumption that any well-regulated and orthodox pirate omitted the business with the pick and shovel and the chart with the significant crosses and compass bearings, but the prosaic facts of history are due to have their innings.

For example, there was Jean Lafitte who amassed great riches in the pursuit of his profession and whose memory has inspired innumerable treasure-seeking expeditions in the Gulf of Mexico and along the coast of Central America. After ravaging the commerce of the East India Company in the waters of the Far East, he set up his headquarters on an island among the bayous and cypress swamps of that desolate region below New Orleans that is known as Barrataria. A deep-water pass ran to the open sea, only two leagues distant, and on the shores of the sheltered harbor of Grand Terre, Lafitte organized the activities of a large number of pirates and smugglers and formed a flourishing colony; a corporation, in its way, for disposing of the merchandise filched from honest shipping. These marauders posed as privateers, and some of them had French and other commissions for sailing against the Spanish, but there was a great deal of laxity in such trifles as living up to the letter of the law.

At Grand Terre, Lafitte and his people sold the cargoes of their prizes by public auction, and from all parts of lower Louisiana bargain-hunters flocked to Barrataria to deal in this tempting traffic. The goods thus purchased were smuggled into New Orleans and other nearby ports, and Lafitte's piratical enterprises became so notorious that the government of the United States sent an expedition against him in 1814, commanded by Commodore Patterson. At Grand Terre he found a settlement so great in force and numbers as to constitute a small kingdom ruled by Lafitte. The commodore described the encounter in a letter to the Secretary of War, and said in part:

"At half-past eight o'clock A.M. on the 16th of June, made the Island of Barrataria, and discovered a number of vessels in the harbor some of which showed the colors of Carthagena. At two o'clock, perceived the pirates forming their vessels, ten in number, including prizes, into a line of battle near the entrance of the harbor, and making every preparation to offer battle. At ten o'clock, wind light and variable, formed the order of battle with six gun boats and the *Sea Horse* tender, mounting one six pounder and fifteen men, and a launch mounting one twelve pound carronade; the schooner *Carolina* drawing too much water to cross the bar.

"At half-past ten o'clock, perceived several smokes along the coasts as signals, and at the same time a white flag hoisted on board a schooner at the fort, an American flag at the mainmast head, and a Carthagenian flag (under which the pirates cruise) at her topping-lift. I replied with a white flag at my main. At eleven o'clock discovered that the pirates had fired two of their best schooners; hauled down my white flag and made the signal for battle; hoisting a large flag bearing the words *Pardon for Deserters*, having heard there was a number on shore from our army and navy. At a quarter past eleven o'clock, two gun-boats grounded, and were passed, agreeably to my previous orders, by the other four which entered the harbor, manned by my barge and the boats belonging to the grounded vessels, and proceeded in. To my great disappointment, I perceived that the pirates had abandoned their vessels and were flying in all directions. I immediately sent the launch and two barges with small boats in pursuit of them.

"At meridian, took possession of all their vessels in the harbor, consisting of six schooners and one felucca, cruisers and prizes of the pirates, one brig, a prize, and two armed schooners under the Carthagenian flag, both in the line of battle with the armed vessels of the pirates, and apparently with an intention to aid them in any resistance they might make against me, as their crews were at quarters, tompions out of their guns, and matches lighted. Colonel Ross (with seventy-five infantry) at the same time landed and took possession of their establishment on

SPOOKY TREASURE TROVES

shore, consisting of about forty houses of different sizes, badly constructed and thatched with palmetto leaves.

"When I perceived the enemy forming their vessels into a line of battle, I felt confident from their number, and very advantageous position, and their number of men, that they would have fought me. Their not doing so I regret, for had they, I should have been able more effectually to destroy or make prisoners of them and their leaders. The enemy had mounted on their vessels twenty pieces of cannon of different caliber, and as I have since learned, had from eight hundred to one thousand men of all nations and colors."

Notwithstanding this unfriendly visit, Lafitte was a patriot after his own fashion and during the War of 1812 his sympathies were with the American forces. In September, 1814, Captain Lockyer, of a British naval vessel, anchored in the pass at Barrataria, and delivered to Lafitte a packet of documents comprising a proclamation addressed to the inhabitants of Louisiana by Colonel Edward Nichalls, commander of the English forces on the coast of Florida, a letter from him to Lafitte, and another from the Honorable W. H. Percy, captain of the sloop-of-war *Hermes*. The upshot of all this was a proposal that Lafitte enter the British naval service in command of a frigate, and if he would take his men with him he should have thirty thousand dollars, payable at Pensacola.

Lafitte refused the tempting bait, and two days later sent the following letter to Governor Claiborne of the state of Louisiana:

BARRATARIA, Sept. 4th. 1814.
"*Sir:*

"In the firm persuasion that the choice made of you to fill the office of first magistrate of this state, was dictated by the esteem of your fellow citizens, and was conferred on merit, I confidently address you on an affair on which may depend the safety of this country. I offer to restore to this state several citizens who perhaps in your eyes have lost that sacred title. I offer you them, however, such as you could wish to find them, ready to exert their utmost efforts in defense of the country. This point of Louisiana which I occupy is of great importance in the present crisis. I tender my services to defend it; and the only reward I ask is that a stop be put to the proscription against me and my adherents, by an act of oblivion, for all that has been done hitherto. I am the stray sheep wishing to return to the fold. If you are thoroughly acquainted with the nature of my offenses, I shall appear to you much less guilty, and still worthy to discharge the duties of a good citizen. I have never sailed under any flag but that of the republic of Carthagena, and my vessels are perfectly regular in that respect. If I could have brought my lawful prizes into the ports of this state, I should not have employed the illicit means that have caused me to be proscribed. I decline saying more on the subject, until I have the honor of your Excellency's answer, which I am persuaded can be dictated only by wisdom. Should your answer not be favorable to my desires, I declare to you that I will instantly leave the country, to avoid the imputation of having coöperated towards an invasion of this point, which cannot fail to take place, and to rest secure in the acquittal of my conscience.

"I have the honor to be"Your Excellency's, etc."J. LAFITTE."

This highly commendable document so favorably impressed Governor Claiborne that he offered Lafitte safe conduct to come to New Orleans and meet General Andrew Jackson. After a conference of this trio, the following order was issued:

"The Governor of Louisiana, being informed that many individuals implicated in the offenses heretofore committed against the United States at Barrataria, express a willingness at the present crisis to enroll themselves and march against the enemy:

"He does hereby invite them to join the standard of the United States and is authorized to say, should their conduct in the field meet the approbation of the Major General, that that officer will unite with the Governor in a request to the President of the United States, to extend to each and every individual so marching and acting, a free and full pardon."

At the battle of New Orleans, on January 8th, 1815, Lafitte and his lieutenant, Dominique, commanded a large force of what Jackson called the "Corsairs of Barrataria," and defended their breastworks and served their batteries with such desperate gallantry that they nobly earned the promised pardons. These were granted by President James Madison on February 6th, and he took occasion to say:

"But it has since been represented that the offenders have manifested a sincere repentance; that they have abandoned the prosecution of the worst cause for the support of the best, and particularly, that they have exhibited in the defense of New Orleans, unequivocal traits of courage and fidelity. Offenders, who have refused to become the associates of the enemy in the war, upon the most seductive terms of invitation; and who have aided to repel his hostile invasion of the territory of the United States, can no longer be considered as objects of punishment, but as objects of a generous forgiveness."

The foregoing evidence is ample to prove that Lafitte had no occasion to bury any of his treasure, but like Kidd along the New England coast, legend has been busy with his name and is blind to the facts of record. He later made a settlement on the island of Galveston and his history becomes obscured. One version is that the love of the old trade was in his blood, and he fitted out a large privateer to have a farewell fling with fortune. A British sloop-of-war overhauled him in the Gulf of Mexico, hailed him as a pirate, and opened fire. The engagement was

SPOOKY TREASURE TROVES

terrifically hot, and Jean Lafitte was killed at the head of his men while resisting a boarding party.

Take next the case of that noted pirate Captain Avery "whose adventures were the subject of general conversation in Europe." He captured one of the Great Mogul's ships laden with treasure; it was reported that he had wedded a daughter of that magnificent ruler and was about to found a new monarchy; that he gave commissions in his own name to the captains of his ships and the commanders of his forces and was acknowledged by them as their prince. With sixteen stout fellows of his own kidney, he ran off with a ship in which he had sailed from England as mate, and steered for Madagascar in the year 1715. "The Pirates' Own Book" tells the story of Captain Avery, his treasure, and the melancholy fate of both, and the author is, as a rule, such a well-informed historian of these matters, that he should be allowed to set it forth in his own words, which are framed in a style admirably befitting the theme.

"Near the river Indus the man at the mast-head espied a sail upon which they gave chase; as they came nearer to her they discovered that she was a tall vessel, and might turn out to be an East Indiaman. She, however, proved a better prize; for when they fired at her, she hoisted Mogul colors, and seemed to stand upon her defense. Avery only cannonaded at a distance, when some of the men began to suspect he was not the hero they had supposed. His sloops, however, attacked, the one on the bow, and another upon the quarter of the ship, and so boarded her. She then struck her colors. She was one of the Great Mogul's own ships, and there were in her several of the greatest persons in his court, among whom, it was said, was one of his daughters going upon a pilgrimage to Mecca; and they were carrying with them rich offerings to present at the shrine of Mahomet. It is a well-known fact that the people of the East travel with great magnificence, so that these had along with them all their slaves and attendants, with a large quantity of vessels of gold and silver, and immense sums of money to defray their expenses by land. The spoil, therefore, which they received from that ship was almost incalculable.

"Our adventurers made the best of their way back to Madagascar, intending to make that place the deposit of all their treasure, to build a small fort, and to keep always a few men there for its protection. Avery, however, disconcerted this plan, and rendered it altogether unnecessary. While steering their course, he sent a boat to each of the sloops, requesting that the chiefs would come on board his ship to hold a conference. He suggested to them the necessity of securing the property which they had acquired, and observed that the main difficulty was to get it safe on shore; adding that if either of the sloops should be attacked alone, they would not be able to make any great resistance. That, for his part, his ship was so strong, so well manned, and such a swift-sailing vessel, that he did not think it possible for any other ship to take or overcome her. Accordingly, he proposed that all their treasure should be sealed up in three chests,—that each of the captains should have a key, and that they should not be opened until all were present;—that the chests should be then put on board his ship and afterwards lodged in some safe place on land.

"This proposal seemed so reasonable, and so much for the common good that it was agreed to without hesitation, and all the treasure was deposited in three chests and carried to Avery's ship. The weather being favorable, they remained all three in company during that and the next day; meanwhile Avery, tampering with his men, suggested that they had now on board what was sufficient to make them all happy; 'and what,' continued he, 'should hinder us from going to some country where we are not known, and living on shore all the rest of our days in plenty!' They soon understood his hint, and all readily consented to deceive the men of the sloops, and fly with all the booty. This they effected during the darkness of the following night. The reader may easily conjecture what were the feelings and indignation of the other two crews in the morning when they discovered that Avery had made off with all their property.

"Avery and his men hastened towards America, and being strangers in that country, agreed to divide the booty, to change their names, and each separately to take up his residence and live in affluence and honor.... Avery had been careful to conceal the greater part of the jewels and other valuable articles, so that his own riches were immense. Arriving at Boston, he was almost resolved to settle there, but as the greater part of his wealth consisted of diamonds, he was apprehensive that he could not dispose of them at that place, without being taken up as a pirate. Upon reflection, therefore, he resolved to sail for Ireland, and in a short time arrived in the northern part of that kingdom, and his men dispersed into several places. Some of them obtained the pardon of King William and settled in that country.

"The wealth of Avery, however, now proved of small service and occasioned him great uneasiness. He could not offer his diamonds for sale in that country without being suspected. Considering, therefore, what was best to be done, he thought there might be some person in Bristol he could venture to trust. Upon this he resolved, and going to Devonshire, sent to one of his friends to meet him at a town called Bideford. When he had unbosomed himself to him and other pretended friends, they agreed that the safest plan was to put his effects in the hands of some wealthy merchants, and no inquiry would be made how they came by them.

"One of these friends told him he was acquainted with some who were very fit for the purpose, and if he would allow them a handsome commission, they would do the business faithfully. Avery liked the proposal, particularly as he could think of no other way of managing this matter, since he could not appear to act for himself. Accordingly, the merchants paid Avery a visit at Bideford, where after strong protestations of honor and integrity, he delivered them his effects, consisting of diamonds and some vessels of gold. After giving him a little money for his present subsistence, they departed.

"He changed his name and lived quietly at Bideford, so that no notice was taken of him. In a short time his money was all spent, and he heard nothing from his merchants though he wrote to them repeatedly. At last they sent him a small supply, but it was not sufficient to pay his debts. In short, the remittances they sent him were so trifling that he could with difficulty exist. He therefore determined to go privately to Bristol, and have an interview with the merchants himself,—where instead of money, he met with a mortifying repulse. For when he desired them to come to an account with him, they silenced him by threatening to disclose his character; the merchants thus proving themselves as good pirates on land as he was at sea.

"Whether he was frightened by these menaces, or had seen some other person who recognized him, is not known. However, he went immediately to Ireland, and from thence solicited his merchants very strongly for a supply, but to no purpose; so that he was reduced to beggary. In this extremity he was determined to return and cast himself upon the mercy of these honest Bristol merchants, let the consequence be what it would. He went on board a trading vessel, and worked his passage over to Plymouth, from whence he traveled on foot to Bideford. He had been there but a few days when he fell sick and died; not being worth so much as would buy a coffin."

That very atrocious pirate, Charles Gibbs, squandered most of his treasure, but it may be some consolation to know that $20,000 of it, in silver coin, was buried on the beach of Long Island, a few miles from Southampton, as attested by the records of the United States Court of the Southern District of New York. Captain Gibbs was a thoroughly bad egg, from first to last, and quite modern, it is interesting to note, for he was hanged as recently as 1831. He was born in Rhode Island, raised on a farm, and ran away to sea in the navy. It is to his credit that he is said to have served on board the *Chesapeake* in her famous battle with the *Shannon*, but after his release from Dartmoor as a British prisoner of war, he fell from grace and opened a grogery in Ann Street, called the Tin Pot, "a place full of abandoned women and dissolute fellows." He drank up all the profits, so went to sea again and found a berth in a South American privateer. Leading a mutiny, he gained the ship and made a pirate of her, frequenting Havana, and plundering merchant vessels along the Cuban coast. He slaughtered their crews in cold blood and earned an infamous reputation for cruelty. In his confession written while he was under sentence of death in New York, he stated "that some time in the course of the year 1819, he left Havana and came to the United States, bringing with him about $30,000 in gold. He passed several weeks in the city of New York, and then went to Boston, whence he took passage for Liverpool in the ship *Emerald*. Before he sailed, however, he had squandered a large amount of his money by dissipation and gambling. He remained in Liverpool a few months, and then returned to Boston. His residence in Liverpool at that time is satisfactorily ascertained from another source beside his own confession. A female now in New York was well acquainted with him there, where, she says, he lived like a gentleman, apparently with abundant means of support. In speaking of his acquaintance with this female, he says, 'I fell in with a woman who I thought was all virtue, but she deceived me, and I am sorry to say that a heart that never felt abashed at scenes of carnage and blood, was made a child of for a time by her, and I gave way to dissipation to drown the torment. How often when the fumes of liquor have subsided have I thought of my good and affectionate parents, and of their Godlike advice! My friends advised me to behave myself like a man, and promised me their assistance, but the demon still haunted me, and I spurned their advice.'"[1]

After the adventure with the deceitful female, Gibbs was not as successful as formerly in his profession of piracy, and appears to have lost his grip. For several years he knocked about the Seven Seas, in one sort of shady escapade or another, but he flung away whatever gold he harvested and was driven to commit the sordid crime which brought him to the gallows. In November of 1830, he shipped as a seaman in the brig *Vineyard*, Captain William Thornby, from New Orleans to Philadelphia with a cargo of cotton and molasses, and $54,000 in specie. Learning of the money on board, Gibbs cooked up a conspiracy to kill the captain and the mate and persuaded Thomas Wansley, the steward, to help him put them out of the way. According to the testimony, others of the crew were implicated, but the court convicted only these two. The sworn statement of Seaman Robert Dawes is as red-handed a treasure story as could be imagined:

"When about five days out, I was told that there was money on board. Charles Gibbs, E. Church, and the steward then determined to take possession of the brig. They asked James Talbot, another member of the crew, to join them. He said no, as he did not believe there was money in the vessel. They concluded to kill the captain and mate, and if Talbot and John Brownrigg would not join them, to kill them also. The next night they talked of doing it, and got their clubs ready. I dared not say a word, as they declared they would kill me if I did. As they did not agree about killing Talbot and Brownrigg, their two shipmates, it was put off. They next concluded to kill the captain and mate on the night of November 22nd but did not get ready; but on the night of the 23rd, between twelve and one o 'clock, when I was at the helm, the steward came up with a light and a knife in his hand. He dropped the light and seizing the pump-break, struck the captain with it over the head or back of the neck. The captain was sent forward by the blow and halloed, 'Oh' and 'Murder' once.

"He was then seized by Gibbs and the cook, one by the head and the other

SPOOKY TREASURE TROVES

by the heels and thrown overboard. Atwell and Church stood at the companion way, to strike down the mate when he should come up. As he came up and enquired what was the matter, they struck him over the head,—he ran back into the cabin, and Charles Gibbs followed him down; but as it was dark, he could not find him. Gibbs then came on deck for the light with which he returned below. I left the helm to see what was going on in the cabin. Gibbs found the mate and seized him, while Atwell and Church came down and struck him with a pump break and club.

"The mate was then dragged upon deck. They called for me to help them and as I came up, the mate seized my hand and gave me a death grip. Three of them hove him overboard, but which three I do not know. The mate was not dead when cast overboard, but called after us twice while in the water. I was so frightened that I hardly knew what to do. They then asked me to call Talbot, who was in the forecastle saying his prayers. He came up and said it would be his turn next, but they gave him some grog and told him not to be afraid, as they would not hurt him. If he was true to them, he should fare as well as they did. One of those who had been engaged in the bloody deed got drunk and another became crazy.

"After killing the captain and mate they set about overhauling the vessel, and got up one keg of Mexican dollars. Then they divided the captain's clothes and money,—about forty dollars and a gold watch. Talbot, Brownrigg and I, who were all innocent men, were obliged to do as we were commanded. I was sent to the helm and ordered to steer for Long Island. On the day following, they divided several kegs of the specie, amounting to five thousand dollars each, and made bags and sewed the money up. After this division, they divided the rest of the money without counting it.

"On Sunday, when about fifteen miles S.S.E. of Southampton Light, they got the boats out and put half the money in each, and then they scuttled the vessel and set fire to it in the cabin, and took to the boats. Gibbs, after the murder, took charge of the vessel as captain. From the papers on board, we learned that the money belonged to Stephen Girard.[2]

"With the boats we made the land about daylight. I was in the long-boat with three others. The rest with Atwell were in the jolly-boat. On coming to the bar the boats stuck, and we threw overboard a great deal of money, in all about five thousand dollars. The jolly-boat foundered. We saw it fill and heard them cry out, and saw them clinging to the masts. We went ashore on Barron Island, and buried the money in the sand, but very lightly. Soon after, we met with a gunner, whom we requested to conduct us where we could get some refreshments. They were by him conducted to Johnson's (the only man living on the island) where we stayed all night. I went to bed about ten o'clock. Jack Brownrigg sat up with Johnson, and in the morning told me that he had told Johnson all about the murders. Johnson went in the morning with the steward for the clothes, which were left on the top of

SPOOKY TREASURE TROVES

the place where they buried the money, but I don't believe they took away the money."

Here was genuine buried treasure, but the circumstances were such as to make the once terrible Captain Charles Gibbs cut a wretched figure. To the ignominious crime of killing the captain and the mate of a little trading brig had descended this freebooter of renown who had numbered his prizes by the score and boasted of slaying their crews wholesale. As for the specie looted from the brig *Vineyard*, half the amount was lost in the surf when the jolly-boat foundered, and the remainder buried where doubtless that hospitable resident, Johnson, was able to find most of it. Silver dollars were too heavy to be carried away in bulk by stranded pirates, fleeing the law, and these rascals got no good of their plunder.

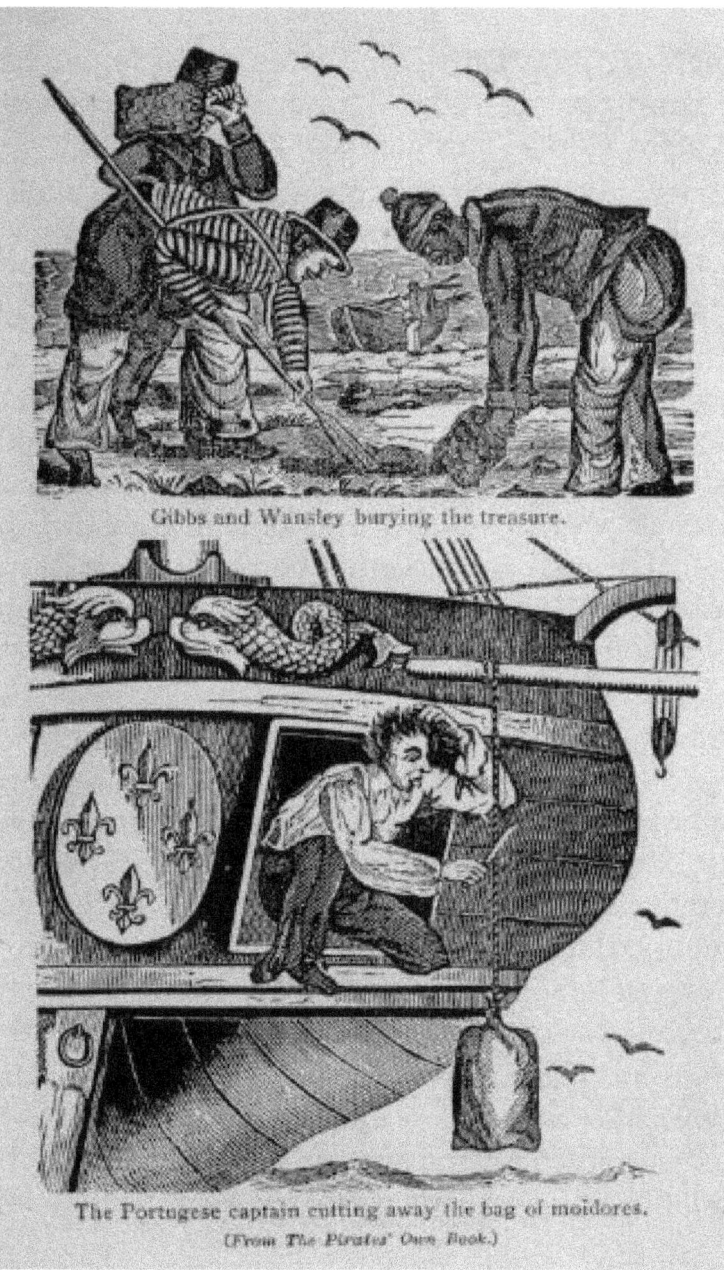

Gibbs and Wansley burying the treasure.

The Portugese captain cutting away the bag of moidores.

(From *The Pirates' Own Book*.)

Gibbs and Wansley burying the treasure.

The Portugese captain cutting away the bag of moidores.

Glance at the sin-stained roster of famous pirates, Edward Low, Captain England, Captain Thomas White, Benito De Soto, Captain Roberts, Captain John Rackham, Captain Thomas Tew, and most of the bloody crew, and it will be found that either they wasted their treasure in debaucheries, or were hanged, shot, or drowned with empty pockets. Of them all, Blackbeard[3] fills the eye most struttingly as the proper pirate to have buried treasure. He was immensely theatrical, fond of playing the part right up to the hilt, and we may rest assured that unless his sudden taking-off prevented, he was at pains to bury at least one sea-chest full of treasure in order to live up to the best traditions of his calling. He was prosperous, and unlike most of his lesser brethren, suffered no low tides of fortune. By rights, he should be a far more famous character than Captain William Kidd whose commonplace career was so signally devoid of purple patches. Blackbeard was a pirate "right out of a book," as the saying is. How this Captain Edward Teach swaggered through the streets of Charleston and terrorized the Carolinas and Bermuda is an old story, as is also the thrilling narrative of his capture, after a desperate battle, by brave Lieutenant Maynard, who hung the pirate's head from his bowsprit and sailed home in triumph. There are touches here and there, however, in the authentic biography of Blackbeard which seem to belong in a discussion of buried treasure, for he was so very much the kind of flamboyant rogue that legend paints as infernally busy with pick and shovel on dark and lonely beaches.

Blackbeard is the hero of such extremely diverting tales as these, which sundry writers have not scrupled to appropriate, either for purposes of fiction or unblushingly to fit them to poor Captain Kidd as chronicles of fact:

"In the commonwealth of pirates, he who goes the greatest length of wickedness is looked upon with a kind of envy amongst them, as a person of a most extraordinary gallantry. He is therefore entitled to be distinguished by some post, and if such a one has but courage, he must certainly be a great man. The hero of whom we are writing was thoroughly accomplished in this way, and some of his frolics of wickedness were as extravagant as if he aimed at making his men believe he was a devil incarnate. Being one day, at sea, and a little flushed with drink; 'Come,' said he, 'let us make a hell of our own, and try how long we can bear it.' Accordingly he, with two or three others, went down into the hold, and closing up all the hatches, filled several pots full of brimstone, and other combustible matter. They then set it on fire, and so continued till they were almost suffocated, when some of the men cried out for air. At length he opened the hatches, not a little pleased that he had held out the longest.

"One night, Blackbeard, drinking in his cabin with Israel Hands,[4] and the pilot, and another man, without any pretense took a small pair of pistols, and cocked them under the table. Which being perceived by the man, he went on deck, leaving the captain, Hands, and the pilot together. When his pistols were prepared, he extinguished the candle, crossed his arms and fired at the company, under the table. The one pistol did no execution, but the other wounded Hands in the knee. Interrogated concerning the meaning of this, he answered with an imprecation, 'That if he did not now and then kill one of them, they would forget who he was.'"

"In Blackbeard's journal, which was taken, there were several memoranda of the following nature, all written with his own hand.—'Such a day, rum all out;—our company somewhat sober;—a damned confusion amongst us! rogues a-plotting;—great talk of separation;—so I looked sharp for a prize; such a day took one with a great deal of liquor on board; so kept the company hot, damned hot, then all things went well again.'"

"Blackbeard derived his name from his long black beard, which, like a frightful meteor, covered his whole face, and terrified all America more than any comet that has ever appeared. He was accustomed to twist it with ribbon in small quantities, and turn them about his ears. In time of action he wore a sling over his shoulder with three braces of pistols. He stuck lighted matches under his hat, which appearing on both sides of his face and eyes, naturally fierce and wild, made him such a figure that the human imagination cannot form a conception of a fury more terrible and alarming."[5]

In the best account of his melodramatic exit from the life which he had adorned with so much distinction, there is a reference to buried treasure that must be set down as a classic of its kind.

"Upon the 17th of November, 1717, Lieutenant Maynard left James's River in quest of Blackbeard, and on the evening of the 21st came in sight of the pirate. This expedition was fitted out with all possible secrecy, no boat being permitted to pass that might convey any intelligence, while care was taken to discover where the pirates were lurking.... The hardened and infatuated pirate, having been often deceived by false intelligence, was the less attentive, nor was he convinced of his danger until he saw the sloops sent to apprehend him. Though he had then only twenty men on board, he prepared to give battle. Lieutenant Maynard arrived with his sloops in the evening and anchored, as he could not venture, under cloud of night, to go into the place where Blackbeard lay.

"The latter spent the night in drinking with the master of a trading vessel, with the same indifference as if no danger had been near. Nay, such was the desperate wickedness of this villain, that, it is reported, during the carousals of that night, one of his men asked him, 'In case anything should happen to him during the engagement with the two sloops which were waiting to attack him in the morning, whether his wife knew where he had buried his money!' To this he impiously replied, 'That nobody but himself and the devil knew where it was, and the longest liver should take all.'

"In the morning Maynard weighed, and sent his boat to take soundings, which, coming near the pirate, received her fire. Maynard then hoisted royal colors, and directly toward Blackbeard with every sail and oar. In a little while the pirate ran aground, and so did the king's vessels. Maynard lightened his vessel of the ballast and water and made towards Blackbeard. Upon this, the pirate hailed in his own rude style. 'Damn you for villains, who are you, and from whence come you?' The lieutenant answered, 'You may see from our colors we are no pirates.' Blackbeard bade him send his boat on board, that he might see who he was. But Maynard replied, 'I cannot spare my boat, but I will come on board of you as soon

SPOOKY TREASURE TROVES

as I can with my sloop.' Upon this Blackbeard took a glass of liquor and drank to him, saying, 'I'll give no quarter nor take any from you.' Maynard replied, 'He expected no quarter from him, nor should he take any.'"[6]

It is to be presumed that the devil fell heir to Blackbeard's treasure, inasmuch as Lieutenant Maynard and his men fairly cut the pirate and his crew to pieces. Turn we now from such marauders as this to that greater generation of buccaneers, so called, who harried the Spanish treasure fleets and towns in the West Indies and on the coasts of the Isthmus and South and Central America. During the period when Port Royal, Jamaica, was the headquarters and recruiting station for these picturesque cut-throats, and Sir Henry Morgan was their bright, particular star, there is the testimony of an eye-witness and participant to show that the blood-stained gold seldom tarried long enough with its owners to permit of burying it, and that they bothered their wicked heads very little about safeguarding the future.

Captain Bartholomew Roberts, that "tall, black man, nearly forty years old, whose favorite toast was 'Damnation to him who ever lives to wear a halter,'" was snuffed out in an action with a King's ship, and the manner of his life and melodramatic quality of his death suggest that he be mentioned herein as worthy of a place beside Blackbeard himself. Roberts has been overlooked by buried treasure legend, and this is odd, for he was a figure to inspire such tales. His flamboyant career opened in 1719 and was successful until the British man-of-war *Swallow* overhauled

Interview between Lafitte, General Andrew Jackson, and Governor Claiborne.

The death of Black Beard. (From *The Pirates' Own Book*.)

him on the African coast. His biographer, Captain Charles Johnson, writing while the episode was less than a decade old and when the facts were readily obtainable, left us this fine picture of the fight:

"Roberts himself made a gallant figure at the time of the engagement, being dressed in a rich crimson damask waistcoat and breeches, a red feather in his hat, a gold chain round his neck, with a diamond cross hanging to it, a sword in his hand, and two pair of pistols hanging at the end of a silk sling flung over his shoulder (according to the fashion of the pirates). He is said to have given his orders with boldness and spirit; coming, according to what he had purposed, close to the man of war, received her fire, and then hoisted his black flag[7] and returned it; shooting away from her with all the sail he could pack.... But keeping his tacks down, either by the wind's shifting or ill steerage, or both, he was taken aback with his sails, and the *Swallow* came a second time very nigh to him. He had now perhaps finished the fight very desperately if Death, who took a swift passage in a grapeshot, had not interposed and struck him directly on the throat.

"He settled himself on the tackles of a gun, which one Stephenson from the helm, observing, ran to his assistance, and not perceiving him wounded, swore at him and bid him stand up like a man. But when he found his mistake, and that Captain Roberts was certainly dead, he gushed into tears and wished the next shot might be his lot. They presently threw him overboard, with his arms and ornaments on, according to the repeated requests he had made in his life."

There was no treasure for the stout-hearted scoundrels who were captured by the *Swallow*. They had diced with fortune and lost, and Execution Dock was waiting for them, but they are worth a passing acquaintance and it gives one a certain satisfaction to learn that "they were impudently merry, saying when they viewed their nakedness, 'That they had not one half penny left to give old Charon to ferry them over the Styx,' and at their thin commons they would observe that they fell away so fast that they should not have weight enough to hang them. Sutton used to be very profane, and he happening to be in the same irons with another prisoner who was more serious than ordinary and read and prayed often, as became his condition, this man Sutton used to swear and ask him, 'What he proposed by so much noise and devotion?' 'Heaven, I hope,' says the other. 'Heaven, you fool,' says Sutton, 'Did you ever hear of any pirate going thither? Give me Hell. It is a merrier place. I'll give Roberts a salute of thirteen guns at entrance.'"

After Morgan had sacked the rich city of Porto Bello, John Esquemeling wrote of the expedition:[8]

"With these (ships) he arrived in a few days at the Island of Cuba, where he sought out a place wherein with all quiet and repose he might make the dividend of the spoil they had got. They found in ready money two hundred and fifty thousand pieces of eight, besides all other merchandises, as cloth, linen, silks, and

SPOOKY TREASURE TROVES

other goods. With this rich booty they sailed again thence to their common place of rendezvous, Jamaica. Being arrived, they passed here some time in all sorts of vices and debauchery, according to their common manner of doing, spending with huge prodigality what others had gained with no small labor and toil."

"... Such of these Pirates are found who will spend two or three thousand pieces of eight in one night, not leaving themselves, peradventure, a good shirt to wear on their backs in the morning. My own master would buy, on like occasions, a whole pipe of wine, and placing it in the street, would force everyone that passed by to drink with him; threatening also to pistol them in case they would not do it. At other times, he would do the same with barrels of ale or beer. And, very often, with both his hands, he would throw these liquors about the streets and wet the clothes of such as walked by, without regarding whether he spoiled their apparel or not, were they men or women.

"Among themselves, and to each other, these Pirates are extremely liberal and free. If any one of them has lost his goods, which often happens in their manner of life, they freely give him, and make him partaker of what they have. In taverns and ale-houses they always have great credit; but in such houses at Jamaica they ought not to run very deep in debt, seeing the inhabitants of that island easily sell one another for debt. Thus it happened to my patron, or master, to be sold for a debt of a tavern wherein he had spent the greater part of his money. This man had, within the space of three months before, three thousand pieces of eight in ready cash, all which he wasted in that short space of time, and became as poor as I have told you."

The same free-handed and lurid manner of life prevailed on the little island of Tortuga, off the coast of Hayti, where the French and English buccaneers had a lawless kingdom of their own. In his account of the career of the infamous L'Ollonais, Esquemeling goes on to say:

"Departing therefore thence, they took their course towards the island Hispaniola, and arrived thither in eight days, casting anchor in a port called Isla de la Vaca, or Cow Island. This isle is inhabited by French buccaneers[9] who most commonly sell the flesh they hunt to Pirates and others who now and then put in there with intent of victualing or trading with them. Here they unladed the whole cargo of riches which they had robbed; the usual storehouse of the Pirates being commonly under the shelter of the buccaneers. Here also they made a dividend amongst them of all of their prizes and gains, according to that order and degree which belonged to everyone. Having cast up the account and made exact calculation of all they had purchased, they found in ready money two hundred and three-score thousand pieces of eight. Whereupon, this being divided, everyone received to his share in money, and also in pieces of silk, linen and other commodities, the value of above hundred pieces of eight. Those who had been wounded in this expedition received their part before all the rest; I mean such recompenses as I spoke of the first Book, for the loss of their limbs which many sustained.[10]

"Afterwards they weighed all the plate that was uncoined, reckoning after the rate of ten pieces of eight for every pound. The jewels were prized with much variety, either at too high or too low rates; being thus occasioned by their own ignorance. This being done, everyone was put to his oath again, that he had not concealed anything nor subtracted from the common stock. Hence they proceeded to the dividend of what shares belonged to such as were dead amongst them, either in battle or otherwise. These shares were given to their friends to be kept entire for them, and to be delivered in due time to their nearest relatives, or whomsoever should appear to be their lawful heirs.

"The whole dividend being entirely finished, they set sail thence for the Isle of Tortuga. Here they arrived one month after, to the great joy of most that were upon the island. For as to the common Pirates, in three weeks they had scarce any money left them; having spent it all in things of little value, or at play either at cards or dice. Here also arrived, not long before them, two French ships laden with wine and brandy and other things of this kind; whereby these liquors, at the arrival of the Pirates, were sold indifferent cheap. But this lasted not long; for soon after they were enhanced extremely, a gallon of brandy being sold for four pieces of eight. The Governor of the island bought of the Pirates the whole cargo of the ship laden with cacao, giving them for that rich commodity scarce the twentieth part of what it was worth. Thus they made shift to lose and spend the riches they had got in much less time than they were purchased by robbing. The taverns, according to the custom of Pirates, got the greatest part thereof; insomuch that soon after they were constrained to seek more by the same unlawful means they had obtained the preceding."

Morgan himself buried none of his vast treasure, although legend persists in saying so, nor did he waste it in riotous living. From the looting of Panama alone he took booty to the value of two million dollars as his share, and he had no need to hide it. He was thought so well of in England that Charles II knighted him, and he was appointed Commissary of the Admiralty. For some time he lived in England, published his *Voyage to Panama* in 1683, and spent his remaining years in Jamaica as an opulent and influential person in high favor with the ruling powers, and a terror to the luckless, beggared comrades who had helped him win his fortune. As governor of the island he hanged as many as he could lay hands on, a kind of ingratitude not at all inconsistent with the traits of character he had displayed as a pirate. He did not hesitate to rob his own men, according to Esquemeling from whose narrative of the great expedition against Panama the following paragraphs are taken as indicative of the methods of this great freebooter of the Spanish Main:

SPOOKY TREASURE TROVES

"Not long after Captain Morgan arrived at Jamaica, he found many of his chief officers and soldiers reduced to their former state of indigence through their immoderate vices and debauchery. Hence they ceased not to importune him for new invasions and exploits, thereby to get something to expend anew in wine, as they had already wasted what was secured so little before. Captain Morgan being willing to follow fortune while she called him, hereupon stopped the mouths of many of the inhabitants of Jamaica, who were creditors to his men for large sums of money, with the hopes and promises he gave them of greater achievements than ever, by a new expedition he was going about. This being done, he needed not give himself much concern to levy men for this or any other enterprise, his name being now so famous through all those islands that that alone would readily bring him in more men than he could readily employ. He undertook therefore to equip a new fleet of ships; for which purpose he assigned the south side of the Isle of Tortuga as a place of rendezvous. With this resolution he wrote divers letters to all the ancient and expert Pirates there inhabiting, as also to the Governor of the said Isle, and to the planters and hunters of Hispaniola, giving them to understand his intentions, and desiring their appearance at the said place, in case they intended to go with him. All these people had no sooner understood his designs than they flocked to the place assigned in huge numbers, with ships, canoes, and boats, being desirous to obey his commands.... Thus all were present at the place assigned, and in readiness, against the 24th day of October, 1670."

Special articles of agreement for the division of the treasure of Panama were drawn up by Morgan before his fleet sailed. "Herein it was stipulated that he should have the hundredth part of all that was gotten to himself alone: That every captain should draw the shares of eight men, for the expenses of his ship, besides his own: That the surgeon, besides his ordinary pay, should have two hundred pieces of eight, for his chest of medicine: And every carpenter, above his common salary, should draw one hundred pieces of eight. Lastly, unto him that in any battle should signalize himself, either by entering the first any castle, or taking down the Spanish colors and setting up the English, they constituted fifty pieces of eight for a reward. In the head of these articles it was stipulated that all these extraordinary salaries, recompenses and rewards should be paid out of the first spoil or purchase they should take, according as every one should then occur to be either rewarded or paid."

The expedition was a gorgeous success, for "on the 24th of February, of the year 1671, Captain Morgan departed from the city of Panama, or rather from the place where the said city of Panama had stood; of the spoils whereof he carried with him one hundred and seventy-five beasts of carriage, laden with silver, gold and other precious things, besides six hundred prisoners, more or less, between men, women, children and slaves.... About the middle of the way to the castle of Chagre, Captain Morgan commanded his men to be placed in due order, according to their custom, and caused every one to be sworn that they had reserved nor concealed nothing privately to themselves, even not so much as the value of sixpence. This being done, Captain Morgan, having had some experience that those lewd fellows would not much stickle to swear falsely in points of interest, he commanded every one to be searched very strictly both in their clothes and satchels and everywhere it might be presumed they had reserved anything. Yea, to the intent this order might not be ill taken by his companions, he permitted himself to be searched, even to the very soles of his shoes. To this office, by common consent, there was assigned one out of every company to be the searcher of all the rest. The French Pirates that went on this expedition with Captain Morgan were not well satisfied with this new custom of searching.

"From Chagre, Captain Morgan sent presently after his arrival a great boat to Porto Bello, wherein were all the prisoners he had taken at the Isle of St. Catharine, demanding by them a considerable ransom for the castle of Chagre, where he then was, threatening otherwise to ruin and demolish it even to the ground. To this message those of Porto Bello made answer: That they would not give one farthing towards the ransom of the said castle, and that the English might do with it as they pleased. The answer being come, the dividend was made of all the spoil they had purchased in that voyage. Thus every company and every particular person therein included, received their portion of what was got; or rather, what part thereof Captain Morgan was pleased to give them. For so it was, that the rest of his companions, even of his own nation, complained of his proceedings in this particular, and feared not to tell him openly to his face that he had reserved the best jewels to himself. For they judged it impossible that no greater share should belong to them than two hundred pieces of eight per capita, of so many valuable booties and robberies as they had obtained. Which small sum they thought too little reward for so much labor and such huge and manifest dangers as they had so often exposed their lives to. But Captain Morgan was deaf to all these and many other complaints of this kind, having designed in his mind to cheat them of as much as he could.

"At last, Captain Morgan finding himself obnoxious to many obloquies and detractions among his people, began to fear the consequences thereof, and hereupon thinking it unsafe to remain any longer time at Chagre, he commanded the ordnance of the said castle to be carried on board his ship. Afterwards he caused the greatest part of the walls to be demolished, and the edifices to be burnt, and as many other things spoiled and ruined as could conveniently be done in a short while. These orders being performed, he went secretly on board his own ship, without giving any notice of his departure to his Companions, nor calling any council, as he used to do. Thus he set sail and put out to sea, not bidding anybody adieu, being only followed by three or four vessels of the whole fleet.

"These were such (as the French Pirates believed) as went shares with Cap-

SPOOKY TREASURE TROVES

tain Morgan, towards the best and greatest part of the spoil which had been concealed from them in the dividend. The Frenchmen could very willingly have revenged this affront upon Captain Morgan and those that followed him, had they found themselves with sufficient means to encounter him at sea. But they were destitute of most things necessary thereto. Yea, they had much ado to find sufficient victuals and provisions for their voyage to Panama, he having left them totally unprovided of all things."

Esquemeling's commentary on this base conduct of the leader is surprisingly pious: "Captain Morgan left us all in such a miserable condition as might serve for a lively representation of what reward attends wickedness at the latter end of life. Whence we ought to have learned how to regulate and amend our actions for the future."

Sir Francis Drake, "sea king of the sixteenth century," the greatest admiral of the time, belongs not with the catalogue of pirates and buccaneers, yet he left a true tale of buried treasure among his exploits and it is highly probable that some of that rich plunder is hidden to-day in the steaming jungle of the road he took to Panama. There were only forty-eight Englishmen in the band which he led on the famous raid to ambush the Spanish treasure train bound to Nombre-de-Dios, a century before Morgan's raiders crossed the Isthmus. This first attempt resulted in failure, but after sundry adventures, Drake returned and hid his little force close by that famous treasure port of Nombre-de-Dios, where they waited to hear the bells of the pack-mule caravan moving along the trail from Panama. It was at dawn when this distant, tinkling music was first heard, and the Cimaroons, or Indian guides, were jubilant. "Now they assured us we should have more Gold and Silver than all of us could bear away." Soon the Englishmen had glimpses of three royal treasure trains plodding along the leafy road, one of fifty mules, the others of seventy each, and every one of them laden with three hundred pounds weight of silver bullion, or thirty tons in all. The guard of forty-five Spanish soldiers loafed carelessly in front and rear, their guns slung on their backs.

Drake and his bold seamen poured down from a hill, put the guard to flight, and captured the caravan with the loss of only two men. There was more plunder than they could carry back to their ships in a hasty retreat, and "being weary, they were content with a few bars and quoits of gold." The silver was buried in the expectation of returning for it later, "partly in the burrows which the great landcrabs have made in the earth, and partly under old trees which are fallen thereabouts, and partly in the sand and gravel of a river not very deep of water."

Then began a forced march, every man burdened with all the treasure he could carry, and behind them the noise of "both horse and foot coming, as it seemed, to the mules." Presently a wounded French captain became so exhausted that he had to drop out, refusing to delay the march and telling the company that

SPOOKY TREASURE TROVES

he would remain behind in the woods with two of his men, "in hope that some rest would recover his better strength." Ere long another Frenchman was missed, and investigation discovered that he had "drunk much wine," and doubtless desired to sleep it off.

Reaching Rio Francisco, Drake was dismayed to find his pinnaces gone, and his party stranded. The vessels were recovered after delay and perilous adventure, whereupon Drake hastened to prepare another expedition "to get intelligence in what case the country stood, and if might be, recover Monsieur Tetu, the French captain, and leastwise bring away the buried silver." The party was just about to start inland when on the beach appeared one of the two men who had stayed behind with the French captain. At sight of Drake he "fell down on his knees, blessing God for the time that ever our Captain was born, who now beyond all his hope, was become his deliverer."

He related that soon after they had been left behind in the forest, the Spaniards had captured Captain Tetu and the other man. He himself had escaped by throwing down his treasure and taking to his heels. Concerning the buried silver, he had lamentable tidings to impart. The Spanish had got wind of it, and he "thought there had been near two thousand Spaniards and Negroes there to dig and search for it." However, the expedition pushed forward, and the news was confirmed. "The earth every way a mile distant had been digged and turned up in every place of any likelihood to have anything hidden in it." It was learned that the general location of the silver had been divulged to the Spaniards by that rascally Frenchman who had got drunk and deserted during the march to the coast. He had been caught while asleep, and the soldiers from Nombre-de-Dios tortured him until he told all that he knew about the treasure.

The Englishmen poked around and quickly found "thirteen bars of silver and some few quoits of gold," with which they posted back to Rio Francisco, not daring to linger in the neighborhood of an overwhelming force of the enemy. It was their belief that the Spanish recovered by no means all of those precious tons of silver bullion, and Drake made sail very reluctantly. It may well be that a handsome hoard still awaits the search of some modern argonauts, or that the steam shovels of the workmen of the Panama canal may sometime swing aloft a burden of "bars of silver and quoits of gold" in their mighty buckets. Certain it is that Sir Francis Drake is to be numbered among that romantic company of sea rovers of other days who buried vast treasure upon the Spanish Main.

[1] *The Pirates' Own Book*.

[2] The famous merchant and philanthropist of Philadelphia.

[3] "I happen to know the fact that Blackbeard, whose family name was given as Teach, was in reality named Drumond, a native of Bristol. I have learned this fact from one of his family and name, of respectable standing in Virginia, near

SPOOKY TREASURE TROVES

Hampton." (Watson's Annals of Philadelphia.)

In the contemporary court records of the Carolina colony, the name of Blackbeard is given as Thatch.

[4] Israel Hands was tried and condemned with Blackboard's crew, but was pardoned by royal proclamation, and, according to Captain Johnson, "was alive some time ago in London, begging his bread." This would indicate that he had buried no treasure of his own, and had not fathomed Blackbeard's secret. Stevenson borrowed the name of Israel Hands for one of his crew of pirates in "Treasure Island."

[5] *The Pirates' Own Book.*

[6] This is from *The Pirates' Own Book*. Captain Johnson's version is unexpurgated and to be preferred, for he declares that Blackbeard cried out, "Damnation seize my soul if I give you quarter, or take any from you."

[7] As showing the fanciful tastes in sinister flags, Captain Johnson records that Captain Roberts flew "a black silk flag at the mizzen peak, and a jack and pendant at the same. The flag had a death's head on it, with an hour glass in one hand, and cross bones in the other, a dart by one, and underneath a heart dropping three drops of blood."

[8] *The Buccaneers of America*. A True Account of the Most Remarkable Assaults Committed of Late Years Upon the Coasts of the West Indies by the Buccaneers of Jamaica and Tortuga (Both English and French). Wherein are contained more especially the Unparalleled Exploits of Sir Henry Morgan, our English Jamaican hero who sacked Porto Bello, burnt Panama, etc. (Published in 1684.)

[9] The buccaneers derived their name from the process of drying beef over a wood fire, or *boucane* in French. They were at first hunters of wild cattle in the island of Hispaniola or Hayti who disposed of their product to smugglers, traders, and pirates, but they were a distinct class from the *filibustiers* or sea rovers. As cattle became scarce and the Spanish more hostile and cruel foes, the buccaneers, French and English, forsook their trade and took to the sea, to harry the common foe.

[10] The schedule thus referred to stipulated that for the crew, except the officers specified, it was a case of "no prey, no pay." For the loss of a right arm, the consolation money was six hundred pieces of eight, or six slaves; for the loss of a left arm, five hundred pieces of eight, or five slaves; for the left leg, four hundred pieces of eight, or four slaves; for an eye one hundred pieces of eight, or one slave; for a finger of the hand the same reward as for the eye. "All which sums of money, as I have said before, are taken out of the capital sum or common stock of what is got by their piracy."

SPOOKY TREASURE TROVES

CHAPTER XVI
PRACTICAL HINTS FOR TREASURE SEEKERS

Faith, imagination, and a vigorous physique comprise the essential equipment of a treasure seeker. Capital is desirable, but not absolutely necessary, for it would be hard indeed to find a neighborhood in which some legend or other of buried gold is not current. If one is unable to finance an expedition aboard a swift, black-hulled schooner, it is always possible to dig for the treasure of poor Captain Kidd and it is really a matter of small importance that he left no treasure in his wake. The zest of the game is in seeking. A pick and a shovel are to be obtained in the wood-shed or can be purchased at the nearest hardware store for a modest outlay. A pirate's chart is to be highly esteemed, but if the genuine article cannot be found, there are elderly seafaring men in every port who will furnish one just as good and perjure themselves as to the information thereof with all the cheerfulness in the world.

It has occurred to the author that a concise directory of the best-known lost and buried treasure might be of some service to persons of an adventurous turn of mind, and the following tabloid guide for ready reference may perhaps prove helpful, particularly to parents of small boys who have designs on pirate hoards, as well as to boys who have never grown up.

Cocos Island. In the Pacific Ocean off the coast of Costa Rica. Twelve million dollars in plate, coin, bar gold, and jewels buried by buccaneers and by seamen who pirated the treasure of Lima.

Trinidad. In the South Atlantic off the coast of Brazil. The vast booty of sea-rovers who plundered the richest cities of South America. A very delectable and well-authenticated treasure, indeed, with all the proper charts and appurtenances. Specially recommendeded.

The Salvages. A group of small islands to the southward of Madeira. Two million dollars of silver in chests, buried by the crew of a Spanish ship in 1804. They killed their captain and laid him on top of the treasure, wherefore proper

SPOOKY TREASURE TROVES

precautions must be taken to appease his ghost before beginning to dig.

Cape St. Vincent. West coast of Madagascar. The wreck of a Dutch-built ship of great age is jammed fast between the rocks. Gold and silver money has been washed from her and cast up on the beach, and a large fortune still remains among her timbers. Expeditions are advised to fit out at Mozambique.

Venanguebe Bay, thirty-five miles south south-west of Ngoncy Island on the east coast of Madagascar. A sunken treasure is supposed to be not far from the wreck of the French frigate *Gloire* lost in 1761. Expeditions will do well to keep a weather eye lifted along all this coast for the treasures of the pirates who infested these waters in the days of Captain Kidd.

Gough Island, sometimes called Diego Alvarez. Latitude 40° 19' S. Longitude 9° 44' W. It is well known that on this unfrequented bit of sea-washed real estate, a very wicked pirate or pirates deposited ill-gotten gains. The place to dig is close to a conspicuous spire or pinnacle of stone on the western end of the island, the name of which natural landmark is set down on the charts as Church Rock.

Juan Fernandez. South Pacific. Famed as the abode of Robinson Crusoe who was too busy writing the story of his life to find the buccaneer's wealth concealed in a cave, also the wreck of a Spanish galleon reputed to have been laden with bullion from the mines of Peru.

Auckland Islands. Remote and far to the southward and hardly to be recommended to the amateur treasure seeker who had better serve his apprenticeship nearer home. Frequently visited by expeditions from Melbourne and Sydney. In 1866, the sailing ship *General Grant*, bound from Australia to London, was lost here. In her cargo were fifty thousand ounces of gold. In a most extraordinary manner the vessel was driven by the seas into a great cavern in the cliff from which only a handful of her people managed to escape. They lived for eighteen months on this desert island before being taken off. The hulk of the *General Grant* is still within the cave, but the undertow and the great combers have thus far baffled the divers.

Luzon. One of the Philippine Islands. Near Calumpit, in the swamps of the Rio Grande, the Chinese Mandarin, Chan Lee Suey, buried his incalculable wealth soon after the British captured Manila in 1762. His jewels were dazzling, and a string of pearls, bought from the Sultan of Sulu, was said to be the finest in the Orient.

Nightingale Island. Near Tristan da Cunha. South Atlantic. One chest of pirate's silver was found here and brought to the United States, but much more is said to remain hidden.

Tobermory Bay. Island of Mull. Western Scotland. Wreck of the galleon *Florencia* of the Spanish Armada. Said to have contained thirty millions of trea-

SPOOKY TREASURE TROVES

sure. Permission to investigate must be obtained from His Grace, the Duke of Argyll.

Vigo Bay. Coast of Spain. Spanish plate fleet sunk by the English and Dutch. A trifling matter of a hundred million dollars or more are waiting for the right man to come along and fish them up. Treasure seekers had better first consult the Spanish Government at Madrid in order to avoid misunderstandings with the local officials.

East River. Manhattan Island, New York. Wreck of the British frigate *Hussar* which carried to the bottom, in 1780, more than two and a half million dollars in gold consigned to the paymasters of the army and naval forces that were fighting the American forces of George Washington. She was sailing for Newport and struck a rock nearly opposite the upper end of Randall's Island, sinking one hundred yards from shore.

Oak Island. Nova Scotia. Near Chester. Unmistakable remains of a deep shaft sunk by pirates and an underground connection with the bay. A company is now digging, and will probably sell shares at a reasonable price. Buying shares in a treasure company is less fatiguing than handling the pick and shovel oneself.

Isthmus of Panama. Directions somewhat vague. Sir Francis Drake left part of the loot of old Panama concealed along his line of retreat, but none of his crew was considerate enough to transmit to posterity a chart marked with the proper crosses and bearings.

Dollar Cove. Mount's Bay, Cornwall. Wreck of treasure ship *Saint Andrew*, belonging to the king of Portugal. Driven out of her course from Flanders to a home port in 1526. An ancient document written by one Thomas Porson, an Englishman on board states that "by the Grace and Mercy of God, the greater part of the crew got safely to land," and that, assisted by some of the inhabitants, they also saved part of the cargo including blocks of silver bullion, silver vessels and plate, precious stones, brooches and chains of gold, cloth of Arras, tapestry, satins, velvets, and four sets of armor for the king of Portugal. According to Porson, no sooner had these treasures been carried to the top of the cliffs than three local squires with sixty armed retainers attacked the shipwrecked men and carried off the booty.

Modern treasure seekers disbelieve this document and prefer the statement of one of the squires concerned, St. Aubyn by name, that they rode to the place to give what help they could, but the cargo of treasure could not be saved.

Cape Vidal. Coast of Zululand. Wreck of mysterious sailing vessel *Dorothea* said to have had a huge fortune in gold bricks cemented under his floor, stolen gold from the mines of the Rand. In 1900, May 21st, an item in the Government Estimates of the Legislative Assembly in the Natal Parliament was discussed under the heading, "Expenditure in connection with buried gold at Cape Vidal,

SPOOKY TREASURE TROVES

search for discovery, £173 19s. 3d." "Mr. Evans asked if a syndicate had been formed and what expectations the Government had to give. (Hear, hear.) The Prime Minister said there were several syndicates formed to raise the treasure. The government had reason to believe that they knew where the treasure was hidden, and started an expedition on their own account. But unfortunately they had not been able to find the treasure. Mr. Evans: The Government was in for a bad spec. (Laughter.) The item passed."

Space is given to the foregoing because it stamps with official authority the story of the treasure of Cape Vidal. When a government goes treasure hunting there must be something in it.

Lake Guatavita. Near Bogotá. Republic of Colombia. The treasure of El Dorado, the Gilded Man. To find this gold involves driving a tunnel through the side of a mountain and draining the lake. This is such a formidable undertaking that it will not appeal to the average treasure seeker unless, perchance, he might pick up a second hand tunnel somewhere at a bargain price. Even then, transportation from the sea coast to Bogotá is so difficult and costly that it would hardly be practicable to saw the tunnel into sections and have it carried over the mountains on mule-back.

THE END

SPOOKY TREASURE TROVES

TIMOTHY GREEN BECKLEY - UFO AND PARANORMAL PIONEER

Tim Beckley has had so many careers that even his own girlfriend doesn't know what he does for a living..

Beckley has been described as the Hunter Thompson of UFOlogy by the editor of UFO magazine Nancy Birnes.

Since an early age his life has more or less revolved around the paranormal. At the age of three his life was saved by an invisible force. The house he was raised in was thought to be haunted. His grandfather saw a headless horseman. Beckley also underwent out of body experiences starting at age six.

And saw his first of three UFOs when he was but ten, and has had two more sightings since - including an attempt to communicate with one of these objects.

Tim grew up listening to the only all night talk show in the country that revolved around the strange and unexplained. Long John Nebel's guests included the early UFO contactees who claimed to have visited other planets and built time machines in the desert. Tim was fascinated by everything that went bump in the night - or even in the daylight for that matter. Years later, Tim was to appear on Long John's show numerous times and over the years has been a frequent guest on hundreds of programs which have come and gone just like ghosts in the night. He is a popular guest on Coast to Coast AM. Has appeared on William Shatner's Weird Or What? And an episode of UFO Hunters regarding the dreaded Men In Black. He currently co-hosts a popular podcast, Exploring The Bizarre on the KCOR Digital Radio Network His YouTube channel Mr UFOs Secret Files, houses over seventy interviews with the greats of the paranormal.

SPOOKY TREASURE TROVES

He is one of the few Americans ever to be invited to speak before closed door meetings on UFOs presided over by the late Earl of Clancarty at the House of Lords in England. He visited Loch Ness in Scotland while in the UK and went home with a belief that Nessie was somehow connected with dragons of mythology as well as strange discs engraved on cathedrals and ghostly phenomenon.

The Inner Light Publications and Global Communications' catalog of books and video titles now number over 200, including the works of Tim Swartz, T. Lobsang Rampa, Commander X, Brad Steiger, John Keel, Tracy Twyman, Wendelle Stevens and a host of many other authors.

Tim is known among horror movie fans as Mr. Creepo. When asked his major cinema influences he mentions Nancy Reagan as having gotten him involved as a horror host. During the heyday of double features and Time Square grind houses, he worked as a movie review critic as well as a publicist for several small film companies. His recent efforts include **Skin Eating Jungle Vampires** and **Blood Sucking Vampire Freaks.**

SPOOKY TREASURE TROVES

SEAN CASTEEL

Sean Casteel has written about UFOs, alien abduction, and related phenomena since 1989 when he interviewed Whitley Strieber, around the time that the movie version of "Communion" was released. He was a contributor for several years to UFO UNIVERSE and was eventually given the title of Associate Editor. Later he began to write special reports and books for both of Tim Beckley's publishing companies, Inner Light Publications and Global Communications. The books he has written include **"UFOs, Prophecy and the End of Time," "The Heretic's UFO Guidebook"** and **"Signs and Symbols of the Second Coming."** His work has also been published in the U.K., Italy, Romania and Australia.

SPOOKY TREASURE TROVES

DR. NANDOR FODOR

Dr. Nandor Fodor, born in 1895, was a British and American parapsychologist, psychoanalyst, author and journalist of Hungarian origin. After receiving a doctorate in law from the Royal Hungarian University of Science in Budapest, he moved to New York to work as a journalist and to Britain in 1929, where he worked for a newspaper company.

Fodor became one of the leading authorities on poltergeists, hauntings and paranormal phenomena. He was also an associate of Dr. Sigmund Freud. The field of psychoanalysis, as pioneered by Freud, was, on the surface, disdainful of the occult, but it is said that even Freud secretly believed that there could be paranormal aspects to some cases of mental illness and neuroses.

Fodor began to embrace paranormal phenomena in the 1930s and by the next decade was advocating a psychoanalytic approach to psychic phenomena, which quickly drew the ire of the spiritualist community. So virulent were the attacks that Fodor eventually filed a lawsuit for libel against a spiritualist newspaper called "The Psychic News."

He is best known for his magnum opus, "Encyclopedia of Psychic Science," first published in 1934. His other titles include "The Haunted Mind: A Psychoanalyst Looks at the Supernatural" and "Haunted People: The Story of the Poltergeist Down the Centuries," the latter being coauthored with Hereward Carrington. Fodor died in 1964 shortly after his 69th birthday.

SPOOKY TREASURE TROVES

TED OWENS

Was he the "voice of doom" or the soothsayer of the Space Generation? The life and career of Ted Owens was often the focus of controversy and wonder. Even Otto Binder, a sci-fi writer who also worked for NASA, was forced to confront issues in regard to Owens' "powers," and his apparently genuine relationship with the UFO occupants. Binder openly asked if the ETs had sent messages through Owens that were being foolishly ignored and whether these same aliens were in control of our very lives by virtue of their incredibly advanced science.

When the original edition of Owens' game-changing book, "*HOW TO CONTACT SPACE PEOPLE,*" appeared in 1969, courtesy of Gray Barker's Saucerian Press, hundreds reported "miracles" and supernatural experiences after carrying or wearing one of the special "Space Intelligence" discs that were provided by Owens. Says one researcher, who calls himself simply "Jinn" and believes the UFOs are extra-dimensional: "Many people who investigated Ted Owens testified that he could predict and control lightning, hurricanes, tornadoes, earthquakes and volcanoes. He claimed he was in telepathic contact with other-dimensional beings he called Space Intelligences, who had trained him since early childhood to communicate with them and co-create tremendous large scale psychokinetic effects."

Jinn goes on to say that Ted Owens could have been one of the greatest parapsychological finds in history. Owens performed about 200 "miracles" in association with the SI's, considered himself to be the "Earth ambassador of UFO intelligences," and compared himself to Moses, whom he said also worked with the SI's. Some people thought Owens delusional; others believed something dramatic had happened in his life to cause these telekinetic events to occur around him with such regularity. Owens died in 1987, leaving behind an untold number of unanswered questions.

SPOOKY TREASURE TROVES

SCOTT CORRALES

Scott Corrales is a writer and translator of UFO and paranormal subjects, with a keen interest in the "high strangeness" aspects of the these and related topics. His books include "Chupacabras and Other Mysteries;" "Flashpoint: High Strangeness in Puerto Rico;" and "Forbidden Mexico." Scott's translation of Salvador Freixedo's landmark "Visionaries, Mystics and Contactees" appeared in 1992 and created a hotbed of controversy due to the nature of the revelations made by the onetime Spanish Catholic priest and former member of the Jesuit Order.

Currently, Corrales directs the institute of Hispanic UFOlogy, which provides daily updates on UFO and paranormal events in Latin America and Spain to the English-reading public, and contributes regularly to Paranoia, Australian UFOlogist and other publications worldwide.

The latest postings of INEXPLICATA-THE JOURNAL OF HISPANIC UFOLOGY can be found at http://inexplicata.blogspot.com/

SPOOKY TREASURE TROVES

PAUL ENO

Co-author of *"The Bell Witch Project: Poltergeists, Ghosts, Exorcism and the Supernatural In Early American History"*

One of the earliest paranormal investigators, Paul has had a distinguished career as a newspaper and magazine reporter and editor. He is the author of seven books, some of which are considered classics of the paranormal genre. Paul has appeared multiple times on "Coast To Coast AM" with Art Bell and George Noory, as well as appearing on the Travel, Discovery and History Channels. Paul's unusually long experience in the field (nearly 45 years), his hair-raising adventures with famous hauntings, along with his unique theories about the paranormal and its meaning for our understanding of the world and ourselves, make him a major draw on the lecture circuit. He co-hosts, along with his son, Ben, a radio program called *"Behind the Paranormal"* that boasts an estimated three million listeners. His latest works include *"The Bell Witch Project," "Footsteps In The Attic,"* and *"Faces At The Window."*

To find out more about Paul Eno and his work, go to:

www.newenglandghosts.com

The website for his radio show is at: www.behindtheparanormal.com

SPOOKY TREASURE TROVES

PAUL DALE ROBERTS

Roberts is a Fortean investigator, meaning he investigates ALL things paranormal, to include Mothman, Chupacabra, UFOs, Crop Circles, Ghosts, Poltergeists, Demons and more. Roberts heads the research group HPI (Hegelianism Paranormal Intelligence – International). https://www.facebook.com/groups/HPIinternational/ Significant investigations conducted by HPI include the Skinwalker Ranch in Utah, looking for Natalee Holloway's ghost in Aruba, UFOs and Bigfoot at Mount Shasta, UFOs and USOs at Monterey Bay, Area 51, and Guatemala City, Guatemala.

Writing Career: Roberts writes community-related stories and is a former columnist for the Sacramento Press, former columnist for Haunted Times Magazine, and has written small blurbs for Newsweek, Time, National Geographic Traveler and People Magazine. Roberts is a former columnist for Vamperotica by www.vamperatica.com/Brainstorm Comics; Writer's Digest; WebBound; and Just Comics and More by Genesis Publications. Roberts now writes for online magazines such as Chatterbrew Magazine www.chatterbrew.com; Lorena's Angels http://www.lorenasangels.com/; and Ceri Clark's All Destiny Magazine. Roberts was recently picked up by Paranormal Magazine UK and works for the online national news site, Before its News. Roberts' articles are featured in legendary Brad Steiger's books and Timothy Green Beckley's books. Roberts has now published 4 books – HPI Chronicles series with Lulu.

SPOOKY TREASURE TROVES

PRESTON DENNETT

Preston is one of the most respected and prolific writers doing field work in the paranormal today. He began investigating UFOs and the paranormal in 1986 when he discovered that his family, friends and co-workers were having dramatic unexplained encounters. Since then, he has interviewed hundreds of witnesses and investigated a wide variety of extraordinary phenomena. Dennett is a field investigator for the Mutual UFO Network (MUFON), a ghost hunter, a paranormal researcher, and author of more than 100 articles on UFOs and the paranormal. His articles have appeared in numerous magazines including Fate, Atlantis Rising, MUFON UFO Journal, Nexus, Paranormal Magazine, UFO Magazine, Mysteries Magazine, Ufologist and others. His writing has been translated into several different languages including German, French, Portuguese, Russian, Chinese and Icelandic. He has appeared on numerous radio and television programs, including Midnight in the Desert with Art Bell, Coast-to-Coast and also the History Channel's Deep Sea UFOs and UFO Hunters.

Among his 17 books published to date which are of particular significance include – ***UFOs Over Arizona, UFOs Over Nevada* and *UFOs Over New Mexico.***

www.prestondennett.weebly.com

ADVERTISEMENT

TWO BOOK SPECIAL: ( ) ADMIRAL BYRD'S JOURNEY BEYOND THE POLES and THE SECRET LOST DIARY OF ADMIRAL BYRD—$20.00 EACH OR BOTH FOR ONLY $29.00 + $5 S/H

EMMY AWARD-WINNING PRODUCER CLAIMS FAMED EXPLORER DISCOVERED ENTRANCE TO HOLLOW EARTH!

One of the world's most enduring mysteries, a legend that stretches from ancient times to the present, is that of the Hollow Earth. As one learns from reading Tim R. Swartz's two excellent offerings from Global Communications, the mythology concerning a world inside our own dates back to pre-Biblical times. So is the Earth hollow, as some believe? Calling on expert testimony from scientists, Emmy Award winning producer Tim Swartz skillfully makes the case that it is more than scientifically possible for our planet to be hollow – it is in fact probable that we share our world with a hidden race who lives beneath our feet and occasionally interacts with us mere surface dwellers for good or evil. Admiral Richard Byrd's trips to both the North and South Poles in the early part of the 20th century are covered in great detail by Swartz. Byrd claimed to have located large openings at the poles that serve as doorways into the interior of the planet, as well as strange landscapes of lush green vegetation and animals roaming freely on the surface where we have long been told there is only snow and ice. It is said that a media cover-up was quickly put into place and Byrd ceased to talk about his discoveries publicly.

THE NAZIS IN SHAMBALLAH

Swartz provides further clues about the government's knowledge of the Inner Earth, along with some fascinating speculation about why such tight secrecy is maintained. Is the shadow government of the New World Order already in contact with the beings down below? The Nazis, according to Swartz, made an expedition to Antarctica before the outbreak of World War II for just such a purpose, hoping to establish relations with the Aryan supermen said to dwell under the surface there. There have also been reports of flying saucer-type craft being seen in the vicinity displaying a swastika on their outer skin. Swartz contrasts that dark tale with a sunnier interpretation of the Hollow Earth theory, namely the existence of a hidden paradise in the planet's interior called Agharta or Shamballah. It is said this mythical wonderland is lighted by a small internal sun, and that wondrous vegetation and animal life abound there, as well as a race of gentle, technologically advanced people who are very concerned about our possible self-destruction through misuse of nuclear weapons. **Admiral Byrd's Secret Journey Beyond the Poles** strikes just the right balance between pragmatic scientific inquiry into the tantalizing notion that the Earth is hollow and stories of the fascinating assortment of creatures that are said to reside there. Swartz has also written another book called **The Secret Lost Diary of Admiral Richard E. Byrd and the Phantom of the Poles** which deals more directly with how Byrd's discovery of the Hollow Earth was quickly covered up by the press and radio outlets of his day.

In his real-life "secret diary," Byrd wrote, "There comes a time when the rationality of men must fade into insignificance and one must accept the inevitability of the Truth! I am not at liberty to disclose the following documentation at this writing. Perhaps it shall never see the light of public scrutiny, but I must do my duty and record it here for all to read one day."

The truths we finally learn are so completely unbelievable that there is no need to question why Byrd hesitated to reveal them publicly, no doubt fearing he would be locked away in a madhouse, protesting the accusation of insanity to deaf ears.

In any case, Tim R. Swartz has put together a pair of winners in the always interesting stream of new books coming out from Inner Light/Global Communications.

TIM R SWARTZ

An Indiana native, a photojournalist and Emmy Award-winning television news producer, Tim Swartz has traveled extensively and investigated paranormal phenomena and other unusual mysteries in such diverse locations as the Great Pyramid in Egypt and the Great Wall of China.

ADVERTISEMENT

NEW BLOCKBUSTER AS HEARD ON COAST TO COAST AM

$18 + $5 S/H

SENSATIONAL NEW BOOK ON THE AFTERLIFE ASKS:

"IS HEAVEN JUST ANOTHER UFO DESTINATION?"

Diane Tessman, and Timothy Green Beckley, ask – and answer! – some potentially fearless questions in U.F.O.S. Are They Your Passport To Heaven And Other Unearthly Realms?

** – Where is Heaven?

** – Is it more easily accessible than we have been taught?

** – Is there such a thing as a UFO/Afterlife "connection"? ** – Is it possible to enter Heaven through the Pearly Gates on a UFO?

** – Can our loved ones return to earth to visit us onboard what we might think of as a "Spaceship"?

** – Do aliens, angels and spirit beings share the same place in the cosmos? What else might they have in common?

** – Can our departed loved ones pick up the telephone and literally call us from the afterlife?

** – Is it possible that we can use our home computer to send an email to our deceased friends?

** – Do our late friends and family provide proof that they still love us by leaving "hidden" objects around the house that they have teleported from paradise?

** – Do our beloved animal friends reincarnate and come back to us as the "new pets" in our life?

NEWS FLASH! – In England a group known as The Scole Afterlife Project held closely-controlled séances for almost a decade. They set up cameras and other electronic devices to record apparitions that manifested themselves; deceased friends and family members of the experimenters materialized on film, and images of the typical gray aliens were captured as well. Also recorded were scenes that look as if they had originated on other worlds, and when played back, seemed to prove the existence of other realms and realities.

AND DISCOVER the secret of the JUNE 24TH ENIGMA and why certain UFO researchers have died on the anniversary of the first modern day UFO sighting, including comedian Jackie Gleason who had one of the world's largest occult libraries.

( ) **UFOS – ARE THEY YOUR PASSPORT TO HEAVEN?** Just $18.00 +$5.00 S/H

WANT TO LEARN MORE? ORDER THESE OTHER BOOKS BY DIANE TESSMAN

( ) **UFO AGENDA: SO DO YOU WANT TO KNOW THE TRUTH?**

Diane brings us face to face with some startling truths about the alien agenda. Why are some people chosen for contact? Are the visitors from far-flung other worlds, or quantum projections of our own mysterious consciousness? – $17.00

( ) **THE TRANSFORMATION: WITH CHANNELING FROM TIBUS**

Written from the heart and soul of UFO researcher and well known spiritual channel, Diane Tessman. It offers a detailed account of her childhood encounter with UFO being, Tibus, with notes on her regression memories by Dr. R. Leo Sprinkle, Ph.D – $15.00

Diane Was Recently On Shirley MacLaine's Radio Program Where She Discussed This Book

SPECIAL: ALL 3 BOOKS $42.00 + $6 S/H

Order From: TIMOTHY G BECKLEY, Box 753, New Brunswick, NJ. 08903

ADVERTISEMENT

WHO IS THE MYSTERIOUS INDIVIDUAL KNOWN ONLY AS BRANTON?
CIA "SLEEPER?" – ILLUMINATI HENCHMAN? – A FORMER AREA 51 WORKER GONE ROGUE?

You Decide After Reading This Series Of Shocking Works That Have Made Branton The Most Compelling Whistle Blower In The Nation Today

$21.95 Each / Set of four books for $88.00 + $8 S/H – All Printed In Large Format Editions
BONUS! – Order all titles and receive a special Audio CD on the Reptilians as narrated by Commander X, Secret Underground Intelligence Operative

---

( ) # 1 – THE MOJAVE DESERT'S MYSTERIOUS SECRETS—(NEW! 365 Pages!) It has been suggested he was given an alternative "double life" which gave him access to underground UFO and MILAB bases, and apparently had been "tagged" by the Greys with a series of alien implants placed in various parts of his body. It is also claimed that he had a number of hybrid children who are now part of the NWO resistance movement. "To the Christians," insists Branton, "the Underworld is Hell. To many, the world of caverns are the abodes of their ancestors, a truism common, perhaps to all of us, if we believe our forebearers were cave men and women. To Richard S. Shaver the Hollow Earth was the abode of debauched Dero; to others it was the home of the Serpent Race of Agharta; still others saw it inhabited by a society with a Utopian model. To some the Inner Earth may represent only caverns, a few hundred feet, or a few miles down. To other theorists it may represent a miniature cosmos of its own, complete with a Central Sun. But however we view it, the Inner Earth remains one of our strongest, if unproved, traditions." A weird but telling book meant only for the serious student.

( ) # 2 – THE OMEGA FILES: SECRET NAZI UFOS BASES REVEALED! —Describes how German engineers actually flew flying saucers shortly before the end of World War Two, and how some of the depraved Nazis actually escaped due to help from America's own version of the Secret Government...and how they actually do their work today from underground bases around the world. SPECIAL SECTION OF PHOTOGRAPHS OF NAZI BUILT FLYING SAUCERS and stories told by our own pilots of encounters with so-called Foo Fighters during the war. Here is final proof that not all UFOS come from outer space!

( ) # 3 – REALITY OF THE SERPENT RACE AND THE SUBTERRANEAN ORIGIN OF UFOS
—WARNING: TO BE USED BY MEMBERS OF THE 'HUMAN RESISTANCE' AS A GUIDE TO ALIEN STRATEGY! This manuscript contains expositions of an extremely revealing and concentrated nature. There are powers of spiritual origin that will attempt to interfere with the dissemination of this information. In the event that the reader begins to sense such an oppressive influence while reading this book, the author strongly recommends that they stop and read the 23rd Psalm aloud and then continue. This will break the power of the spiritual attacks. Learn Of: The great cosmic conflict between humans and the REPTILIANS. * The Serpent Race and its influence throughout history. * The Missing Link between Lizards and Snakes. * Horrible battle between humans and aliens.

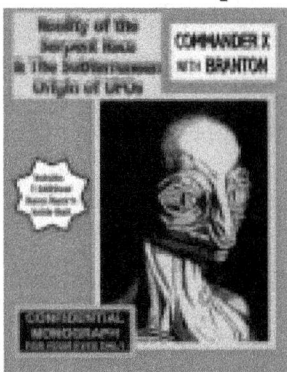

( ) # 4 – UNDERGROUND ALIEN BIO LAB AT DULCE—Is the town of Dulce, NM the location of an underground base guarded by U.S. Forces and inhabited by a group of sinister Ets? Or is all the UFO and paranormal activity in the area merely a "False Flag" designed to act as a convenient cover story for secret black project operations? Or perhaps as suggested by radio host JC Johnson when he asks, "are the beings working with the government there in fact demons whose evil exceeds anything we may think we know about aliens in Dulce?"

TIMOTHY G BECKLEY, BOX 753, NEW BRUNSWICK, NJ 08903

www.ingramcontent.com/pod-product-compliance
Lightning Source LLC
Chambersburg PA
CBHW081915180426
43198CB00038B/2611